Rivals for Power

Rivals for Power

Presidential-Congressional Relations

Fourth Edition

James A. Thurber

ROWMAN & LITTLEFIELD PUBLISHERS, INC.
Lanham • Boulder • New York • Toronto • Plymouth, UK

ROWMAN & LITTLEFIELD PUBLISHERS, INC.

Published in the United States of America
by Rowman & Littlefield Publishers, Inc.
A wholly owned subsidiary of The Rowman & Littlefield Publishing Group, Inc.
4501 Forbes Boulevard, Suite 200, Lanham, Maryland 20706
www.rowmanlittlefield.com

Estover Road
Plymouth PL6 7PY
United Kingdom

British Library Cataloguing in Publication Information Available

Library of Congress Cataloging-in-Publication Data:

Rivals for power : presidential-congressional relations / edited by James A. Thurber.
— 4th ed.
    p. cm.
  Includes bibliographical references and index.
  ISBN 978-0-7425-6141-0 (cloth : alk. paper) — ISBN 978-0-7425-6142-7 (pbk. : alk.
paper) — ISBN 978-1-4422-0019-7 (electronic)
  1. Presidents—United States. 2. United States. Congress. 3. United States—Politics
and government—20th century. I. Thurber, James A., 1943–
  JK585.R59 2009
  320.973—dc22   2009013651

Printed in the United States of America

∞ ™ The paper used in this publication meets the minimum requirements of American
National Standard for Information Sciences—Permanence of Paper for Printed Library
Materials, ANSI/NISO Z39.48-1992.

For my wife, Claudia

And my family,
Mark, Kathryn, Greg, Tristan, Bryan, and Kelsey

Contents

Tables and Figures

TABLES

FIGURES

Preface

This book builds on the knowledge of a variety of scholars and practitioners from the White House and the Hill and is designed to explain the political dynamic between the president and the U.S. Congress. The examination of the rivalry between the president and Congress uses a variety of approaches and perspectives. The title *Rivals for Power: Presidential-Congressional Relations* highlights the continued competition between the two branches, whether the White House and Congress are controlled by the same party or by different parties. The book focuses on the divisions in our democracy that create the rivalries between the president and Congress. It explores the structural, political, and behavioral factors that establish incentives for cooperation between the two branches.

As director of the Center for Congressional and Presidential Studies at American University and as a former congressional staff member, I have spent several decades studying and teaching about the relationship between the White House and Congress. Much of my understanding of this complex rivalry comes from a combination of my independent research and the knowledge from scholars, White House staff, members of Congress and staff, the press, and students. All of these are essential sources for this book. I have many people from the White House and the Hill to thank for sharing their knowledge and expertise, not the least are U.S. Senator Hubert H. Humphrey, U.S. Representative David Obey, and former U.S. Representative Lee Hamilton for whom I worked. Many interviews with persons in Congress and the White House were helpful to me in preparing this book. The hundreds of former students who are or have worked for Congress and in the White House have all been a source of knowledge and wisdom for my research.

The fourth edition of *Rivals for Power* is intended for students, scholars, public officials, the media, and the general public. Each chapter is new since the last edition and reports on original research on Congress and the relationship between the president and Congress from unique viewpoints often as players from inside the policy making process. Scholars and political practitioners have contributed to this volume. Most of the scholars are also experienced hands who have worked in Congress and the White House.

This book relies on the support of Niels Aaboe, Michelle Cassidy, Melissa McNitt, and others from Rowman & Littlefield and American University who contributed their expertise and dedication to assure its publication. I thank Rowman & Littlefield for its support of this work.

At American University, I first want to thank the dedication and help from the staff of the Center for Congressional and Presidential Studies (CCPS), especially Olga Gallardo, Erik Cooke, and Alicia Prevost. I would also like to thank the CCPS scholars, especially Patrick Griffin, Gary Andres, Chuck Brain, and Michael Berman whose many years of experience on the Hill and in the White House have helped me to better understand the two institutions and their relationship.

I have special thanks for the support of the center and this project from William LeoGrande, dean of the School of Public Affairs. As chair of the Department of Government, Candice J. Nelson has been a friend and strong supporter of the work of the center. My close friend and colleague, Neil Kerwin, president of American University, has been a friend and unfailing and enthusiastic proponent of my efforts to build the Center for Congressional and Presidential Studies and to continue our scholarship about the president and Congress.

Sean Singer of the Woodrow Wilson Center was of great assistance for the chapter submitted by the Honorable Lee Hamilton.

This book is clearly a collective effort. I thank all the contributors who have contributed original and important scholarship to each chapter. As editor and author, I take full responsibility for any omissions or errors of fact and interpretation.

I dedicate this book to my family. Thank you, Claudia, Mark, Kathryn, Greg, Tristan, Bryan, and Kelsey for your gifts of love, inspiration, support, and humor.

James A. Thurber

Chapter One

An Introduction to Presidential-Congressional Rivalry

James A. Thurber

The journey from campaigning to governing is always quick for newly elected presidents, but it was especially rapid for President Barack Obama. Presidential campaigns are a test of a candidate's style, strategy, message, organization, and leadership. Ultimately campaigns are a way for voters to judge how the president will lead and what policies he will attempt to implement. Campaigns are as dynamic as a president's relationship with Congress. The 2008 Obama campaign was the longest, most expensive, and may be one of the best-run presidential campaigns in the history of the United States. *Washington Post* veteran reporter, David S. Broder, declared it was the "best campaign I've ever covered."[1] The passage of the $787 economic stimulus bill three weeks into Obama's presidency and his introduction of a transformational $3.6 trillion federal government budget a month into his administration were also swift and historic. Campaigns do not happen in a vacuum, and they are not predetermined by economic or political circumstances. Governing is the same. Successful campaigns must develop a clear message that mobilizes groups of voters that will help the candidate win, that is, the party loyalists ("the base") and the swing voters (often moderate and ideologically in the middle). President Obama initially tried to find support in Congress in the same way, build a solid base of votes from his party and then try to reach out for votes from moderate Republicans. In one month, President Obama asked 139 lawmakers to visit the White House. Candidate Obama had the organization, strategy, and a massive amount of money (over $745 million) to run a "perfect campaign."

The political environment undoubtedly benefited the Obama campaign, with a historically unpopular president, two ongoing wars, and a damaged economy all being tied to Republicans and their president. Obama's unwavering message, discipline, and outstanding organization innovated and used technological advancements to target and mobilize voters on the ground and inspired voters through the air war using Obama's extraordinary charismatic communication skills. All of this combined to elect the first African American as president of the United States and became the foundation of his "mandate" to govern during one of the worst economic crises in the history of the United States.

The 2008–2009 economic recession and two wars matched the stagflation and cold war that confronted President Ronald Reagan in 1981. These challenges may have exceeded any previous president since FDR. Even with these challenges, and to a certain extent because of them, most careful observers of the 2008 campaign have concluded that it was the best-run campaign in modern history, and students of campaign management will study its strategy and tactics for years to come.

From the day of his inauguration, January 20, 2009, President Obama attempted to use his "political capital" from his successful election campaign, that is, the size of his election victory (53 percent), his popularity as shown in early high poll ratings (mid-80 percent job approval ratings the first month in office), and the natural breath of partisan support in unified party government (solid Democratic majorities in the House and Senate) to build a strong relationship with Congress. However, this important presidential resource of "political capital" is often an intangible and transient force that flows from many sources as will be described by the authors in this book.

There was no honeymoon for incumbent President Obama stemming from his impressive electoral win. His political momentum was undermined by events, the staggering economic woes of the United States and the world, the war in Afghanistan, and the unified political opposition of the Republican congressional leadership to his policy agenda. Other unplanned events outside the president's control, such as former Senator Daschle's tax problems and withdrawal from his nomination to be Secretary of the Department of Human and Health Services and Senator Gregg's and New Mexico Governor Richardson's withdrawal from their nominations to be commerce secretary also took away from President Obama's political drive.

It behooves candidates and their campaign managers and, after elected, presidents and their political advisers to evaluate environmental conditions early and develop campaign plans and governing strategies that take advantage of the conditions and to revise those plans when events call for it. Campaign (and presidential leadership) strategy, planning, and tactics must take objective economic and political facts into account. Candidate and President Obama learned these lessons quickly and well in the campaign and in the early months of his administration.

Campaign strategy charts the path to win the election and recognizes that campaigns are dynamic and in constant change, reacting to events and opponents. Presidential coalition building strategies to get votes in Congress for presidential initiatives have similar dynamics. Campaigns are frequently underfunded, disorganized, and understaffed, and their personnel lack enough information to make rational decisions, but that was not the case of candidate Obama. Presidential initiatives such as President Obama's 2009 economic stimulus bill have similar characteristics as many campaigns. Early in an administration, the president is understaffed with personnel that may not have enough information to make quick decisions that are not always completely rational choices, but have a long-lasting impact. Well-run campaigns and successful governing strategies start with a plan, with a theme and message, making the best use of resources (e.g., a candidate's or a president's time), reducing liabilities (marginalizing opposition), and establishing a set of objectives whose achievement will maximize the probability of winning an election or getting the votes needed to pass a president's legislative agenda in Congress. This sounds simple, but the key elements of a campaign or leadership strategy and plan are complex and dynamic. Campaign strategies and plans and governing style must take into account a vast number of factors, such as the candidate or president's personality/charisma, the constituencies in the nation and on the Hill, the nature of the policies being advocated, party discipline (or lack of it), the strength of party leadership, the economic situation, political resources/capital available, and the nature of the electorate and the preferences of key members of Congress.

Successful presidential election campaigns must develop a message that is focused on groups of voters who will help the candidate win, the party loyal ("the base") and swing voters (often moderate and ideologically in the middle). Successful presidential governing strategies must focus on the base of the president's party and then the other votes that are needed for success in the House (218) and in the Senate (60). Successful campaigns have similar functions to successful governing: they must analyze the political environment, decide what tactics or tools will be used to implement the strategy, and set the "budget" for the allocation of time and personnel to each element of the plan.

Until Obama's 2008 presidential campaign, the 2004 campaign was one of the most intense, expensive, longest, and closely contested campaigns. President George W. Bush was reelected to the presidency in 2004 with 51 percent of the vote. Bush won both the popular vote against Senator John Kerry by a margin of over 3.5 million people and the Electoral College vote, unlike the 2000 election when Bush received 500,000 fewer votes than Al Gore. The 2004 election showed once again that presidents are chosen by Electoral College votes, thus the candidates focused their resources of time, people, and money on a handful of battleground states where the contest was close and made a difference in the outcome of the election. The 2004 campaign (just like the 2000 and 2008 campaigns) was waged primarily in Florida, Pennsylvania, Ohio, Michigan, Minnesota, Wisconsin, Iowa, and New Mexico. The Republicans increased their majority in the U.S. Senate and the U.S. House of Representatives with 55 GOP senators and 231 representatives.

Unlike the 2008 and 2004 elections, in just about every respect the 2000 election made history. In 2000 George W. Bush was elected to the presidency in one of the closest national elections of all time, on the promise that he would reach across the aisle to be a reformer working in the middle of the political spectrum. Having lost the popular vote to Al Gore, George W. Bush entered the White House with very little political capital and a closely divided Congress, but he passed large income tax cuts that became his signature economic policy for his presidency. The result of the 2000 election was power sharing in the Senate with 50 Democrats and 50 Republicans and a House with an exceedingly narrow margin for the Republicans, 212 to 211 with two independents. George W. Bush won the presidency without a majority of the popular vote, with no clear mandate or overwhelming majority in the Senate or House. The reality of the president's first year in office was not bipartisanship but a development of a conservative political agenda that alienated the very lawmakers the president had pledged to work with during his campaign. Senator Jeffords of Vermont changed parties and became an independent voting with the Democrats, giving them the majority and the chairmanships in the Senate, and stopping or seriously slowing down Bush's legislative agenda. However, nine months into his first year, the 9/11 attacks gave Bush enough popular support with the American people and influence with Congress to take the nation into war against Iraq. Events, especially in the realm of foreign policy, can drain or replenish a president's power as we saw with the unpopularity of President Bush and the Iraq War by 2008.

Over 40 percent of all presidential elections since the early nineteenth century have produced "minority" winners, including Abraham Lincoln, Grover Cleveland (twice), Woodrow Wilson (twice), Harry S. Truman, John F. Kennedy, Richard M. Nixon, Bill Clinton (twice), and George W. Bush (in 2000). These sub-50 percent winners often have at least one of the following three factors to help them govern: a clear-cut edge in the popular vote, a decisive advantage in the Electoral College, or party allies firmly in command on Capitol Hill. President George W. Bush in 2000 had none of these advantages at the beginning of his administration and faced a unique problem involving legitimacy considering the outcome of the five-week Florida recount and the ultimate forum, the courts. That changed dramatically with the 9/11 terrorist attack on the United States with a rallying of U.S. citizens, Congress, and the world community behind President Bush. President Obama had all of the three key factors to help him govern: a large majority of the popular vote, a decisive advantage in the Electoral College, and party allies firmly in command on Capitol Hill.

Congressional Democrats lost ground politically during the Clinton presidency both in the Senate and the House, but it did not guarantee a new Congress that would work easily with President George W. Bush. The 2000 elections left the Democrats with 46 fewer House seats and seven fewer Senate seats than when Clinton was first elected in 1992. Every two-term president in the twentieth century has lost seats in the House and the Senate (save for FDR's first eight years when the Democrats picked up seven Senate seats), and Clinton was no exception to this trend. President Bush was an exception to this trend with Republican gains in the House and Senate midterm elections in 2002 (and with Republican gains in 2004).

The historic 1994 midterm congressional election reversed a generation of Democratic dominance in the House, brought divided party control of government again, and dramatically reshaped the rivalry between the president and Congress. Every election since 1996 has reinforced the dominance of the Republicans on Capitol Hill except in 1994 when Senator Jeffords switched parties and gave the Democrats a majority of one in the Senate from mid-2001 to 2002. The 1994 election not only brought an overwhelming victory for the Republican Party and major changes in the policy agenda and the structure of Congress, but it also dramatically changed the balance of power between the president and Congress.[2] Having received an electoral mandate to implement their legislative program of cutbacks, devolution, and deregulation, Republicans in Congress boldly set about dictating the policy agenda. In contrast, President Clinton found that his negotiating power had been significantly diminished after the 1994 election. The Republicans centralized the decision-making system in the House of Representatives and, in the process, limited the president's ability to influence Congress. These changes did not last long.

After the historic 1994 midterm election, President Clinton was compelled to reach out to the new Republican leadership in the House and the Senate. Speaker Newt Gingrich (R-GA) received a boost in power from a highly unified House Republican Conference and the structural reforms that it imposed upon the House. President Clinton's activist agenda during the 103d Congress was overshadowed by the Contract with America and the GOP-led drive to balance the budget and cut back the federal government.[3] However, ultimately, neither President Clinton nor the new Republican leadership could govern effectively without the cooperation of the other. Elections can have an impact on presidential and congressional relations, as shown so clearly in the dramatic shift in political mood and policy agenda from 1992 to 1994.

The 1992 presidential election brought President Clinton (Democrat) to the White House and unified party control of government for the first time in twelve years. At the heart of the 1992 presidential campaign was President Clinton's promise to fix the economy and to use the presidency to do so. He believed in an activist role for the federal government. The election produced the largest turnover of membership in the House of Representatives in more than forty years; 110 new members took office in January 1993. President Clinton had a majority of Democrats in the House and Senate, unified party control of government, and many new members of Congress who wanted change. However, he discovered quickly that 43 percent support in the election (all but four House members ran ahead of him in absolute votes) did not translate into a mandate or easy coalition to push his activist agenda.[4] Although he was a "New" Democrat from the Democratic Leadership Council (DLC), Clinton sent strong signals to the Hill that he wanted to cooperate with a policy agenda along centrist lines. However, it was difficult for the president to find common ground for his centrist agenda with the Republicans and liberal or "Old" Democrats who were aligned with organized labor (opposing the DLC).

Unified party control of government did not bring an end to the rivalry between the president and Congress for President Clinton (in 1993–1994) nor did it for President George W. Bush. Within a few months, bitter struggles had broken out pitting both of these presidents with their own parties and against opposition party leaders. Although Presidents George W. Bush and Bill Clinton presented themselves as moderates, pragmatic, and bipartisan, they had serious problems building centrist coalitions to support their programs. Both had to work with the majority of their party members, whose centers of gravity had moved to the left on the political spectrum for the Democrats and to the right for the Republicans and who, as a result, frequently opposed the presidents' policies. For example, in 2001, President Bush had major opposition within his party from key committee chairs to his first legislative initiatives: a $1.6 trillion tax cut proposal and major changes in education policy (No Child Left Behind Act). In 2005 Bush was also confronted with opposition to his social security privatization reforms and to certain budget cuts and permanent tax cuts. Although Clinton also had unified party government for his first two years in office (1993–1994), eleven Democratic House subcommittee chairs voted against President Clinton's economic package in May 1993, and the president's program barely survived. In a clear indication of the lack of discipline in the Democratic Party, after a subsequent demand by some House members, especially freshmen, the House leadership rejected the proposal that the eleven be stripped of their chairmanships.[5] Clinton also had to build cross-party coalitions with more conservative Republican leaders to pass several major bills on his agenda, such as the North American Free Trade Agreement (NAFTA), the General Agreement on Tariffs and Trade (GATT), and normal trade relations for the People's Republic of China. Many of President Clinton's initiatives were stopped or amended so thoroughly that they bore little resemblance to his original proposals. Unified government did not guarantee presidential dominance in Clinton's relationship with Congress.

In 1989 President George Bush (senior) had similar conflicts with Congress. Immediately after his inauguration, President Bush, also in a gesture of goodwill like his son George W. Bush, praised Congress: "To the Members of the Congress, to the institution of the House of Representatives and the Senate of the United States, may they flourish and may they prosper."[6] In response to President Bush's efforts to build better relations with Congress, Thomas S. Foley (D-WA), then House majority leader, said, "That's another example of President Bush reaching out. We're going to respond very positively to that."[7] Despite all this, President Bush went on to have one of the lowest records of support for his policy initiatives in Congress in the last fifty years (average 51.6 percent presidential success in Congress, see table 1.1). President Obama, Clinton, and the two Bush presidents had every good intention to work with broad bipartisan centrist coalitions in Congress, but whether with unified or divided party control of government, it did not work out that way.[8]

Goodwill does not generally characterize the institutional relationship between Congress and the president. In his first four years in office, President George W. Bush earned the highest presidential support scores (the percentage of presidential proposals that are approved by Congress calculated annually by *Congressional Quarterly Weekly Report*) since President Jimmy Carter (see table 1.1). President Clinton also earned high presidential support in his first two years of office, but they dropped for the last six years during divided party and government.[9] He was impeached stemming from an affair with a White House intern and his health care reform failed. Personal scandal followed him from his political career in Arkansas through his eight years in office into retirement, which affected his ability to build support in Congress. However, while in office he did continue to reduce the federal budget deficit, to build bipartisan support for successful passage of NAFTA and GATT, the family and medical leave law, normal trade relations with the People's Republic of China, and a variety of other programs.

In his eight years in office, President George W. Bush faired better in his first six years than most presidents elected in the postwar era, winning over 80 percent of the roll-call votes on which he took an unambiguous position. That overall average dropped to 71 percent for eight years when he was faced

Table 1.1. Presidential Success in Congress, 1953–2008

Presidential Success Scores: History			
Year/President	*Success Scores*	*Year/President*	*Success Scores*
1953 Eisenhower	89.16	1981 Reagan	82.35
1954	78.26	1982	72.45
1955	75.27	1983	67.07
1956	69.70	1984	65.79
1957	68.38	1985	59.89
1958	75.68	1986	56.07
1959	52.00	1987	43.50
1960	65.12	1988	47.40
1961 Kennedy	81.38	1989 G. Bush	62.57
1962	85.41	1990	46.77
1963	87.10	1991	54.17
1964 Johnson	87.92	1992	43.03
1965	93.07	1993 Clinton	86.39
1966	78.95	1994	86.43
1967	78.77	1995	36.17
1968	74.53	1996	55.07
1969 Nixon	73.95	1997	53.62
1970	76.92	1998	50.65
1971	74.82	1999	37.80
1972	66.27	2000	55.05
1973	50.65	2001 G. W. Bush	86.67
1974 Nixon	59.56	2001	87.76
1974 Ford	58.20	2003	78.74
1975	60.99	2004	72.62
1976	53.85	2005	78.00
1977 Carter	75.45	2006	80.90
1978	78.33	2007	38.30
1979	76.80	2008	47.80
1980	75.11		

Source: CQ Data, 2008

with strong Democratic Party opposition in his last two years. Bush's success rate dropped during the last two years of his presidency to 43 percent, the lowest in the past fifty-five years for the final two years of a presidency.[10] On the other hand, despite President George H. W. Bush's popularity with the American people during Desert Storm (the highest in the polls of any postwar president at the end of his first year), and his sincere efforts to build bridges between the White House and Capitol Hill, executive-legislative relations during his presidency remained deeply rooted in political and institutional divisions, a divided party government. His presidential success score for 1992 (his fourth year in office) was tied with his son's rate, the lowest in the past fifty-five years at 43 percent. The partisan divisions that George H. W. Bush experienced did not evaporate for President Clinton with unified government in 1993–1994, and they were clearly revealed in Clinton's relationship with Congress until he left office January 20, 2001. Clinton's fourth-year presidential success scores were 55.1 percent.

President George W. Bush called for bipartisanship, comity, and a more civil relationship with Congress in his 2000 campaign as did President Barack Obama in his 2008 campaign. President Obama reached out to the Republicans in Congress in an unprecedented act of meeting with them on the Hill during his first week of his presidency in an attempt to build a bipartisan coalition in support of his historic $787 billion economic stimulus package. He ended up getting only three Republican senators to support the bill and no Republican votes in the House. Both Presidents Obama and Bush sought more comity and bipartisan support during the early days in office only to be rebuffed. Both Presidents Obama and Bush inherited a long-seated partisan rivalry and difficulty in building across party coalitions around their policy initiatives. Where does this conflict come from? What are the roots of the rivalry between the president and Congress? Why does the president's success with Congress vary over time? Why in both unified or divided party government are the president and Congress prone to rivalry?

"The relationship between Congress and the presidency has been one of the abiding mysteries of the American system of government," according to Arthur M. Schlesinger Jr.[11] In this introduction, I will examine several root causes of the rivalry between the president and Congress: the constitutional design with its formal presidential and congressional powers; different electoral constituencies for the president, the House, and the Senate; varying terms of office; increased partisanship and polarization of Congress; the ongoing competition for power between Congress and the president; the permanent election campaign; narrow majorities in both houses; congressional individualism; the impact of the "increasingly microscopic nature of political analysis" of the media (especially cable television and the Internet) in the twenty-four hour seven days a week news cycle; and the nature of interest groups and American pluralism.

The framers of the Constitution bequeathed to Americans one of the most enduring rivalries in government, that between the president and Congress.[12] The Constitution separates the three branches of government (legislative, executive, and judicial) but combines their functions, creating conflict and shared powers.[13] As Richard Neustadt observed, the Constitution created a government "of separated institutions sharing powers," which makes it difficult for presidents to bridge the constitutional gap even in the best of political circumstances. The Constitution gives the president and the Congress different powers, and each is jealous of the other's constitutional prerogatives regardless of context.

The Constitution invests Congress with "all legislative Powers" (lawmaking) but it also authorizes the president to veto legislation. If the president vetoes a bill, "it shall be reposed by two-thirds of the Senate and the House of Representatives" (article I, section 7). Because it is so difficult for Congress to gain a two-thirds' vote, presidential vetoes are usually sustained. Through 2008, presidents had used the veto 2,560 times; 1,066 of these were "pocket vetoes" not subject to congressional override. Congress only overrode presidential vetoes 6 percent of the time (109 times) when it had the opportunity to vote on them.[14] President George W. Bush did not use a veto in his first four years in office and used it only ten times in his last four years of office, fewer than any president since President Harding. The threat of a veto in the legislative process gives the president a potent bargaining tool; however, George W. Bush did not use this tool in his first term and President Clinton did not use this tool until 1995, when he vetoed a $16 billion rescission bill. Clinton also used the veto in his confrontation with the Republican-led Congress over the cuts in Medicaid, Medicare, welfare, education, and federal environmental programs in the fiscal year 1996 federal budget. This showdown ultimately helped to shut down government and stop the power of the Contract with America supporters in the House and Senate. The greatest tool of the president in divided government is often the power to say no as President Clinton did in his last six years of office and George W. Bush did in his last two years of office. It is easier to stop legislation than it is to pass it. President Clinton embraced that notion in his historic budget battle in 1995 when he said: "This is one of those moments in history when I'm grateful for the wisdom of our Founding Fathers. The Congress gets to propose, but the president has to sign or veto, and that Constitution gave me that authority and one of the reasons for the veto is to prevent excess. They knew what they were doing and we're going to use the Constitution they gave us to stand up for what's right."[15]

Congress is given broad powers in article I, section 8 of the Constitution, but the greatest power of Congress is its authority to pass laws directly binding upon all citizens (lawmaking). Also of great importance is the power of the purse, the power to authorize and appropriate funds for the president and executive branch agencies. Presidents may propose budgets for the federal government, but Congress has the final say on spending. This creates an automatic rivalry between the two and conflict over spending priorities. Congress also has the power to levy and collect taxes, to borrow and coin money, and to regulate foreign and interstate commerce. A central element of the rivalry between the president and Congress has been battles over spending, tax, and trade policy. The powers to declare war, to provide for a militia, and to adopt laws concerning bankruptcy, naturalization, patents, and copyrights are also bestowed on Congress. The interpretation of presidential and congressional war power has changed over time and is another contemporary source of conflict. Congress has the authority to establish or eliminate executive branch agencies (e.g., intelligence reform of 2004) and create new departments (e.g., Department of Homeland Security in 2002) and to oversee their operations. The Senate must approve cabinet nominees, ambassadors, and Supreme Court and federal judicial appointees before they can take office. A president cannot enter into a binding treaty with a foreign government without a two-thirds' vote of the Senate, nor can the president "declare war," a power the Constitution purposely gives to Congress. All of these constitutional congressional and presidential powers force both institutions to confront each other in governance, which more often than not creates rivalry and conflict.

A dramatic but rarely employed check on the president is impeachment. President Clinton's impeachment was rare and historic. The president and executive branch officials can be impeached (formally accused) by a majority vote in the House and tried in the Senate. If two-thirds of the senators vote to convict, the official is removed from office. Only President Andrew Johnson and Bill Clinton have been tried on impeachment charges. The vote fell one short of the number required to convict Johnson and the Senate did not convict Clinton by a significant majority. The House Judiciary Committee recommended that Richard M. Nixon be impeached for transgressions in connection with the Watergate burglary involving the Democratic National Committee offices and the ensuing cover-up. Nixon, however, resigned the presidency before a full session of the House could vote on the impeachment issue. The threat of impeachment establishes an important check on the president and executive branch officials, limiting the power of the president.

The framers of the Constitution deliberately fragmented power between the national government and the states (federalism) and among the executive, legislative, and judicial branches (separation of powers).[16] They also divided legislative powers by creating two coequal houses, a bicameral Congress with different constituencies, which further magnifies rivalry and conflict. Although divided, Congress was designed to be independent and powerful, able to check the power of the executive and to be directly linked with the people through popular, periodic elections. The framers wanted an effective and powerful federal government, but they also wanted to limit its power in order to protect personal and property rights. Having experienced the abuses of British monarchs and their colonial governors, the framers were wary of excessive executive authority. They also feared "elective despotism," or excessive legislative power, something the Articles of Confederation had given their own state legislatures.

The framers created three branches of government with none having a monopoly. This separation of powers restricted the power of any one branch, and it required cooperation among the three in order for them to govern effectively. Today, as then, political action requires cooperation between the president and Congress. Yet the Constitution, in the way it divided power between the two branches, created an open invitation for conflict.[17] In sum, in creating a separated presidency and two equal legislative chambers, the framers guaranteed checks and an ongoing rivalry between executive and legislative power.

DIFFERENT ELECTORAL CONSTITUENCIES

The U.S. system of government, unlike parliamentary systems throughout the world, elects the executive and members of the legislature independently. The president is elected from vastly broader electoral coalitions (271 electoral votes, generally from "battleground" or competitive states) than are representatives and senators, who have narrow constituencies and in homogenous congressional districts or heterogeneous states. Members of Congress, even those who belong to the president's party or hail from his home state, represent specific interests that can conflict with the interests of the president who represents the nation as a whole. James Madison well understood this dichotomy of interest as an important source of conflict between the president and Congress: "The members of the federal legislature will be likely to attach themselves too much to local objects. . . . Measures will too often be decided according to their probable effect, not on the national prosperity and happiness, but on the prejudices, interests, and pursuits of the governments and the people of the individual States."[18] Members of Congress often live in discrete communities and cleverly drawn House districts favoring one party or the other, but especially favoring incumbents. Those incumbents who run for reelection are overwhelmingly successful, in the mid-90th percentile for House members and mid-80th for senators in the last twenty-five years.

VARYING TERMS OF OFFICE

The interaction of Congress and the president is shaped not only by their different constituencies and electoral competitiveness but by their different terms in office. The constitutional structure of U.S. government, which separates the Congress and the president, sets different terms of office for representatives (two-year terms), senators (six-year terms), and the president (four-year terms), and ensures they will be chosen from different constituency bases. Term limited presidents have only four years, possibly eight, in which to establish their programs. They are expected to set the national policy agenda and usually move rapidly in the first year before their decline in popularity, as done by President Obama.[19] Presidents are not concerned about reelection after the first four years of office. They focus on legacy, establishing lasting good public policy and an honored place in history as their first priority. Other interests are certainly operative, but the drive for reelection for members of Congress is most important.[20] Legislators, then, are often reluctant to allow their workload and policy agenda to be dictated by a president who has no political clout or perceived electoral mandate to do so. Members of Congress are often driven by the short-term motivation to be reelected rather than the long-term goals of a president.

Congress moves more slowly than the president; it is deliberative and inefficient primarily because it represents a vast array of local interests. Congress passes new laws slowly and reviews old ones carefully. For example, the Republican House of Representatives of the 104th through the 109th Congresses centralized power and was more efficient than the House of any other modern Congress, but this too caused conflict with President Clinton's and President Bush's agenda. The decision-making pace of Congress and of the president is not the same because of their different terms of office, electoral base, and perceived constituency mandates. Confronted with major economic problems and two wars, President Obama pursued an ambitious domestic agenda through his stimulus legislation and his first budget, something he laid out in his election campaign. He did not back off his campaign promises of redeployment in Iraq and quick action to turn the economy around. However, Congress had its own pace and its own ideas on the Iraq War, health care, energy, environment, and education. The result of these varying terms of office is rivalry, conflict, extreme partisanship, and often deadlock over major policies, something Obama promised to change.

POLITICAL PARTIES

Another factor influencing the relationship between the president and Congress is the federal system of state-based political parties. They contribute to the independence of members of Congress from the president. The president must work with decentralized political party organizations that often exercise little control over recruitment of candidates who run under their party label, mete out weak discipline, and hold even less leverage over members. Senators and representatives usually run their own races with their own financing. The way they respond to local conditions has little to do with national party platforms or presidential politics. Members often freely pursue their own interests without fear of discipline from the president.

Independence from political parties and the president allows legislators to seek benefits for their own constituents and to serve specialized interests. Thomas Mann argues further:

> The changes that swept through the political system during the 1960s and 1970s—the increase in split-ticket voting, the growing cost of campaigns and reliance on contributions from special interests, the rise of television, the expansion and growing political sophistication of interest groups in Washington, and the democratization and decentralization of Congress—may well have weakened the classic iron triangles, but they also heightened the sensitivity of politicians to all forms of outside pressure.[21]

However, for Republican members of the House the 1994 election deviated from the normal individualistic election. The Contract with America, signed by three hundred Republican candidates for the House, "nationalized" the campaign for most of those candidates. No incumbent Republican House member lost in the 1994 election. Republicans earned a net gain of seventeen in the fifty-two open-seat House contests and lost only four Republican-controlled House open seats to the Democrats. Thirty-five House incumbent Democrats lost. With the Democrats losing fifty-two seats in the House and eight Senate seats, the mandate of the new Republicans was to be loyal to the contract, to the House Republican leadership, and to the reduction of individualism in the House. Party discipline came from the congressional party leaders, not from the grassroots party organizations throughout the United States. This was unique in modern congressional elections and created the basis of more discipline and centralized power in the House of Representatives and conflict with President Clinton, and party leadership helped President George W. Bush's agenda into the 109th Congress.

There is a continuing trend in both chambers away from bipartisan cooperation and toward ideological and political loyalty as President Obama so clearly saw early in his administration. An analysis of party unity votes, defined by *Congressional Quarterly* as votes where a majority of one party votes against a majority of the other, shows that Republicans and Democrats have record levels of polarization. Party unity has steadily increased since 1960, from the low average party unity score of the mid-60s to the high 80s from 1993 to 2008 (see table 1.2). For example, in the eight years of the Bush presidency, on votes in which party leaders took clear opposing positions, House and Senate Republicans voted to support the party position almost

Table 1.2. Party Unity: Average Unity Score by Party, 1960–2008

Year/President	Republicans	Democrats	Year/President	Republicans	Democrats
1960 Eisenhower	68	64	1985	75	79
1961 Kennedy	72	71	1986	71	78
1962	68	69	1987	74	81
1963	72	71	1988	73	79
1964 Johnson	69	67	1989 G. Bush	73	81
1965	70	69	1990	74	81
1966	67	61	1991	78	81
1967	71	66	1992	79	79
1968	63	57	1993 Clinton	84	85
1969 Nixon	62	62	1994	83	83
1970	59	57	1995	91	80
1971	66	62	1996	87	80
1972	64	57	1997	88	82
1973	68	68	1998	86	83
1974 Nixon/Ford	62	63	1999	86	84
1975	70	69	2000	87	83
1976	66	65	2001 G. W. Bush	90	85
1977 Carter	70	67	2002	89	86
1978	67	64	2003	92	87
1979	72	69	2004	89	86
1980	70	68	2005	90	88
1981	76	69	2006	88	86
1982	71	72	2007	85	91
1983	74	76	2008	87	92
1984	72	74			

Source: CQ Data, 2008

89 percent of the time and House and Senate Democrats supported the party position 88 percent of the time. These party voting patterns have revealed the parties to be much more ideological and polarized.

PARTY CONTROL OF GOVERNMENT

With President Obama unified party government returned to America. Unified and divided party governments have a most important impact on the relationship between the president and Congress. A major electoral base impediment to legislative-executive cooperation is divided government, as shown by the dramatic election of 1994, which left a Democrat in the White House working with Republican majorities in the House and Senate, and the midterm election of 2006, which forced President Bush to work with the opposition party in the House and Senate in the 110th Congress.[22] There are two varieties of divided government (the condition that exists when the majority party in either or both houses of Congress differs from the party of the president): divided party control of Congress and split control of Congress and the White House. From 1901 through 2008, we have had unified party control of government for sixty-five years (60 percent of the time) and divided party control of government for forty-three years or almost 40 percent of the time (see table 1.3).

Opposing parties have controlled the presidency and one or both houses of Congress in twenty-two of the past twenty-eight years (79 percent of the time from 1969 through 1996), with the Republicans mainly controlling the White House and the Democrats controlling Congress. From 1887 to 1954, divided party control of government occurred only eight years (14 percent of the time), but from President Dwight D. Eisenhower's first year (1953) through President Clinton's fourth year in office (1996), it occurred twenty-eight years (56 percent of the time). Although President George W. Bush has had unified party government most of the time, divided party control of government at the federal level has been the norm in modern U.S. politics.

Presidents are more likely to be successful in their relationship with Congress with unified party government than with divided government. This has been especially true since the post-1980 resurgence of party-line voting and

Table 1.3. Unified and Divided Party Control of Government, 1901–2008

Year	Party Control	Number of Years	Percentage
Unified party control of government (65 years): 60.2%			
Divided party control of government (43 years): 39.8%			
1901–1920	Unified	16	80
	Divided	4	20
1921–1940	Unified	18	90
	Divided	2	10
1941–1960	Unified	12	60
	Divided	8	40
1961–1980	Unified	12	60
	Divided	8	40
1981–2000	Unified	2	10
	Divided	18	90
2001–2008	Unified	5	62.5
	Divided	3	37.5

party cohesion in Congress. *Congressional Quarterly* defines its measure of party-line voting as the percentage of all votes when a majority of voting Democrats opposes a majority of voting Republicans. Overall, Reagan and Bush had low presidential support scores in Congress because of divided party government. Clinton's victories on votes in Congress during his first two years (1993–1994) in office averaged over 86 percent in the House and Senate and dropped to 36 percent in 1995 when the Republicans captured the Congress. Although President George W. Bush had unified Republican government for the first time since 1954, the closeness of the election and the tie in the Senate created the foundation for conflict and in effect divided government until he had to face actual divided party government in 2007. Although President Obama had a significant electoral victory in 2008, he faced tough opposition from the House Republicans and few Senate Republicans willing to support his policies (only three voted for his 2009 stimulus package). The necessity for sixty votes to stop a filibuster made Obama's margin of support very thin in the Senate with Senator Specter becoming the sixtieth shifting party affiliation to caucus with the Democrats.

The trend toward ticket splitting between presidential and congressional candidates further exacerbates already strained relations. Election returns for Congress have increasingly diverged from national presidential returns, until 2008. During the past forty years, as the power of political parties has declined significantly, there has been a corresponding rise in individualistic candidacies for the presidency, the Senate, and the House. Fewer and fewer members of Congress ride into office on the electoral "coattails" of the president. This has led to the election of presidents who find it difficult to translate electoral support into governing support. This was even the case with Obama's historic 2008 election. The scarcity of presidential coattails by Bush I in 1988, Clinton in 1992 and 1998, and Bush II in 2000 and 2004 brings the conclusion that "the emperor has no coat."[23] Bush I was the first candidate since John F. Kennedy to win the White House whiie his party lost seats in the House. Clinton ran behind all but four members of the House. With the decline of presidential coattails, strong-willed members of Congress are largely beyond the president's control. They are often more responsive to district and specialized interests than to the national agenda of the president. The 2006 and 2008 elections have increased the power of Democrats with a gain of 53 House seats and 12 Senate seats. The gains in 2008, 23 House seats for a total of 257 Democrats to 178 Republicans and 8 Democratic seats in the Senate for a total of 59 (including two independents), still made it difficult for President Obama to build support for his policies without Senator Specter's partisan change to make the 60-seat majority.

Unified party control of government does not mean the two branches will work closely together. Divided government does not always mean that the two branches will fight. David Mayhew found that when it comes to passing major legislation or conducting investigations, it "does not seem to make all that much difference whether party control of the American government happens to be unified or divided."[24] However, we do know that it was generally easier for presidents to govern during periods of unified party government.

The balance of power between and within the institutions of Congress and the presidency is dynamic and conflict is inevitable, another root cause of the rivalry between the president and Congress, no matter of the same party or not. The congressional institutions of a stable committee system, party leadership organizations, the seniority system, member individualism, and behavioral norms such as reciprocity all have an impact on congressional-presidential relationships. What the public expects from each institution varies over time, as dramatically shown by the differences between the 103d and 104th Congresses and the 110th and 111th Congresses.[25] For over two hundred years Congress has continued to represent local interest and to respond (some think too much) to political preferences and public pressures.[26] Nevertheless, the institution has changed dramatically. The reforms of the past thirty-five years have made Congress even more representative and accountable. These reforms have changed the way it makes laws, passes budgets, oversees the executive branch, and confronts or cooperates with presidents. The degree of party centralization or fragmentation of power among committees and individualism among members has major consequences for Congress's power vis-à-vis the president. It is difficult for the president to build predictable coalitions around a highly fragmented legislature and weak leadership, but it can also play into his favor if divided party government exists.

As the congressional leadership is centralized and made more effective by one party, the power of a president of the opposition party is often diminished. This creates more tension between the two branches, with a clash between the president's national policy agenda and the agenda of Congress. President Clinton's legislative successes during the 103d Congress (1993–1994) and unified party government were impressive, with a remarkable 86 percent win record on the votes on which he took a position. The 1994 election changed his success and the competitive environment with Congress; he was overshadowed by the Contract with America, the leadership of Speaker Newt Gingrich, and the Republican drive to balance the budget. Unified government and a decentralized Congress helped his legislative successes in 1993 and 1994; a massive loss in the midterm elections to the Republicans created conflict and a deadlock between the two branches. If the president is popular with the American public, he has electoral coattails bringing many new members into Congress that are beholden to him, and if he has a well-organized and well-run White House and administration, he is more able to control the national policy agenda. An example of a president meeting these criteria is President Lyndon Johnson during his first two years of office, before the war in Vietnam undermined his influence in Congress and popularity with the American voters. His central core of authority in dealing with Congress reduced conflict between the two branches. Structural reforms within the presidency (for example, the establishment of the Bureau of the Budget and, later, the creation of the Office of Management and Budget (OMB) and the expansion of the post–World War II White House staff, or policy czars under President Obama) and change in Congress (for example, the centralization of power by the Republican Party's congressional leadership and increased parity unity in the 104th Congress) have direct impacts on the ability of the president to dominate the legislative agenda and for the Congress to act independently from the president.

Pressure to check the power of the president through the War Powers Resolution of 1973 and the Budget and Impoundment Control Act of 1974 brought changes that helped Congress reclaim some of the power it had lost to the president during the previous decades. Many institutional reforms of the 1970s, however, resulted in decentralization, which made Congress more democratic but also less efficient. With the new openness came greater accountability and responsiveness but at the price of efficiency and effectiveness as a lawmaking body. Modern presidents find Congress harder to influence than did their predecessors in the White House. Members of Congress are more independent. And with the weakening of strict seniority rules wielded by strong parties, coordinating the legislative process was more difficult for congressional party leaders until the House reforms of the 104th Congress that centralized power with the Republican leadership.

Although Congress created new ways of checking presidential power in the 1970s and in 2007–2008, ultimately legislative-executive relationships are not zero-sum games. If one branch gains power, the other does not necessarily lose it. The expansion of the federal government since World War II has given vast new power to both branches. Problems like the terrorist attack on the United States on 9/11 and the economic crisis of 2008 contribute to the policy-making power of both the president and Congress. The war on terrorism, the war in Iraq, the economic crisis of 2008 and beyond, failing banks and financial institutions, and continuing large budget deficits have led to new administrative (and legislative) powers expanding the scope of both branches. Even these crises, however, are not enough to reduce the rivalry between the two institutions and the two parties.

The decentralization and fragmentation of power within Congress was dramatically altered as a result of the 1994 election. The Speaker, the only structural feature of the House dictated by the Constitution, had significant power before Speaker Gingrich expanded that power even more. Gingrich appointed the committee chairs and increased his influence over committee assignments, placing freshman on the Ways and Means, Appropriations, Rules, and Commerce Committees. Of the eleven Republican openings on the Appropriations Committee, Speaker Gingrich appointed nine freshmen, thus assuring cohesion and loyalty from the new Republicans in the House. Gingrich's control over committee assignments for freshmen and over the selection of chairs was a dramatic break from the decentralized and more democratic House of the last twenty years. He abolished proxy voting in committees, which limited the power of committee chairs. He reduced committee staffing, abolished independent subcommittee staff, and placed six-year term limits on committee chairs, thus reducing the power of the chairs and increasing the power of the leadership. Gingrich, with the support of the Republican Conference, also limited committee assignments and restructured the committee system generally. All of these reforms helped to centralize power in the speakership. Under the reformed House of Representatives, Speaker Gingrich gained substantial power to control the policy agenda using key provisions in the GOP Contract with America. He was able to overshadow President Clinton (and the Senate) and pass far-reaching legislation that projected a balanced budget in seven years, cut taxes, cut back spending on Medicare, Medicaid, and welfare, and decentralized federal government, sending more programs and money to the states. Republican Party dominance of the House and Senate and internal change in the House power structure fundamentally changed the relationship with the president in 1995.[27] However, after the shutdown of government as a result of a conflict over the budget in 1995, the committee chairs and members reasserted themselves in the House and the normal decentralized system of policy making was reestablished. The power of the committee and subcommittee chairs became the locus of decision making and President Clinton had to build coalitions in a highly fragmented individualistic House for the next five years of his administration, but that changed dramatically in 2001, after the election of President George W. Bush.

The House Republican leadership continued to transform the organization and processes of the House. That helped President Bush achieve his legislative successes under unified party government. There was a greater concentration of power in the hands of House leaders. There was an increasing use of the House rules to deny the minority a full debate or votes on its views. There was a disintegration of the committee process in the House. During the first weeks, the Obama administration also ignored the "regular process" when considering the historic stimulus bill.

Candidate Obama promised to "change the way Washington works" with respect to Congress and lobbyists. He promised to stop the heavy reliance on riders and "ear marks" to the appropriations bills as a way to act on significant policy issues. There were promises to stop the abuse of the conference committee by the majority party. There were promises to fix the breakdown in the budget process, passing large omnibus spending bills well after the start of the fiscal year (October 1).[28] Importantly President Obama tried to reduce the polarization and lack of comity and civility in the House and Senate.[29] The Imperial Presidency was dormant from the late 1970s through the Clinton administration, but it returned with President Bush's elections in 2000 and 2004 and was assisted by the Republican House and Senate leadership and unified party government until the 110th Congress (2007–2008) when divided party government faced President Bush. The 2008 election of President Barack Obama changed Congress yet again. It brought back Democratic Party unified government with a large majority in the House and a highly competitive Senate and the decentralization of power to the committees again in the House and Senate. The economic crisis also brought demands for President Obama to act quickly and forcefully to pass his legislation to address the nation's problems.

INTEREST GROUPS AND PLURALISM

Candidate Barack Obama ran against interest groups and lobbyists claiming that he would change the way Washington works. He promised the following in the 2008 campaign: "I intend to tell the corporate lobbyists that their days of setting the agenda in Washington are over, that they had not funded my campaigns, and from my first day as president, I will launch the most sweeping ethics reform in U.S. history. We will make government more open, more accountable and more responsive to the problems of the American people" (www.nhpr.org/node/14408).

"Today as the Democratic nominee for president, I am announcing that going forward, the Democratic National Committee will uphold the same standard—we will not take a dime from Washington lobbyists," Obama said at a town hall meeting in Bristol, Virginia. He later said, "We are going to change how Washington works. They will not run our party. They will not run our White House. They will not drown out the views of the American people" (www.msnbc.msn.com/id/24989468/wid/7468326/).

"My argument is not that we're perfect. I suffer from the same original sin of all politicians, which is we've got to raise money," Obama said. "But my argument has been and will continue to be that the disproportionate influence of lobbyists and special interest is a problem in Washington (and) in state capitals" (www.iht.com/articles/ap/2007/08/17/america/NA-POL-US-White-House-Obama.php).

No matter what his promises, the passage of the 2008 stimulus package was greatly dependent upon the input and support of many interest groups and lobbyists. It is impossible to govern in the American pluralist representative democracy without federal registered lobbyists, interest groups, and advocates of all kinds. When a president's policy agenda is proposed, especially through his budget, there is a mobilization of interests for and against the thousands of policy decisions and proposals embedded in his fiscal plan, as shown in the lobbying around President Obama's proposed $3.6 trillion budget, his health care reforms, and environment-energy policy initiatives. The competition among a variety of interests has often produced deadlock and stalemate on the nation's most pressing problems. President Obama promised to change that by reducing the role of lobbyists and campaign money for special interest groups in his administration. Commentators stated that "while his budget incorporates bold proposals to rescue the financial system, stabilize the auto industry, jump-start the economy, reform the health care system and eventually bring down the deficit, he knows he is unlikely to win any of it if he cannot change the way business is done in Washington." Obama's and all presidents' challenge is to get Americans and their advocates in Washington to take a broader view of their own self-interest. Obama's early agenda was to persuade Americans and their interest groups that the benefits they will get from finally balancing the budget or cleaning up the air or reforming health care or changing America's addiction to carbon fuels are so great that they will accept the sacrifices of paying higher taxes or losing a subsidy or accepting increased government regulation. This is a massive fight with interest groups and their lobbyists and their connections in Congress.

Interest groups play a central role in the relationship between the president and Congress. This was clearly the case with the Bush administration and Congress. Passage of the 2003 Medicare Prescription Drug bill was dependent upon the strong support of three major associations, the AARP, the pharmaceutical companies, and the health insurance companies of America. The battle to reform Social Security was also directly linked to the battle of special interests in the United States, the AARP (and associated groups), and the U.S. Chamber of Commerce/National Association of Manufacturers coalition (and other association allies). Medicare and Social Security reform are examples of the importance of organized interest groups in the relationship between the president and Congress, something President Obama understood clearly when he proposed major changes in both entitlement programs at the beginning of his administration. Without the help of well-organized groups the president and Congress cannot easily enact legislation. With them against the president, it is exceedingly difficult to bring about reform. Pluralism (group-based politics) limits the power of the president and Congress to pursue their own agendas and thereby increases the competition between them. Policy-making gridlock (hyperpluralism) often comes from competition among organized interests in society, not from divided party control of government as has been seen with all presidents, including Obama. Deadlock over clean air policy, energy policy, health care policy, immigration, education, delays in passing annual budgets, the refusal by appropriators to fully fund authorization bills, the tendency toward "government by continuing resolution" are all examples of the consequences of deadlock among groups. As more people are organized (there are over 140,000 associations in the United States and over one million groups), as the political process is opened to more groups, industries, regions, and classes than ever before, and as the demands and needs of those competing interests are weighed and mediated in the political process, the power of the president and Congress to control the policy agenda is reduced. The constitutional First Amendment rights, especially freedom of speech, freedom of assembly, freedom of the press, and freedom to petition government for grievances, are the foundation of pluralism in U.S. politics. The decay of political party organizations in the last thirty years in the United States has helped the growth of pluralism.[30] As political parties have lost power to recruit and elect candidates who are loyal to party leaders in government, interest groups have gained political power. The United States is experiencing "hyperpluralism," or extreme competition among groups that makes it almost impossible to define the public good in terms of anything other than the collection of special narrow interests.[31] Hyperpluralism contributes fundamentally to the rivalry between the president and Congress and often leads to deadlock between the two branches of government by making it difficult to make the necessary compromises between the national interests of the president and the parochial interests of members of Congress.[32] Crisis and presidential leadership can break the deadlock, as seen with President Bush's post-9/11 policy and President Obama's quick action to solve the problem of a failing economy.

CONCLUSIONS AND OVERVIEW OF THE BOOK

Organization theorists suggest that conflict and crisis produces incentives for organizations to centralize decision-making power. President Obama's strong chief of staff Rahm Emanuel and his White House organization structured around health, economic, energy-environment, and national security policy czars are an example of this.[33,34] When an organization is challenged, a premium is placed on efficiency, effectiveness, and cohesiveness in setting strategy. This was the case of the Obama campaign organization and President

Obama's White House. After forty years of Democratic control and two years of conflict from the Clinton White House, the House Republicans also centralized their decision-making power structure (especially in the House of Representatives) in unprecedented ways. The House Republican centralization of decision making, starting in the 104th Congress, reduced individualism and brought about a more efficient, disciplined, and cohesive institution in its battle with President Clinton and more coordination with President Bush in the 108th and 109th Congresses.

Threatened by a unified Republican House and Republican Senate, President Clinton also reorganized and centralized his White House staff through Leon Panetta, his chief of staff. He simplified his policy agenda and built a more tightly knit and effective legislative affairs operation. Faced with a Democratic majority in the House in the 1980s, then minority whip Newt Gingrich helped to build a cohesive, centralized, and efficient opposition that was eventually used as a majority party organization against President Clinton and the congressional Democrats in 1995.

Intense rivalry between the president and Congress is inevitable in an electoral system that can produce divided party control of the two branches. Cooperation may be more likely when both the president and Congress are of the same party; however, it is not guaranteed. Because of the wide range of views within a party, unified government is no safeguard against conflict, as was shown with President Obama, with President Clinton and the congressional Democratic Party in 1993 and 1994, and with the relationship Bush had with Congress (especially the Senate) in 2005. Partisanship may also serve to move legislation. The give-and-take between national and local representation, deliberation and efficiency, openness and accountability, specific interests and the "public good" ensures a certain amount of confrontation between Congress and the president. The relationship between the president and Congress is shaped by an amalgam of factors: constitutional design, different electoral motivations and constituencies, different terms of office, weak political parties, partisanship, divided party control of government, ongoing competition for power, and interest group pluralism. Although the rivalry and conflict between Congress and the president are inherent in our system of government, presidents must build support in Congress and members must seek assistance from the White House. To succeed in office, every president must surmount the constitutional and political obstacles to pass their legislative program and establish a working relationship with Congress.

Separation of powers and the division of political control between presidents and Congresses do not present an insurmountable barrier to good public policy making. Presidents need to lead both public opinion and a consensus among the policy communities in Congress to solve the problems that are so readily visible. Overcoming divided government, changing public opinion, building consensus, keeping party discipline, and establishing the nation's policy priorities calls for leadership from the president or from inside Congress. Congress and the president must work together. Unified partisan control of both branches of government does not guarantee cooperation as President George W. Bush found out early in his administration. Divided government does not guarantee conflict, but it does make governing more difficult. Governing calls for bargaining, accommodation, and compromise by Congress and the president, which are the basis of our "separated" and pluralistic system of government.[35]

The chapters in this book present a balance of views between presidential and congressional scholars. This book presents no one viewpoint, no one dominant ideology for or against Congress or the presidency. Some contributors believe the system is working well and others believe reform is badly needed. Some argue that Congress needs to assert more power to check the president and others conclude the relationship between Congress and the president is working well and as designed in our Constitution. The following chapters address the most important question about the relationship between the president and Congress. Taking a variety of approaches, what are the root causes of their rivalry and their cooperation? Political scientists, legal scholars, historians, journalists, former White House and Capitol Hill staff, and former members of Congress all contribute. Each author brings unique experiences, methodologies, viewpoints, and theoretical backgrounds to the study of the relationship between Congress and the president.

In chapter 2, "Partisan Polarization, Politics, and the Presidency: Structural Sources of Conflict," James P. Pfiffner argues that relations between the president and Congress have recently become even more polarized and combative. In this chapter, Pfiffner describes the structural sources for the highly partisan and volatile politics of the Clinton and Bush presidencies and the beginning of the Obama presidency. The factors leading to the recent increase in polarization between Congress and the president include the fact that the South is no longer the undisputed territory of Democrats and the increased frequency of divided government. He further shows how contemporary presidents do not enjoy the ideological sympathies of some members of the opposing party. Political parties that are more homogeneous—"Rockefeller Republicans" and "Boll Weevils"—are a thing of the past. As a result, presidents find it difficult to build and maintain the support of members from the opposing party for their legislative agenda. Filibusters have also increased, as have presidential threats to veto. Pfiffner argues that all these factors contribute to the contentious relationship between the president and Congress, even during unified party government. He also documents a decline in civility in both chambers since the 1970s and how this affects congressional-presidential relations. Given the continuing reality of predictably safe seats in the House, the polarization in Congress is not likely to go away soon. All these factors leave presidents with no natural coalition partners in the middle in Congress. Presidents often need to cobble together a fluid coalition of policy partners in Congress, but cannot count on their own party's support or cross-over support from members of the opposing party, as shown in the early days of the Obama presidency. This chapter concludes with an examination of the consequences of partisan polarization on public policy making and politics.

Stephen J. Wayne, in chapter 3, "From Washington to Obama: The Evolution of the Legislative Presidency," argues that the constitutional design as set by the framers assigns the president little role in legislating. The framers of the Constitution did not expect the president to be chief legislator.

However, the president's legislative role has increased steadily since Jefferson and Jackson were presidents. Contemporary presidents maintain "public relation teams" and seemingly try to influence legislative activity at every turn. In this chapter Professor Wayne uncovers why this change occurred. He first provides a historical description of how and why presidents first began to enter the legislative arena. He argues that nineteenth-century presidents began to legislate through members of Congress. They also used their veto power, and threats of vetoes, to influence congressional activity. As the twentieth century progressed, presidents went even further into the legislative arena. They developed a two-track agenda for influencing legislation. Major policy decisions received presidential attention while OMB and executive agencies handled more minor legislative activity. Wayne points out that the presidents since Reagan have most dramatically moved away from the framer's intent. Chiefs of staff now focus almost exclusively on the legislative agenda, policy directors have cabinet-level status, and the press is regularly used by presidents and their operatives to influence legislative activity. Presidents seek to sway public opinion and define legislative issues through sophisticated, permanent "public relation teams" centered in the White House. These teams use polling, focus groups, and the press to strategically set priorities, cycle issues, and package proposals in ways most likely to ensure legislative success. This ongoing public relations campaign within the White House stands in contrast to the specified legislative role for the president. To be successful, modern presidents must make their pressure on Congress an extension of a successful election campaign as was the case with the passage of Obama's 2009 economic stimulus bill. Wayne concludes that election campaigning and successful governing is closely linked in American politics, which has major ramifications for presidential and congressional rivalry. Wayne concludes that the personal involvement of the president, as shown by President Obama, is usually necessary to distinguish presidential priorities from other policy initiatives and to gain the votes required to enact them into law. Legislative successes are important criteria for evaluating presidential performance; they contribute to the foundation on which presidential legacies are built.

Chapter 4, "The President and the Congressional Party Leadership in a Polarized Era," written by congressional scholar Barbara Sinclair, examines how presidential-congressional relations look from 1600 Pennsylvania Avenue and from Capitol Hill. Sinclair investigates the relationship under both unified and divided control in recent years to demonstrate the effects of control under conditions of high partisanship and to highlight the varied other determinants of cooperation and conflict. She concludes with an analysis of President Obama's relationship with Congress, House and Senate Republicans and Democrats under the staggering problems and policy challenges facing the United States.

She concludes that the relationship between Obama and the Republican congressional leadership is likely to be rocky throughout his presidency, but by regular communication with them, President Obama can perhaps prevent the relationship from descending into bitter partisanship and distrust. President Obama's relationship with Democratic House and Senate leaderships is likely to remain good under unified party government. However, Sinclair concludes that the Democratic congressional leaders believe that their Republican predecessors' deference to President Bush hurt them, resulting in Bush listening to too few voices and too few opinions. Democrats in Congress also think that the Republican oversight of Bush administration agencies and policies and decisions hurt rather than helped. She concludes that the Obama administration can expect considerably more congressional oversight. Democratic leaders in Congress see their fate and that of their members linked with that of President Obama's. If President Obama maintains high support in the polls, if he makes decisions that are politically popular, and if he consults congressional leaders on a regular basis, he will have the political capital to push an aggressive policy agenda. In this era of high partisan polarization, Obama and the congressional Democrats are in the same boat, and if it sinks, they will go down together.

In chapter 5, "Understanding Presidential Relations with Congress," two former senior-level White House legislative experts, contemporary lobbyists, and political scientists—one Republican, Gary Andres, and one Democrat, Patrick Griffin—use their own experiences to critique existing conceptualizations of presidential "success" and "influence." They analyze the details of managing relations with Congress from inside the White House. Both having worked in the White House or on the last four presidential transitions (George H. W. Bush, Bill Clinton, George W. Bush, and Barack Obama), they have observed the process up close. They show that the constitutional framework of separation of powers and the political and policy context matters a lot in shaping presidential tactics and success. Presidents with large majorities in Congress face a different set of opportunities and challenges than those in mixed-party government situations. Further, these factors also shape the approach deployed in managing White House relations with the Hill. Presidential success is not always guaranteed, even if with unified party government.

Andres and Griffin also demonstrate why "personalities" and strategic goals of the actors involved contribute to the quality of a president's relations with Congress. They conclude by outlining a host of critical process variables that impact the quality of presidential relations with Capitol Hill. They analyze the importance of "political conditions" (such as the strength of the president's party control in Congress and presidential popularity) versus a president's personal leadership skills and his power to persuade. From their experience in the White House and on the Hill, they conclude that political conditions are more important determinants of success with Congress and that leadership skills only impact legislative achievement at the margins. Presidential success in Congress is largely determined by the political conditions faced by the White House and the president's ability to exploit them. From their practical experience with hundreds of legislative battles between the White House and the Hill, they highlight the most important factors in understanding presidential success in Congress. They raise questions about the dynamic relationship between the branches and conclude that whether presidents are successful in their relations with Congress should be evaluated using the broader criteria they propose in the chapter.

Congressional scholar, Roger H. Davidson, in chapter 6, "The Presidency and Congressional Time," argues that rather than measuring political time in terms of successive presidencies, one should analyze congressional eras. He tracks several factors, including legislative workload and productivity figures, and identifies four distinctive congressional regimes. By examining legislative attributes within each era, and between succeeding eras, Davidson casts new light on interbranch policy making since the New Deal to President Obama. He reveals two generalizations about legislative activity and productivity. First, legislative productivity does not necessarily coincide with the tenure of individual presidents. Second, legislative productivity is less determined by party control that one would think. By taking the viewpoint of Capitol Hill rather than that of the Oval Office, he offers a useful and nonconventional perspective of congressional-presidential relations. Davidson shows how strong party leadership saw its zenith in the late nineteenth and early twentieth centuries, the structural and partisan factors that lead to its erosion, and the gradual reemergence of strong party leadership in the 1970s. On the Senate side, strong party leadership emerged roughly during the same period. Davidson argues that the increased prominence and power of party leaders, especially since the 1950s, can be traced directly to the need for Senate leaders to confer with activist presidents and to help them manage their legislative agenda. He analyzes legislative productivity and presidential-congressional relations over time, in four distinct periods, the bipartisan conservative era (1937–1964), the liberal activist party government era (1965–1978), the postreform era (1979–1992), and the conservative party government era (1995–2008). Davidson concludes his analysis with comments on the Obama-congressional relationships and states that legislative productivity is not always linked with the tenure of individual presidents and is less determined by party control than one might assume. Davidson argues that party control is an incomplete guide to legislative activity and productivity; thus, casting doubt on the assumption of many observers that unified party control raises legislative output and divided government leads to stalemate.

Richard Conley adds a different perspective on presidential legislative power, political time, and unified and divided party control of government in chapter 7, "The Legislative Presidency in Political Time: Unified Government, Divided Government, and Presidential Leverage in Congress." Conley focuses on the ways in which unified or divided government matters for presidential legislative leadership. He concludes that single-party control facilitates more success for presidents. Presidents prevail more often on congressional votes on which they express a position in unified party government. He argues that scholars who have focused solely on congressional lawmaking have overlooked the advantages of unified government for the legislative presidency.

Split-party control has had a much more variable impact on presidents' success in Congress. In the early post–World War II period, presidents were often able to reach across the aisle to the opposition majority and its leadership to cobble together winning coalitions on floor votes. It is in the last several decades that assertive opposition majorities have set more of the policy agenda and have forced presidents to preempt Congress or take a more defensive role in the legislative game. Heightened partisanship and organizational reforms in Congress have hampered presidents' efforts to construct cross-party coalitions. These factors have hurt presidents' legislative success rates and complicated agenda control. Conley offers an historical analysis of party control and presidential-congressional relations. He proposes a theory of presidential leadership of Congress. His framework helps to explain the intersection of elections on organization and voting patterns in Congress since

World War II. His longitudinal data analysis of presidential success on floor votes in Congress as well as presidents' involvement in significant legislation shows the importance of party control of Congress for the legislative presidency. He analyzes how party control of the Congress and the presidency since 1953 has influenced both the president's legislative priorities and the relationship between the White House and the Congress. In defining "eras" of party unity and reform, Conley helps us to better understand presidential legislative successes and failures. More specifically, this chapter identifies how ideological agendas throughout history have contributed to the advancement of legislative priorities from presidents who have shared and differed in party identification from peers in Congress and what specific benefits resulted from such collaboration or opposition. Conley concludes with comments of how the institutional context following the 2008 presidential and congressional elections has shaped President Obama's potential for legislative leadership.

In chapter 8, "The Imperial Presidency vs. the Hill," Andrew Rudalevige argues with an historical and legal analysis that an imperial presidency requires an "invisible Congress," something that occurred from 2001 through 2006. The theory of the "unitary executive" has been an important justification for disregarding the very relevance of the legislative branch during the Bush presidency. Rudalevige's chapter explores that assessment, in theory and practice, with concluding comments about the Obama presidency and Congress. He shows that the risks that face the United States are real and that the temptation to take shortcuts correspondingly strong and, in the short term, always justifiable. He argues, for example, that the tragedies of September 11 made it clear that strong presidential leadership is essential to the nation. He also concludes that Congress has a critical role to play in determining policy in times of crisis. Rudalevige argues that if government must efficiently carry out national priorities, those priorities must themselves be arrived at through a deliberative process grounded in coalition and consensus between the president and Congress, not command solely by the president. He concludes the chapter with an application of these lessons to the Obama presidency during times of economic crisis.

Chapter 9 by Mark J. Rozell and Mitchel A. Sollenberger, "Executive Privilege and the Unitary Executive Theory in the George W. Bush Administration," describes and analyzes attempts by the Bush administration to employ the "unitary executive" theory in its efforts to conceal information from Congress and the public. They describe and critique a variety of attempts by the Bush administration to use executive privilege under the broader theory of a unitary executive. They conclude with an analysis of the future implications of Bush's actions and why it is essential that the Obama and other new administrations avoid the pitfalls of overreaching in the use of executive privilege.

Budgets are not just numbers and program priorities; they are politics and reveal a great deal about the relationship between the Congress and the president. In chapter 10, "The President's Budget vs. Congressional Budgeting: Institutionalizing the Adversarial Presidency?" Joseph White explains the political relationship between the White House and Congress in the federal budgetary process. He analyzes the role of the executive and legislative branches in budgeting. He describes the time each branch uses to act on budgetary issues and reveals the considerable differences in style when it comes to budgetary politics. The actions of executive branch offices and the White House are predictable and the president is always the ultimate arbiter. Congress is different. There is no central authority, each member tries to get his or her pet projects through and to influence the process. As a result, congressional action surrounding the budget is more unpredictable. With these broad differences delineated, White offers a discussion of budget development and implementation, noting the relative strength of presidents and Congress at each stage. This chapter pays particular attention to how the budgetary process has been shaped by deficit politics over the last twenty years. White argues that the battle over budgets has become more contentious and highlights a number of factors that contribute to this bitterness. He also argues that the budget process is only effective if those involved are willing to take the risks necessary to make it work. Presidents and the Congress have sought many agreements and reforms to strengthen their ability to discipline spending and establish priorities, but in the end, the process cannot work unless leaders are willing to lead. White concludes by stating the budget process is the essence of our democracy.

In chapter 11, "Congress and the President: 'Yes We Can!' or 'Can We?'" Mark Oleszek and Walter Oleszek focus on factors that influence the relationship between the president and Congress. They describe several major structural elements that make it difficult for the House, the Senate, and the president to act collectively, to build the winning coalitions required to make tough policy decisions, even during crisis. They also discuss the personal and environmental factors that influence legislative-presidential relationships. They review three presidencies—Franklin Delano Roosevelt (FDR), Lyndon Baines Johnson (LBJ), and Ronald Reagan—and evaluate the factors that influenced their success in winning congressional approval of their policy priorities during their first year in office. They conclude with an assessment of the relevance of these factors for President Obama. They conclude with an analysis of basic conditions necessary for Obama to be the "Yes we can" president. President Obama should take advantage of the fact that the public wants change. President Obama should use his rhetorical and bargaining skills to rally the citizenry and the Congress to his side. President Obama and congressional leaders should use their political skill to implement a governing vision that resonates with members of Congress and the populace. President Obama should push an activist agenda strongly and early during this economic crisis.

In chapter 12, "Relations between the President and Congress in Wartime," The Honorable Lee H. Hamilton evaluates the role of the president and Congress in making war. As a former member of Congress (from 1965 to 1998), former chair of the House Select Committee on Intelligence and chair of the House Foreign Affairs Committee, and his recent work as cochairman of the 9/11 and the Iraq Study Group Commissions, Hamilton uses his extensive experience in foreign and defense policy making on the Hill and off to discuss the appropriate role of the president and Congress in the decision to go to war. It is the most serious decision our government makes, but our Constitution and more than two hundred years of debate and legislation have not clarified the respective roles of the president and Congress. Hamilton's chapter does not resolve this constitutional dilemma, but tries to help future presidents and Congresses find an answer. He argues that the key question is: how can we assure that the president gets the best advice possible before embarking on war, and not just from a president's key advisers, but also from Congress? He argues that presidents are still the chief actor when it comes to war making, but that their dominance is no longer uncontested. He makes the case for providing genuinely independent counsel in the decision to go to war. He suggests that it is crucial for the president and the Congress to consult meaningfully and deliberate exhaustively before committing the nation to war. He does not refute the constitutional arguments advocates of congressional and presidential authority make about the scope of each branch's powers, but wants to enhance the role of Congress in making war. He recognizes that the president will make the final decisions about war; he want to increase the likelihood of consultation and congressional oversight during war. He wants Congress to use its power of the purse to shape the conduct and termination of armed conflict when necessary.

In the wake of the horrific attacks upon the United States on September 11, 2001, members of Congress were asked to stand side by side with the commander in chief in his defense of our great nation. In the days that followed the attacks of September 11, 2001, our nation learned much more about the mission carried out by Al Qaeda terrorists who sought to destroy our society's collective way of life and the individual lives of thousands of innocent civilians in the process. What we did not know during the months that followed was that our government would respond quickly to combat the terrorists while also establishing an agenda to further develop the "war on terror" in countries that had little or no connection with the horrific attacks on our homeland. In chapter 13, "Rivals Only Sometimes: Presidentialism, Unilateralism, and Congressional Acquiescence in the U.S. 'War on Terror,'" John E. Owens also argues that the terrorist attacks on New York and Washington signaled not only new directions in U.S. foreign and domestic policy but also a new presidential era in U.S. government. It brought a new phase in the aggrandizement of presidential power at a cost to civil liberties and the system's checks and balances. President Bush's actions shifted institutional power further to the White House and away from Congress. His historical analysis documents that many presidents in time of crisis, including George W. Bush, have made policy unilaterally by exploiting the notorious vagueness and ambiguities of the vesting clauses in article II of the Constitution, especially in times of war and emergency.

One indication of whether a new constitutional equilibrium between the president and Congress will be reached may be determined by whether and to what extent the Congress collectively challenges President Obama on the Bush counterterrorist issues, particularly in the new context of global economic recession. He concludes that presidential power is not only the power to persuade; it is also a question of what a president can get away with. Whether the Congress and the courts will stop him is the test of his power. He thinks that within a decade we should know the lasting legacy of George W. Bush's shift of power to the executive.

As a complement to Owens's chapter on the president's expansion of power during the war on terror and Hamilton's chapter on the role of Congress and the president in time of war, Louis Fisher's historical-legal-constitutional analysis in chapter 14, "The President, Congress, Military Tribunals, and Guantanamo" describes President George W. Bush's justification and authorization of the creation of military tribunals to try individuals who assisted in the terrorist attacks of 9/11. Military tribunals had not been used since World War II. President Bush invoked "inherent" powers of the president as legal authority for the tribunals. Congress acquiesced to these initiatives, but the detention of hundreds of suspects at the U.S. naval base in Guantanamo, Cuba, met repeated defeats in the courts. Fisher argues that with false historical precedents and "strained" arguments, the Bush administration claimed it could indefinitely hold U.S. citizens and aliens at Guantanamo naval base with few procedural safeguards. Fisher shows that as detention continued for years, without trial or even bringing charges against the suspects, the Bush administration's position grew progressively weaker in court, in the country, and in the eyes of the world community. He concludes his analysis by reminding readers that 2008 candidate Barack Obama promised to close the detention facility at Guantanamo and in his first few days in office, on January 22, 2009, President Obama issued several executive orders related to the detainees and closing Guantanamo, directly changing President Bush's actions and challenging his justifications for detention of suspects at the naval base.

In the concluding chapter 15, "The President and Congress: Separate, Independent, and Completely Equal," former member of Congress and constitutional scholar, Mickey Edwards argues that American democracy is designed not for happy harmony but for deliberate conflict. Democracy is dependent on the full consideration of alternatives: on the ability of the people, through their representatives, to weigh options and consider which best serve the interests of the nation. Partisanship and conflict is a natural state in a rigorous democracy. His essay presents the case for a vigorous, energetic, and effective president and a strong, representative Congress. Edwards argues that such a presidency and Congress enables a rivalry that serves American liberty rather than threatening it. Congress and the president should have a rivalry for primacy in the court of public opinion and conduct their battle for public policy bounded by the constraints of the Constitution. Given this necessity of vigorous debate, it is easy to see why the president and Congress come into such regular conflict. If our democracy is to thrive, the Congress should be (and is) at the heart of a public participation in the public policy-making process. Congress must challenge the president and be able to put issues forward and engage in serious discussion about their relative merits. Edwards argues that merely following the direction of the president diminishes democracy; it does not enhance it. He concludes his essay on the necessary balance between the president and Congress by pointing out that President Obama has put his own stamp on the nature of the rivalry between the legislative and executive branches of government during a time of crisis.

NOTES

1. David S. Broder, "The Amazing Race," *Washington Post*, November 2, 2008, B1.

2. James A. Thurber, "Thunder from the Right: Observations about the Elections," *The Public Manager* (Winter 1994–1995): 13–16.

3. On September 27, 1994, Republican congressional candidates signed the Contract with America, pledging that if elected they would support changes in congressional procedures and bring votes in the House on a series of proposals such as a balanced budget amendment, a line-item veto, and term limits for members of Congress. For more on the Contract with America, see Ed Gillespie and Bob Schellhas, eds. *Contract with America* (New York: Times Books, 1994).

4. For more on the 1992 elections, see Michael Nelson, ed., *The Elections of 1992* (Washington, DC: CQ Press, 1993).

5. Beth Donovan, "Maverick Chairman Forgiven as Clinton Reworks Bill," *Congressional Quarterly Weekly Report*, June 12, 1993, 1251–52.

6. Erwin C. Hargrove, "The Presidency: George Bush and the Cycle of Politics and Policy," in *The Elections of 1988*, ed. Michael Nelson (Washington, DC: CQ Press, 1989), 175.

7. Quoted in James A. Barnes, "Political Focus," *National Journal*, February 11, 1989, 377.

8. For a description of presidential-congressional policy battles, see Lance T. LeLoup and Steven A. Shull, *Congress and the President: The Policy Connection* (Belmont, CA: Wadsworth, Inc., 1993).

9. See Joseph J. Schatz, "With a Deft and Light Touch, Bush Finds Ways to Win," *CQ Weekly*, December 11, 2004, 2900–2905.

10. Schatz, "With a Deft and Light Touch," 2901.

11. Arthur M. Schlesinger Jr. and Alfred De Grazia, *Congress and the Presidency: Their Role in Modern Times* (Washington, DC: American Enterprise Institute, 1976), 1.

12. See James A. Thurber, "Congress and the Constitution: Two Hundred Years of Stability and Change," in *Reflections on the Constitution*, ed. Richard Maidment (Manchester, UK: University of Manchester Press, 1989), 51–75.

13. For this constitutional basis of conflict, see Richard E. Neustadt, *Presidential Power and the Modern Presidents: The Politics of Leadership from Roosevelt to Reagan* (New York: Free Press, 1990); James L. Sunquist, *The Decline and Resurgence of Congress* (Washington, DC: The Brookings Institution, 1981); Steven A. Shull, *Domestic Policy Formation: Presidential-Congressional Partnership?* (Westport, CT: Greenwood Press, 1983); Michael L. Mezey, *Congress, the President, and Public Policy* (Boulder, CO: Westview Press, 1985); Louis Fisher, *Constitutional Conflicts Between Congress and the President*, 4th ed. rev. (Lawrence: University of Kansas Press, 1996); Louis Fisher, *The Politics of Shared Power: Congress and the Executive* (Washington, DC: CQ Press, 1993); Charles O. Jones, *The Presidency in a Separated System* (Washington, DC: The Brookings Institution, 1994); Charles O. Jones, *Separate But Equal Branches: Congress and the Presidency* (New York: Chatham House, 1999); Charles O. Jones, *Clinton and Congress: Risk, Restoration, and Reelection* (Norman: University of Oklahoma Press, 1999).

14. A pocket veto is the act of the president withholding his approval of a bill after Congress has adjourned. See Harold W. Stanley and Richard G. Niemi, *Vital Statistics on American Politics*, 5th ed. (Washington, DC: CQ Press, 1995), 258. For vetoes and overrides from the 80th to the 103d Congresses (1947–1994), see Norman J. Ornstein, Thomas E. Mann, and Michael J. Malbin, *Vital Statistics on Congress, 1995–1996* (Washington, DC: Congressional Quarterly, Inc., 1996), 167.

15. Todd S. Purdum, "President Warns Congress to Drop Some Budget Cuts," *New York Times*, October 29, 1995, 30.

16. See Jones, *The Presidency in a Separated System*.

17. See George C. Edwards III, *Presidential Influence in Congress* (San Francisco: Freeman, 1980); and Cecil V. Crabb Jr. and Pat M. Holt, *Invitation to Struggle: Congress, the President, and Foreign Policy*, 4th ed. (Washington, DC: CQ Press, 1992).

18. James Madison, "Federalist No. 46," in *The Federalist Papers*, ed. Clinton Rossiter (New York: New American Library, 1961), 296.

19. See Stephen Wayne, *The Legislative Presidency* (New York: Harper and Row, 1978).

20. David R. Mayhew, *Congress: The Electoral Connection* (New Haven, CT: Yale University Press, 1974).

21. Thomas E. Mann, "Breaking the Political Impasse," in *Setting National Priorities: Policy for the Nineties*, ed. Henry J. Aaron (Washington, DC: The Brookings Institution, 1990), 302.

22. On divided party control of government, see David R. Mayhew, *Divided We Govern: Party Control, Lawmaking, and Investigations, 1946–1990* (New Haven, CT: Yale University Press, 1991); James A. Thurber, ed., *Divided Democracy: Cooperation and Conflict between the President and Congress* (Washington, DC: CQ Press, 1991); and Gary C. Jacobson, *The Electoral Origins of Divided Government* (Boulder, CO: Westview Press, 1990).

23. Nelson Polsby quoted in *Congress and the Nation*, vol. VII, 1985–1988 (Washington, DC: Congressional Quarterly Inc., 1990), 21–22.

24. Mayhew, *Divided We Govern*, 198.

25. See Stephen J. Wayne, "Great Expectations: What People Want from Presidents," in *Rethinking the Presidency*, ed. Thomas E. Cronin (Boston: Little, Brown, 1982), 185–199; and Glen R. Parker, "Some Themes in Congressional Opportunity," *American Journal of Political Science* 21 (February 1977): 93–119.

26. See Committee on the Constitutional System, *A Bicentennial Analysis of the American Political Structure* (Washington, DC: Committee on the Constitutional System, 1987).

27. James A. Thurber, "The 104th Congress Is Fast and Efficient, But at What Cost?" *Roll Call*, March 4, 1995, 16; and James A. Thurber, "Republican Centralization of the Congressional Budget Process," *Extensions of Remarks*, December 1995.

28. James A. Thurber, "Twenty-five years of Deficit and Conflict: Partisan Roles in Congressional Budget Reform," in *New Majority or Old Minority: The Impact of Republicans in Congress,* eds. Nicole C. Rae and Colton Campbell (Lanham, MD: Rowman & Littlefield, 1999).

29. Richard E. Cohen, Kirk Victor, and David Bauman, "The State of Congress," *National Journal*, January 10, 2004, 83–105.

30. See Joel H. Sibley, "The Rise and Fall of American Political Parties," in *The Parties Respond: Changes in American Parties and Campaigns*, ed. L. Sandy Maisel (Boulder, CO: Westview Press, 1994), 3–18.

31. James A. Thurber, "Political Power and Policy Subsystems in American Politics," in *Agenda for Excellence: Administering the State*, eds. B. Guy Peters and Bert A. Rockman (Chatham, NJ: Chatham House Publishers, 1996), 76–104.

32. See Jonathan Rauch, *Demosclerosis* (New York: Times Books, 1994).

33. Ryan Lizza, "The Gatekeeper," *New Yorker*, March 2, 2009, 24–29.

34. See James G. March and Herbert A. Simon, *Organizations* (New York: John Wiley and Sons, 1958).

35. See Jones, *The Presidency in a Separated System*.

Chapter Two

Partisan Polarization, Politics, and the Presidency: Structural Sources of Conflict

James P. Pfiffner

Bill Clinton's presidency began in 1993 with great optimism in the Democratic Party. The Democrats controlled both houses of Congress and the presidency for the first time since the Carter administration. In his campaign Clinton promised to "end welfare as we know it," provide a middle-class tax cut, and reform the nation's health care system. But health care reform did not even get to a vote in Congress, and in the 1994 elections, a Republican wave swept many Democrats out of office. This gave Republicans control of Congress for the first time in forty years. The aggressive policy agenda of the 104th Congress threatened to dismantle many central programs from the New Deal and the Great Society. But Clinton used his veto power to face down the challenge from the Republican Congress and got reelected in 1996. The Monica Lewinsky scandal erupted in 1998, and the Republican House impeached President Clinton, although there were not enough votes in the Senate to remove him from office.

In the campaign of 2000 President Bush campaigned as a "compassionate conservative," said that he would pursue a "humble" foreign policy, and promised to be a "uniter, not a divider." Rather than trying to build a moderate coalition of Democrats and Republicans in his policy agenda, he played to his base in the electorate and the cohesive Republican Congress on the Hill. The terrorist attacks of 9/11 gave him tremendous political capital and public approval ratings in the 90 percent range, the highest in the modern presidency. He successfully displaced the Taliban regime in Afghanistan, but before the war was over, decided to pursue "regime change" in Iraq. After deposing Saddam Hussein in Iraq, the U.S. occupation of the country faced a deadly insurgency that dragged on for the rest of his presidency. Rather than being a uniter, President Bush turned out to be the most divisive president in at least a half century.[1] His low public approval ratings led Republicans in

Congress to avoid appearing with him during the 2008 elections, and John McCain took care to distance his candidacy from the Bush administration.

Some of the difficulties in these two presidencies were due to the individual personalities of the two presidents and their differing policy agendas. But a good portion of their difficulties was the result of an extremely polarized Congress. The country as a whole began voting more along party lines than in previous decades, and political elites, particularly the two parties in Congress, were more polarized than they had been since the late nineteenth century.

In addition to the partisan and policy rivalry between president and Congress, the two branches also struggle with each other over their institutional power in the separation of powers system. The framers of the Constitution built into the government sources of friction between the president and Congress that have been played out over the history of the republic. As Madison said in "Federalist No. 51," "ambition must be made to counteract ambition." This necessary and often healthful competition for power between the president and Congress sometimes degenerates into struggles for power that stretch the bounds of the separation of powers system. Congress pushes the envelope when it attempts to tie the president's hands too narrowly in the normal execution of public policy, a practice often known as "micromanagement." In the twentieth century, however, the executive was most often the branch pushing the envelope. In the twenty-first century, George W. Bush challenged the role of Congress by claiming extraordinary constitutional authority in several areas of public policy.

This chapter will first examine the roots of partisan polarization and its consequences for public policy and politics. It will then look at the consequences of that polarization for the two contentious presidencies of Bill Clinton and George W. Bush. Finally, it will briefly address the fundamental constitutional challenge that President Bush presented to Congress. His claims to constitutional authority were in some ways unprecedented, and his assertions struck at the very base of the constitutional separation of powers and the rule of law in the United States.

THE ORIGINS OF CONGRESSIONAL POLARIZATION

In the latter quarter of the twentieth-century, Congress was transformed from a relatively consensual institution with significant overlap between the Democratic and Republican parties to an ideological, polarized battlefield with virtually no middle ground. The path to partisan polarization was begun with the political revolution that turned the U.S. South from a Democratic bastion to a conservative stronghold; Republicans dominated the region, with pockets of liberal and African American strength.

Congressional polarization has ebbed and flowed over the history of the United States. It reached a high mark in the latter decades of the nineteenth century. In the first third of the twentieth century, the parties began to converge, with more cross-pressured members of each party voting with the other party. During the middle third of the twentieth century, from the early 1930s to the early 1970s, Congress enjoyed an unusual period of voting overlap in the middle of the ideological spectrum. During this period conservative Democrats (Boll Weevils) from the South often combined with Republicans in the "conservative coalition" to defeat civil rights and other liberal legislative proposals. So there was plenty of ideological confrontation, but ideology did not reinforce partisanship, because there were significant numbers of conservative Democrats and liberal Republicans who often crossed party lines in voting on important legislation.

During this era relative power in Congress devolved to committee chairs who dominated their separate fiefdoms, and consequently party leaders presided over the two houses but did not dominate the legislative agenda. During this period of relative stability between the parties, Democrats controlled Congress for the most part. But in their voting records, 36 percent of Democrats were more conservative than the most liberal Republicans, and 95 percent of the Republicans were more liberal than the most conservative Democrats.[2] This significant overlap prompted George Wallace in his 1968 campaign for the presidency to declare that there was "not a dime's worth of difference" between the two parties.

But beginning in 1973 members of Congress began to vote increasingly along party lines, leading to the intense polarization that marked the end of the twentieth century and the beginning of the twenty-first century in Congress. The steady polarization began with the breakup of Democratic domination of the "Solid South." From the 1950s to the 1980s migration of whites from the North to southern cities and suburbs led to the gradual ascendancy of the Republican Party. Many of these immigrants brought with them Republican voting habits. From the 1960s to the 1980s, approximately 40 to 50 percent of southern Republicans were born outside of the South.[3] Along with general urbanization in the South and black migration to the North, the partisan complexion of the South began to change. The Republican Party was becoming a viable political party and beginning to attract more voters.[4] Partisan realignment in the South was further encouraged by the Civil Rights Act of 1964 and the Voting Rights Act of 1965, both of which increased the number of black voters who voted overwhelmingly Democratic.[5]

Conservative whites began to identify with the Republican Party, and to send more Republican representatives to Congress. The creation of majority-minority districts concentrated more liberal blacks in districts while more conservative whites ended up in districts that voted Republican. The result of this realignment was that the Democratic Party in Congress lost its "Dixicrat" (conservative southern Democrats) members and became more homogeneously liberal.[6] The conservative coalition, which had been thwarting Democratic presidents since FDR, began to decline in importance, because the conservative southerners were now in the Republican Party.

The transformation of the South from domination by the Democratic Party to Republican control was only one of the factors that led to congressional polarization. House delegations outside the South as well as senators became more polarized during the same time period. One of the important factors in the process was the ideological "sorting" of voters in which those who labeled themselves liberal began voting more consistently for Democrats and conservatives voted regularly for Republicans. In addition, congressional districts became more politically homogeneous, with Democrats and Republicans tending to live near each other. In 1976, 26.8 percent of voters lived in districts where one congressional candidate won by a margin of more than 20 percent; by 2004 that percentage had increased to 48.3.[7]

Along with homogeneous districts, redistricting led to safer seats in which members won reelection by large margins and did not have to worry much about losing to the opposing party. As a result, there were fewer congressional districts "in play," that is, seats that might be won by either party. According to Gary Jacobson's analysis, the number of safe seats increased significantly between 1992 and 2002: Democrats' safe seats increased from 142 to 158, and Republicans' safe seats increased from 139 to 198.[8] Thus the total number of safe seats was 356 of 435, but the number of House races that were actually competitive was significantly less than that.[9] In the 2004 elections 83 percent of House races were won by margins of 20 percent or more, and 95 percent of districts were won by more than 10 percent. In the 2006 and 2008 congressional elections Democrats were able to put more seats in play because of voter disenchantment with the Bush presidency.

Redistricting, however, was only part of the cause of polarization in Congress.[10] Before the 1960s, party elites who were active in politics (as office holders, convention delegates, or active participants in partisan political activities) were concerned primarily with winning elections and were often willing to compromise on policy issues. But beginning in the 1960s a different type of elite began to dominate political parties. The new elites were more ideologically committed to particular causes or policy issues. They were less willing to compromise and were even willing to risk losing an election in order to make ideological statements. These Democratic and Republican partisan elites were also those who were most likely to turn out to vote in primary elections, and they favored more extreme candidates from their own party.[11]

Safer districts, the advantages of incumbency, and the influence of party activists led to the election of more liberal Democrats and more conservative Republicans. Safe seats put moderate candidates of both parties at a disadvantage. Turnout for primary elections is predictably low, and most of those who actually vote are committed partisans, that is, true believers who hold more extreme views than most voters in their parties. Thus in order to get nominated and then to remain in office, members must please those on the wings of their parties or be outflanked by more extreme candidates.

Congressman Jim Leach (R-IA), with some exaggeration, explained the problem this way:

> A little less than four hundred seats are totally safe, which means that there is competition between Democrats and Republicans only in about ten or fifteen per cent of the seats. So the important question is who controls the safe seats. Currently, about a third of the over-all population is Democrat, a third is Republican, and a third is no party [independent]. If you ask yourself some mathematical questions, what is a half of a third?—one-sixth. That's who decides the nominee in each district. But only a fourth participates in primaries. What's a fourth of a sixth? A twenty-fourth. So it's one twenty-fourth of the population that controls the seat in each party.[12]

The changes in the partisanship of members of Congress over the several decades included both the replacement of moderate members with more partisan candidates as well as individual members changing their own ideological perspectives and becoming less moderate in order to head off a challenge in the primaries.[13] The retirement of many moderate senators and their replacement with more extreme senators, who often moved from the more polarized House and brought with them their more confrontational ways, increased the polarization in the Senate.[14]

The advantages of incumbents who sought reelection, always considerable, have become even more pronounced. From 1984 to 1990 House members seeking reelection were successful 97 percent of the time and in 2002, 98 percent successful. Senators were a bit more vulnerable, but still quite successful, winning 86 percent of bids for reelection from 1982 to 2003 and 95 percent in 1996.[15] In 2004, aside from the redistricted Texas, 99 percent of House incumbents won reelection, with only three incumbents being defeated.[16] In 2006 Democrats were partially successful in nationalizing the elections by treating them as a referendum on the war in Iraq and were able to drive the reelection rate down to 94 percent.[17]

As Congress became more polarized the two party caucuses became more homogeneous internally at the same time that the two parties diverged more sharply on ideological and policy issues. The transformation of the South from the Democratic to a Republican stronghold, ironically, led to a more successful Democratic control of the House. The increasing liberal consensus among the Democrats in Congress led the Democratic caucus in the House to become more cohesive and, through control of committee membership, assert its liberal policy views more effectively (e.g., on civil rights, old-age assistance, health care, housing, and other federal programs). According to David E. Price, Democratic representative from North Carolina,

> Revitalizing the House Democratic Caucus proved necessary in order to rewrite the rules, depose recalcitrant chairmen, and otherwise effect the desired transfer of power. The leadership, moreover, was the only available counterweight to conservative bastions like the House Rules and Ways and Means Committees. Therefore, two key early reforms removed the committee-assignment function from Ways and Means Democrats and placed [it] in a leadership-dominated Steering and Policy Committee and gave the Speaker the power to nominate the chair and the Democratic members of the Rules Committee.[18]

The number of Democrats in the House began to increase in 1958, and particularly in the Democratic landslides in 1964 and 1974. In order for the Democratic caucus to gain more effective policy control, more power was delegated to its leadership in the 1970s and 1980s.[19] As the Democrats in the House became more ideologically similar, their leadership became more assertive in the use of parliamentary tactics and provoked the ire of Republicans by denying them procedural rights in ways that were perceived as unfair.[20] Newt Gingrich led the outraged Republicans in the House to develop Republican candidates, particularly in the South. Their organizational efforts culminated in the 1994 election landslide that put the Republicans in charge of Congress for the first time in forty years.[21]

Thus the Republican domination of southern congressional delegations led to a more homogeneous, liberal Democratic party in Congress, which led to more polarized parties and finally to the Republican takeover of Congress in 1994.[22]

Polarizing parties with more internal cohesion combined with near parity of party balance in Congress led to the delegation of more power to the leadership of both houses but particularly the House. Thus in the 1980s Democrats used heavy-handed parliamentary tactics to keep Republicans from delaying and obstructing the legislative process. Republicans denounced these Democratic practices, yet when they came to power in 1995, they resorted to the same tactics in order to prevail in passing their own priority legislation.

The Democrats, in turn, complained, but when they came back to power in 2007, they again used similar tactics to assure their legislative success. This negative spiral of parliamentary warfare in Congress feeds on itself, making procedural voting more important and makes Congress a contentious battleground with fewer opportunities for cooperation.[23]

We turn now to the consequences of polarization: the decline of the center and its impact of civility in Congress.

THE WANING CENTER AND DECLINE OF CIVILITY

In the middle of the twentieth century the two political parties in Congress were not ideologically monolithic. That is, each party had a significant number of members who were ideologically sympathetic to the other party. The Democratic Party contained a strong conservative wing of members, the southern Boll Weevils, who often voted with the conservative Republicans. The Republican Party contained a noticeable number of moderates, mostly from the northeast, the "Rockefeller Republicans," who would often vote with the Democrats. These cross-pressured members of Congress made up between one-fifth and one-third of each house of Congress from 1950 to the mid-1980s.[24]

In the last fifteen years of the twentieth century the cross-pressured members of each party all but disappeared. Bond and Fleisher have calculated the number of liberal Republicans and conservative Democrats in Congress from the 1950s through the 1990s and have documented their decline. The number of conservative Democrats in the House has decreased from a high of 91 in 1965–1966 to a low of 11 in 1995–1996. In the Senate the high of 22 in the early 1960s was reduced to zero in 1995–1996. Liberal Republicans similarly fell from a high of 35 in the early 1970s to a low of 1 in 1993–1994 in the House, and a high of 14 in 1973–1974 to a low of 2 in 1995–1996 in the Senate.[25] This disappearance of the middle is a convincing demonstration of ideological polarization in Congress.

Sarah Binder has also found that the area of ideological overlap between the two parties in Congress has drastically decreased from a relatively high level of overlap in 1970 to "virtually no ideological common ground shared by the two parties."[26] The *National Journal* developed its own ideological scale of liberal and conservative voting and has calculated individual scores for members of Congress. Since 1981, most House Democrats would be on the liberal end of the spectrum and most Republicans on the right. There was always a number of members of each party whose voting record put them in the middle, overlapping ideological space. In 1999, however, only two Republicans and two Democrats shared the middle ground.

Theriault reports that in the 93d Congress 252 members of the House could be placed ideologically between the most liberal Republicans and the most conservative Democrats. By the 108th Congress no member of the House could be placed similarly. In the Senate of the 93d Congress forty senators could be placed in this middle portion of the ideological spectrum, and by the 108th Congress, there were only four.[27] The percentage of Republicans who were moderate decreased from 49 percent in 1977 to 3 percent in 2005. And in the 2006 elections, eight of the most moderate Republicans were defeated for reelection, leaving the 110th Congress with the fewest moderates since the nineteenth century.[28]

What the above data mean in a practical sense is that each of the political parties in Congress is more ideologically homogenous and that there is greater ideological distance between the two parties. Thus there is less need to compromise in a moderate direction when reaching a consensus within each party. And it is correspondingly more difficult to bridge the ideological gap between the contrasting perspectives of the two parties. Finding middle ground where compromise is possible becomes much more difficult. It is more likely that votes will be set up to highlight partisan differences and used for rhetorical and electoral purposes rather than to arrive at compromise policies.

According to Sarah Binder systematic comparisons of the ratio of actual laws enacted to important issues considered by the political system, two dimensions of polarization outweighed even the effect of divided government: the ideological gap between the parties and the ideological distance between the two houses of Congress. Thus if one is concerned with the problem of *gridlock* (which she defines as "the share of salient issues on the nation's agenda left in limbo at the close of each Congress"), ideological polarization in Congress is even more important than divided government (when the president's party does not control both houses of Congress).[29]

From this rather abstract discussion of the consequences of polarization, we now turn to the more human consequences: the decline of civility in Congress.

The traditional norms of courtesy, reciprocity, and comity that marked the 1950s and 1960s in Congress began to break down in the 1970s.[30] Reflecting broader divisions in U.S. politics over the Vietnam War and Watergate, life in Congress became more contentious. Legislative language had traditionally been marked by overly elaborate politeness in order to manage partisan and sometimes personal conflict. But instances of harsh language and incivility became more common and more partisan in the 1970s and 1980s. In the House the Republicans felt increasingly suppressed by the majority Democrats through the rules of debate and legislative scheduling and, under the leadership of Newt Gingrich, began to use obstructionist tactics to clog up the legislative process.[31] The predictable Democratic response was to tighten up the rules even more to deal with disruptive tactics. After Republicans took control of Congress in 1994, relations between the parties continued to deteriorate.

Even the usually more decorous Senate suffered from declining civility. As long ago as the early 1980s Senator Joseph Biden remarked, "There's much less civility than when I came there ten years ago. There aren't as many nice people as there were before. . . . Ten years ago you didn't have people calling each other sons of bitches and vowing to get at each other."[32]

Scholars David Brady and Morris Fiorina summarize the political context during the 1990s:

> In a context in which members themselves have stronger and more distinct policy preferences, where they scarcely know each other personally because every spare moment is spend fund-raising or cultivating constituents, where interest groups monitor every word a members speaks and levy harsh attacks upon the slightest deviation from group orthodoxy, where the media provide coverage in direct proportion to the negativity and conflict contained in one's messages, where money is desperately needed and is best raised by scaring the bejesus out of people, is it any wonder that comity and courtesy are among the first casualties?[33]

The decline in civility that marked the end of the 1990s continued into the early twenty-first century, as the polarized politics of the era continued to erode the relatively more decorous times of the mid-twentieth century. With the narrow Republican control of the Senate at stake, Majority Leader Bill Frist of Tennessee decided to go to South Dakota to campaign against Minority Leader Tom Daschle. Such personal campaigning by the Senate majority leader in the minority leader's home state was unprecedented in the twentieth century and highlighted the animosity that marked the polarization in Congress.[34] Frist was successful when Daschle lost his bid for reelection in 2004.

On the floor of the Senate, the personal animosity resulting from the polarization was illustrated when Vice President Cheney publicly said to Democrat Senator Patrick Leahy, "Fuck yourself." Although such insults are common among politicians (and nonpoliticians), they are most often expressed in private. This particular insult was particularly egregious because it was not a comment about a third party but stated directly to the person insulted; it was not private, but public; it was said on the floor of Congress; and it was said publicly by the president of the Senate, the vice president of the United States. In explaining his remark, the vice president did not address a substantive difference between the two men, but said that it correctly expressed his feelings, "I expressed myself forcefully, felt better after I had done it."[35]

Democrats in 2004 also complained that Republicans systematically excluded them from important conference committee negotiations between the two houses and that the procedural rules were used against them in ways that exceeded the Democrats' partisan use of procedures in the later years of their domination of Congress. Republican Senator John McCain commented on the partisanship of the procedural battles, "The Republicans had better hope that the Democrats never regain the majority."[36] Sure enough, when the Democrats returned to power in 2007, they also used heavy-handed parliamentary tactics to ensure that their legislative priorities were enacted.

PRESIDENT AND CONGRESS IN
AN ERA OF POLARIZED POLITICS

The Clinton era was a contentious time for relations between the president and Congress. At one level the conflict reflected a personal rivalry between Bill Clinton and Newt Gingrich. Clinton, a self-described "New Democrat," pulled the Democratic Party in a more moderate direction and "captured" some issues from the Republicans, for example, support for crime control, fiscal prudence, family values (at least in rhetoric). Gingrich, on the other side, had led the Republicans from the wilderness of minority status to the promised land of majority control of Congress, and sought to dismantle much of the liberal Great Society legislation that Democrats had passed in the 1960s.

President Bush campaigned for the presidency in 2000 as a moderate, "compassionate conservative," but once in office he pursued a conservative policy agenda of tax cuts and a unilateral foreign policy. Immediately after the 9/11 terrorist attacks on the United States, Bush enjoyed some of the highest approval ratings of the modern presidency and support for the United States throughout the world. By the end of his second term, his approval ratings were among the lowest of the modern presidency, and international attitudes toward the United States had dropped precipitously because of the Iraq war and U.S. treatment of detainees in the war on terror. This section will examine the polarized politics of the Clinton and Bush presidencies.

President Clinton and Congress:
Partisan Conflict and Impeachment

In the 103d Congress (1993–1995) the Democrats still held a majority in Congress and had high hopes that they would achieve a positive policy record that would mark a resurgence of Democratic hegemony after twelve years of

Republican control of the presidency.[37] But the dream was not to come true. Clinton's first major policy push was for deficit reduction, which he won with no Republican votes, but which was bitter medicine for congressional Democrats who would rather have pushed new programs. Then, Clinton's big initiative for universal health care coverage was defeated by the Republicans in 1994. The huge and complex plan favored by the administration was framed by the Republicans as more "big government" and too costly. In 1994 the Republicans were able to use the Clinton record to "nationalize" the midterm congressional elections and take control of Congress for the first time in forty years.

The Gingrich-led Republican victory was so overwhelming that at the beginning of the 104th Congress they were able to push the Contract with America agenda through the House in the spring of 1995 and roll over the Democrats in doing so. The national agenda was so dominated by the Republican contract that on April 18, 1995, President Clinton had to argue that, as president, he was still "relevant" to the policy process. "The President is relevant. . . . The Constitution gives me relevance; the power of our ideas gives me relevance; the record we have built up over the last two years and the things we're trying to do give me relevance."[38] But when many of the Contract with America proposals foundered in the Senate, the Republicans decided to build into the appropriations process provisions that would go far beyond the contract in trying to reduce severely many of the government programs of which they disapproved. They wanted to abolish three cabinet departments and cut back severely programs in education, environmental protection, Medicare, and Medicaid as well as eliminate smaller programs such as the National Endowments for the Arts and Humanities.

These priorities were packaged in omnibus legislation in the fall of 1995, and President Clinton vetoed the bills several times. When the Republicans did not change the provisions, much of the government was shut down for lack of appropriations. When it became clear that the public saw the Republican Congress rather than President Clinton as responsible for the shutdown, Robert Dole, who was running for president, convinced Congress to pass appropriations bills and negotiate the budget bills. Clinton was reelected in 1996, and the Republicans retained control of Congress by narrow margins.[39]

The 105th Congress (1998–1999) began with Clinton's plans to propose a number of "small bore" policy proposals that would be acceptable across the political spectrum, but in late January the Monica Lewinsky scandal hit. The rest of the spring was dominated by the efforts of Kenneth Starr to collect evidence for the Republican impeachment of Clinton in the fall of 1998. The articles of impeachment passed on party-line votes, with only a few members from each party defecting on the two articles that were adopted. The 106th Congress began with the Senate trial of the president and its decision not to remove him from office. The rest of the session was taken up with the aftermath of the impeachment trial and partisan battles over policy priorities. The second session began in an election year (2000) and was not marked by major policy victories or an impressive legislative record.

As bitter as the battles between Clinton and Gingrich were, the argument of this chapter is that the fundamental causes of the partisan battles that dominated the four Congresses of the Clinton era were driven by the polarization of Congress rather than by the personalities of the two men. It must also be kept in mind that the whole political spectrum had shifted in a conservative direction in the 1980s, just as it shifted in a more liberal direction in the 1960s.

Partisan conflict and battles between the president and Congress, however, do not mean that no important legislation gets passed. Stalemate is a relative term, and the government keeps operating (even during a shutdown) during intensely partisan periods. Thus President Clinton and Congress were able to pass a number of important policy initiatives. In 1993 President Clinton fought for congressional approval of the North American Free Trade Agreement (NAFTA). But he was able to get it passed only by knitting together a coalition of more Republicans than Democrats.

Similarly, although he thought the measure too harsh, President Clinton decided to sign the Republican welfare reform bill in the summer of 1996, despite opposition of the Democrats in Congress (and some in his own administration). It was an election year, and Clinton did not want to give Republicans the opportunity to argue that he vetoed three welfare bills after promising to "end welfare as we know it."

In 1997 President Clinton and the Republican Congress were able to compromise in order to come to an agreement that would balance the budget within five years. This impressive agreement was achieved by the willingness of each side to set aside partisan warfare and negotiate an outcome in which each side could claim victory. The 1997 deal was followed by a FY 1998 budget that was actually balanced—four years earlier than had been projected, and surpluses continued in 1999, 2000, and 2001.[40] This historic turnaround was based on the groundwork laid by Presidents Bush in 1990 and Clinton in 1993 with their deficit reducing agreements and spending constraints. But it was made possible by a booming economy and historically high stock market.[41]

In the spring and summer of 2000 President Clinton was able to work with Republicans in Congress to win approval of permanent normal trade relations with China. In the House more than twice as many Republicans as Democrats supported the measure, echoing the coalition that passed NAFTA in 1993. The above policy achievements were possible only through bipartisan cooperation and the willingness to share credit. But such cross-party victories have been unusual; the primary pattern has been one of partisan rancor and stalemate.

Clinton ended his terms in office with a limited, but creditable legislative record. His overall legacy, however, was marked by policy struggles with the Republican Congress and his impeachment in 1998. Eight years later, President Bush would also leave office with a mixed legislative record.

President Bush and Congress:
Two Wars and Constitutional Challenges

President Bush's terms in office were marked by his initial conservative policy agenda, historic public support after 9/11, the divisive war in Iraq, and his aggressive assertions of presidential power.

During the presidential campaign of 2000 candidate Bush set a moderate tone by asserting that he was a "compassionate conservative" and advocating educational proposals that often appealed to Democratic voters. He promised to "change the tone" in Washington by taking a bipartisan approach to governing, as he had in Texas. While arguing for more defense spending and a national missile defense, privatizing part of Social Security, and a large tax cut, the emphasis was not on the more conservative aspects of his policy agenda.

In his initial months in office, however, he pursued a conservative agenda that appealed to his Republican base in the House of Representatives and the electorate. In January 2001 Republicans controlled both houses of Congress and the presidency for the first time since the beginning of the Eisenhower administration, but their control of Congress was narrow, with a 221 to 212 margin in the House (with two independents) and a 50–50 tie in the Senate (with the vice president able to cast the tie-breaking vote).

President Bush's first and largest legislative initiative was to propose a large tax cut, as he had promised in the campaign. The administration's proposal was for a $1.6 trillion cut over ten years; Congress gave him a tax cut of $1.3 trillion, an important policy victory for the president. In another of Bush's top priorities he established by executive action a White House Office of Faith-Based and Community Initiatives to facilitate the use of federal funds for social purposes to be administered by faith-based organizations. He also won approval of the No Child Left Behind program and a new Medicare drug benefit by compromising with the Democrats. But the Bush administration was transformed on September 11, 2001.

The terrorist attacks on the World Trade Towers and the Pentagon created a surge of public unity that gave President Bush unprecedented public support and a compliant Congress willing to support the administration's war on terrorism. The first and most important political effect of the terrorist bombings of September 11 was a huge jump in public approval of President Bush. In the September 7–10 Gallup poll public approval of the president stood at 51 percent; the next poll, on September 14–15, registered 86 percent approval—a 35 percent jump, virtually overnight.

Congress quickly passed a bill providing $40 billion in emergency appropriations for funding military action, beefing up domestic security, and rebuilding New York City. Congress also passed antiterrorism measures proposed by Attorney General John Ashcroft with broad, bipartisan support. The administration also asked for and got sweeping authority to pursue an international war on terrorism. On September 14 Congress passed a joint resolution giving President Bush broad discretion in his direction of the military response to the terrorist attacks. The grant of power was sweeping in that it allowed the president to decide as "he determines" which "nations, organizations, or persons" U.S. forces may attack.

The president used his authority to attack the Taliban regime in Afghanistan, which had harbored the Al Qaeda terrorists. After U.S. air power and the ground forces of the Northern Alliance successfully defeated Taliban forces, the United States and allied troops occupied the country. As the war in Afghanistan went on and Osama bin Laden was being pursued, secret planning was under way for war with Iraq.[42] But the partisan unity that marked the administration's immediate reaction to the 9/11 attacks and the war in Afghanistan began to erode as the administration's plans for war in Iraq came to be debated in 2002.

In the fall of 2002 President Bush decided to go to the United Nations for a resolution demanding that Saddam Hussein disclose his weapons of mass destruction (WMD). He then went to Congress for a resolution giving him authority to take the country to war with Saddam. The president framed the issue as the necessity of standing up to Saddam Hussein and backing the president in his attempt to get Saddam to back down. With an eye to the upcoming 2002 elections, the implication was that if Democrats in Congress did not support the president, they would be attacked in the campaign as weak on national security. The final resolution passed Congress by large margins in the House and Senate.

After the administration convinced Congress to give the president authority to attack Iraq, the UN Security Council passed Resolution 1441, which ordered UN weapons inspectors into Iraq and gave them until February 21, 2003, at the latest, to report back on Iraq's compliance. The UN weapons inspectors searched Iraq with seeming carte blanche and surprise visits to sites of possible weapons manufacture, but by late January had found no "smoking gun." Chief UN inspector, Hans Blix, said that he needed more time to do a thorough job. But President Bush became increasingly impatient with the inability of the UN inspection team to locate evidence of Iraq's weapons of mass destruction.

In his State of the Union address on January 28, 2003, President Bush said that the UN had given Saddam Hussein his "final chance to disarm." On March 19 U.S. forces attacked Saddam, and after three weeks had prevailed over Saddam's forces in the battle for Baghdad. Winning the initial military battle was relatively easy for U.S. forces, but controlling the country after the initial victory was another matter. Paul Bremer, the U.S. person in charge of the occupation, decided to disband the Iraqi army and eliminate all Baathist party members from the top levels of the Iraq state bureaucracy. These decisions threw hundreds of thousands of Iraqis out of work and deprived the U.S. occupation of the capacity to provide security for the country.

As a result, an insurgency against U.S. forces grew, and sectarian fighting between Sunni and Shiite factions became very bloody. For the rest of the Bush administration, U.S. forces fought the insurgency, losing more than four thousand U.S. soldiers and killing tens of thousands of Iraqis. The weapons of mass destruction that justified the war to the American people were never found. Nevertheless, in a campaign in which President Bush emphasized the terrorist threat to national security, he was able to defeat Democrat John Kerry in the 2004 election. But the deteriorating situation in Iraq dominated President Bush's second term in office.

After his election victory in 2004, President Bush declared "I earned capital in the campaign, political capital, and now I intend to spend it."[43] In early 2005 he launched a campaign to introduce private accounts into the Social Security system and traveled throughout the country to win support for it. Public opinion, however, was not swayed, and he admitted defeat and dropped the proposal. Then in August 2005 Hurricane Katrina devastated the Gulf Coast and particularly New Orleans. The administration was not able to deal effectively with the aftermath, and President Bush did not give the impression of being closely engaged in the federal response. Though the resulting disaster was not all its fault, the administration was blamed for its inability to deal expeditiously with the disaster.

The failure of the president's Social Security initiative and the aftermath of Hurricane Katrina began a decline in President Bush's public approval and support in Congress, even among Republicans. Republicans in Congress passed a harsh immigration bill, and Bush eventually signed a law to create a fence along the southern border between the United States and Mexico. Congress also passed a bill to allow the government to fund research using stem cell research, and President Bush used the first veto of his presidency to stop it. With the president's public support eroding, the Republicans went into the 2006 elections at a disadvantage, and the Democrats were able to recapture control of Congress. They picked up thirty seats in the House and six seats in the Senate, giving them significant majorities in both chambers. Thus President Bush received little legislative support during the 110th Congress, but he was able to stymie Democratic attempts to slow the war in Iraq.

In Barbara Sinclair's analysis, Bush sought large changes in public policy and used a partisan strategy to achieve them, and he was partially successful with his partisan approach. Sinclair describes Bush's approach to winning legislation in Congress in his first term: he pursued a few major priorities "compromising only late in the process and when absolutely necessary, and having the House go first and to the right, Bush got more of what he wanted on those bills that passed than he would have with a more accommodating strategy."[44]

Constitutional Challenges to Congressional Authority

Apart from President Bush's legislative record with Congress, he mounted an aggressive campaign to enhance executive power at the expense of the other two branches. From the beginning of the administration, both President Bush and Vice President Cheney argued that Congress had usurped presidential power in the 1970s and they intended to right the balance. The attacks of 9/11 gave them the opportunity to assert executive power and use the commander in chief clause of the Constitution to exclude Congress from important national security policies. Among other assertions of presidential power, President Bush pushed further than other presidents in four policy areas: he asserted the authority to detain suspects of terrorism indefinitely without charging them with crimes, he suspended the Geneva Conventions on the treatment of prisoners, he ordered the national security agency to monitor communications involving Americans without the warrants required by law, and he used signing statements to an unprecedented extent. A brief explanation of each of these claims to presidential power follows.[45]

After the U.S. invasion of Afghanistan, the administration faced the problem of what to do with the many prisoners that were captured by U.S. and allied forces. Some of these prisoners were suspected of aiding Al Qaeda and posed a danger to the United States. The administration decided to fly the detainees to Guantanamo Bay, Cuba, an area of the island under complete U.S. control. Ordinarily, prisoners of war would be imprisoned to keep them off the battlefield and released at the end of the war. But the Bush administration envisioned the war on terror lasting for decades, with no sharp ending where the enemy surrendered. Some of the detainees who were incarcerated at Guantanamo for an indefinite period argued that they did not oppose the United States and committed no terrorist acts and applied for writs of habeas corpus. Such an appeal would allow judges to decide whether the administration had sufficient evidence to keep them in custody.

The administration argued in court that the detainees had no right to habeas corpus appeals, in effect suspending the right of appeal that the Constitution says can only be suspended by Congress in cases of invasion or insurrection. After years of appeals, the Supreme Court decided that detainees did have the right to appeal to the court system and present arguments that they were detained without sufficient evidence of their guilt. After this legal defeat, President Bush was able to persuade Congress to strip the courts of jurisdiction over the detainee cases. But in the end, the Supreme Court decided that the president does not have the right to suspend habeas corpus and that the laws that stripped the courts of jurisdiction were unconstitutional. Thus President Bush's assertion of the unenviable right to hold detainees in prison indefinitely without charging them with a crime was eventually overturned by the Supreme Court.

Implied in the administration's decision not to charge suspected terrorists with crimes was the decision that obtaining intelligence from them was more important than convicting them of crimes and punishing those found guilty. The administration feared that there would be future attacks on the United States by Al Qaeda and that those plans could be discovered by interrogating detainees at Guantanamo. When intelligence was slow in coming, the administration decided to use harsh interrogation methods that were forbidden by the Geneva Conventions, which were signed by the United States in 1955. To allow such harsh interrogations, President Bush suspended the Geneva Conventions for Al Qaeda suspects on February 7, 2002.

The administration trained interrogators in techniques that had been developed by the Chinese and North Koreans and used on U.S. prisoners during the Korean War in order to force them to make false confessions that they committed atrocities. These techniques were used at Guantanamo and then were imitated at Bagram Air Force Base in Afghanistan and Abu Ghraib prison in Iraq. In April 2004 photographs of U.S. soldiers grossly abusing Iraqi prisoners at Abu Ghraib became public and investigations of the origins of the abuses were begun. A number of official government reports were issued that documented the harsh techniques, and Congress, in spite of veto threats by President Bush, passed the Detainee Treatment Act of 2005 that forbade torture or cruel and degrading treatment of detainees. Nevertheless, the Bush administration maintained that the CIA could continue to use harsh interrogation techniques that were denied to the U.S. military. Critics of the administration argued that the Supreme Court made it clear that the United States was bound by the Geneva Conventions, and that any CIA secret techniques that violated the treaty were illegal.

Shortly after the 9/11 attacks, President Bush secretly ordered the National Security Agency to undertake surveillance of communications between foreign and U.S. persons that might involve terrorism. The Foreign Intelligence Surveillance Act allows surveillance of U.S. communications only after a warrant is secured from a special court. Despite the denial of only five of more than 18,000 applications for warrants from 1978 to 2006, President Bush decided that the law was too cumbersome and he did not have to obtain the warrants required by law.

The issue raised one of constitutional presidential authority versus the constitutional rights and duties of the other two branches. The Constitution does not give the president the authority to ignore the law. The wisdom of surveillance policy is a separate issue. In 2007 President Bush convinced Congress to amend the law so that he could continue to conduct the surveillance that he had previously been doing illegally. Despite this political victory, President Bush did not admit that he did not have the constitutional right to ignore the law as he had before the new law was passed.

Since early in the Republic, presidents have issued statements upon their signing bills into laws. Usually these statements have been hortatory, often praising members of Congress for their participation or touting the importance of the new law to the country. By the late twentieth century, presidents occasionally issued signing statements that challenged the constitutionality of the laws they were signing, and the Reagan administration tried to establish them as a regular part of the legislative process. President Bush, however, used signing statements very aggressively to challenge the idea that laws could constrain his actions as president. For instance, he used them to indicate that he did not feel bound by all of the provisions of laws regarding: reporting to Congress pursuant to the PATRIOT Act; the torture of prisoners; whistleblower protections for the Department of Energy; the number of U.S. troops in Colombia; the use of illegally gathered intelligence; and the publication of educational data gathered by the Department of Education. He issued more than twelve hundred signing statements during his two terms, more than twice as many as all other previous presidents combined.

The implications of these sweeping claims to presidential authority are profound and undermine the very meaning of the rule of law. Despite the Constitution's granting lawmaking power to the Congress, the Bush administration maintained that executive authority and the commander in chief clause can overcome virtually any law that constrains the executive. President Bush was thus claiming unilateral control of the laws. If the executive claims that it is not subject to the law as it is written but can pick and choose which provisions to enforce, it is essentially claiming the unitary power to say what the law is. The "take care" clause of article II can thus be effectively nullified.

Even though there may occur some limited circumstances in which the president is not bound by a law, expanding that limited, legitimate practice to more than one thousand threats to not execute the law constitutes an arrogation of power by the president. The Constitution does not give the president the option to decide *not* to faithfully execute the law. If there is a dispute about the interpretation of a law, the interaction of the three branches in the constitutional process is the appropriate way to settle the issue. The politics of passage, the choice to veto or not, and the right to challenge laws in court all are legitimate ways to deal with differences in interpretation. But the assertion by the executive that it alone has the authority to interpret the law and that it will enforce the law at its own discretion threatens the constitutional balance set up by the Constitution.

CONCLUSION

The Clinton and Bush presidencies each experienced difficult relations with Congress. Clinton did not get much of what he wanted from the Democratically controlled Congress in his first two years in office. Ironically, his major achievements in office resulted from six years of his contentious relations with the Republican-controlled Congress of the late 1990s. He was able to blunt the more extreme cuts in domestic programs sought by the Gingrich-led House, and in negotiations with them achieved a series of four budget surpluses, the only surpluses the United States enjoyed since 1969. His impeachment by the House marked the low point of his administration, one of the most hostile incidents in president-Congress relations since the Nixon administration.

George W. Bush got most of what he wanted from the Republican-controlled Congress for his first six years in office. He did not even use his veto power until his sixth year in office. His relative success reflected the willingness of Democrats to vote for Bush's national security priorities as well as the care that Republicans in Congress took to shape legislation to his liking. He might also have felt little need to issue vetoes because his signing statements declared that he did not feel bound by many provisions of the laws that Congress passed and he signed. When the Democrats took over Congress in the 2006 elections, he was still able to stymie them on the national security issues that were important to him.

Barack Obama took office in 2009 promising to change the partisan tone in Washington. He carefully courted Congress and paid particular attention to Republicans as he sought support for his first policy initiatives. First among them was the huge expenditure proposal that totaled more than $750 billion that he hoped would blunt the economic downturn set off by the financial crisis in the fall of 2008. Republicans in Congress signaled that they would oppose Obama on that and other issues. Although the Democrats controlled both houses of Congress by significant margins because of the 2008 elections, Obama was not likely to have an easy time with Congress. New Democrats who were elected in 2008 were often moderates who defeated liberal Republicans, so the Democratic caucus was not as unified as the Republicans were in the House. And in the Senate the Democrats lacked the necessary votes to invoke cloture to shut off a Republican filibuster.

Thus, despite the sizable Democratic majorities in Congress and President Obama's overtures to Republicans, the polarization that had characterized the previous three decades was likely to guarantee continuing friction between the president and Congress in their rivalry for power.

NOTES

1. See Gary C. Jacobson, *A Divider, Not a Uniter* (New York: Longman, 2006).
2. Sean M. Theriault, *Party Polarization in Congress* (New York: Cambridge University Press, 2008), 26. The Wallace quote is also from Theriault.
3. Nelson Polsby, *How Congress Evolves* (Oxford: Oxford University Press, 2004), 87–93.
4. Polsby, *How Congress Evolves*, 80–94.
5. For analyses of the changing electoral makeup of the South and the partisan implications, see: Earl Black and Merle Black, *The Vital South* (Cambridge, MA: Harvard University Press, 1992); Bruce Oppenheimer, "The Importance of Elections in a Strong Congressional Party Era," in *Do Elections Matter?* eds. Benjamin Ginsberg and Alan Stone (Armonk, NY: M. E. Sharpe, 1996); Gary Jacobson, "The 1994 House Elections in Perspective," in *Midterm: The Elections of 1994 in Context*, ed. Philip A. Klinker (Boulder, CO: Westview Press, 1996); Gary C. Jacobson, "Reversal of Fortune: The Transformation of U.S. House Elections in the 1990s" (paper presented at the Midwest Political Science Meeting, Chicago, April 10–12, 1997); Paul Frymer, "The 1994 Electoral Aftershock: Dealignment or Realignment in the South," in *Midterm: The Elections of 1994 in Context*, ed. Philip Klinker (Boulder, CO: Westview Press, 1996); Lawrence C. Dodd and Bruce I. Oppenheimer, "Revolution in the House: Testing the Limits of Party Government," in *Congress Reconsidered*, Dodd and Oppenheimer (Washington, DC: CQ Press, 1997), 29–60, and "Congress and the Emerging Order: Conditional Party Government or Constructive Partisanship?" 371–89.

6. Polsby, *How Congress Evolves*, 94.

7. Theriault, *Party Polarization*, 50.

8. Gary C. Jacobson, *The Politics of Congressional Elections*, 6th ed. (New York: Pearson Longman, 2004), 252.

9. Charlie Cook, "Value of Incumbency Seems to Be Growing," *National Journal*, March 20, 2004, 906.

10. Theriault concludes that redistricting led to 16 to 48 percent of safe seats and accounts for 10–20 percent of the polarization in Congress. *Party Polarization*, 83.

11. Theriault, *Party Polarization*, 111. See also Morris Fiorina, *Culture War?* (New York: Pearson Longman, 2006).

12. Quoted in Jeffrey Toobin, "The Great Election Grab," *New Yorker*, December 8, 2003, 76.

13. See Gary C. Jacobson, "Explaining the Ideological Polarization of the Congressional Parties Since the 1970s," in *Parties, Procedure, and Policy Choice: A History of Congress*, eds. David Brady and Mathew McCubbins (Palo Alto, CA: Stanford University Press, forthcoming), draft of June 2004, 10–12. For an argument that individual shifts in ideology contributed to the overall shift, see Sean M. Theriault, "The Case of the Vanishing Moderates: Party Polarization in the Modern Congress" (manuscript, Austin, University of Texas, April 15, 2004).

14. Theriault, *Party Polarization*, 130.

15. Burdett A. Loomis and Wendy J. Schiller, *The Contemporary Congress*, 4th ed. (Belmont, CA: Wadsworth/Thomson Learning, 2004), 66.

16. In Florida, if an incumbent is not opposed, his or her name does not appear on the ballot. Thus the candidate is "automatically reinstated in Washington" without any constituent having to cast a ballot in his or her favor. David S. Broder, "No Vote Necessary," *Washington Post*, November 11, 2004, A37.

17. See Russell Renka, "The Incumbency Advantage in the U.S. Congress," at cstl-cla.semo.edu/renka/ps103/Fall2007/congressional_incumbency.htm (accessed January 13, 2009).

18. David E. Price, "House Democrats under Republican Rule," *Miller Center Report* 20, no. 1 (Spring/Summer 2004): 21.

19. Polsby, *How Congress Evolves*, 80, 150.

20. See Loomis and Schiller, *Contemporary Congress*, 150–60.

21. For an analysis of the 1994 elections and the 104th Congress, see James P. Pfiffner, "President Clinton, Newt Gingrich, and the 104th Congress," in *On Parties: Essays Honoring Austin Ranney*, eds. Nelson W. Polsby and Raymond E. Wolfinger (Berkeley, CA: Institute of Governmental Studies Press, 1999), 135–68.

22. Polsby puts it this way, "Air conditioning (plus other things) caused the population of the southern states to change [which] changed the political parties of the South [which] changed the composition and in due course the performance of the U.S. House of Representatives leading first to its liberalization and later to its transformation into an arena of sharp partisanship, visible among both Democrats and Republicans." *How Congress Evolves*, 3.

23. See Sarah Binder, et al., "Assessing the 110th Congress, Anticipating the 111th," in the "Mending the Broken Branch" series, vol. 3 (January 2009),

at www.brookings.edu/~/media/Files/rc/papers/2009/0108_broken_branch_binder_
mann/0108_broken_branch_binder_mann.pdf (accessed January 13, 2009).

24. Jon R. Bond and Richard Fleisher, "The Disappearing Middle and the President's Quest for Votes in Congress," *PRG Report* (Fall 1999): 6.

25. Bond and Fleisher, "The Disappearing Middle," 7. The authors calculate their ideological scores from the rankings of liberal and conservative groups, Americans for Democratic Action (liberal) and American Conservative Union (conservative).

26. Sarah Binder, *Stalemate: Causes and Consequences of Legislative Gridlock* (Washington, DC: The Brookings Institution, 2003), 24, 66.

27. Theriault, *Party Polarization*, 226.

28. Calculation by Keith Poole, reported by Zachary A. Goldfarb, "Democratic Wave in Congress Further Erodes Moderation in GOP," *Washington Post,* December 7, 2006, A29.

29. Sarah A. Binder, "Going Nowhere: A Gridlocked Congress?" *Brookings Review* (Winter 2000): 17.

30. See Eric M. Uslaner, *The Decline of Comity in Congress* (Ann Arbor: University of Michigan Press, 1993).

31. Eric M. Uslaner, "Is the Senate More Civil than the House?" in *Esteemed Colleagues: Civility and Deliberation in the U.S. Senate,* ed. Burdett A. Loomis (Washington, DC: The Brookings Institution, 2000), 32–55.

32. Uslaner, "Is the Senate More Civil than the House?" 39.

33. David Brady and Morris Fiorina, "Congress in the Era of the Permanent Campaign," in *The Permanent Campaign and Its Future,* eds. Norman Ornstein and Thomas Mann (Washington, DC: The Brookings Institution-AEI, 2000), 147.

34. Carl Hulse, "A Longtime Courtesy Loses in the Closely Split Senate," *New York Times,* April 24, 2004, A7; Sheryl Gay Stolberg, "Daschle Has Race on His Hands and Interloper on His Turf," *New York Times,* May 23, 2004, 18.

35. Dana Milbank and Helen Dewar, "Cheney Defends Use of Four-Letter Word," *Washington Post,* June 26, 2004, A4.

36. Charles Babington, "Hey, They're Taking Slash-and-Burn to Extremes!" *Washington Post,* December 21, 2003, B1, B4.

37. See James P. Pfiffner, "President Clinton and the 103rd Congress: Winning Battles and Losing Wars," in *Rivals for Power: Presidential-Congressional Relations,* ed. James Thurber (Washington, DC: CQ Press, 1996), 170–90.

38. Quoted in Joe Klein, "Eight Years: Bill Clinton and the Politics of Persistence," *New Yorker,* October 16 and 23, 2000, 209.

39. For an analysis of the shutdown and the partisan battles surrounding it, see Pfiffner, "President Clinton, Newt Gingrich, and the 104th Congress," 135–68.

40. See Allan Schick, *The Federal Budget: Politics, Policy, Process* (Washington, DC: The Brookings Institution, 2000), 26–30.

41. See Louis Uchitelle, "Taxes, the Market, and Luck Underlie the Budget Surplus," *New York Times,* October 20, 2000, 1.

42. Bob Woodward, *Plan of Attack* (New York: Simon and Schuster, 2004), 77, 80, 96, 98. In the spring of 2002, President Bush said several times in news conferences, "I have no war plans on my desk." Woodward, *Plan of Attack,* 120, 127.

43. Quoted in Barbara Sinclair, "Living (and Dying?) by the Sword," in *The George W. Bush Legacy*, eds. Colin Campbell, Bert Rockman, and Andrew Rudalevige (Washington, DC: CQ Press, 2008), 181.

44. Sinclair, "Living (and Dying?) by the Sword," 184.

45. For a more thorough analysis of these constitutional issues, see James P. Pfiffner, *Power Play* (Washington, DC: The Brookings Institution, 2008).

Chapter Three

From Washington to Obama: The Evolution of the Legislative Presidency

Stephen J. Wayne

THE CONSTITUTIONAL DESIGN

The framers of the American Constitution did not expect or want the president to be chief legislator. They did not expect the president to set Congress's policy agenda except in times of crisis, particularly in situations when Congress was not in session. The emergency triggering mechanism devised by the delegates gave the president the authority to call a special session, provide Congress with the information it needed on the state of the union, and then, if the president thought it desirable, recommend necessary and expedient legislation.

Nor did the framers anticipate or want the president to be the principal domestic policy maker, although in conjunction with the Senate, the chief executive was given responsibility to formulate treaties and alliances. But Congress had a role here as well—to enact legislation necessary for the implementation of treaties and alliances.

The veto power, a traditional executive prerogative and the president's only other legislative instrument granted by the Constitution, was intended primarily as a defensive check on a Congress that intruded into the executive's sphere of authority or a device the president could use to negate unwise and ill-conceived legislation. It was not intended as a tool for imposing a presidential policy judgment on the legislature. In "Federalist No. 73," Alexander Hamilton writes: "The primary inducement to conferring the power in question [the veto power] upon the Executive is, to enable him to defend himself; the secondary one is to increase the chances in favour of the community against the passing of bad laws through haste, inadvertence, or design."[1] As a hedge against misuse by the president, an overwhelming majority in

Congress, a minimum of two-thirds of each house, could override the veto. In this sense, a unified Congress had the last word.

Legislative draftsman, congressional lobbyist, and coalition builder—there is little indication that the framers expected or wanted the president to assume any of these roles on a regular basis. The policy-making authority of the national government appears in the same constitutional article that gives the Congress "all legislative powers herein granted." Although a president could affect the legislature's exercise of its authority through information, recommendations, and as a final resort, the veto, the executive could not assume legislative powers by virtue of any inherent or implied constitutional grant.

Nor did the concept of separation of powers anticipate a major, ongoing legislative role for the president beyond the sharing of the appointment and treaty-making powers with the Senate. George Washington, chair of the Constitutional Convention, had limited contact with Congress and much of it was formal: his State of the Union addresses, several dinners and events in which members of Congress were present, and three legislative proposals submitted to Congress. [2] Washington even refused a House committee's request for his advice on the grounds that it would violate the constitutional separation of legislative and executive authority.

As far as lobbying and coalition building were concerned, there was no expectation and no formal or informal authority by which the president should or could exercise these functions. The debate over presidential selection suggests that framers were fearful of demagogues, equated popular leadership with them, and saw the constitutional structure as a hedge against a plebiscitary president. Going public was viewed as undesirable, even dangerous.[3]

The good news is that the Constitution and the framework it established are alive and well. The bad news is that this framework inhibits presidential leadership of Congress in an era in which the public, press, and Congress expects and wants that leadership. This expectation fuels the president's contemporary legislative leadership challenge.[4]

THE NINETEENTH CENTURY:
EXERCISING INFORMAL INFLUENCE

Despite the constitutional investiture of legislative powers to the Congress, the president's legislative role expanded in the nineteenth century. Jefferson and Jackson used their party leadership to influence Congress. Jefferson met informally with his partisans, had two of his cabinet members, James Madison and Albert Gallatin, attend his party's congressional caucus meetings, used the appointment process to satisfy members of Congress's personnel requests, and engaged in social lobbying. Jackson too exerted partisan influence in Congress, but he also threatened and used the veto to get his way. He exercised twelve vetoes, two more than all his predecessors combined. By doing so, he opened up the veto as a powerful presidential weapon that could be used to affect the content of legislative policy making.

Lincoln too enhanced the president's legislative role, but he did so in times of crisis. So his actions, which included the first bill actually drafted in the White House and sent to Congress as well as emergency measures that he initiated on his own, were not seen initially as precedents by those who followed him in office. In fact, by the end of the nineteenth century the conventional wisdom, as described by Professor Woodrow Wilson, was that Congress was the dominant policy-making institution.[5] Wilson saw the president's legislative powers as no greater than his prerogative of the veto.

THE TWENTIETH CENTURY:
SETTING THE POLICY AGENDA

Theodore Roosevelt's actions in the domestic and foreign policy arenas forced Wilson to modify his initial judgment. In a series of lectures given at Columbia University, Wilson acknowledged that the president had the greatest potential to provide policy leadership by virtue of his power to affect public opinion from his "bully pulpit" and to influence international events. As president, Wilson exploited this potential with his New Freedoms program and his public and private diplomacy before, during, and after World War I.

Although the Senate rejected the Versailles Treaty and League of Nations that Wilson had helped draft, it could not prevent future presidents from assuming a more active policy-making role in foreign affairs if they chose to do so, a role the Supreme Court acknowledged they had the power to exercise in 1936.[6] Legislators also turned to the president for imposing fiscal responsibility. The Budget and Accounting Act of 1921 made it a presidential responsibility to provide Congress with an annual executive branch budget.

Franklin Roosevelt's new economic initiatives,[7] his lobbying of Congress, and his public appeals added a new dimension to presidential leadership of Congress while the Executive Office of the President provided an institutional structure to facilitate the president's expanded legislative presence and influence.[8] Both Truman and Eisenhower continued to depend on these units in the new Executive Office to perform clearance functions for the executive branch. In addition, Truman converted the State of the Union message into an annual agenda-setter for Congress and political address to the country. Eisenhower created the first White House legislative affairs office to explain his program to members of Congress, and later, after the Democrats gained control of both houses, to dissuade them from enacting proposals he opposed.[9]

Kennedy and Johnson expanded the president's domestic policy-making sphere to include civil rights and social welfare legislation. They also created staffs in the White House to develop priority policy initiatives. Outside task forces generated ideas that were "staffed out" by executive branch personnel under the coordination of White House while an expanded congressional legislative operation, working out of the east wing of the White House, pushed presidential proposals on Capitol Hill. In coordination with their party's congressional leadership, Kennedy and Johnson's White House liaison staffs counted heads, twisted arms, and involved the president on an individual basis with committee chairs and other critical members of Congress.[10]

In effect a two-track legislative system was created with priority legislation on track one, initiated, coordinated, and pushed by the White House, and less important legislation on track two, initiated by the executive departments, coordinated by the Bureau of the Budget, and monitored by the departments' legislative affairs offices. There was considerable presidential involvement in track-one lobbying activities. Johnson, especially, enjoyed the give and take of legislative relations, and according to most reports, was very good at it.[11]

Whether Johnson's civil rights and Great Society programs were enacted because of the president's legislative skills, the Democrats overwhelming majority in both houses, and/or public support is difficult to determine. What is clear, however, is that the structure of power in Congress in the 1960s, the committee system controlled by southern Democrats, Johnson's personal relations with them, and the closed-door style of decision making facilitated the exercise of presidential influence in a way that today's more decentralized, more individualistic, more transparent congressional decision-making process does not.

From the perspective of the president's legislative goals and operations, the Nixon-Ford presidency was transitional. The White House, enlarged and more centrally managed during the Nixon administration, had internal policy staffs develop, coordinate, and oversee track-one legislation. A more politicized, management-oriented Office of Management and Budget (OMB), the successor to the Bureau of the Budget, ran the executive clearance processes while the White House legislative liaison operation continued in much the same manner as it had during previous Democratic administrations.

Changes began to occur during the Carter period when White House offices were established to interact with increasingly active interest groups and state and local governments that wanted a larger share of the federal largess. Finding that his legislative liaison office alone did not have sufficient clout to do his bidding, Carter was forced to involve senior White House aides Stuart

Eisenstat, the architect of many of Carter's domestic programs, and Hamilton Jordan, de facto chief of staff, in a legislative lobbying role. The president, however, refrained from doing so on a regular basis. Carter believed that his proposals should be judged on their merits, not on their politics.

Carter's strained relations with Congress prompted the incoming Reagan administration to adopt a new, top-down approach, one in which the president played an active role. Reagan called or met frequently with members of Congress identified by his staff as needing a little extra "encouragement" to support his administration's policy positions on key votes.

James Baker III, Reagan's first chief of staff, ran a legislative strategy group out of his own office to monitor and push the administration's program on Capitol Hill. In addition to the chief of staff, the group included one of Baker's deputies, the policy director from the appropriate cabinet council, the head of congressional liaison, and the president's chief political adviser. Meetings, which occurred almost daily, were designed to coordinate the administration's outreach to members of Congress, involving cabinet members as needed. Baker made it a practice to stay in close touch with the congressional leadership. He also promoted the president's program in his daily contacts with the press, with whom he would speak on an off-the-record basis.[12]

Donald Regan, Baker's successor as chief of staff, had less patience negotiating with the Republican leadership. His penchant for tightly filtering congressional input to the Oval Office proved to be his downfall. Frustrated members of Congress who could not reach the president through Regan and his aides took a back channel to the Oval Office in the form of anonymous leaks to the press, leaks that undercut and infuriated Regan and decreased his tolerance for dealing with Congress even further. The result was a chilly relationship that lasted until a new chief of staff, Howard Baker, was named. Baker and his deputy and later successor, Ken Duberstein, both had extensive congressional experience, many contacts with members and their aides, and were well liked. As a consequence, presidential-congressional relations improved even though by 1987 both houses of Congress were controlled by the Democrats. Setting priorities, cycling issues, and packaging proposals were keys to Reagan's legislative policy successes.

George H. W. Bush's administration was not as effective in its relations with Congress. Part of Bush's problem stemmed from his lack of a comprehensive legislative agenda and part from chief of staff problems. As in the Reagan White House, Bush's top aides, especially chief of staff John Sununu, were expected to be heavily involved in pursuing the president's interests on Capitol Hill. But in doing so, Sununu's abrasive style antagonized members of Congress who perceived him as overbearing, condescending, and intolerant. After Sununu fell from presidential grace, he was replaced by aides who lacked the skills and stature to deal effectively with Congress. With the exception of gaining support for the Persian Gulf War, Bush had to compromise on many of his major policy goals, irritating both Republicans and Democrats in the process.

The desire of members of Congress to deal directly with the president and his top aides presented a problem in the early months of the Clinton administration because lines of authority in the White House were fuzzy. Although top staff met regularly with members of Congress, it was unclear which of these aides, chief of staff Mac McLarty, communications director George Stephanopoulos, liaison chief Robert Paster, economic adviser Robert Rubin, or treasury secretary Lloyd Bentsen was speaking for the president. Clinton and vice president Al Gore were also heavily involved in policy formulation and legislative promotion.

After the defeat of Clinton's first legislative priority, a proposal to stimulate the economy, the White House tried to impose order on its legislative operations. Bentsen was designated as the principal point man to deal with the House and Senate tax committees on the deficit reduction bill, the assistant treasury secretary, Robert Altman, was put in charge of a war room to forge and promote a coherent, public position while Clinton engaged in behind-the-scenes lobbying. According to David Gergen, a senior adviser in the Clinton White House, the lesson that the president learned from the defeat of his first legislative priority was to keep control himself and get the bills through on his own.[13]

Clinton's partisan attitude and negotiating style contributed to his legislative problems. His dependence on Democratic support and willingness to bargain for it encouraged members of Congress, particularly Democrats, to feign opposition or indecision in order to gain favors from the White House. According to Treasury Secretary Bentsen, "Clinton had made it too desirable for congressmen to hold out, to appear to make up their minds in the end game when they had maximum leverage. Clinton needs more discipline and should not keep paying off the holdouts."[14] End runs to the president were tolerated, even encouraged; partisan support in Congress for the president's policy proposals lagged until members were given constituency-related projects that were written into the legislation. "Rolling" Clinton became a popular sport on Capitol Hill; both Republicans and Democrats played the "I-will-support-you, if" game.

Late in the spring of 1994, Clinton restructured his White House organization and the way it operated with the appointment of Leon Panetta as chief of staff. Panetta played a key role in negotiations with Congress on budget matters and other policy initiatives. He describes his contact in the following way: "I knew most of the players up there. I would go up and brief our caucus. . . . I would go to their luncheons. I would go to their meetings. Usually we tried to tie it to major issues [and votes] that were coming up so that we could make the case for why they should support the administration."[15] Panetta was also conscious of the need to coordinate his activities with others in the White House and departmental legislative affairs offices.[16] Throughout, Clinton stayed heavily involved in legislative matters.

Panetta's successors, chiefs of staff Erskine Bowles and John Podesta, operated in much the same manner. They too engaged in negotiations with the congressional leadership; they too served as spokesmen for the administration; they too coordinated the president's legislative operation on major initiatives.

THE TWENTY-FIRST CENTURY: MOBILIZING CONGRESSIONAL SUPPORT

The administration of George W. Bush began with a sizable legislative agenda, but a bare Republican majority. Despite the controversy surrounding his election victory, Bush was determined to push his conservative agenda, which consisted of tax relief, educational reform, a defense buildup, national energy policy, and the president's faith-based initiative. During the first six months of his presidency, only one of these goals, a major tax reduction, was enacted into law. The rest of Bush's policy initiatives got mired in partisan controversy.

The president had initially thought that he could adopt the legislative style he employed as governor of Texas—a light hand and cooperative attitude. In the aftermath of the 2000 election, such an approach seemed appropriate. However, the conservative House and more moderate Senate were too far apart ideologically for the White House to find common ground on most of Bush's legislative policy initiatives, particularly after Senator James Jeffords announced his defection from the Republican Party and voted with the Democrats to reorganize the Senate. Only one other major domestic priority, educational reform, was enacted during the administration's first year, and it succeeded primarily because of the national unity the terrorist attacks produced.

The war on terror shifted the administration's focus from domestic to national security policy for the remainder of Bush's first term in office. During most of this period, Congress played follow-the-leader, partisanship was muted, and the country unified behind its president. Congress enacted most of Bush's national security agenda in the form and with the content he desired with the exception of the creation of a Department of Homeland Security and an insurance indemnification plan, which were not passed until after the

Republican victory in the 2002 midterm elections. The president was not a particularly active lobbyist on behalf of his own administration, but the vice president was. Cheney regularly attended his party's policy caucuses in the House and the Senate and presented the administration's position.

Using Political Capital

The president's reelection and Republican gains in Congress raised Bush's domestic policy aspirations for term two. Claiming that he earned political capital from the election, Bush pursued an expansive domestic agenda that included reforming Social Security; simplifying the tax code; limiting class action lawsuits and medical malpractice damages; and promoting a new national energy policy, telecommunications legislation, and a bill to replace the USA PATRIOT Act, which was about to expire.

In pursuing these objectives, the president ran into trouble. Republicans, angry with the administration's failure to consult them on policy issues during the president's first term and eager to distance themselves from an increasingly unpopular president, revolted after the 2004 elections and refused to support a congressional compromise on the creation of a national intelligence director. House Speaker, Dennis Hastert, said that he would not bring that bill and others like it to the floor without the support of a majority of his party. The Speaker's position embarrassed the newly reelected president, undercut his claim of having additional political capital, and forced the White House once again to send Vice President Cheney to negotiate a deal with recalcitrant members of his own party.

The episode placed the administration in an ideological straitjacket at the beginning of its second term and gave House conservatives, in effect, a veto over presidential policy. The majority of the majority rule also made bipartisan coalitions on controversial measures less likely, thereby diminishing the administration's influence in Congress. The Democrats' victory in the 2006 midterm elections reduced that influence even further. Only the magnitude of the economic problems in the fall of 2008 and the support of a government bailout by both major parties' presidential candidates gave the administration leverage it needed to get its rescue package approved by both houses. Even before he had reached lame duck status in the last year of his term of office, Bush's legislative clout had effectively dissipated.

The incoming Obama administration understood the legislative lessons of the three administrations that preceded it. Political capital was not a commodity that could be put aside for safekeeping. It had to be earned and employed skillfully by the White House. Moreover, the president's top aides had to coordinate priority policy making within the executive branch as well as between it and Congress.

Obama moved quickly to appoint his legislative team. He chose White House and cabinet officials who had considerable legislative experience in addition to his own and Vice President Biden's; both were former senators. Obama's chief of staff had been a member of Congress and the fourth in the chain of Democratic leadership in the House. His legislative director and deputies had all worked for many years as congressional staff aides. There were two ex-senators and two ex-representatives in his cabinet. Even before he became president, Obama worked closely with Democratic leaders in the Senate to speed their confirmation.

As president-elect, Obama consulted regularly with House and Senate leaders. He wanted the Democratically controlled Congress to release the second stage of the bailout funds that had been authorized by previous legislation to prevent the recession from getting worse. He and his economic aides worked with Congress's Democratic leadership to fashion an economic stimulus package, which was designated as the new administration's first major legislative priority.

Once Obama became president, he continued to meet with members of Congress. He adopted a bipartisan approach in an effort to moderate the ideological division that characterized national politics for the last three decades, build support for his stimulus package, and gain the goodwill necessary to govern from the middle.

Obama stated his priorities early and clearly. He wished to avoid the ambiguity that encourages members of Congress to pursue their parochial interests at the expense of national policy. He reached out to Republicans and Democrats alike to build a policy consensus, understanding that ideological, constituency, and regional diversity generates interest-based politics, which the president and vice president as the only nationally elected public officials must try to overcome. His goal was to find common ground on the basis of shared values and interests, but how to achieve that goal was the issue.

Obama relied primarily on three strategic opportunities. He emphasized the country's national needs during the economic crisis and went public in much the same manner as he had during his 2008 election campaign.

Taking Advantage of a Crisis

Presidential influence is enhanced in times of peril. Members of Congress, much like the general public, tend to look to the president for leadership. President George W. Bush benefited from this "rally round the flag" effect in dealing with Congress following the terrorist attacks and throughout his first term. Bush used his bully pulpit to articulate and reinforce the administration's antiterrorism campaign. During this period from September 11, 2001, to the end of the president's first term, legislation that pertained to national and homeland security received more attention and congressional backing than it would have in a "politics as usual" environment. The crisis atmosphere enhanced the president's influence and enabled him to get his way on most of the measures he proposed within the national security arena.

"Never waste a crisis" was Rahm Emanuel's advice to Barack Obama after his electoral victory in 2008. Obama took that advice and used the dire economic situation—job losses, credit difficulties, and potential bankruptcy of large investment firms, insurance companies, and automobile manufacturers—to quicken Congress's deliberation of his economic stimulus program as well as to mobilize public and congressional support for it. He also used the crisis to deflect criticism that his plan would greatly enlarge the budget deficit and national debt.

Obama was not alone in adopting this tactic. Presidents have frequently defined problems in crisis terms to enhance backing for their legislative proposals. Lyndon Johnson's war on poverty, Jimmy Carter's energy crisis, Bill Clinton's health care reforms, and George W. Bush's partial privatization of Social Security are examples.

Presidents also tend to prolong crises to extend their public support. Through terrorism alerts, announcements of extra security measures, and media coverage of terrorist activities around the world, the Bush administration successfully kept the terrorism issue front and center throughout the president's first term and reelection campaign. Over time, however, if the objectives are not achieved, or if the cost becomes too high, presidential influence is apt to decrease as it did for Bush during his second term.

Much of the president's power in declaring and extending crises comes from maximizing the symbolism and voice of the office. The public relations dimension of the modern presidency has been an important instrument of presidential power, or at least presidents have thought it to be. In the words of Lyndon Johnson, "presidential popularity is a major source of strength in gaining cooperation from Congress."[17] Richard Nixon put it this way: "No leader survives simply by doing well. A leader survives when people have confidence in him when he is not doing well."[18] Presidents and their advisers believe that high popularity encourages members of Congress to support the president while low popularity does not.

These beliefs, for the most part, have been reinforced by the political science literature on presidential power. In his seminal work, Richard E. Neustadt argues that presidential prestige contributes to a president's ability to bargain successfully with members of the Washington community.[19] Samuel Kernell notes in his revision of Neustadt's thesis that "Going public becomes the preferred course when protocoalitions are weak, when individual politicians are susceptible to public pressures, and when politicians in the White House appreciate the requirements of television better than the needs of committee chairs."[20] George Edwards, another presidential scholar, is less optimistic about presidential popularity's impact on congressional decision making when he wrote, "The impact of public approval for the president on congressional support for the president occurs at the margins, within the confines of other influences. . . . Approval gives a president leverage, but not control."[21]

In a more recent study, this one focusing on White House attempts to alter public opinion on policy issues, Edwards also found little evidence that presidents, even those who are judged to be effective communicators, can affect public opinion very much.

> Chief executives are not directors who lead the public where it otherwise refuses to go. . . . Instead, presidents are facilitators who reflect, and may intensify, widely held views. In the process, they may endow the views of their supporters with structure and purpose, and exploit opportunities in their environment to accomplish their joint goals.[22]

Going Public

Despite Edwards's finding, contemporary presidents and their advisers have increasingly emphasized the public dimensions of their office to enhance their influence with Congress, their popularity, their reelectability, and their place in history. They have done so by creating "PR" offices in the White House, appointing media experts to advise them, and spending a greater portion of their time out of the White House on the road in full public view.

The development of institutional mechanisms in the White House to build public support began during the Nixon administration when an office of communications was established. That office tried to control or at least monitor the flow of information into and out of the White House. Nixon, the first president to appoint a liaison to business and labor, viewed public outreach as essential to leverage Congress, buttress the administration against its real and imagined political enemies, and provide a broad constituency on which to build his reelection campaign.

Ford and Carter took limited forays into the public arena. Ford was deterred by Watergate, his pardon of Nixon, and his own unpolished speaking style. He went public when he had to do so: when he became president; when he pardoned Nixon; and when he campaigned for election in 1976. Similarly, Jimmy Carter never developed a strong public persona. His halting manner of speaking, desire to downplay the pomp and majesty of the office, and unease with Washington, especially with the White House press corps, led him to deemphasize the public dimensions of his presidency, much to his own disadvantage in leading Congress and affecting public opinion.

Carter's failings, a product of his personal style, his dislike of "politics as usual," and his unwillingness to lobby members of Congress eventually led his administration to modify the ways it dealt with Washington. Legislative lobbying became more centralized in the White House and outreach activities were expanded. By 1978, two additional liaison offices were established. The public liaison office linked and coordinated interest group activity for the president while the intergovernmental affairs office had a similar mission for and with state and local governments.

The people who advised Ronald Reagan understood the lessons of Ford's and Carter's legislative experiences. They brought in skilled media managers to develop and implement a communications strategy to enhance the president's legislative influence on key administration priorities. Michael Deaver, deputy chief of staff, oversaw the operation. He used the president as the administration's key salesman, choreographing Reagan's public activities for the news media. The object was to present pictures and words that the news networks would feel compelled to air. According to Samuel Kernell:

> Polls were taken; speeches incorporating the resulting insights were drafted; the press was briefed, either directly or via leaks. Meanwhile in the field, the ultimate recipients of the president's message, members of Congress, were softened up by presidential travel into their states and districts and by grassroot lobbying campaigns, initiated and orchestrated by the White House but including the RNC [Republican National Committee] and sympathetic business organizations. [23]

Major speeches were timed to coincide with key votes. Prior to the speeches, the public liaison office working with outside groups, such as the Business Roundtable, would establish telephone banks that went into action the moment the speech ended. By generating a seemingly spontaneous and favorable public response and by doing so on a constituency by constituency basis, the White House was able to provide Democrats with the political cover they needed to support the president's position on key legislation.

George H. W. Bush, Reagan's successor, was much less desirous of conducting a continuous PR campaign. He lacked Reagan's skills and confidence as a communicator. Downplaying the president's public role, the elder Bush sought to govern in the old bargaining environment of the pretelevision age. Needless to add, he was not particularly successful within the domestic policy arena although his numerous trips abroad, diplomatic initiatives, responses to international humanitarian crises, and use of force in Panama and the Persian Gulf commanded public attention and worked to his short-term political advantage.

Initially the Clinton White House failed to coordinate its public campaign with the president's legislative goals. The president's first legislative initiative, an economic stimulus bill, was defeated by a Senate filibuster while his second major initiative, a major reduction in the annual budget deficit, was significantly altered by Congress, before it was enacted by the barest of margins. Although the administration did have some legislative successes in its first year, the North American Free Trade Agreement (NAFTA) being the most noteworthy, most of its policy accomplishments resulted from Democratic congressional initiatives that the president supported rather than the other way around.

Clinton's initial failure to use his bully pulpit effectively in his first two years forced him and his legislative aides to bargain with Democrats in Congress on an issue-by-issue basis. His second year was even worse as the administration was unable to sustain public support for its health care reform proposal. The failure of that proposal, which had pushed other domestic initiatives off the congressional calendar, along with allegations and scandals involving top White House aides, the First Lady, and the president himself led to the Republican takeover of Congress in the 1994 midterm elections and a decrease in the president's ability to influence priority policy making.

Instead of pursuing liberal Democratic policy goals, the president had to modify his policy stances, taking a more centrist approach. Instead of setting the congressional agenda, he was forced to react to the Republican's Contract with America. Instead of emphasizing his role as head of government, Clinton had to devote more attention to his position as head of state and to his ceremonial and symbolic functions. He turned increasingly to foreign affairs. In making these adjustments, Clinton and his aides finally figured out how to use the president's bully pulpit, presidential seal, and White House communications office to better legislative advantage. What followed was a public relations extravaganza, as calculated and as orchestrated as Reagan's, but one that was very different.

Whereas the Reagan White House used its outreach and public relations to build support for the president's congressional initiatives, the Clinton White House used them to build support for the president's legislative vetoes and his reelection campaign. Whereas the Reagan White House emphasized the distinctiveness of the president's legislative goals, the need to reverse the course of government, the Clinton White House repositioned the president on Republican issues, claimed the middle ground for itself, and put the president in a position to take credit for some major legislative enactments, such as the balanced budget, welfare reform, and incremental health care policies, which the Republican Congress proposed and enacted.

The Reagan and Clinton models were similar in that both used foreign travel to enhance the president's image, particularly in the light of the scandals that afflicted both presidents in their second term. Both PR campaigns showed an active and powerful president, thereby countering the allegations that they would be crippled as lame ducks with the opposition party controlling both houses of Congress. Clinton also took advantage of man-made and natural disasters to play the role of a visible crisis manager and empathic leader. In short, both White Houses used the public relations presidency to offset their policy weaknesses and enhance presidential images. The public responded with high approval ratings.

George W. Bush followed the Reagan and Clinton examples. Determined not to repeat his father's mistakes, one of which was to deemphasize public relations, the younger Bush made PR a top priority. Under the leadership of Karen Hughes, Dan Bartlett, and Karl Rove, the White House carefully coordinated policy initiatives with presidential events. The president traveled widely at the beginning of his first term, preaching to the faithful and whomever would listen.

Prior to the terrorist attacks of September 11, 2001, the White House reported 71 presidential statements and news releases and pictures from 21 photo ops on its website. During the same period, the president addressed 62 groups and gave 20 radio addresses. After 9/11, it was more of the same except the focus of the public presidency turned to national and homeland security. Of the 223 presidential statements and press releases, 40 photo ops, and 12 radio addresses that occurred between September 11, 2001 and December 31, 2002, more than half dealt with terrorism at home or abroad. With domestic policies a lower priority, the president met with fewer outside groups than he did in the previous period.[24]

The public relations initiative continued through Bush's first term, merging with his reelection campaign. The focus remained on terrorism and its threat to the United States. Iraq policy was front and center with most of the president's public pronouncements dealing with national security issues in general and Iraq in particular. However, the failure to find weapons of mass destruction in Iraq, continuing resistance to the American occupation, U.S. prison abuse, Iraqi sectarian violence, and the cost of the war in American lives and wealth led to a disconnect between the president's words and public perceptions of the situation, and eventually, to a steep decline in the president's approval ratings. These consequences demonstrate the difficulties of sustaining a public relations campaign in the light of increasing public dissatisfaction with the president and his policy.

Obama began his legislative presidency mired in the economic meltdown that had contributed to his electoral victory. As previously noted, he used the crisis as an action-forcing mechanism to get the Senate to move quickly on the confirmation of his cabinet and Congress to expedite consideration of his economic stimulus proposal and his budget, to reinforce his nonpartisan style of policy making and coalition building, and to emphasize the economic consequences of his other domestic policy goals. Moreover, he continued his political campaign after the election, using his "Yes, we can" theme and hopeful rhetoric to advance his legislative policy agenda. Obama's White House even adopted some of the new technology, which his campaign had pioneered, to reach the millions who had left their e-mail addresses, cell phone numbers, and postal zip codes with his election organization now housed in the offices of the Democratic National Committee. Transition and White House websites encouraged people to communicate their experiences and ideas for policy change, thereby enhancing their perception of participatory democracy, the responsiveness of the Obama administration, and the merits of its policy goals.

The Permanent Campaign

The Clinton, Bush, and Obama presidencies indicate how the permanent legislative campaign and public relations agenda have now become inextricably linked to one another. In 1995, a new team of political operatives joined with ongoing White House staff to recast Clinton as a plebiscitary president. With the pulse of the public measured by continuous polling, the administration repositioned itself within the political center and used its presidential podium to cast the congressional Republicans as extreme and mean-spirited and to stereotype the GOP policy orientation as one that was designed to benefit the rich. Focus groups were used to capture emotionally laden words and phrases while presidential travels, meetings, and events highlighted the active, publicly oriented Clinton presidency.

Much of the White House–generated public activity was intended to benefit Clinton politically, to set the stage for his reelection, maintain his high approval ratings, and shield him from personal scandal. His public relations' campaigns, however, were also designed to further his legislative policy goals. Clinton had attributed the defeat of his health care initiative, and later, fast-track authority, to the administration's failure to mount and maintain a successful public relations campaign for these issues, while in the case of health care, opponents of the Clinton plan, such as the Health Insurance Association of America, spent in excess of $13 million on advertising to defeat his plan. Obviously there were other factors that contributed to the defeat of these initiatives, but the president saw public relations as the key variable.[25] Lessons of these failures were not lost on his administration and the ones that followed it.

George W. Bush mirrored Clinton's strategy. On a political level, he raised money to deter a primary opponent, respond to Democratic criticism, and be in position to mount his reelection in the spring of 2004. On a policy level, he articulated his terrorism theme, defended his Iraqi policy, and took advantage of social issues on gay marriage, abortion, and religion to energize his Christian coalition base. Throughout his public relations campaign, Bush and his communication advisers emphasized those character attributes that coincided with the public's image of strong presidential leadership during crisis: strength, courage, conviction, consistency, and vision based on moral values. For a person who entered office with an underwhelming leadership image, the president had come full circle by the end of his first term.

But then the public's perceptions of reality began to change. Its mood soured; people believed the country was moving in the wrong direction. The president did not and refused to modify his policy. Before long, the personal attributes that contributed to Bush's popularity in term one became liabilities in term two. His forcefulness was seen as precipitous, his policy consistency as inflexibility, his worldview and actions in Iraq as simplistic, incorrect, and particularly inappropriate for a non-Western culture.

Similarly, Barack Obama began his term in office with a flourish of public activities aimed at differentiating his presidency from his predecessor's in terms of his governing style, policy orientation, and leadership attributes. He consulted rather than commanded, compromised rather than resisted changes to his proposals, surrounded himself with a staff of diverse policy experts rather than simply loyal true believers—pragmatists rather than ideologues. Obama encouraged debate rather than shielding himself from it. He emphasized the needs of main street, not Wall Street; saw government as a positive force rather than a negative one in regulating critical industries, helping to achieve greater economic and social opportunities for all Americans, and for stimulating economic growth, environmental protection, and energy independence. Obama advocated diplomacy over force in resolving international disputes and sought to restore America's leadership in the community of nations on the basis of shared values and interests rather than unilateral actions. He stressed his willingness to listen, advocated transparency and accountability in government, and encouraged public participation and responsive government. He demonstrated intellectual curiosity, exuded confidence, maintained an even temper and cool demeanor, and for the most part, exercised a considered judgment. Perceiving the power of words, Obama used them to build and sustain public support for his legislative policy choices as well as political advantage and personal popularity. He emphasized and excelled in the public dimensions of his job.

The Pros and Cons of Public Legislative Diplomacy

But how important is this dimension to presidential success within the legislative arena? Can presidents actually mold, even change public opinion? Can they use the public sector to advance their policy proposals in Congress? Does their popularity affect legislative influence and policy outcomes? Despite the findings of George Edwards and others that presidential influence in Congress is marginal at best, most contemporary White Houses see their public dimension as an essential component of presidential power, a key ingredient for exercising presidential leadership.[26]

Presidential public relations campaigns on behalf of their legislative agenda are important for several reasons:

1. They signify to Congress the high priority to which the president attaches to an issue.

2. They bring issues to the attention of more people than would otherwise be the case, thereby upping the ante for members of Congress.

3. They enable a president to use his bully pulpit, to set and control the Congress's and news media's agendas, define the issues to the administration's advantage, and even target appeals to groups that are likely to be more responsive to them. The other side is usually unable to argue as loudly and clearly because it lacks the reach and status of the president's bully pulpit.

The negative side of going public, however, is that compromise may become more difficult if presidents attempt to present their policy agenda before they invite input from Congress, interest groups, and the general public. It is harder to negotiate in full public view. Electoral calculations become more salient; interest group participation may unleash forces that an administration cannot control, as was the case with Clinton's health care reform and Bush's attempt to privatize Social Security. Moreover, the public mood may change if there appears to be a disconnect between the president's words and external events as the decline in American support for the war in Iraq and Bush's approval ratings indicates.

Going public raises the stakes and makes defeat more politically, and perhaps psychologically, devastating. It also may impede compromise by solidifying positions, heighten rhetoric, personalize issues, and increase incivility, thereby making relations with members of Congress more difficult in the future. Nasty rhetoric can burn bridges that presidents may have to cross later in their administration.

But PR is easy, easier than engaging in hard bargaining. It is merely an extension of a successful election campaign. It accords with public expectations. It feeds the news media, often diverting their attention from less favorable pictures and events. Presidents become actors; they read scripts; they speak to friendly groups and crowds, carefully selected by the White House, to provide a supportive environment and a sympathetic hearing. The event is choreographed for television; the president speaks behind the seal; the audience responds positively. Even if the president's remarks do not change public opinion, even if Congress does not respond as the administration desires, the president still gets a favorable sound bite, a good picture, and probably an inflated ego. The benefits outweigh the costs, at least that is what most White House communication aides believe.

SUMMARY

The legislative presidency has gone through several stages, becoming increasingly important for governmental policy making and presidential leadership within the legislative arena. Presidents are now expected to set Congress's agenda, influence its deliberations, and shape policy outcomes. To do so, they must overcome the constitutional, political, and institutional hurdles that impede external leadership of Congress. They need to propose legislative goals, consult and bargain primarily with the congressional leadership to shape those goals, and then wage an inside and outside lobbying campaign to achieve them. The process involves White House policy staffs, OMB coordination, executive liaison activities, and major, ongoing public relations efforts in which the appeals and techniques of electioneering are used to build and sustain public support and direct it toward individual members of Congress identified as potential targets of opportunity. The personal involvement of the president is usually necessary to distinguish presidential priorities from other executive policy initiatives and to gain the votes required to enact them into law. These legislative achievements have become criteria for evaluating presidential performance; they contribute to the foundation on which presidential legacies are built.

NOTES

1. Alexander Hamilton, "Federalist No. 73" in *The Federalist* (New York: Modern Library), 477.

2. Louis Fisher, *The Politics of Shared Power* (Washington, DC: Congressional Quarterly, 1993), 18, 29.

3. Jeffrey K. Tulis, *The Rhetorical Presidency* (Princeton, NJ: Princeton University Press, 1987), 25–49.

4. Charles O. Jones in his book, *The Presidency in a Separated System* (Washington, DC: Brookings Institution, 1994) draws the opposite conclusion: it is good news that the Constitution constrains the president's legislative leadership but bad news that the public, Congress, and the president do not understand, much less appreciate, a more constrained presidential role.

5. Wilson titled his study of the American constitutional system, *Congressional Government*. Woodrow Wilson, *Congressional Government* (New York: Meridan Books, 1885).

6. In *United States v. Curtiss Wright Corporation* (299 U.S.304, 1936) the Supreme Court acknowledges the president as "sole organ of the federal government in the field of international relations" with constitutionally based "plenary and exclusive power" within the realm of foreign affairs.

7. In the first phase of the New Deal, Roosevelt submitted to Congress an emergency banking bill, the Truth in Security Act, Agricultural Adjustment Act, National Industrial Recovery Act, Federal Deposit Insurance Corporation Act, to name but some of his initiatives to deal with the exigencies of the Great Depression. In the second phase from 1934–1936, Roosevelt got a Democratic Congress to enact the Wagner Act, Social Security Act, Soil Conservation and Domestic Allotments Act as well as the National Labor Relations Act. New bureaucracies were created to implement this legislation and provide for ongoing regulatory activities.

8. It was during this period that the legislative clearance and enrolled bill processes were established by the Bureau of the Budget to coordinate and control the executive departments and agencies. See Stephen J. Wayne, *The Legislative Presidency* (New York: Harper & Row, 1978), 70–107.

9. Wayne, *The Legislative Presidency*, 41–42.

10. The liaison office also began to service members' constituency needs, thereby necessitating an increase in size.

11. However, George C. Edwards III found that Johnson's legislative success on a whole (as measured by the percent of legislative support he received on all bills in which he took a public position) was not much greater than Carter's even though Carter was seen as a much less effective legislator by Congress, the press, and the public. As a consequence, Edwards contends, legislative skills are overrated as an instrument of presidential power. They do not have a systemic effect on increasing congressional support for the president although he admits that in individual cases they may matter. See George C. Edwards III, *At the Margins* (New Haven, CT: Yale University Press, 1989), 176–89.

I contend that Edwards's methodological assumptions and his aggregate analysis of roll-call voting patterns forces these conclusions. For a discussion of the limitation of this type of analysis of presidential influence in Congress, see the author's response in his book, *The Legislative Presidency* (New York: Harper & Row, 1978), 168–72.

12. Interview with James Baker III, conducted by Martha Kumar for the Presidency Research Group's Transition Project, November 16, 1999.

13. David Gergen, *Eyewitness to Power* (New York: Simon & Schuster, 2000), 278.

14. Gergen, *Eyewitness to Power*, 279.

15. Interview with Leon Panetta, conducted by Martha Kumar for the Presidency Research Group's Transition Project, May 4, 2000.

16. "I had to be very careful that I didn't just go out there and do it on my own without coordinating with the people who had a responsibility. And they also had a lot of responsibility to come up with a lot of the backup material. . . . They had a responsibility to provide all the material and supporting documents every time we developed policy." Panetta added: "Anytime I was dealing with something on Capitol Hill, I would normally call that person [the president's assistant for legislative affairs] into my office so that they would know what I was doing and were supportive of it." Interview with Panetta.

17. Lyndon Johnson, *The Vantage Point: Perspectives of the Presidency, 1963–1969* (New York: Popular Library, 1971), 443.

18. Richard M. Nixon, *In the Arena: A Memoir of Victory, Defeat, and Renewal* (New York: Simon & Schuster, 1990), 282.

19. Richard E. Neustadt, *Presidential Power and the Modern Presidents* (New York: Free Press, 1990), 29–49.

20. Samuel Kernell, *Going Public*, 4th ed. (Washington, DC: CQ Press, 2007).

21. Edwards, *At the Margins*, 113.

22. George C. Edwards III, *On Deaf Ears* (New Haven, CT: Yale University Press, 2003), 74.

23. Kernell, *Going Public*, 169–70.

24. The George W. Bush Library. http: georgewbush-whitehouse.archives.gov.

25. Health care reform died in part because the administration did not mount a coordinated effort for the legislation. A separate health care group, which did not include most of the president's principal West Wing aides, managed the bill and oversaw the public relations campaign. Although President Clinton delivered a major address on health care before Congress in September 1993, the actual legislation did not arrive until almost one month later. The bill, large and complex, made it difficult to sell but easy to attack. Meanwhile as the president's focus was diverted by foreign policy matters, Mrs. Clinton became the public advocate and major critic of those industries that opposed it. Her involvement, her advocacy, and her criticism made compromise difficult. No single person coordinated the administration's campaign as the opposition to the plan mounted, the "Harry and Louise" ads were aired, and Congress was increasingly divided over various health care proposals. With the opponents of the plan spending heavily to defeat it, with the administration unable to organize a counter attack, and with the 1994 election approaching and the Republicans seeing

the demise of health care as the road to their electoral success, the proposal died on the floor of Congress, and with it, Democratic control of both houses.

26. See also George C. Edwards III and Andrew Barrett, "Presidential Agenda Setting in Congress in *Polarized Politics*, eds. Jon R. Bond and Richard Fleisher (Washington, DC: Congressional Quarterly, 2000), 109–133; Barbara Sinclair, "Hostile Partners: The President, Congress, and Lawmaking in the Partisan 1990s," in *Polarized Politics*, 134–53.

Chapter Four

The President and the Congressional Party Leadership in a Polarized Era

Barbara Sinclair

As candidate, president-elect, and new president, Barack Obama promised action on an ambitious policy agenda and an end to the "brain-dead" hyper-partisanship that had characterized Washington for years. Aiming to set a post-partisan and "Hill-friendly" tone, he and his top advisers met frequently with members of Congress, Republican as well as Democratic, vowed to take their ideas and concerns seriously, and to work in partnership with them. When, in 2012, we look back at Obama's first presidential term, how likely are we to find that he succeeded in these efforts? And what will make the difference?

A good president, most voters will tell you, is one who keeps his promises; and that requires, at minimum, enacting his agenda. The politically attentive know that the president is dependent on Congress for legislative success. In the highly polarized political world of the early twenty-first century that means the president is dependent on the majority party leaderships in the House and Senate. The president plays no role in choosing congressional party leaders, even those of his own party, and yet whether they promote or oppose his agenda is a key determinant of his likely legislative success. The dependence, however, is mutual; the party leaders also want things from the president. The character of the relationship depends on a number of factors, preeminently whether the president and the congressional majority leader-ships are of the same or opposing parties. Yet, even if they are of the same party, differences in their perspectives and goals can make for an uneasy partnership.

This chapter examines how the relationship looks from 1600 Pennsylvania and how it looks from Capitol Hill; it then investigates the relationship under both unified and divided control in recent years to demonstrate the effects of control under conditions of high partisanship and to highlight the varied other determinants of cooperation and conflict. In the final section, I consider what this portends for the relationship between President Obama and the congressional leadership.

THE VIEW FROM 1600 PENNSYLVANIA

Whether the president's immediate goal is enhancing his chances of reelection, burnishing his legacy, or bringing about policy change he believes in, passing his program is a critical means toward accomplishing any of those ends. Consequently, congressional action is essential to presidential success. So what does a contemporary president see when he looks down Pennsylvania Avenue to Capitol Hill? Like his predecessors, he sees two legislative bodies with different memberships and rules, both of which need to pass a bill for it to become law. Unlike many of his predecessors, he sees congressional parties that are highly polarized along ideological, that is, policy preference, lines, with most congressional Republicans being strongly conservative and most Democrats, liberal or moderate.[1] Furthermore, this polarization is not simply a Washington phenomenon; rather, constituency sentiment at both the activist and voter level underlies congressional partisan polarization, especially in the House with its smaller and more homogeneous districts.

In the House of Representatives, greater ideological homogeneity made possible the development of a stronger and more activist party leadership.[2] The House is a majority-rule institution; decisions are made by simple majorities and opportunities for minorities to delay, much less block, action are exceedingly limited. The Speaker is both the presiding officer of the chamber and the leader of the majority party. When the majority party is homogeneous, its members have the incentive to grant the Speaker significant new powers and resources and to allow him or her to use them aggressively, because the legislation the Speaker will use them to pass is broadly supported in the party. By the mid-1980s, majority party members had granted their party leadership such new authority and the leadership did employ it assertively to pass legislation the members wanted. With the Republican takeover of the House in the 1994 elections, the trend only accelerated.

The majority party leadership oversees the referral of bills to committee, determines the floor schedule, and controls the drafting of special rules that govern how bills are considered on the floor. The leaders can bypass committees when they consider it necessary or orchestrate postcommittee adjustments to legislation. The leadership can serve as an extremely valuable ally for the president. The leaders can work with (and, if necessary, lean on) the committees to report out the president's program in a form acceptable to him and in a timely fashion; deploy the extensive whip system to rally the votes needed to pass the legislation; bring the bills to the floor at the most favorable time and under floor procedures that gives them the best possible chance for success; and, if necessary, use the powers of the presiding officer to advantage the legislation.[3]

Senate rules are a great deal more permissive that House rules and give individual members much greater prerogatives; consequently the Senate majority leader lacks many of the institutional tools the Speaker possesses. Still the majority leader does command the initiative in floor scheduling and is the elected leader of the majority party in the chamber. Over the course of the 1980s and 1990s, the Senate parties like their House counterparts organized themselves for joint action and for member participation.[4] Thus the Senate majority leadership too is potentially a useful ally for the president.

The president, then, sees majority party leaderships that can be valuable allies but, by the same token, may alternatively be formidable opponents. Given the high partisan polarization that underlies leadership strength, he can expect a majority party leadership of his own party to be a great deal more inclined to cooperate with him than one of the other party. If the opposition party controls one or both houses, he knows he and his program have a much rockier road ahead; he may be able to use his own substantial resources to induce Congress to act in the manner he prefers but he very likely will need to do so through the majority party leadership, especially in the House.

THE VIEW FROM CAPITOL HILL

Congressional party leaders are elected by their fellow party members in the chamber and need to meet their members' expectations to keep their positions. Members have both electoral and policy goals and expect their leaders to promote those goals by enacting legislation and by engaging in other activities that serve to maintain the party's majority in the chamber and further individual members' reelection. From the leadership's perspective, the question is: does passing the president's program promote those goals?

In a time of high partisan polarization, when the president is of the same party, the answer is usually yes. Members of Congress are likely to have similar policy goals to those of a president of their party—not infrequently his program includes policy proposals that originated with them; furthermore, members are aware that the president's success or failure will shape the party's reputation and so affect their own electoral fates. To be sure, there will always be differences about particulars and sometimes also about priorities. Having different constituencies assures that.

Nevertheless, when control is unified, the House leadership will usually see it is in its own interest to act on the president's behalf and employ the formidable resources discussed above to enact the president's program. The incentives are similar for the Senate majority leader but the resources at his command are less. Precedent and tradition give the majority leader the task of scheduling legislation for the floor but because sixty votes are required to cut off debate—even on a motion to consider a bill—a unified minority party of forty-one or greater can act as a major barrier to passing legislation in a form the majority party—and often the president—prefers. Since the 1990s, with the increase in partisan polarization, Senate minorities have routinely used filibuster strategies to extract concessions and to kill legislation.

When the congressional majority in a chamber faces a president of the other party, the members' policy and electoral goals are much less likely to impel the leadership toward cooperation with the president. With the parties so polarized along ideological lines, members of a congressional majority party are likely to strongly oppose many of the legislative initiatives of a president of the opposition party. Furthermore they are likely to see his success as a threat to their electoral goals. The party leadership, thus, may consider blocking the president's agenda as the best way of furthering their members' goals.

Still, even under divided control, political circumstance may give party leaders incentives to work with the president. If a newly elected president is perceived to have received a mandate for his agenda, blocking its enactment may be seen as politically perilous, especially for electorally marginal members of the majority. Similarly, a congressional leader has to think hard and long before strongly opposing a broadly popular presidential proposal; among other considerations is whether, even in this period of high partisan polarization, the leader can keep his or her members in line. A crisis can confront both the president and members of Congress with the necessity of responding or appearing incompetent and indifferent; and swift legislative action demands cooperation. Just doing the minimum necessary to keep the government functioning by enacting appropriations (e.g., money) legislation requires that the leadership and the president deal with each other.

Conversely, political circumstance may sometimes make it difficult or even impossible for party leaders to cooperate with a president of their own party. If supporting the president fundamentally conflicts with furthering member goals, congressional leaders are likely to put their members first, to "dance with the one that brung them."

Congressional party leaders expect a president of their own party to avoid putting them in such a predicament. They expect access and information, to be consulted and to be informed about presidential decisions that affect them and their members. They expect his administration to be flexible about the details of policy proposals when those are important to their members. They expect the president to use his resources to help them pass his program and they want him to employ the bully pulpit effectively so as to make passing his initiatives easier. A president who treats the congressional leaders with respect and never blindsides them maximizes the cooperation that political circumstances allow. Indeed, showing respect and scrupulously keeping his promises can lubricate the president's relations with the leaders of the opposition party as well.

In sum, we expect unified versus divided control to be the single most important determinant of cooperation versus conflict between the congressional majority party leadership and the president, but not the sole determinant.

COOPERATION OR CONFLICT

In the following sections, I examine the relationship between the president and the congressional leadership under conditions of unified and divided control in recent years to highlight the effect of control and to identify other factors that affect that relationship.[5]

Unified Control

When Bill Clinton was elected president in 1992, Democrats controlled the presidency and both houses of Congress for the first time in twelve years. The Reagan years had seen both political parties become more ideologically homogeneous internally and more polarized—both in the country and in Congress. Consequently a president and the members of Congress of his party were more likely to agree on policy than in the pre-1980 period. Congressional Democrats believed that the party's reputation—and to some extent their own reelection—hinged on the new administration's success. Most believed that, given unified control, the public would hold them collectively responsible if they failed. "Bill Clinton's success is our success, his failure is our failure," said Representative Bob Matsui (D-CA). "The public wants the elimination of gridlock."[6] The incentives for cooperation are even greater for the president and the congressional leadership of his party than for the president and rank and file members. As guardians of their party's image, congressional leaders have a major stake in the president's success; and the president has resources—favors and the bully pulpit—that make him an invaluable ally.

From the beginning of Clinton's presidency, the working relationship between him and the Democratic congressional leadership was cooperative and close, if not always smooth. Both Speaker Tom Foley and Senate Majority Leader George Mitchell were convinced that congressional Democrats' fate was closely linked to the Clinton administration's success. "Nobody's going to have divided government to blame anymore," Foley said as the new congress convened. "We will have the first opportunity we've had in a long time to prove government can work—and people will be watching."[7]

The leaders met frequently with the president at the White House and contact below the presidential level was still more common. On the House side, the White House congressional liaison attended the regular Thursday morning whip meetings and the meetings of those whip task forces set up to mobilize votes on legislation of interest to the president. The Speaker provided a desk and phone in his Capitol working office to the White House liaison people. Agency liaisons also worked closely with the whip operation when their legislation was under floor consideration. Similarly, on the Senate side, contact between the leadership and the top liaison people was an everyday occurrence. At the senior staff level, consultation and coordination with the executive branch became a major part of the job.

The incentives for cooperation between newly elected president George W. Bush and the Republican congressional leaders in 2001 were even greater. Fifty years had passed since Republicans enjoyed unified control and the Republican Party was considerably more ideologically homogeneous than the Democratic Party of the early 1990s. As Senator Phil Gramm (R-TX) expressed it, "I've been waiting all my life to have a Republican president and a Republican Congress."[8] Congressional Republicans wanted to cooperate and work with Bush, to help him pass his agenda with which they largely agreed, and to see him succeed. The congressional leaders, especially Speaker Dennis Hastert and the other House leaders, saw passing the president's priorities as their number one job and worked closely with the administration. As staffers explained, contact, most often by phone, was "continuous." One said in 2001, "The Speaker is at the White House every week, we have enormous amounts of contact with the Administration, there's coordination and we now know ahead of time what's going to happen."

Their close working relationship with their party's congressional leaders was instrumental to the early successes of both Clinton and Bush. Some legislative victories came relatively easy. In 1993, Congress passed family and medical leave legislation and "motor voter" legislation to make registering to vote easier. Both were major elements of Clinton's agenda but also top priorities of congressional Democrats. The "motor voter" bill does demonstrate how the differences between House and Senate rules affect the help the majority leaderships can give the president. Republicans used Senate rules, which require a super-majority of sixty votes to cut off debate, to delay and exact some concessions on a bill clearly supported by a simple majority.

For both presidents, passing the budget was the first major test; for both, the budget resolution and the reconciliation bill implementing it carried their top priorities. Clinton had run on the economy and his program included targeted investments in areas such as education and infrastructure and also deficit reduction through tax increases on the wealthy and spending cuts in less essential programs. Bush's number one priority was a large tax cut. In both cases the congressional leaderships perceived passing their president's proposal as essential to showing the party could govern and so to the party's reputation. Although Clinton and the Democratic leaders had the harder task—increasing taxes is always more difficult politically than cutting them—both sets of leaders knew they could expect little support from across the aisle; by 1993 opposition to any new taxes had become a core tenant of Republican ideology; Democrats saw the Bush tax cut proposal as primarily a giveaway to the rich.

The party leaders used every tool at their disposal to pass their president's economic program. In the House, the majority leaderships oversaw the drafting of the legislation to keep it on track in terms of timing and substance; they whipped the key votes intensely. In 1993, Whip David Bonior himself headed the whip task force set up to pass the bill. Starting work several weeks before the bill got to the floor, members of the task force and then the top leaders themselves unrelentingly pursued every House Democrat; anyone who might have influence with an undecided or recalcitrant member—state party chairmen, governors, union officials, personal friends—were enlisted whenever possible to help in the persuasion effort. The leaders used their scheduling power and their control over the character of the special rule under which a measure is considered on the floor to advantage the president's policy. In both 1993 and 2001, the special rule used protected the measure by prohibiting most floor amendments.

Senate leaders likewise maximally employed their tools; thus, in 2001, Senate Majority Leader Trent Lott bypassed the deadlocked Budget Committee and brought the budget resolution directly to the floor. Yet, although budget rules protect budget resolutions and reconciliation bills from filibusters and nongermane amendments, the leadership cannot prohibit germane amendments. In both years, despite the leaders' best efforts, the Senate changed the bills in ways the president disliked. Well before Senate floor consideration in 1993, maverick Democrat David Boren's opposition had killed the Btu tax, a central element of the Clinton proposal. More conservative southern Democrats still made up a significant proportion of the Senate Democratic membership in 1993–1994 and they often proved a problem for Clinton and the Democratic leadership. In 2001, three moderate Republicans defected from Bush's position on a Democratic floor amendment reducing the tax cut and it passed. Although moderates made up a relatively small part of the party's Senate membership, the Republicans could afford no defections. The Senate was split 50–50 and Republicans controlled the chamber only because of Vice President Dick Cheney's vote. Despite these hitches in the Senate, passage represented a major win for the president in both these cases.

The effort to pass these bills was by no means one-sided. Congressional party leaders expected their president to be fully engaged in the campaign and both presidents delivered. Clinton worked hard to win over Democratic votes, meeting with members in groups and as individuals, sending his cabinet members to the Hill, making myriad phone calls, and showing flexibility in bargaining to get the last necessary votes. Although passing his tax cut was easier, Bush sent his vice president to the Hill to oversee the legislative process; he himself worked to sell it to the public through many public appearances; and his senior staff persuaded Republican-leaning interest groups to work for it even if it did not include their favorite provisions. Although congressional leaders and their members had some complaints about their president's performance, by and large, the cooperation between the president and his party's congressional party leaders on the early budget battles set a good precedent for the future.

For House Republican leaders, passing the Bush tax cut was relatively uncomplicated because this was an issue on which their members strongly supported Bush's proposal. Two major Bush priorities—the No Child Left Behind education bill in 2001 and the Medicare Prescription Drug bill in 2003—raised more problems. In both cases, the leadership had to ask many of their members to vote for the president's proposal despite their opposition to it on ideological grounds. The more conservative Republicans were unhappy with increased federal intervention in education policy and with the lack of school vouchers in the education bill; two years later, many of the same members opposed establishing a new entitlement program for prescription drugs for seniors under Medicare. In both cases, the leadership did what was necessary to pass the bills because they believed failure would damage not just the Bush presidency but also the Republican Party's reputation and so the likelihood of holding their majority. On the Medicare bill, House passage of the conference report required that Speaker Hastert hold the normally fifteen-minute vote open for almost three hours while the leadership, through persuasion and pressure, rounded up the votes. While dramatic, such instances of leaders pressuring their members to vote against their own strongly held views are infrequent. Republican members' strong support for Bush's legislative priorities and the leaders' success in passing them rested on basic policy agreement.

The effort to enact the Medicare prescription drug legislation illustrated the ways in which a Senate majority leader can assist a president of his party even though his tools are considerably less formidable than those of his House counterpart. Bill Frist became majority leader in early 2003 replacing Trent Lott who was forced to step down after making remarks that could be interpreted as racist. Frist was seen as Bush's pick and lacked long experience and deep ties to colleagues, problems that would manifest themselves often during his tenure. On health care policy, however, Frist's status as a physician gave him credibility and it was an issue in which he was deeply interested. Frist began meetings with key senators at the beginning of the Congress; he and

Charles Grassley, chairman of the Finance Committee with jurisdiction over the issue, met weekly with the other Republican members of the committee. Knowing he would need sixty votes, Frist also conferred with Max Baucus, the committee's ranking Democrat, and with Ted Kennedy, long the Senate Democrats' lead person on health issues. Frist's negotiating efforts helped the committee to report out a bipartisan bill that commanded Kennedy's support. Frist was never able to negotiate a unanimous consent agreement that limited amendments but the committee deal largely held up on the floor and Frist's patience was rewarded when the bill passed 76 to 21 after nine days of floor consideration. Frist appointed himself to the conference committee and, when negotiations bogged down, he and Speaker Hastert took over and put together the final deal. As a Senate leadership aide explained, "In Conference it was really threading a needle between what the House needed, so that the conservatives would vote for the bill, and what we needed in the Senate, so we could get our 60 votes." Getting the sixty votes required keeping on board Baucus; Louisiana moderate Democrat John Breaux, another influential member of the Finance Committee; and the AARP, the powerful senior citizens' lobby—Frist managed all that. Although Kennedy and many other Democrats opposed the final bill, the party did not mount a serious filibuster. Frist's motion to invoke cloture on the conference report was approved 70 to 29; the conference report won 54 to 44. Given AARP support and a divided party, the Democratic Senate leadership decided that, even if they could which was far from certain, killing the bill was simply too politically risky. Thus Frist and Hastert were instrumental to delivering a huge legislative victory to President Bush.

Even the most strenuous efforts of skillful leaders do not guarantee success, as the fight over Clinton's health care proposal shows. Speaker Tom Foley, House Majority Leader Richard Gephardt, and Senate Majority Leader George Mitchell did everything they could to try to negotiate a bill that could pass; yet their best efforts failed. When, influenced by the intense public relations campaign waged by opponents, the constituents of Democratic members turned against action, members could not be budged; they knew they might be punished at the polls for doing nothing on health care but feared that passing an unpopular program would hurt them more. At that point, there was simply nothing the leadership could do.

At about the same time, the House Democratic leadership's inability to pass the rule for consideration of the Clinton crime bill revealed that the Democratic membership, although certainly more ideologically homogeneous and more inclined to work cooperatively that it had been in the 1970s, was not always willing to be led. Democrats on the left, disgruntled by their support for Clinton and the leadership seemingly being taken for granted and unhappy with provisions in the bill, voted against the rule and defeated it. That well-publicized debacle, combined with the bigger health care failure, had major repercussions in the 1994 midterm elections. House Democrats, who had controlled the chamber for forty years and had come to take that control for granted, lost their majority.

There are instances when majority party leaders do not cooperate with a president of their own party on one of his top priorities but they have been rare in recent years. On the North American Free Trade Agreement in 1993, the House Democratic leadership split. Reflecting the divisions in the Democratic Party, Whip David Bonior, from a rustbelt Michigan district, and Majority Leader Richard Gephardt of St. Louis, opposed NAFTA; Speaker Tom Foley of Washington state supported it. While Gephardt's opposition was relatively low key, Bonior organized and led the House effort to defeat the pact. In deference to his lieutenants, Foley took a behind- the-scenes role in marshalling votes; other House Democrats, including Chief Deputy Whip Bill Richardson (D-NM), were the public face of the effort. Republicans' own policy preferences and crucially those of their strongest supporters were much more likely to favor NAFTA; Clinton's victory in the House on NAFTA depended on Republican votes. After the fight was over, the administration worked hard to repair the breech; thus both the President and Hillary Clinton called David Bonior personally.

The Republican leadership did not actively oppose President George W. Bush's proposal to allow workers to set up private accounts and invest part of their Social Security taxes in the stock market; in fact, a substantial majority of congressional Republicans favored private accounts on policy grounds. But Social Security is considered the "third rail" of American politics: touch it and you die! The leaders complained privately that they had not been consulted on making the Social Security plan Bush's top 2005 priority and basically waited to see if Bush could build public support for it. When, instead, opponents of the plan revved up major opposition, the leaders let the plan die. No legislation emerged from any congressional committee. The leaders were not about to ask their members to commit political suicide.

Responding to constituent concern about illegal immigrants, House Republicans in December of 2005 passed a harsh enforcement-only immigration bill that they knew the president opposed. Big business, a core component of the Republican coalition, favored a bill with a guest worker program and a route to legal status for the millions of undocumented workers currently working in the United States. Bush also feared a punitive approach would alienate Latino voters. With the Republican base split between the two approaches, Senate Republicans also split, but a bipartisan coalition managed to pass a bill acceptable to Bush in the Senate in mid-2006. However, House Republicans, who had repeatedly fallen in line behind Bush, refused to go along. Instead of agreeing to a conference to work out differences between the two bills, House Republicans scheduled a flurry of public hearings, in Washington and around the country, on illegal immigration with the intention of pressuring the Senate and the president to consent to a bill emphasizing enforcement. Shortly before the 2006 elections, both chambers passed and Bush signed a bill to build a seven hundred–mile fence along the U.S.-Mexican border. Clearly, even relatively ideologically homogeneous parties are not monolithic; both policy preferences and political considerations sometimes lead to differences between the president and the members of his party in Congress. When the president sees it as being in his interest to advocate a policy course that many of the members of his party in Congress oppose, the party leaders have to balance their members' interests as individuals, in attaining their policy goals and in securing reelection, against the damage to the party's reputation—and its possible impact on keeping the majority—when the president fails. But even when the leadership decides to oppose the president, the leaders and the president make every effort to keep the relationship civil. Few congressional majority party leaders criticize a president of their own party publicly nor do presidents disparage their party's congressional leadership.

To be sure, congressional leaders are often annoyed with the White House and the administration even when they are working together. Leaders—and more often their staffs—may criticize anonymously; they frequently complain about poor communication, often blaming it on White House staff not the president himself. They are not consulted enough; they are not informed before important decisions are made public. People in the administration are insufficiently responsive to members of Congress whose votes they will need. Too many White House decision makers do not understand how Congress functions; some have contempt for the legislative branch. And, of course, the president's aides have complaints of their own. The Congress leaks like a sieve; members ask for too much, seldom see the big picture, and are never satisfied. However, when control is unified, the president and the leaders of his party in Congress know they have to work together for either to succeed and—in this period of relatively homogeneous, polarized parties—they know they will agree much more frequently than they will disagree. Both attempt to maintain as smooth a working relationship as the structure of the U.S. government allows because it is in both of their interests.

Divided Control

Even in this period of high polarization, a president and a Congress controlled by the opposition party are not always in conflict; sometimes their interests do coincide. An examination of recent instances shows, however, that the circumstances conducive to cooperation are not everyday occurrences. After a year of high-stakes confrontation and conflict, both President Clinton and the Republican congressional majority party leadership needed legislative accomplishments to take into the 1996 elections and that required that they deal with each other. Trent Lott had replaced Bob Dole as Senate majority leader and he was eager to make his mark; Newt Gingrich, Speaker of the House, faced an election in which Republicans could loose their new majority. Compromises were reached on minimum wage legislation, modest health care reform, a safe drinking water measure, and a rewrite of the pesticide law. In the summer of 1996, Republicans, eager for a big accomplishment, stripped alterations in the Medicaid and food stamps programs unacceptable to Clinton from the welfare overhaul bill and softened some other provisions. Clinton signed the bill.

In 1997, after Clinton and Republican congressional majorities had been reelected, the president and the Republican congressional leadership negotiated a deal to balance the budget by 2003 while still increasing funding for a number of Clinton priorities, including a new children's health care program.[9] Clinton and the leaders were eager to burnish their legacies and the increasingly robust economy made a deal that both could tout possible.

When a president confronts a Congress controlled by the opposition party in this period of high polarization, he is forced to deal with that party's leadership if he wants legislative accomplishments as Clinton did in 1996 and 1997. Doing so, however, creates problems for his relationship with his own party and its leaders, even when he tries to include them in the negotiations. They tend to see themselves as being relegated to a minor role, which to some extent they are, and their electoral interests may conflict with the president's interest in getting legislation enacted. If the majority party appears incompetent and "do nothing," the minority may benefit. In 1996, many Democrats, especially House Democrats, opposed the deals Clinton struck. He gave away too much substantively, especially on welfare, many believed, and, by handing the Republicans legislative accomplishments, he reduced Democrats' chances of retaking the House. In 1997, House Minority Leader Dick Gephardt opposed Clinton's course throughout the convoluted process of enactment; he argued that Republicans should be forced to try to pass a balanced budget on their own and, when they failed, Democrats could pass their plan by picking off a few moderate Republicans.[10] The White House believed that scenario was unrealistic and worked around Gephardt. The Senate Democratic leadership was friendlier to Clinton's approach, seeing legislative accomplishments in their own interest, and worked with the White House in negotiating the deal.

In the 110th Congress (2007–2008), cooperation between the new Democratic majorities and President Bush was still less frequent. The Bush administration seems to have decided that, given the gaping ideological divide between the parties, little was to be gained and made little effort; the Democratic congressional leaders deeply distrusted Bush because they believed he had engaged in "bait and switch" tactics in the past. Nevertheless, two crises forced some cooperation. In early 2008 the economy was weakening significantly and both the Bush administration and the Democratic leadership believed a stimulus package was essential; neither wanted to be responsible for doing nothing in the face of a recession. The administration negotiated a stimulus package with Speaker Nancy Pelosi and House Minority Leader John Boehner; the Senate leaders were not included. It was the House leadership that could—and did—deliver; in the end, the Senate was largely forced to go along. The credit crisis in the fall of 2008 again forced a level of cooperation between the administration and a broader group of congressional leaders. When disaster seemed imminent, the administration asked Congress to pass a three-page bill that gave it the authority to do almost anything with the $700 billion authorized. The Democratic leaders—and Republicans as well—balked and insisted on more specificity. Treasury Secretary Hank Paulson and his aides and the congressional leadership, including the Banking Committee chairs, negotiated an agreement over the course of several days. When the House turned down the resulting bill, the Senate Democratic leadership stepped in to take the lead. Senate Majority Leader Harry Reid negotiated a time agreement with his Republican counterpart and brought to the floor a sweetened bill he and committee chairmen had put together. The Senate's overwhelming passage margin—as well as the stock market's huge drop—put enough pressure on the House to pass the bill as well.

An analysis of the first House vote sheds considerable light on how the relationship between leaders and their members conditions the relationship between the leadership and the president. The initial bailout bill failed because two-thirds of Republicans—and 40 percent of Democrats—voted against it. The House Republican leadership had participated in the negotiations and had attempted to round up the votes to pass the package that the Republican president argued was essential to stabilizing the financial markets. Many Republican members, however, opposed the bailout on substance and, when a firestorm of anger from their constituents rained down on their offices, they saw no reason to bail out a president that many felt had let them down. He was asking them to endanger their reelection for his mistakes. When Boehner comprehended how deep the opposition among his members was, he pulled back. After the failure, the Democratic leadership was criticized as well; Speaker Pelosi gave a floor speech blaming the crisis on the Bush administration and, when the bill was going down to a narrow defeat, the Democratic leaders made no attempt to twist enough Democrats' arms to rescue it. In fact, the Democratic leadership was asking its members to take a politically perilous vote and needed to provide them with cover. The Democratic House leaders had reached an agreement with their Republican counterparts: half of the House Democrats and half of the Republicans would vote for the bailout, thus taking the vote off the table as an election issue. When Republicans voted overwhelmingly against the bill, Democratic leaders were not about to pressure their members into taking a vote that might defeat them. And similarly, Pelosi's speech was aimed at providing cover for—and expressing the deep frustration of—those Democrats that did vote for the bill.

These dramatic instances of often imperfect cooperation notwithstanding, conflict has much more frequently characterized the relationship between presidents and congresses controlled by the opposition party in recent times. With the parties so polarized, with disagreement on policy preferences running so deep, compromises that both sides consider better than the status quo often do not exist. Even when both sides know some deal will eventually need to be reached, such as on appropriations bills to fund the government, both have strong incentives to use their resources to try to back the other into a corner that puts them at a disadvantage in the bargaining that will come. That often means a PR offensive to gain the public opinion high ground.

The budget battle between President Clinton and the new Republican Congress in 1995 exemplifies the factors that lead to conflict in its most extreme form. [11] Congressional Republicans led by Newt Gingrich believed they had received a mandate in the 1994 elections and that therefore they could force the president to accept their program. Republicans managed to get through both chambers a massive reconciliation bill that cut taxes and balanced the budget in seven years by drastically reducing domestic spending and restructuring a number of the biggest federal entitlement programs including Medicare. Because budget bills are protected by law from the filibuster, Democrats were unable to stop the legislation in the Senate. Clinton, however, threatened to veto the bill because it cut too much from education, the environment, Medicare, and Medicaid. Using a traditional congressional strategy, Republicans had attached provisions to appropriations bills that they knew Clinton would veto if they came to him as free-standing legislation. Clinton objected to funding cuts and to the extraneous provisions and threatened vetoes. Appropriations bills fund the government; if they do not become law by the beginning of the fiscal year, much of the government shuts down. Clinton vetoed the reconciliation bill and several appropriations bills and threatened to veto others. Negotiations between the Republican leadership and the White House failed to produce an agreement congressional Republicans considered satisfactory and Republicans, still convinced Clinton would cave, several times let appropriations lapse and shut down the government, in one case for twenty-two days over Christmas. Not only did Clinton hold fast, the public reaction was the opposite of what House Republicans had expected; the public blamed the Republicans, not the president and Clinton's public job approval ratings went up. When in early 1996 Republicans voted to reopen the government without having gotten Clinton to agree to a budget deal on their terms, they tacitly admitted that their strategy had been a failure.

The congressional Republicans' failure in the budget battle set the stage for the cooperation between the branches in 1996 and 1997 discussed earlier, but for most of the remainder of Clinton's term, the relationship remained conflictual; although liberal Democrats sometimes accused Clinton of "triangulation," in fact his policy preferences and those of the typical congressional Republican were far apart. The White House did frequently deal directly with the Republican leadership, especially in bargaining over appropriations bills. After the 1995 budget debacle, the Republican leadership knew it could not allow the government to shut down again and Clinton became highly adept at extracting policy victories in return for agreeing to sign appropriations bills. This veto bargaining, of course, depended on congressional Democrats' willingness to uphold Clinton vetoes.

However annoyed they sometimes were with Clinton, congressional Democrats backed him up on all but one veto he cast because it was in their interest to do so. Not only were their own policy views much closer to Clinton's than to those of congressional Republicans, their only path toward any positive policy influence was via Clinton's veto bargaining. The days in which minority party members could significantly influence major policy at the committee level were long gone, killed off by polarization. Consequently the Democratic congressional leadership could not let disputes such as that between Clinton and Gephardt on the 1997 budget deal derail their working relationship.

At the beginning of the 110th Congress (2007–2008), the circumstances were highly conducive to interbranch conflict and conflict was, in fact, the predominant relationship. A new Democratic majority with an ambitious program had gained control; the parties were even more polarized than they had been in the mid-1990s when Clinton first confronted an opposition party–controlled Congress and Bush was serving the last two years of his presidency and consequently reelection was not a concern.

The House Democratic leadership used the tools at its disposal aggressively to ensure passage—in the House at least—of policy measures their members wanted and the party had promised. The new Speaker, Nancy Pelosi, also employed both her control over floor procedures and her persuasive and fundraising prowess to protect her new members, especially those from "red" districts. Both were seen as essential to maintaining the new Democratic majority. Passing legislation in a form most House Democrats preferred and in a timely fashion, holding together carefully constructed compromises among the party's factions on difficult issues, and protecting marginal members from having to take potentially politically disastrous votes often dictated using tightly controlled floor procedures. Doing so exacerbated the hostility between the parties in the House; but on the big issues, policy preference differences between the parties was a much greater barrier to bipartisan cooperation.

The Democrats' Senate margin was agonizingly close—51-49—and, in any case, the majority party's agenda and floor control is much more tenuous in the Senate than in the House. Through a combination of bipartisan negotiations often including concessions and occasional hardball, Majority Leader Reid and the Senate Democrats managed to pass a number of the party's priorities—a minimum wage increase, the State Children's Health Insurance Program (SCHIP), an energy bill, and lobbying reform. But the process was agonizingly slow and a number of cherished measures were blocked by Republican obstruction.

President Bush largely continued the partisan strategy he had pursued during his first six years in office, making few attempts to work with the Democratic leadership. In any case, neither the Democratic leadership nor the rank and file trusted Bush, putting another impediment into the path of cooperation. Bush's strategy relied on veto threats, the Senate filibuster and, on security and defense policy, PR efforts painting Democratic nonsupport as unpatriotic. Two of the three prongs of the strategy depended on the support of the Republican congressional minority. Again, as was the case in 1995–2000, the minority were often unhappy with their president, but most of the time the party leadership supported him. Thus House Republicans upheld most of Bush's vetoes, even when, as on SCHIP, Senate Republicans failed. However, Senate Republican Leader Mitch McConnell and his leadership team came through for Bush over and over again by blocking or extracting concessions on legislation Bush opposed. When the president's party controls both chambers, the House leadership is the president's most valuable ally; when the opposition party controls, it is the Senate minority leadership that can help the president most. Under current circumstances it is usually in the minority party leadership's interests to provide the support. Despite Bush's low poll numbers, abandoning Bush would likely have alienated the party base and damaged the party's reputation; in the Senate, blocking Democrats' initiatives gave Republicans major leverage; and furthermore, most congressional Republicans agreed with Bush on most issues. The bill allowing Medicare to negotiate prescription drug prices, a bill making labor organizing easier, one giving the District of Columbia voting representation in the House, and another overturning a Supreme Court decision severely narrowing plaintiffs' ability to sue in job discrimination cases all died when Republicans filibustered the motion to proceed. Republicans also blocked most clean votes on disapproving of Iraq policy and advocating a withdrawal timetable. Before the 2008 August recess, Republicans blocked action on almost all bills the Democratic leadership wanted to consider; their demand was a simple majority vote on lifting the moratorium on off-shore drilling.

When, on policy or political grounds, their members did not agree with Bush, the Republican leadership did abandon Bush or at least made little effort to hold their members. Thus Bush's vetoes of the farm bill, of water projects legislation, and of a bill to prevent a cut to physicians' reimbursements under Medicare were overridden. Republicans in both chambers were instrumental in killing an immigration bill that was a top Bush priority. And, in December 2008 in the midst of the financial crisis, Senate Republicans killed by filibuster the auto bailout bill negotiated by Bush and the majority Democrats. After the 2006 elections, congressional Republicans and their leaders were much less willing to support their president when doing so entailed a possible cost to them. He could no longer help them much to attain their goals so Republican members of Congress decided they needed to look out for themselves.

OBAMA AND THE CONGRESSIONAL LEADERSHIP IN THE 111TH CONGRESS

On November 4, 2008, Barack Obama was elected president with 52.9 percent of the popular vote, carrying twenty-eight states. After a gain of 30 seats in the 2006 elections (and 3 subsequently in special elections), House Democrats added a net of 21, giving them a 257 to 178 margin in the 111th Congress. Senate Democrats picked up 8 seats to increase their majority to 59. Thus, the elections determined that the branches would be controlled by copartisans and that the majorities in both chambers would be ample.

Obama and congressional Democrats ran on quite similar issues as one would expect when the political parties are relatively ideologically homogeneous; thus they began with considerable agreement on a policy agenda. The economic crisis fueled a sense of urgency in the public and among policy makers alike, further focusing the attention of the new president and his congressional partisans on the same agenda. Obama was the first nonincumbent president elected with a majority of the popular vote since 1988. His team's adept handling of the transition further increased his public support and he began his presidency with great expectations and a lot of goodwill. With the economy souring even more in late 2008 and early 2009, there was broad public support for the sort of swift and decisive action that Obama and many Democratic candidates had proposed during the campaign.

In sum, for Democrats the stars are better aligned for a cooperative relationship and legislative success than at any time since 1965. At the same time, they face a sobering set of policy challenges.

Occupying the top congressional leadership positions are experienced, savvy politicians eager to work with the new president. Pelosi and Reid had often found their attempts to legislate in the 110th Congress frustrated by a president who profoundly disagreed with them and their membership on most major policy disputes. Now they have a president with whom they and their members mostly agree and, perhaps even more important, they see Obama's success as essential to their own success—to satisfying their members' policy and electoral goals and to maintaining their majorities. Most of the senior Democratic leaders, committee as well as party, served in Congress during the early Clinton presidency and are determined to avoid the mistakes made then. They know that they must deliver policy change and that will require discipline. They also expect to be partners not underlings in the formidable enterprise.

In his relations with Congress, Obama, a legislator himself, began well. He and his team started consulting with the Democratic congressional leadership even before the elections and continued throughout the transition period. He chose for important jobs in the new administration people with extensive congressional know-how and high respect on the Hill—Rahm Emanuel, a House member who had served as chair of the Democratic Congressional Campaign Committee and chair of the Democratic Caucus, as his chief of staff; former Senate Democratic Leader Tom Daschle as secretary of health and human services and health care policy czar; Peter Orszag, director of the Congressional Budget Office, as head of the Office of Management and Budget; and, as his head of congressional liaison, Phil Schiliro, formerly chief of staff for senior House Democrat Henry Waxman, incoming chairman of the Energy and Commerce Committee.

Obama reached out to Republicans as well as fellow Democrats in Congress, attempting to deliver on his promise of tamping down the partisan hostility in Washington. He sent Emanuel to meet with the Republican leadership soon after election; he himself called a number of the Republican ranking committee members; vice president elect Joe Biden talked to some of his former Senate colleagues; Obama himself consulted Olympia Snowe, a key Senate moderate, on the stimulus package; and on January 5, two days after the new Congress convened, Obama met first with Pelosi and Reid, and then with the Republican and Democratic leadership teams. And he has continued his outreach, even going to the Hill after he became president to meet with Republicans on the stimulus package.

To give President Obama popular legislation to sign soon after his swearing in, the House quickly passed the SCHIP reauthorization and the Lilly Ledbetter Fair Pay Act and the Senate followed—though more slowly as is its want. After skillful lobbying by Obama and his economic team, Senate Democrats with a little help from across the aisle voted to allow the incoming administration to use the remaining half of the $700 billion approved in the fall for the Troubled Asset Relief Program (TARP). Despite the unpopularity of the program, all but one of the Democratic freshmen senators supported Obama's position.

Passing the stimulus plan was the most crucial early test of the relationship between the new administration and Congress. The process demonstrated a willingness on the part of the Obama team to listen to members of Congress and to adjust its proposals in response; for example, when Democrats argued that the $3,000 employee hiring tax credit would be impossible to administer as intended, Obama gave it up even though it had been a campaign promise. Obama left most of the details of crafting the package to Congress. The process further showed the extent to which Democrats and their leaders see their fates as intertwined with Obama's and the extent of agenda agreement. Thus the House committees marked up the stimulus bill during the first week of the Obama presidency and the House passed it in the second. Pelosi made clear she would use the tools at her command to enact the bill when she vowed there would be no mid-February President's Day recess until the bill was finished. Obama demonstrated his desire for a bipartisan bill by proposing a large tax-cut component; and the House Democratic leadership, in response to Obama's desire for comity and Republican demands, agreed to holding hearings and marking up the bill in committee rather than bringing the bill directly to the floor. From his radio—and web—addresses, begun not long after the elections, his decision to maintain at ready the huge e-mail list of supporters amassed during the campaign, his inaugural address, and his deploying of senior advisers and officials on the Sunday talk shows, Obama made clear that he was going to employ the bully pulpit aggressively.

Action on the stimulus bill also showed the difficulty of making major policy change through a truly bipartisan process. Although encouraged by Obama's initial proposal to dedicate 40 percent of the stimulus package to tax cuts, congressional Republicans did not signal support for the package but demanded more tax cuts and less spending. House Democrats, unconvinced that business tax cuts would stimulate the economy as much as spending, decreased the proportion of tax cuts. Republicans complained they were not given enough input and attempted to portray the Democratic leaders as dictatorial and out of step with Obama. When the Republican leaders met with Obama, they argued against a core element of his tax proposals (Obama pointed out he had won the election!). In an era of high partisan polarization, genuine and severe policy disagreement impedes bipartisanship. Furthermore when the minority party faces unified government as the Republicans do in 2009, they may also perceive bipartisanship to conflict with their electoral interests. Obama and the congressional Democrats would get credit for any successes but, if they supported the bills, Republicans would share the blame for any failures.

Consequently, the relationship between Obama and the Republican congressional leadership is likely to be rocky throughout his presidency. By communicating with them regularly, Obama can perhaps prevent the relationship from descending into bitter distrust. Opportunities for genuine cooperation will arise occasionally. But the Republican leaders' job is furthering their members' policy and electoral goals and a majority of those members will not see supporting Obama as furthering either of those goals.

In contrast, the relationship between the Democratic House and Senate leaderships and Obama is likely to remain good. However, Pelosi and Reid are leaders of a separate branch of government; and they almost certainly give a higher priority to protecting the prerogatives of the legislative branch than the Republican congressional leaders during the Bush administration did. Reid, for example, made it clear to then vice president elect Joe Biden that he should not expect to attend the weekly closed lunch of Democratic senators; vice president Dick Cheney had attended the Republican senators' lunch and, unlike Cheney, Biden had been a senator for over thirty years. Pelosi early on made it clear to incoming chief of staff Rahm Emanuel that, although he is a former House leader, he is no long a member of the legislative branch and that she expects "no surprises, and no backdoor efforts to go around her and other Democratic leaders by cutting deals with moderate New Democrats or conservative Blue Dogs."[12] The current Democratic congressional leaders believe that their Republican predecessors' deference to President Bush hurt not only Congress as an institution but did no favors for the Republican Party in Congress or the White House. The result was that Bush heard too few voices and too few opinions and so made more mistakes. Similarly congressional Democrats believe that the Republican Congress's meager oversight of Bush administration agencies and decisions hurt rather than helped the administration. Thus the Obama administration can expect considerably more scrutiny. Still the Democratic congressional leaders see their fate and that of their members and their majority as entwined with that of Obama's; if Obama maintains his high public support, if he makes decisions that are politically as well as substantively wise, if he continues to consult the congressional leaders and keep their members' varied interests in mind, he will make it much easier for the congressional leaders to deliver for him legislatively but, even if not, they will have little choice but to try. In this era of high partisan polarization, Obama and the congressional Democrats are in the same boat, and if it sinks, they will go down together.

NOTES

In addition to the sources cited, this chapter is based on the author's interviews with members of Congress, congressional staff, and informed observers.

1. See Barbara Sinclair, *Party Wars: Polarization and the Politics of National Policy Making*, Julian Rothbaum Lecture Series (Norman: University of Oklahoma Press, 2006); Pietro Nivola and David Brady, eds., *Red and Blue Nation: Characteristics and Causes of America's Polarized Politics* (Stanford, CA: Hoover Institution; Washington, DC: Brookings Institution Press, 2006); Pietro Nivola and David Brady, eds., *Red and Blue Nation: Consequences and Correction of America's Polarized Politics* (Hoover and Brookings, 2008).

2. David Rohde, *Parties and Leaders in the Postreform House* (Chicago: University of Chicago Press, 1991); Barbara Sinclair, *Legislators, Leaders, and Lawmaking* (Baltimore: Johns Hopkins University Press, 1995).

3. See Barbara Sinclair, "Trying to Govern Positively in a Negative Era: Clinton and the 103rd Congress" in *The Clinton Presidency: First Appraisals,* eds. Colin Campbell and Bert A. Rockman (Chatham, NJ: Chatham House Publishers, 1996); Barbara Sinclair, "Context, Strategy, and Chance: George W. Bush and the 107th Congress," in *The George W. Bush Presidency: An Early Appraisal,* eds. Colin Campbell and Bert Rockman (Chatham, NJ: Chatham House Publishers, 2003).

4. Steven S. Smith, "Forces of Change in Senate Party Leadership and Organization," in *Congress Reconsidered,* 5th ed., eds. Lawrence C. Dodd and Bruce I. Oppenheimer (Washington, DC: CQ Press, 1993).

5. For a more detailed discussion of Clinton's relations with Congress, see Sinclair, "Trying to Govern Positively in a Negative Era: Clinton and the 103rd Congress," and Barbara Sinclair, "The President as Legislative Leader," in *The Clinton Legacy,* eds. Colin Campbell and Bert A. Rockman (Chatham, NJ: Chatham House Publishers, 1999). For the same on George W. Bush, see Sinclair, "Context, Strategy, and Chance: George W. Bush and the 107th Congress," and Barbara Sinclair, "Living (and Dying?) by the Sword: George W. Bush as Legislative Leader," in *The Bush Legacy,* eds. Colin Campbell and Bert Rockman (Washington, DC: CQ Press, 2007).

6. Pamela Fessler, "If People Get Behind the President, Congress Is Likely to Follow," *Congressional Quarterly Weekly Report,* February 20, 1993, 380–81.

7. David Hess, "100 New Faces Start in Congress Today," *Riverside Press Enterprise,* January 5, 1993.

8. Alison Mitchell, "Conservatives to Lead Senate; Gore Says He'll Continue to Fight," *New York Times,* December 6, 2000.

9. John Hilley, *The Challenge of Legislation* (Washington, DC: The Brookings Institution, 2008).

10. Hilley, *The Challenge of Legislation.*

11. Elizabeth Drew, *Showdown: The Struggle between the Gingrich Congress and the Clinton White House* (New York: Simon & Schuster, 1996).

12. John Bresnahan, "Pelosi Lays Down the Law with Rahm," Politico.com, December 16, 2008.

Chapter Five

Understanding Presidential Relations with Congress

Gary Andres and Patrick Griffin

When Barack Obama began his first term as president of the United States, he experienced some early and dramatic legislative successes. Congress passed a massive economic stimulus bill and legislation to expand insurance coverage to four million low income children, and overturned a ban on federal funding of embryonic stem cell research and other measures, boosting spending on Democratic priorities long stymied by Obama's predecessor, President George W. Bush.

What accounted for these early achievements? Was Barack Obama—a new president with relatively little legislative experience—a naturally skilled and savvy congressional negotiator? Was he just cashing in on the political capital generated by his November 2008 victory? Or was he aided by other factors like his large majorities in the House or Senate?

How about his success at attaining bipartisanship? During the 2008 presidential campaign, he promised to end the culture of partisan polarization in Washington. He tried to keep his word by courting congressional Republicans early. He traveled to Capitol Hill to meet with the GOP Conference. He and his staff communicated often with lawmakers by phone during his first months in office, regularly inviting them for business and social meetings at the White House, trying to set a tone of conciliation and outreach across the aisle. These efforts yielded more goodwill than solid votes. So were his efforts at bipartisan bridge building a failure?

We can also generalize these questions about President Obama's dealings with Capitol Hill. Doing so provides a window to better understand presidential-congressional relations. Some observers believe presidents succeed or fail in terms of influence with Congress based largely on political context (mixed versus unified party government, presidential popularity, time in office, and so on).[1] Others argue it has more to do with presidential leadership and persuasive skills.[2]

In this chapter, we address these questions, analyzing the details of managing relations with Congress from the inside. Having worked in the White House or on the last four presidential transitions (George H. W. Bush, Bill Clinton, George W. Bush, and Barack Obama), we observed the process up close. Yet as professionally trained social scientists, we are also keenly aware of the questions frequently posed by scholars and students of American government. Measuring the president's influence on Congress is one popular area of inquiry. We argue this view is important, but incomplete. Fully grasping White House congressional relations demands first an appreciation of the separation of powers that our forefathers carefully and deliberately designed and the impact it has on *both* how presidents try to influence Congress, but also how lawmakers attempt to push back or even pursue their own separate agendas.

Next, we show that *context* (party control of Congress and the type of policy) matters a lot in shaping presidential tactics and success. Presidents with large majorities in Congress face a different set of opportunities and challenges than those in mixed-party government situations. Further, these factors also shape the approach deployed in managing White House relations with the Hill. But as we discuss later in the chapter, presidential success is not always guaranteed, even if the same party controls the executive and legislative branches.

We also demonstrate why "personalities" and strategic goals of the actors involved contribute to the quality of a president's relations with Congress, as well as the product produced by the joint efforts of the White House and the Hill. These variables are hard to quantify and measure; yet our experience suggests they require close scrutiny because they also shape outcomes and the tone of interbranch relations. For example, a president whose party controls the Congress may signal he wants to produce a lot of legislative accomplishments. So he tells his party leadership—"just pass whatever you want and I'll sign it." To use the terminology of political scientists Jon R. Bond and Richard Fleisher, this style may demonstrate a lot of "success" but not necessarily much "influence."[3] On the other hand, former White House chief of staff John Sununu once famously remarked that his agenda for Congress was "I hope they do nothing." For his boss, President George H. W. Bush, legislative success meant stopping the Democrats from passing what was in his opinion bad public policy. Vetoing legislation was the way to do that. In Congress, then, the White House staff would consider sustaining a veto by garnering one-third plus one votes a victory, a strategy called "winning by losing."

In other words, strategic goals matter in evaluating success.

Finally, after examining all these influential factors, we conclude by outlining a host of critical process variables that impact the quality of presidential relations with Capitol Hill. By analyzing these factors, we dive into a long-standing debate among political scientists about the importance of "political conditions" (such as the strength of the president's party control in Congress and presidential popularity) versus a president's personal leadership skills and his power to persuade. Most political scientists conclude political conditions are more important determinants of success with Congress and that leadership skills only impact legislative achievement at the margin.[4]

This conclusion comports with our experience. Presidential success in Congress is largely determined by the political conditions faced by the White House and the president's ability to exploit them. But these research findings also raise a troubling real-world question. If presidential success is largely predetermined by the partisan or ideological makeup of Congress, why should the White House even try? And our experience further suggests presidents try a lot.

We have some answers to these questions and explore them in greater detail in the final section of this chapter. How the White House manages these tasks—like consultation, engaging the leadership, addressing the needs of rank-and-file members, and more—determines the degree of success. For example, close relations with Congress might help the White House propose unpopular legislation that Congress would reject. Close relations with the leadership can help get certain initiatives on the agenda that might not occur if left in the hands of Congress. Looking at the president's role more broadly than just success in legislation, the White House can help build the president's party on Capitol Hill. Or, the White House might choose to work hard developing a line of communication with the opposition. These relations might not yield votes from the opposition, but they can set a cordial tone that could result in future support (depending on the issue or circumstance). Further, it could reduce polarization and conflict in Washington, which might also raise the president's approval numbers, thus helping him indirectly with success in Congress. There are circumstances when a president is seen publicly reaching out to the opposition so he can demonstrate, if desired, that he is captive of neither party and serving only the country's interest. This has recently come to be known as *triangulation*.

Taken together, these process tasks in which the White House engages (outlined at the end of the chapter) are important. They may not directly produce votes, but they do contribute to presidential influence in a variety of indirect ways.

INFLUENCE FLOWS BOTH WAYS—PRESIDENTS PERSUADE, BUT SO DOES CONGRESS

Understanding the relationship between the White House and Congress must begin with a simple premise—influence flows both ways. Too often when scholars and students consider executive-legislative relations they only analyze the flow of power and influence in one direction—the president's success in getting Congress to do what he wants it to do. A more accurate description acknowledges the rivalry and the power-sharing relationship between the branches embedded in the U.S. Constitution. Presidents press Congress and lawmakers push back. Sometimes the president leads the dance, other times lawmakers do. Viewing the relationship as a reciprocal dialogue, rather than a one-way monologue, is key to a complete understanding of the dynamics of White House–congressional relations. This back and forth power struggle is a constant, one that doesn't shift even in different contexts like mixed-versus unified-party control or differing policy situations.

Acknowledging that "influence" flows both ways is one of the keys to understanding executive-legislative relations. It's unrealistic to assume only the president tries to shape outcomes in Congress. Political scientist Mark Peterson makes a similar point.[5] He notes that conventional wisdom among the press, the public, and scholars about presidential-congressional relations is "president centered."[6] He paints a picture of the president standing before Congress, giving his State of the Union message with his agenda on the line. If the president can convince Congress to pass it, he wins; if not, he loses. It is all about the president, and it is all about passing his agenda—a one-way series of inputs from the president into the Congress to achieve legislative outputs.

However, presidential-congressional relations are best understood as a two-way street with pressure, influence, success, and failure flowing freely in both directions. And sometimes this two-way street causes the White House to shift gears somewhere in the middle of the process. Two relatively recent examples make this point. First, most observers agree welfare reform was never a top priority in the Clinton White House, yet congressional Republicans continued to push for this legislation. After rejecting broader legislation that included welfare reform, President Clinton not only signed a modified version of the measure but also shifted strategy to embrace the bill and share in the political credit with the Republicans.

Creating a Department of Homeland Security was a similar example for George W. Bush. After resisting creation of the new department, Mr. Bush pivoted due to continued congressional prodding, signed the legislation, and used its creation as a political benefit in his reelection bid.

Both examples underscore how presidents are not only occasionally led by Congress, but can also shift strategies (if they are politically facile and astute) and claim credit for legislative initiatives.

Models of presidential-congressional relations based on a unidirectional influence flow also tend to view presidential success or influence in constant as opposed to dynamic terms. Charles Jones, for example, notes this short-coming in extant scholarship and argues for a dynamic approach. He argues that the "strategies of presidents in dealing with Congress will depend on the advantages they have available at any one time. One cannot employ a constant model of an activist president leading a party government. Conditions may encourage the president to work at the margins of president-congressional interaction (for example where he judges that he has an advantage, as with foreign and defense issues)."[7] Again, using the example of the presidency of George W. Bush, his ability to successfully influence Congress on matters related to defense, national security, and homeland security changed dramatically after the 9/11 terrorist attacks.

Looking to Mr. Bush's second term, times changed again. Many of his legislative initiatives stalled in his first two years after reelection (2005 and 2006). And then his opportunities to go on offense almost ground to a halt in 2007 and 2008, as the Democrats took over the majority in Congress after the 2006 election. Times changed and so did the White House–legislative dynamics.

A COLLECTION OF CONTEXTS

So far we've established that understanding the White House–congressional relationship requires acknowledging that power and influence flow both ways. The basic interests and rivalries driving this reciprocal relationship don't change. But they do play out in a variety of contexts—unified versus split-party control, institutional factors like differences between the House and the Senate, and various policy domains all shape the tactics deployed. The next section outlines how this collection of contexts affects relations between the branches.

Party Control of Congress

Whoever controls the majority in the House and Senate has a significant impact on the tactics, style, and content of managing presidential relations with Congress. President George W. Bush's administration faced markedly different circumstances in its relations with the Hill in its last two years in office following the 2006 election after Republicans lost control of the majority in the House and Senate. On the other hand, President Barack Obama faced a situation of unified party control in 2009. These two different contexts produced vastly different strategies and tactics on both ends of Pennsylvania Avenue, for both the minority and majority parties.

Mixed versus Unified Party Governments

To begin, consider mixed (or divided) versus unified party government. Barack Obama in 2009 had the privilege of serving with unified party government, as did George W. Bush in 2001 and Bill Clinton in 1993.

For both Presidents Clinton and Bush, their experience with unified government was relatively short-lived. The Clinton administration served its first two years with its own party as the majority, but spent the next six years working with a Republican majority in Congress. President George W. Bush's experience was even shorter. He lost the majority in six months in June of 2001 when Senator James Jeffords changed parties. Mr. Bush regained a Senate majority eighteen months later following the 2002 midterm elections.

Unified party control can help produce some quick legislative victories, as they did for presidents Clinton, Bush, and Obama. But these wins tend to be on "low hanging fruit," items a previous party's president may have stymied.

In some respects, the president's political prowess in legislative affairs during periods of unified party government may be overrated. Recent presidents facing unified party control experienced some notable legislative successes. However, there were also glaring examples of failure by unified government, most notably in the form of President Clinton's health care reform package, which languished in a Democrat-controlled Congress and ultimately became fodder for a successful Republican campaign to take over Congress in the 1994 elections. President Bush campaigned hard for Social Security reform with a unified Republican majority in 2005, following his reelection. But after months of barnstorming the country, Congress never acted on the president's idea.

As David Mayhew and others point out, unified control is not a sufficient criterion to predict significant differences in legislative accomplishment.[8] Entire chapters or books could he written about different strategies to deal with unified party government. In the short space remaining, we make two points based on our experiences and those of others who have worked in the White House. First, we agree that there are structural components to gridlock that make it difficult to enact major legislative accomplishments, even under conditions of unified party government.[9] Given factors such as intrachamber member and committee rivalries, competition between the House and the Senate, rule XXII in the Senate that requires sixty votes to break a filibuster, and the two-thirds majority required in both chambers to pass a bill over the president's objections, enacting any piece of legislation is difficult.

Second, given the difficulty moving an agenda through Congress with the president's party in control, too little time is spent cultivating relationships and reaching out to members of the opposition party. Building strong relationships with the opposite party is one of the most challenging aspects of leadership in the legislative arena. From majority leaders in the Senate, to Speakers of the House, to presidents of the United States, finding a successful formula for working with the other party without alienating allies in one's own party eludes most modern-day political leaders in Washington. These efforts are also sometimes stymied when the opposition takes the strategic view that they do not want to cooperate with the president in a given instance. Yet presidents who take a longer view and do make authentic connections usually reap large benefits. If there is one common thread of underachievement running through all modern presidents, it is that the challenge of working with the opposition has gotten the better of most of them.

We conclude with one suggestion: presidents should not measure success merely in votes, but in positive relations and trust. Barack Obama diligently courted Republicans during his first weeks in office. Even though the efforts resulted in few GOP votes on the president's initial priorities, he kept the lines of communications open and set a tone of civility. This attitude laid the groundwork for future bipartisan success. As Mr. Obama said in a February 2009 news conference, "I'm more interested in building long-term trust than gaining short-term votes."

Bicameral Effects

Differences between the House and the Senate are another important variable in managing relations with Congress. Institutional rules represent the most glaring difference. In the Senate, some argue that the majority is not really "a majority" without sixty votes, since so much of Senate floor activity is dependent on unanimous consent at achieving a three-fifths supermajority. The minority often blocks majority initiatives without sixty votes in the Senate.

This is not the case in the House. Even a slim majority, such as in the House in the 106th Congress, can process legislation efficiently and effectively using its Rules Committee, as long as it can keep its members unified. Managing the behavior of these institutions is further complicated by the impact different election calendars have on all three institutions, including the president. The Senate has only a third of its members up every two years, the House has the entire body running for reelection while the president runs every four years. Off-year election cycles often create competing concerns and interests that are hard to harmonize, even within your own party.

The White House must incorporate these bicameral differences into its lobbying strategy. Here are a couple examples. The White House may look to different types of personnel to staff the liaison office for positions dealing with the House and Senate. Senators are typically older and may have more difficulty or reticence interacting with younger, former staffers. The president's team should also spend a good portion of its time working aggressively to develop relationships and gather input from a wide array of senators.

Second, given the size of the House and its majority rules, working with the leadership in the House is relatively more important than working with Senate leaders (as power in the Senate is more diffuse). Although no White House should ignore rank-and-file House members, compared with those in the Senate, the rules allow the White House team to focus relatively more attention on the House leadership.

Policy Contexts

The president's attempts to lead and manage relations with Congress also depend on the type of policy under consideration. For example, President George H. W. Bush approached Congress a certain way in January 1991 when he attempted to secure congressional authorization for the use of force in the Persian Gulf War. Alternatively, President Clinton used a different set of tactics in 1993 when he successfully passed his economic-stimulus/deficit-reduction strategy. Finally, both presidents used yet another set of strategies when responding to more specific and particular requests from individual members, trying to secure administration positions on narrower policy questions.

Some issues, by their very nature, in the current political environment are highly partisan. In today's landscape, issues like health care and taxes are difficult policies on which to reach bipartisan consensus. This suggests a more partisan approach to managing these issues. Other policy areas, like certain distributive policies such as transportation funding, military spending, or foreign policy legislation following major economic or foreign policy shocks, like issues immediately following the 9/11 terrorist attacks, are decidedly more bipartisan. In these areas, the president will find reaching bipartisan consensus and gaining support from across the aisle much easier tasks. It is also worth noting that policy debates precipitated by crisis or other external developments cast presidents into promoting policy agendas that may or may not suit or interest them. President George W. Bush was masterful and apparently very comfortable in managing the issues that confronted the country post-9/11. This did not appear to be the case as he and his administration successfully began addressing the financial issues facing the country in the waning days of his administration, in pleading with Congress to give the government massive authority to intervene in capital markets and bail out a host of financial institutions.

STRATEGIC GOALS

Too often in the analysis of U.S. politics, Congress and the president are simply viewed as the targets of outside societal influences. Such views purport that extraneous forces almost exclusively shape their actions. In contrast, our experiences have taught us that individuals, their relationships, and their goals make a difference.

David Mayhew recognizes this shortcoming in contemporary U.S. political analysis when he says,

> Public affairs [meaning significant public actions by individuals and legislators that come to be remembered], moreover, is a highly important realm in that much of what virtually anybody by any standard would consider to be politically important originates, is substantially caused, and happens within it—that is, is endogenous to it. This may be a commonsense view, but it is not all that common within the boundaries of modern social science, where politics tends to be seen as driven or determined by exogenous forces such as classes, interest groups, interests, or otherwise pre-politically caused preferences.[10]

We agree with Mayhew and believe that recognizing the unique role individuals and their strategic goals play helps illuminate many aspects of presidential-congressional relations. Evaluating these objectives and their evolution provides useful insights into the level of success or influence that presidents achieve in legislative outcomes. These strategic goals form part of the context, including the process and institutional variables outlined above, helping us better understand and interpret the meaning of outcome measures.

Analyzing how the Clinton administration and congressional strategic goals interacted is a useful case study. Let us begin in 1993, during a period when Democrats controlled the House, Senate, and White House. Although President Clinton initially urged his Democratic colleagues to involve Republicans early in the deliberations, the congressional Democrats worked to ensure their proposals could pass without Republican support. As noted above, the cornerstone of the early agenda was a $500 billion tax increase and spending cut package to reduce the deficit. This measure was passed by one vote, and no Republicans supported it. The administration and the Democratic congressional leadership's ultimate decision not to move their complex and controversial proposal until they were assured that it could pass without the support of Republicans, particularly in the House, was a strategic disaster. While many Democrats wore this victory as a badge of honor, the Republicans gradually but successfully worked to characterize the Democrats' frenetic legislative agenda as extreme, excessive, and out of touch with most Americans. The Republicans capitalized on the Democrats' decision and crystallized this strategic message: stop the Democrats by putting the Republicans in control of Congress. The Republicans successfully used this message to change the entire political context of the new presidency. They convinced the American public that the Democrats should lose their jobs, not because they had failed to do what they said, but precisely because they were doing what they had promised.

In January 1995, the new Republican majority in the Congress took the lead, attempting to shape the political and legislative agenda of the new Congress. The cornerstone of their strategy was the Contract with America, which included popular initiatives such as litigation reform, tax cuts, and cancellation of many traditional Democrat-sponsored programs. Democrats at both ends of Pennsylvania Avenue were unsure initially how to respond.

Congressional Democrats, particularly in the House, were not needed to pass any of these new proposals, leaving them in the comfortable position of being against everything. Because the House was going to take the lead legislative charge, the Senate Democrats were in a "wait and see" posture. The administration, desperately wanting to remain relevant, was anxious to see if there were policy issues on which staff could work together with the Republicans, knowing that there would be plenty of areas in which they could draw the bright lines of battle.

The House acted quickly and aggressively to implement its agenda. Like the Democrats in the previous Congress, Republicans relied on their own party to pass their proposals. Appearing to take a strategy out of the failed Democrat playbook, the House GOP advanced a partisan set of bills. Soon the president and congressional Democrats realized their best strategic position in response to these legislative proposals was to claim, as the GOP did in the previous Congress, that the Republican proposals were extreme, insensitive, and out of touch with the American people. Democrats pledged to do everything they could to prevent these draconian measures from becoming law. As a result, no major legislation passed into law that entire year except for a continuing resolution that was finally adopted in January 1996.

Victory in this case was not measured by traditional outcome measures. Instead, winning was defined by whose message was more believable to the American public. By most accounts, the administration and congressional Democrats "won," for stopping the Republicans from going too far with the proposals. The boldness of the new Republican agenda fell on deaf ears. The Republicans now had ten months before the next election to decide whether to make a "halftime" strategy correction or stay the course. Especially after the departure of Majority Leader Bob Dole it became apparent that the new GOP leadership team, Lott and Gingrich, wanted to play an entirely new hand. And by doing so, they set in place the third strategic dynamic between President Clinton and the Congress in three short years.

The theme of this strategy was "cooperation." On what issues could the Republican majority work with a Democratic president? How could they quickly show they were not "extreme" and "insensitive" and instead ready to do the people's business? The new congressional majority and the president both thought this was the ticket to their respective reelections in 1996.

This was not a popular view among congressional Democrats. The minority felt it would be far more preferable for the president not to cooperate with the Republican majority, showing the American people that the GOP could not govern. This, the Democrats believed, was their best route to regain power in Congress.

Some conservative Republicans held the same position, though for different reasons. They believed compromise was tantamount to capitulation and working together with the Clinton administration would dilute the Republican cause and only help the president get reelected. Nevertheless the Republican leaders and the Democratic president forged a course of cooperation that resulted in small business tax cuts, minimum wage increases, welfare reform, and a framework for a bipartisan balanced budget package.

The 1996 election returned President Clinton and the House and Senate Republican majorities. Despite the success this strategy produced in the 1996 election, there was serious dissatisfaction among the Republican rank and file. After working with the president to enact a balanced budget and pass welfare reform, Republicans were not sure about the next act of this political play. Many had no desire to continue to work with the president after he won the 1996 election, and in the wake of revelations about campaign financing irregularities and the continuation of the Whitewater investigation. The Republican leadership decided to disengage from a cooperative posture on policy and develop an aggressive strategy to use its oversight and subpoena authority to pursue the new campaign and personal financial investigations.

In addition to pursuing the truth, these investigations served at least two other strategic purposes for Republicans. They continued to fill the negative atmosphere surrounding the Clinton administration, with the GOP hoping to undo the administration's credibility in the eyes of the public and media. Further, these investigations served to keep the administration at arm's length in the legislative arena.

"Scandal as diversion," appeared as a strategic approach through the hearing on Whitewater, through inquiry into the campaign financing of the 1996 election, and ultimately through the impeachment proceedings regarding the Lewinsky matter. It produced very little authorizing legislation of note, except by accident, and an appropriations process that generally served to the disadvantage of the Republicans and to the benefit of the president and Democrats. The 1998 elections were held in the height of this strategy, and the Republican majority in the Senate held its own while the GOP House majority lost a handful of seats, putting an already slim majority in serious jeopardy for 2000.

While the strategy of scandal as diversion was on the wane, the congressional leaders and the president contemplated an appropriate framework for the last dance of a lame-duck president. The nature of the final strategic relationship is still unclear. There is no doubt, however, that clarifying the strategic goals pursued by the actors in the legislative and executive branches is a critical precursor to understanding the legislative outcomes (or lack thereof).

In January of 2007, the parties changed roles. The Democrats now controlled the Congress and George Bush was looking at his two final years in office facing conditions of mixed party government. Little of consequence happened legislatively during those two years. President Bush had just come off of a major defeat of his Social Security reform initiative in 2005 along with a major embarrassment for his administration's handling of Hurricane Katrina in New Orleans. The war in Iraq was not going well and neither political party appeared open to compromise and conciliation.

As the economy deteriorated in 2008, President Bush did work with Congress early in the year to pass a modest economic stimulus package and later in the year a major piece of legislation called the Troubled Asset Relief Program (TARP),[11] but little was accomplished in other areas such as education, climate change, energy, or entitlements.

Thus far, we have examined how factors largely outside the control of the White House affect relations with Congress. House and Senate attempts to influence the president, mixed versus unified party control, and the strategic goals of congressional actors are all outside the control of the White House. Of course, the president and the White House generally set their own strategic goals. But there are other aspects of managing the process of relations with Congress from the standpoint of the president that deserve closer examination. The remainder of this chapter outlines a series of tactics the White

House can pursue—largely within its control—to achieve successful influence with the Congress.

PROCESS—A TAPESTRY OF SUCCESS

The "process" of managing White House–congressional relations has many dimensions. "Success" with Congress is an interwoven tapestry of activity rather than a single strand, such as winning roll-call votes. True legislative success builds an active two-way dialogue between the Congress and the president. Bryce Harlow, who adroitly negotiated the shoals of Congress for Presidents Eisenhower and Nixon, has said, "The presidents legislative affairs office creates a bridge across a yawning Constitutional chasm, a chasm fashioned by our power-fearing Fathers to keep the Congress and the President at a safe distance from one another in the interest of human liberty."[12]

Identifying the tools necessary to build this bridge is the subject of the next section. Most of these recommendations apply to the president and the White House legislative affairs staff. They all fit into what scholars might term *presidential leadership* tactics. They are different from some of the context variables described above. And several scholars have questioned whether they truly "influence" congressional behavior (that is, cause Congress to do something it might not otherwise do anyway). Still, we think these leadership/process tactics matter. We explore the reasons why in the conclusion after we outline these process variables.

Active Consultation

Presidents who put a strong emphasis on consultation with Congress, communicating often personally or through the staff with legislators, will get high marks and succeed in influencing the House and the Senate. The Clinton team got high marks early on with the Democratic leadership in Congress for consulting and working in concert on a variety of measures during 1993. Their initiatives included proposals on education and environment, the Family and Medical Leave Act, and "motor voter" legislation (two initiatives that President Clinton's predecessor, George H. W. Bush, consistently opposed that now could pass under conditions of unified party government), as well as modest institutional reform proposals regarding campaign finance and lobbying registration. Their agenda also included legislative objectives that began to reposition Democrats as supporting a balanced budget while reducing the size of government and expanding efforts to fight crime.

As is often the case in unified government, the Democrats worked to ensure that their proposals passed without Republican support. The cornerstone of this early agenda was a $500 billion tax increase and spending cut package to reduce the deficit. The measure passed the House by a margin of one, with all Republicans opposing it.

President George W. Bush's legislative strategy in the House followed a similar path over his first five years. In the Senate, however, Mr. Bush was also able to secure some Democratic support for most of his major initiatives like tax cuts, Medicare prescription drug legislation, and the No Child Left Behind education bill.

Holding their respective parties in line took Presidents Clinton and Bush many hours of consultation by inviting members to the White House and sending administration personnel to the Hill. Active consultation results in members of Congress believing that someone at the White House is listening and considering their point of view. Often just "hearing people out" and being attentive to their views go a long way toward strengthening and creating positive relations with Congress.

Barack Obama followed an almost identical path in the House of Representatives. While he worked hard trying to win Republican support through phone calls, meetings, and social gatherings, he failed to win any House Republican votes on his first major legislative initiative—an economic stimulus package.

Although these presidents failed to produce a lot of bipartisan votes, they received strong initial marks for trying. At a minimum, these consultations began a dialogue, keeping the door open for future negotiations and bipartisanship in policy areas that did not produce as much polarization. A cynical interpretation of these gestures might be that they were never expected to produce a bipartisan result. The hope in making these gestures was to reinforce a bipartisan image of the president that was carefully forged in the campaign. The president's advisers may have concluded early on that true bipartisanship was necessary or doable for the president to be successful in the long run. What he needed was to get the legislation through the Congress while minimizing a negative impact on his brand.

Creating a Capitol Hill Presence

Building successful bridges with legislators requires accessibility on the part of the White House staff on Capitol Hill. Both Bush (George H. W. and George W.) administration legislative affairs teams stationed their members in critical places around the Capitol during every roll-call vote in the House and the Senate. This allowed senators and congressmen to find the staff and vice versa. It helped develop an image of a White House and administration actively engaged with the Congress, listening to members' concerns and complaints, and feeding information back to lawmakers.

Conversely, the Clinton team spent more time early in the administration in internal policy-development meetings in the White House. Soon many on Capitol Hill began to complain that the White House team was "invisible" on the Hill, and complaints about lack of attentiveness began to mount.

David Hobbs, former assistant to the president for legislative affairs in the second Bush administration, was also a former chief of staff to former House majority leader Dick Armey (R-TX) before joining the White House lobbying team in 2001. As a denizen of the House, Hobbs took creating a presence to a new level by literally sitting in the House Republican cloakroom—normally an area restricted to members only—to listen, learn, and cajole. Without floor access most legislative affairs staff don't have that kind of presence. Yet because of Hobbs's unique background in the House, he was "presence personified."

Congress's, particularly the House Democrats', perception of the Clinton legislative team waxed and waned almost as did their attitudes about him. A very graphic waning moment after the 1994 election is the White House legislative team's workspace being relegated to a small desk and a phone at the end of a leadership corridor. The Senate relationship remained steady and constructive throughout Clinton's tenure, but not without regular lectures on strategy and other not so helpful suggestions.

The actual makeup of the Obama legislative team is unprecedented in that they are a collection of very senior and talented Hill staffers who, all but two, have never lobbied the Congress before. All will have left congressional jobs to join this team. They will have the additional challenge of not only learning the new job of being the president's lobbyists, but they will also have to simultaneously surrender their congressional instincts to serve and protect their former bosses and their institution in service of new loyalties and responsibilities. This will become very apparent when they have to persuade some of their old colleagues to take votes and positions that might promote the president's agenda but may not be easy to explain to a set of voters in a given congressional district.

Creating a Hill presence is a key ingredient for the White House to engage daily in the ebb and flow of congressional culture. Presidents who dispatch their staff to talk to legislators in this manner will win high marks from Congress. It is a tactic that requires a large time commitment; President George H. W. Bush and President Reagan's legislative affairs teams were on Capitol Hill whenever Congress was in session. Yet it is also a tactic that will result in major dividends in creating an effective two-way dialogue with Congress.

Engaging the Leadership

Fostering a constructive relationship with the congressional leadership—both the president's party and the opposition—is one of the most important tasks in which the White House can invest time and energy. As previously discussed, the nature of the relationship with the leadership changes when the president's party is in the majority or minority. For now, it is important to note that the president and his *staff* must cultivate and forge strong relations with the congressional leadership irrespective of the context. The president's legislative affairs staff ignores the minority—of either party—at their own peril.

In George H. W. Bush's administration, the president and his staff worked hard to cultivate these relationships, meeting with the congressional leadership nearly every week when Congress was in session during the president's four-year term. The president and his staff would organize bipartisan, bicameral meetings twice a month, dedicating the other two monthly meetings to only Republicans from the House—and the Senate. Bush consciously tried to convey the impression that he was diligently working with the congressional leadership (on both sides of the aisle), listening to their views, and meeting them halfway on any issue he could.

This strategy had mixed results. Often Bush never moved far enough to accommodate the congressional Democratic leadership, and his Republican allies viewed his actions with suspicion. In the mixed party government environment faced by Bush, engaging the leadership seemed to work best when playing defense. In those cases, he and his staff could rally the GOP leadership to oppose a Democratic initiative. The combination of the Republican leadership whipping its members and the White House working conservative Democrats did result in a few key legislative wins. House passage of a capital gains tax cut and the first authorization of "fast-track" trade–negotiating authority are two primary examples.

Presidents George W. Bush and Barack Obama faced a completely different situation, at least with the House leadership. Instead of constantly trying to get morsels of information from the majority about scheduling and agenda, as the first President Bush did between 1989–1992, the George W. Bush and Barack Obama administrations spent far less time trying to work with the minority. These differences in amount of time, energy, and contact with the minority underscore how differing political and institutional contexts should affect how we evaluate success and influence.

One of the biggest challenges both of these president's faced (at least during Bush's first six years and at the beginning of the Obama administration) was paying enough attention to the minority. As the opposition they rarely agreed with the White House. And the care and feeding of the majority and its leaders took so much time that the president's team rarely had the time to reach out effectively to the minority.

Working with congressional leadership emerges as one of the White House staff's key tasks in any review of process and tactics. It is an important ingredient to any successful legislative strategy. Strong relations with the congressional leadership make every other aspect of relating with the House and the Senate operate more smoothly and efficiently.

Addressing Needs and Wants

When former senator Trent Lott was minority whip in the House, he used to admonish President Reagan's White House staff, "You've got to take care of members' needs and wants." This is both a big and a small request, and it is important to address those needs and wants. This may involve a letter from the president, a trip on Air Force One back to the district or state, a change in an administration position, or a signing pen from a piece of legislation recently enacted into law. There is no better way to build a reservoir of goodwill and develop a reputation of responsiveness than by attending to member needs and wants.

For instance, Nicholas Calio, assistant to the president for legislative affairs for President Bush from 2001 to 2002, used to invite people from the Hill to his office for drinks and sandwiches and then give them private tours of the Oval Office after hours. His actions produced currency in the real world of politics.

M. B. Oglesby, legislative affairs chief for President Reagan, told his staff that responsiveness meant that they should never leave the White House at the end of the day without having returned every phone call. A president can vastly improve his relations with Congress by making it clear that he wants to address member needs and wants. Doing so will pay large dividends when it comes time to spend some political capital—even if it fails to produce active support by the opponents, sometimes it can moderate their attacks.

Access to the President

Effective leadership and influence with Congress includes staff that can speak clearly and authoritatively for the president. In order to do this, White House staff charged with relations with Congress must have unfettered access to the president. Building too many layers of staff between the president and the personnel that must speak for him is a common mistake in the modern White House. A recurrent theme in our own experience and in research by political scientists, such as Ken Collier in his book *Between the Branches,* is that White House staff who lack easy access to the president are diminished in their effectiveness.[13] When the legislative affairs staff members lack access to the president, they lose stature and ultimately effectiveness in influencing Congress.

One of the best examples of this occurred during the first Bush administration and the now infamous 1990 budget agreement in which the president broke his "read my lips, no new taxes" pledge. Office of Management and Budget director Richard Darman concocted the 1990 budget strategy with no input from the White House legislative affairs staff. Darman worked closely with the Democratic leadership, sounding them out repeatedly about the outlines of a budget deal, without consulting with the Republican leadership or his own colleagues. The president and Congress reached a final agreement on the budget deal during a morning meeting in the White House that included Bush, Darman, White House chief of staff John Sununu, Speaker of the House Tom Foley, House Majority Leader Richard Gephardt, and Senate Majority Leader George Mitchell. The only two Republican congressional representatives attending were House Minority Leader Robert Michel and Senate Minority Leader Dole. According to their staffs' recollections, their involvement in the meeting was minimal. No one from the White House legislative affairs staff found out about the meeting and the agreement from lawmakers on Capitol Hill until later that morning as word began to leak out. This lack of access by the legislative affairs staff to the president hurt the Bush team for many months in the future in terms of their reputation on the Hill.

Building Trust

The president and his staff must work to develop trust with legislators. Because of factors like political and institutional rivalries discussed earlier in this chapter, trust between the branches may not be the natural state of affairs. Building effective relations with Congress means constantly assuring lawmakers that one will do what one says one will do. A promise to provide a legislator with a letter of support must be followed up. Promises for a presidential phone call must be delivered.

The ability to "make things happen" is part of the building of trust from the standpoint of the White House staff. A White House staff that does not have the ability or stature to deliver on promises or commitments made will never glean the type of respect and trust from lawmakers to effectively lead or influence Congress. On the other hand, building a trusting relationship doesn't always entail making your congressional colleagues happy by doing what they want. Often that is not possible, nor desirable. What is doable is being direct and not misleading when cooperation does not serve your interest. In the darkest hours between the Clinton White House and the Republican leadership, Dan Meyer, the Speaker's chief of staff, and Clinton's director of legislative affairs, were able to talk regularly and candidly with each about the functioning of the government while their bosses were only throwing barbs—or worse—at one another.

Strategic Coordination

Coordinating with other executive branch agencies and building coalitions with outside groups are other keys to lobbying success. If utilized correctly, both represent powerful tools that can strengthen a president's legislative muscle on Capitol Hill. How and when the White House chooses to coordinate with executive agencies is a key consideration. While the president and his staff want to utilize the agency resources at certain times and make sure that the executive branch departments do not get "off message," the White House also must guard against every agency initiative becoming a presidential priority.

During the first two years of the Clinton administration cabinet officials and agency heads often wanted to make their agency priorities the same as the president's, hoping to give them more leverage on Capitol Hill. White House staff studiously guarded the list of presidential priorities, pushing large pieces of the administration's agenda back to the agencies for implementation. After losing control of the Congress in 1994, the senior staff of the president reversed course with their agency counterparts and brought virtually the entire agenda of the administration inside the West Wing so that they could manage its execution on a daily basis. Coordinating the substance, message, and execution became a very nuanced and complex process in the highly charged political atmosphere of the Republican takeover. The White House wanted maximum control in all phases of its application under these conditions, whereas it allowed and even encouraged a liberal decentralization approach when operating under unified party control of the Congress and executive branch in the prior two years.

Coordination in the administration of George W. Bush was also relatively strong. Many observers noted that his White House and its political appointees normally stayed "on message." And as Mr. Bush began his second term, it appeared that coordination would become even more tightly controlled as the president moved some of his key White House staff out to head cabinet-level agencies like the defense, education, and justice departments.

The Obama administration is not taking any chances in ensuring White House coordination and control of their major policy initiatives and concerns. The president created senior White House positions to drive his two major domestic initiatives on health care and climate change. He also enhanced and expanded the role of his national security adviser to ensure the maximum White House control and coordination of his administration's response to the volatile national security issues exploding around the world.

Communications and Message Coordination

How an issue or policy is talked about is critical. But language matters in some inobvious ways. The president has an enormous advantage in being able to frame an issue. His bully pulpit often gives him the first and last word on a matter, particularly if it is contentious. He can use the bully pulpit to frame a new initiative, for example, the need for normalizing trade relations with China or condemning congressional tardiness in completing business. His voice maximizes when it is coordinated with his political allies on Capitol Hill or sympathetic spokespeople around the country. Presidential communications in all these forms are formidable tools, particularly when used as part of a comprehensive strategy to advance or thwart an issue. However, this is not foolproof, as we saw in the repeated attempts by the Clinton administration to frame the problems and solutions implied in its proposal to solve the health care crisis in 1994.

Our experience suggests, however, that a strong message may do more to bolster the enthusiasm of core supporters rather than move public opinion. This conclusion is consistent with what George Edwards writes in his book *On Deaf Ears* (2003). What we don't know is what impact the president's voice will have when spoken in concert with the some 13 million e-mail addresses of supporters the Obama campaign harvested in the march to the White House. Will they amplify his voice on policy proposals by their willingness to echo it in congressional offices around the country or will it dissipate in the din of Washington give-and-take?

Although building successful congressional relations depends on weaving a tapestry of activities, success also varies based on institutional and policy contexts. Still these elements are only a part of the myriad of variables that affect legislative-executive relations. As discussed in this chapter, party control and policy matter, creating differing contexts for the interbranch dance.

CONCLUSION

Currently, the views of most pundits, scholars, and reporters on presidential-congressional relations are too limited. Understanding the dance between presidents and lawmakers requires a broader perspective. Presidents do not sink or swim, succeed or fail, have influence or not, based solely on outcome-based measures like roll-call votes or sustaining vetoes. A broader perspective on presidential-congressional relations also requires understanding that Congress tries to influence and lead the president as much as the president tries to guide Congress. Not only is too much of the research in this area presidency centered, but there is also not enough emphasis on how Congress and the president try to influence each other through a dynamic process of give-and-take.

A better understanding of the White House–congressional relationship also must take into account contexts like party control or the type of policy where the two branches are interacting.

This chapter also highlights some of the secrets of success in managing presidential-congressional relations given these changing and differing contexts. Viewing presidential-congressional relations in this broader perspective sets the stage for a better and more realistic understanding of how these institutions can and should interact, including their potential and their limits.

Achieving presidential success and influence with Congress is not easy. Based on the variables discussed in this chapter, one might conclude that most presidents are destined to fail. Quadrennial discussions about mandates or what can be done in the first one hundred days simply do not fit reality when it comes to presidential agendas with Congress.

We are not ready to throw in the towel and concede that all future presidents will underachieve. But we do think that someone needs to burst (or at least deflate) the public's overblown expectations about presidential influence in the legislative arena. If a president hopes to produce prodigious legislative accomplishments, many political and institutional stars have to align. He will have to be blessed with large legislative majorities in both chambers of Congress, an activist agenda with wide public support, and a great deal of bargaining skill to overcome a host of potential institutionally based pitfalls in Congress that could thwart pieces of his agenda. Appreciating that these political and institutional stars rarely align will help lower public expectations for future presidents.

President Barack Obama may have one of the best opportunities in recent decades to achieve major legislative accomplishments. His party controls majorities in both the House and Senate. He was elected on a mandate for change. And his ideological commitment is to an activist government agenda. Taken together, these are all ingredients suggesting Obama's work with Congress should resemble more of an FDR or LBJ pattern of success, compared with, say George H. W. Bush or perhaps Clinton and George W. Bush when they faced divided government.

But even with these advantages, success is never guaranteed. We argue that success depends on more than winning votes. We believe the process variables outlined in this chapter also deserve consideration. Presidents set the tone for relations between the branches. Focusing on how well the White House approaches the process suggestions outlined above will set a positive and civil tone, maximizing the possibility of successful influence.

The debate about the importance of presidential leadership/process variables versus context will no doubt continue. We believe both are important in determining a president's influence with Congress. Presidents confronting a conducive context (unified party government, large majorities, an electoral mandate, and an activist agenda) will likely produce a lot of legislative accomplishments. But leadership/process variables—like the tone they set, how well they listen, their openness to ideas from legislators—can make the difference between taking advantage of or squandering this positive context. On the other hand, presidents facing less positive contexts (mixed party government, larger majority opposition, a smaller government agenda) can also find success in a different way by skillful management of the process variables outlined in this chapter. They may define success differently—such as "stopping bad public policy" by a veto/sustain strategy or through party building activities with the minority—but nevertheless these leadership/process variables matter in determining influence and success with Congress. Influence and success are the products of both context and leadership in the real world of presidential-congressional relations.

NOTES

1. Jon R. Bond and Richard Fleisher, *The President in the Legislative Arena* (Chicago: University of Chicago Press, 1990); George C. Edwards III, *At the Margins: Presidential Leadership of Congress* (New Haven, CT: Yale University Press, 1989).

2. Richard Neustadt, *Presidential Power: The Politics of Leadership* (New York: John Wiley and Sons, 1960).

3, Bond and Fleisher, *The President in the Legislative Arena.*

4. See, for example, Edwards, *At the Margins*; or Bond and Fleisher, *The President in the Legislative Arena.*

5. Mark Peterson, *Legislating Together: The White House and Capitol Hill from Eisenhower to Reagan* (Cambridge, MA: Harvard University Press, 1990).

6. Peterson, *Legislating Together.*

7. Charles O. Jones, *The Presidency in a Separated System* (Washington, DC: The Brookings Institution, 1994).

8. David Mayhew, *Divided We Govern: Party Control, Lawmaking, and Investigating, 1946–1990* (New Haven, CT: Yale University Press, 1991.

9. Sarah Binder, *Minority Rights, Majority Rule: Partisanship and the Development of Congress* (Cambridge: Cambridge University Press, 1997).

10. David Mayhew, *America's Congress: Actions in the Public Sphere, James Madison through Newt Gingrich* (New Haven, CT: Yale University Press, 2002).

11. The TARP program was a response to banks not lending money due to a number of bad real estate loans on their books. The legislation called for the Treasury Department to buy these troubled assets and get them off their books.

12. Kenneth Collier, *Between the Branches: The White House Office of Legislative Affairs* (Pittsburgh: University of Pittsburgh Press, 1997).

13. Collier, *Between the Branches*.

Chapter Six

The Presidency
and Congressional Time

Roger H. Davidson

The legislative workload, along with institutional arrangements for coping with it, is a major component of the structure and substance of legislative-executive relations. Given the Constitution and the political history of the United States, it could not be otherwise. Articles I and II, after all, lay out the interleaved lawmaking responsibilities of the two branches—from initiation ("He [the president] shall from time to time recommend to their [Congress's] consideration such measures as he shall judge necessary and expedient . . .") to implementation ("He shall take care that the laws be faithfully executed . . ."). Beginning with George Washington, activist presidents have always inserted themselves into the legislative process. Franklin D. Roosevelt and his modern successors institutionalized "the legislative presidency"; today's chief executives are expected to present their legislative agendas to Congress, and to provide their allies on Capitol Hill with leadership and guidance.

As for Congress, one attribute sets it apart from virtually all of the world's other national assemblies: it is a working body that writes, processes, and re-fines laws that are typically its own handiworks; and it relies to a large degree on "in-house" resources. Until quite recently, scholars paid scant attention to legislative business as a research topic. Yet Congress's agenda and work-load shape not only the behavior and operations of the Senate and House of Representatives, but also the two chambers' relationships with the executive branch. What is more, the legislative workload reminds us of "what Congress actually does and how it does it, with all its duties and all its occupations, with all its devices of management and resources of power."[1]

Legislative activity is, of course, only one aspect of the interactions be-tween presidents and congresses. Executive communications to Congress, for example, have grown so rapidly over the past two generations that almost as many of them are referred to committees as are bills and resolutions. Implementing and overseeing the laws and agencies Congress has created, not to mention scrutinizing administrative and judicial rule making, are other functions that repeatedly propel the president and Congress into joint action. Given the breadth and reach of modern government, these oversight duties remain burdensome even when few new statutes are produced. Yet oversight is closely linked to lawmaking: it flows from previously enacted statutes, it influences how these statutes are carried out or revised.

Making federal appointments is another joint enterprise that has become more burdensome at both ends of Pennsylvania Avenue. In days gone by, presidential nominations were usually handled perfunctorily, following the belief that presidents deserved to have executive-branch leaders of their own choosing. Today, however, nominees' qualifications, records, and financial activities are vetted within the White House by the Presidential Personnel Office and examined on Capitol Hill by the committee having jurisdiction over the relevant agency. Even federal court appointments—whose selection is clearly a joint duty of the president and the Senate (which offers "advice and consent")—historically provoked little congressional participation. No court nominee appeared before the Senate Judiciary Committee before 1925 (Harlan Fiske Stone, who was easily confirmed and then served as Chief Justice 1941–1946). Not until the 1950s did confirmation hearings become common. But they were still not required: Chief Justice Earl Warren (1953–1969), a singular figure in the Court's history, was not asked to testify—when confirmed, he was already sitting on the Court as an interim appointee. Nowadays, writes Robert A. Katzmann (a political scientist/lawyer now serving as a U.S. Circuit Court judge), "[H]earings have become a staple of the confirmation process. The expectation that nominees will testify is firmly rooted."[2] Not only the Senate Judiciary panel, but also numerous lobby groups, study nominees' writings and judicial opinions; the media often cover such hearings. In short, congressional outputs are diverse in content and variable over time.

THINKING ABOUT POLITICAL TIME

Thinking in terms of political time ought to come naturally to students of U.S. politics. After all, the Constitution separates the two policy-making branches, the presidency and Congress, chronologically as well as functionally. The interlocking system of terms of office—four years for the president, two years for representatives, and staggered six-year terms for senators—creates a perpetual timetable for electoral renewal or replacement of officials. The constitutional system was designed as an intricate machine of interlocked moving parts—and that machine could very well be a timepiece.[3]

The two policy-making branches run on different but related time frames; rarely do they experience change at precisely the same moment or at exactly the same rate. Because presidents are limited to four or eight years, they are forced to focus on the most pressing policy issues and to seek quick results. By contrast the houses of Congress display a durable continuity maintained by overlapping tenure and by the presence of experienced careerists. As a result, policies are typically incubated and nurtured by Capitol Hill policy entrepreneurs, oftentimes years or even decades before someone in the White House decides to elevate the item to a short list for urgent action.

These divergent time perspectives suggest why it is misleading to tell political time strictly according to elections. Every new Congress is to some degree unique, but not every election makes substantial changes in the two chambers. As a continuing body the Senate is especially resistant to change; despite respectable turnover rates, the average senator these days has served nearly three six-year terms. The House of Representatives formally reconstitutes itself every two years, but only rarely is it as radically transformed as when the Republicans seized control in 1995, or when the Democrats recaptured it in 2007. Even so, the average representative in 1995 had served nearly four terms; now the average exceeds six terms, or more than twelve years.[4]

Categorizing presidencies might seem a simpler matter, and indeed most historians and political scientists use particular presidencies as their unit of analysis. But even here things are not always what they seem. First, an administration may undergo substantial midcourse corrections—caused by midterm elections, crises, or other events. Bill Clinton's first term was derailed after only two years, when the opposition Republicans won control of Capitol Hill. George W. Bush's first term was transformed by the events of 9/11; his second term was enfeebled by his plunging public support. Such occurrences can alter a president's governing strategy and effectiveness.[5] Second, essential presidential governing strategies or styles may conceivably extend beyond a single administration—as, for example, in the Nixon-Ford or Reagan-Bush successions.

Political scientists tend to measure political time in terms of underlying and enduring political party coalitions. These "party systems" are initiated by realigning elections or periods: most notably, Andrew Jackson's election in 1828, the Republican Party's ascendancy in 1860, the "system of 1896" that strengthened the GOP's dominance, and Franklin D. Roosevelt's election in 1932. To this list we must add two recent shifts: the Republican dominance beginning in 1994 and lasting for a dozen years, and the Democrats' more recent resurgence (2006 and 2008).

Such a categorization assumes the existence of mass-based parties that can effectively mobilize the votes of loyal supporters in elections—unless and until these stable loyalties are disturbed either by short-term forces or by a more permanent reordering of party divisions.[6] The theory conforms to political development during the heyday of U.S. political parties, roughly from the 1830s through the 1960s; and it fits reasonably with events since that time—an era characterized by intense top-down partisan organization and elite mobilization, though with lower overall rates of participation. Despite its flaws, party alignment theory yields interesting insights into changes in presidential and congressional policy making.[7]

A related classification is offered by Stephen Skowronek, who links changing political eras to what he calls "emergent structures" of presidential policy making, depending on whether a given president challenges or adheres to the prevailing political order.[8] Skowronek plants himself right in the middle of the Oval Office: political time is defined as "presidentially driven sequences of change encompassing the generation and degeneration of coalitional systems or partisan regimes."[9] He describes how presidents "make politics" by tirelessly building constituencies for change and striving to remove obstacles that stand in the way of their high-priority agendas.

It is hard to square this president-centered account with, for example, the varied patterns of legislative-executive relations. In truth, presidents are not always at the center of policy making, nor are they invariably agents of change. In our separated system, as the evidence shows, innovation and incubation of major policy departures can occur in many places, not the least of which are on Capitol Hill.

CONGRESSIONAL WORKLOAD AND OUTPUTS

Both the president and Congress today confront a number and variety of demands unmatched in all but the most turbulent years of the past. The history of Congress readily demonstrates that "the volume of output demands as well as . . . their complexity, uniformity, and volatility, vary greatly over time."[10] Aggregate legislative statistics from the last six decades show how variable these workload measures can be.

One workload indicator is the number of bills and resolutions introduced by senators and representatives. In both chambers, bill introduction followed a long-term growth from the mid-1940s through the 1970s, followed by gradual decline. In the House, a portion of the decline can be traced to changes in cosponsorship rules and the rise of megabills. Both chambers, however, have experienced parallel buildup, then a period of extraordinary legislative activity, followed by contraction. Since the late 1990s, there has been a modest rise in the volume of bills: in today's two-year congresses, from eight to ten thousand bills and joint resolutions are introduced. From four hundred to eight hundred laws are enacted.

Bill introduction and sponsorship vary widely among individual senators and representatives. Some lawmakers are inveterate sponsors of bills and resolutions; others shy away from sponsoring measures. In the late 1940s, House members on average authored about eighteen bills or resolutions, compared to thirty-three for senators. Bill sponsorship peaked in the later 1960s, when the average member in both bodies authored almost fifty measures per Congress. Then in the late 1970s the figures plummeted, reaching a plateau that remains to this day. Today's lawmakers introduce fewer measures than those who served in Congress at the beginning of the post–World War II period—some thirty per senator and fewer than half that number per representative.

Legislators today are doubly disadvantaged: not only do they introduce fewer bills and resolutions, but their proposals are less likely to be approved by the full chamber. A Senate measure introduced in the 1940s had better than an even chance of passage in some form; the odds are now less than one in four. A House measure used to have nearly one chance in four of passage; today the odds are about half that.[11] This trend stems from two trends: (1) increased emphasis on broad-scale legislative vehicles—omnibus bills, usually shaped by party or committee leaders, that serve as catch-alls for scores of specific provisions, and (2) gradual elimination or contraction of large numbers of administrative or noncontroversial matters that were once the subject of separate bills.

Overall workload levels reverberate, to a greater or lesser degree, in the committee rooms of the two houses. To be sure, every committee is unique, as Richard F. Fenno Jr. reminded us; one committee's business may soar while other panels are looking for work.[12] Yet most committees confront more or less the same overall boom-and-bust cycle, at least in terms of bills and resolutions referred to them. In the boom years of the 1970s, activity levels reached modern-day peaks. After about 1978 committee workload indicators declined markedly, to a plateau that has persisted to the present day.

Recorded votes on the House and Senate floors underscore these shifts in legislative activity. The numbers of recorded votes, traditionally quite low, accelerated in the 1960s and then exploded in the 1970s. The rise in floor activity was linked directly to changes in rules and procedures that made it easier for members to offer floor amendments and gain recorded votes. This shifted power perceptibly from the committee rooms to the chambers themselves. Party and committee leaders, especially in the House, soon fought back with procedural tactics aimed at limiting contentious floor votes. Accordingly, the number of recorded votes fell off markedly after 1978. In the Senate votes have stabilized to about 600 to 800 per Congress, compared to 1,000 or more in the 1970s. The House has 1,100 or more floor votes during each Congress—a resurgence that nearly matches the peak years of the 1970s.

Finally, consider the end product of lawmaking: bills and resolutions that survive the complex legislative process to become law. Working in tandem, Congress and the executive strictly regulate the flow of legislative outputs. Of the thousands of bills and resolutions introduced in the House and Senate in a given Congress, only about 5.5 percent find their way into the statute books. The size and shape of the legislative product are a function not only of political support or opposition but also of changing rules specifying which matters must be resolved by statute and which can be handled by other means.

Overall legislative output figures—measures passed by the two chambers, measures signed into law—look quite different from the input and activity figures described thus far. The number of enacted public bills (those dealing with general legislative issues) began at a high level after World War II, peaking at midcentury. Levels have descended gradually since then. Only a modest upsurge in the volume of public laws occurred during the activist era of the 1960s and 1970s; since then, there has been only a slight decline.

The number of enacted private bills (that is, granting benefits to named individuals, as in pension or land claims) has slowed to a trickle. In earlier times, private bills typically equaled or exceeded the number of public laws; today they are rare: one to two dozen in each two-year Congress.

The shrinkage in the volume of substantive legislation is commonly attributed to the policy "gridlock" that has resulted from close party competition and heightened cohesion within the two parties. But it was equally a by-product of the increasingly common stratagem of packaging legislative proposals into massive measures—for example, continuing resolutions, reconciliation bills, tax reform packages, and broad-scale reauthorizations. This is attested by the steady growth in the length of public statutes. Between 1947 and the present day, the average public law has ballooned from two and a half pages to more than thirteen pages. As recently as the 1960s, more than two-thirds of all public laws took up no more than a single page; nowadays very few are that brief. And the proportion of truly lengthy enactments—twenty-one pages or more—grew threefold in that same period. Legalistic verbosity is only partly to blame; legislative packaging is also at work.

These statistical trends, especially the activity and workload figures, lend strong support to the thesis that contemporary lawmaking has passed through a series of five distinct stages or eras (see table 6.1). Legislative-executive

Table 6.1. Political/Operational Eras of the Modern Congress

Congressional Era	Approximate Dates*	Environmental Forces	Leadership Mode	Member Goals	Activity and Workload
Bipartisan Conservative	1937–1964	Intraparty divisions	Chairmen of "corporate" committees	Public policy; internal influence sought by careerists; reelection stressed by marginal members	Stable (much of it routine in nature)
Liberal Activist	1965–1978	Liberal majorities	Democratic Caucus	Public policy now competes with reelection for most members; internal influence	Rising rapidly with legislative innovation; jurisdictional expansion
Postreform	1979–1992	Divided government	Party leaders versus committee majorities	Public policy sought by many, internal influence by a few; reelection important for most members	Declining rapidly; (jurisdictional protectionism, oversight stressed)
Partisan Conservative	1993–2007	Interparty conflict	Republican leadership	Public policy predominant; careerism rebounds after initial decline; reelection stressed by marginal members	Short-term rise; party leaders drive committee productivity
Liberal Activist (?)	2007–	Interparty conflict	Democratic majorities/GOP obstruction	(Same as above)	Rising legislative and oversight activity

* These dates are approximations, based on certain turning points that seemed most clearly to herald a passage from one congressional regime to another—for example, the 1964 electoral surge that gave the Democrats two-to-one majorities in both houses, the 1978 revival of the Republicans that led to their wider victories in 1980, and the GOP takeover of both chambers in 1992. Of course, there is a certain arbitrariness in erecting these landmarks. These "regimes" are actually products of gradual and incremental changes in the institution's environment and operations. Democratic gains in 1958, for example, set the stage for an outpouring of liberal legislation following President Kennedy's assassination in 1963. More recently, the Republican regime was not fully operative until the aftermath of the terrorist attacks of September 11, 2001. The most recent era has yet to reveal itself: its dimensions, not to mention its longevity, are yet to be determined.

relations follow different paths during each of these periods. The first was a relatively static era dominated by a bipartisan conservative coalition (roughly 1937–1964); the second was an era of liberal activism and reform (1965–1978); the third was an era of contraction, of fiscal restraint and political stalemate (1979–1994); the fourth congressional era (1993–2007), while marked by elements of stalemate, was increasingly driven by a conservative partisan majority. Most recently, the tectonic plates of U.S. party loyalty have shifted once more—this time toward the Democrats, who—having recaptured the House and Senate—opposed the Bush administration during its fading years (2007–2009), and then responded to the Obama administration's leadership (2009–). This present era has yet to reveal its basic characteristics.

Like any artifacts of historical categorization, these eras are bound to arouse debate over their precise definitions and boundaries, and perhaps even over their utility in illuminating legislative-executive relations. Historical developments, after all, are continuous and multifaceted, rarely yielding unambiguous boundaries. Although our primary data sets begin in 1947, we can extend the first era back to the second Roosevelt administration (1937–1941) by turning to fragmentary statistical indicators and a wealth of qualitative data. The boundaries of the second, liberal era, are also problematic: reformist skirmishes broke out over a period of years starting in the late 1950s; by the time the climax occurred in 1974–1975, the era's energy was already waning. The third, postreform era, was one of instability in which elements of the prior period coexisted uneasily with subsequent adjustments in economic and political trends. The years of the fourth era resist categorization, too, perhaps because they were relatively recent. And the current era offers a big question mark: does it represent something more than a partisan change? And will it change Congress's substantive output?

Despite these caveats, it is intriguing how closely these five eras coincide with changing journalistic and scholarly understandings of the legislative process. The "textbook Congress" that emerged from the first era was well researched and descriptively persuasive.[13] The same can be said for the liberal activist, or reform, era—which produced numerous journalistic and textbook analyses. Scholarly consensus even emerged on the nature and characteristics of the postreform era—with its emphasis on candidate-centered politics and cut-back policy making.[14] The fourth era—marked by close competition between cohesive party cadres—is described by scholars as a state of "conditional party government."[15] The current era as yet lacks convincing definition or boundaries.

THE BIPARTISAN CONSERVATIVE ERA (1937–1964)

According to popular legend, Franklin D. Roosevelt overwhelmed Congress with his New Deal programs, dictating legislation that gained virtually automatic approval. The facts by no means support this legend. Aside from the emergency measures approved quickly in the spring of 1933, during the first months of his administration, Roosevelt's legislative record drew heavily on proposals already introduced and incubated on Capitol Hill. This interbranch cooperation increased in the late 1930s. For the years 1931–1940, Lawrence H. Chamberlain found joint presidential-congressional influence at work in 52 percent of the major pieces of legislation; the president prevailed in 37 percent of the cases and Congress in 11 percent.[16] His findings affirmed "the joint character of the American legislative process," even in years of powerful presidential leadership.

The New Deal soon gave way to a long period of bipartisan conservative dominance, which lasted roughly from the second Roosevelt administration through the mid-1960s. Both parties were split internally between progressive, internationalist wings and reactionary wings. Although the progressives tended to dominate presidential selections, the conservatives held sway on Capitol Hill. An oligarchy of senior leaders, oftentimes called "the barons" or "the old bulls," wielded the gavels and commanded the votes in the committees and on the floor. Whichever party was in power, congressional leaders overrepresented safe one-party regions (the Democratic rural South, the Republican rural Northeast and Midwest). The narrow legislative agenda reflected the will of the conservative bipartisan majority that controlled so much domestic policy making.

This Capitol Hill regime proved a hostile environment for activist presidents and their ambitious legislative agendas. "For God's sake," a congressional spokesman telephoned the White House in April 1938, "don't send us any more controversial legislation!" Recounting this anecdote from Franklin Roosevelt's second term, James MacGregor Burns summed up legislative-executive relations as "deadlock on the Potomac."[17]

Harry Truman's clashes with Congress began early and continued throughout his administration. "Except for the modified Employment Act of 1946," related Robert J. Donovan, "the [Democratic] Seventy-ninth Congress had squelched practically every piece of social and economic legislation Truman had requested."[18] Truman's other congresses were equally frustrating, though in different ways. The Republican 80th Congress (1947–1949) "gave [Truman] his most enduring image. Facing an opposition-controlled legislative body almost certain to reject any domestic program he proposed, he adopted the role of an opportunist."[19]

Truman campaigned successfully in 1948 by attacking the "awful, do-nothing 80th Congress." Yet the Democratic 81st Congress (1949–1951) re-jected virtually all his major Fair Deal initiatives, and the 82nd (1951–1953), marked by depleted Democratic majorities and the Korean War stalemate, was even more hostile to new domestic legislation.

The 1950s were years of outward quiescence accompanied by underly-ing, accelerating demands for action and innovation. Dwight Eisenhower (1953–1961), whose legislative goals were far more modest than Truman's, was increasingly placed in the position of offering scaled-down alternatives to measures launched on Capitol Hill by coalitions of activist Democrats and moderate Republicans.

The legislative workload throughout this era was, accordingly, relatively stable and manageable from year to year. A large proportion of the bills and resolutions were routine and dealt with matters not yet delegated to the execu-tive branch for resolution—for example, immigration cases, land claims, and private legislation. Demands were building, however, for bolder legislation to address civil rights, housing, unemployment, and other concerns of urban and suburban voters.

On Capitol Hill, the powerhouse committees (the taxing and spending panels plus House Rules) were cohesive groups—"corporate," Fenno termed them—with firm leadership and rigorous internal norms of behavior.[20] They put a tight lid on new legislation, especially in fiscal affairs. The appropria-tions committees, in particular, stood as guardians of the U.S. Treasury, hold-ing in check the more ambitious (and costly) goals of the program-oriented authorizing panels.

Power thus gravitated to a cadre of strong committee leaders in both houses. The best of these were able, vivid personalities whose safe constitu-encies enabled them to lavish their time and skills upon their committees' agendas. If they often behaved autocratically, they usually enjoyed the toler-ance if not support of a majority within their committees. Southern Demo-crats, who chaired most of the key panels during those days, reached across the aisle to build their working majorities, often cultivating close bonds with their GOP ranking members and other conservatives. Younger and more lib-eral members, although initially shunned by the old bulls, slowly succeeded in restraining or replacing the committee barons.

Journalists and political scientists closely studied mid-twentieth-century congresses, constructing a detailed and persuasive picture of their operations. Borrowing research concepts and techniques from sociology and anthropol-ogy, behaviorally trained political scientists illuminated Congress's workings through close personal observation, interviews, and statistical analyses. The Senate of that era was lovingly described by journalist William S. White and systematically analyzed by political scientist Donald R. Matthews.[21] Richard F. Fenno Jr. wrote powerful, detailed accounts of committee operations and the budgetary process.[22]

The picture of the midcentury Congress that emerged from the scholars' work on Capitol Hill was so persuasive that one scholar labeled it "the textbook Congress."[23] According to the leading intellectual framework from that period, the institution was viewed as an interlocking pattern of personal relationships in which all the structural and functional parts worked in rough equilibrium. Ironically, by the time observers got around to completing this coherent picture of a tight, closed, internally coherent congressional system, that world was already being turned upside down. Pressures for change and "reform" mounted, heralding a prolonged period of liberal reformist politics.

LIBERAL ACTIVIST PARTY GOVERNMENT (1965–1978)

The cozy committee domains of the barons were eventually demolished by what journalist Hedrick Smith called a "power earthquake."[24] That metaphor is attractive but inexact. Although many observers associated the changes with the post-Watergate "class of 1974" and the subsequent overthrow of three House committee chairmen, these events signaled the high-water mark rather than the outset of the era of liberal legislative activism and procedural reform.

The boundaries of the liberal era, like those of the other eras, are somewhat imprecise. The process of change began in earnest in the last two Eisenhower years—after the 1958 elections, when the Democrats enlarged their ranks by sixteen senators and fifty-one representatives, many of them urban and suburban liberals. The elections had immediate effect in both chambers. Senate Majority Leader Lyndon Johnson's heavy-handed leadership style softened perceptibly; in the House a small band of liberal activists formally organized the Democratic Study Group (DSG), which set about launching a drive for procedural reforms. After John F. Kennedy won the presidency two years later, the Senate majority leader's post passed from Johnson to Mike Mansfield (D-MT), a mild-mannered liberal. In the House, Speaker Sam Rayburn (D-TX) struggled to break the conservatives' control of the powerful Rules Committee, in order to clear the way for the new president's expected agenda. The reform era reached its high-water mark in the mid-1970s with successive waves of changes in committee and floor procedures and, in 1975, the ouster of three of the barons from their committee chairmanships.

One underlying cause of the upheaval was the policy demands of urban and suburban voting blocs as well as minority groups—demands already heeded by activist presidents.[25] The spirit of the era was reflected in the popular movements that came to prominence: civil rights, feminism, environmentalism, consumerism, and growing opposition to the Vietnam War. These movements provided not only an extensive legislative agenda, but also grassroots activists who promoted that agenda—some of whom wound up serving in the House and Senate. Longer-range causes of the era's liberal activism included demographic shifts, widened citizen participation, social upheaval, technological changes in transportation and communications, and Supreme Court–ordered reapportionment and redistricting that made the House more reflective of urban and minority interests.

The resulting changes left Congress more open and participant-friendly, and encouraged legislative innovation and productivity. Individual lawmakers had greater leverage; influence was dispersed among and within the committees. More leaders existed than ever before, and even nonleaders could exert more influence. More staff aides were on hand to extend the legislative reach of even the most junior members.

Individual senators and representatives, while enjoying their enhanced legislative involvement, were forced at the same time to devote increased attention to their constituents back home. No longer was frantic constituency outreach confined to a few senators from large states and a few representatives from swing districts; it was practiced by all members (or their staffs) in order to purchase electoral security in a time of dwindling grassroots party support. In their office-holding activities, members tended to exchange the role of workhorse, or legislative specialist, for that of the showhorse, becoming legislative generalists, advertisers, and credit seekers.

The reforms were propelled by, and in turn helped to facilitate, an ambitious and expansionist policy agenda, as signified by such themes as John F. Kennedy's New Frontier and Lyndon B. Johnson's Great Society. This era witnessed a flood of landmark enactments in civil rights, education, medical insurance, employment and training, science and space, consumer protection, and the environment, not to mention five new cabinet departments and four constitutional amendments. Legislative activity soared by whatever measure one chooses to apply—bills introduced, hearings, reports, hours in session, floor amendments, recorded floor votes, and measures passed. The processing of freestanding bills and resolutions became the centerpiece of committee and subcommittee work.

This legislative outpouring formed a gigantic "bulge in the middle," which David R. Mayhew noticed in his study of lawmaking between 1946 and 1990.[26] Fifty-two percent of the 267 "major" enactments Mayhew identified over the fifty-four-year period were enacted between John F. Kennedy's inauguration in 1961 and the end of Gerald Ford's administration in 1976. Over this period 74 measures were produced under eight years of divided party control (Nixon, Ford) and 66 under eight years of unified control (Kennedy, Johnson). We will presently have more to say about this aspect of our analysis, which bears out Mayhew's thesis that party control made little difference in the congressional output of major enactments or investigations.

The decentralization of the 1960s and 1970s was accompanied by a weakening of the appropriations committees' grip over spending and by a strengthening of the power of the authorizing committees (for example, agriculture, banking, commerce). By ingenious use of "backdoor spending" provisions—such as contract authority, budget authority, direct Treasury borrowing, and especially entitlements—the ascendant authorizing committees stripped the appropriations panels of much of their former fiscal guardianship role.[27] Three-quarters of the domestic spending growth between 1970 and 1983 occurred in budget accounts lying outside annual appropriations—that is, beyond the appropriations committees' reach.[28]

The procedural autonomy of another prereform power center, the House Ways and Means Committee, was not breached until nearly the close of the liberal activist period. "During the congressional revolution of the 1970s," wrote Abner J. Mikva and Patti B. Sarris, "the Ways and Means Committee became a 'bastille' that symbolized the inequities of the old order."[29] The panel's independence was curtailed not only by chamber-wide reforms (caucus ratification of committee chairmanships, modified or open rules for floor deliberation, open committee meetings), but also by provisions aimed explicitly at the committee—enlargement of the committee, transfer of Democratic committee assignments to the Steering and Policy Committee, jurisdictional encroachments and, finally, mandated subcommittees.

Like the earlier period, this reform era was well documented by journalists and scholars.[30] The most popular scholarly paradigm of the era, drawn from economics, focused on Congress's decentralization and fragmentation.[31] Lawmakers were viewed not as role players enmeshed in a complex system of interactions in equilibrium, but as individual entrepreneurs competing in a vast, open marketplace that rewarded self-interested competitiveness with little or no regard for the welfare of the whole institution.

THE POSTREFORM ERA (1979–1992)

During the 1980s Congress again faced an environment that departed in significant ways from what had gone before. Although the shift is popularly associated with the Reagan administration (1981–1989), it was already under way in the last two years of Jimmy Carter's presidency (the 96th Congress, 1979–1981).

The advent of what economist Lester Thurow called the "zero-sum society" no doubt lay at the root of the changed political atmosphere.[32] Between World War II and the early 1970s, the nation's productivity levels had soared, along with real incomes for average citizens. These engines had enabled the nation to raise its standard of living while underwriting an expanding array of public services. After 1973 both the nation's productivity and the individual worker's real income stagnated, in comparison with both our economic rivals and our previous record. Indeed, the 1970s and 1980s were the century's poorest productivity decades.[33] The economy no longer seemed to support the federal government's vast array of services, many of them enacted or enlarged during the liberal activist period.

Lagging productivity affected not only government tax receipts but also citizens' attitudes toward their economic well-being. In the late 1970s the economy was buffeted by *stagflation*, a double-whammy of high inflation and high unemployment. Serious recessions occurred in the early 1980s and again in the early 1990s. Meanwhile, the government's costly and relatively impervious system of entitlements, coupled with President Reagan's 1981 tax cuts and program reallocations, turned the midcentury's "fiscal dividends" into "structural deficits."

Intellectual fashions and political realities repudiated the notion that government could solve all manner of economic and social ills. Disenchantment with the results of government programs, many of which had been shamelessly oversold to glean support for their enactment, led to widespread demands for a statutory cease-fire: disinvestment, deregulation, and privatization. At the same time, "bracket creep" raised the marginal and real tax rates of millions of citizens and spurred a series of tax revolts that swept through the states to Washington.

In the 1980s the president and Congress were fixated on resolving fiscal and revenue issues, rather than on designing new programs or establishing new agencies in response to constituent preferences or national needs. In the domestic realm, the emphasis was on reviewing, adjusting, refining, or cutting back existing programs. "There's not a whole lot of money for any kind of new programs," remarked Senator Thad Cochran (R-MS), "so we're holding oversight hearings on old programs . . . which may not be all that bad an idea."[34] Accordingly, fewer individual members were tempted to put forward their ideas as freestanding bills or resolutions. Such new ideas as were salable were more likely to be contained in amendments to large-scale legislative vehicles: reauthorizations, continuing appropriations, and debt limit or reconciliation bills.

The environmental constraint in the 1980s reversed the previous era's liberal activism. Government revenues were curtailed by lagging economic productivity, exaggerated after 1981 by tax cuts, program reallocations, and soaring deficits. Few new programs were launched, and few domestic programs were awarded additional funding. Although the public continued to expect Congress to take action to solve problems, there was equal sentiment for cutting back "big government" and reducing public sector deficits. Public faith in government's capacity to solve problems plummeted in the wake of criticisms of waste and ineffectiveness of government programs.

Elected officials at both ends of Pennsylvania Avenue sought profit from cutback politics. They engaged in creative bookkeeping to give the appearance of balancing revenues and outlays and trimming the deficit as required by a series of seemingly stringent budgetary process fixes, beginning in 1985. Conservatives seized upon revenue shortfalls as a way of snuffing demands for new programs and new spending. Liberals blamed the situation on the failures of the Reagan and Bush administrations and pledged to protect federal programs favored by middle-class voters. As for the voters, they naturally wanted to have it both ways. As Gary C. Jacobson put it, "They can vote for Republican presidential candidates committed to the diffuse collective goods of low taxes, economic efficiency, and a strong national defense, and for congressional Democrats who promise to minimize the price they have to pay for these goods in forgone benefits."[35]

The phenomenon of cutback politics influenced the postreform Congress in at least six ways. First, fewer bills were sponsored by individual senators and representatives. Second, key policy decisions were packaged into huge megabills, enabling lawmakers to gain support for provisions that would be unlikely to pass as freestanding measures. Third, lawmakers employed techniques of blame avoidance—for example, in closing military bases—to protect themselves from the adverse effects of cutbacks. Fourth, more noncontroversial "commemorative" resolutions were passed—nearly half of all laws produced by congresses in the 1980s. Fifth, party-line voting on Capitol Hill, driven mainly by changes in the parties' demography, soared to modern-day highs. Finally, leadership in the House and Senate was markedly stronger than any time since 1910. Congressional leaders benefited not only from powers conferred by reform-era innovations of the 1960s and 1970s; they also responded to widespread expectations that they were the only people who could, and should, untangle jurisdictional overlaps and orchestrate the legislative schedule.[36]

The House Ways and Means Committee mirrored the shifts of the postreform era in Congress as a whole. Randall Strahan describes the changed agenda that the committee faced after 1978. Following the reform-era assaults on the committee and hiatus in leadership, Chairman Dan Rostenkowski (D-IL) set about systematically to strengthen the panel's position.[37] According to Allen Schick, the chairman's efforts succeeded in the main: "Ways and Means has regained its status and effectiveness by resorting to a simple formula that worked for it in the past: the committee is successful when it controls the House and when the chairman controls the committee."[38]

As the committee's exhaustive bicentennial history explained, the chairman "centralized control over staff and substantially diminished the autonomy of subcommittee chairs."[39] Rostenkowski's personal leverage was enhanced by his influence over Democratic assignments to the panel as well as his selective use of sanctions. To promote cohesiveness, he scheduled more closed meetings and arranged for weekend retreats and seminars to discuss policy questions.[40] The panel's internal politics settled somewhere between the extremes of bipartisan consensus of the prereform mills and the reform period's divisive partisanship.[41]

Confronted by a lagging economy, a divided government, and the public's doubts about the efficacy of government programs, the president and Congress in the postreform era changed the way they approached the legislative workload. Presidents trimmed their agendas and hampered congressional initiatives through a combination of curtailed revenue and veto threats. Interbranch negotiations frequently took the form of high-level summitry. Divided control of the White House and Congress, along with rising party voting on the Hill, placed a premium on tough bargaining between the president, Senate leaders, and House leaders. Congress, for its part, moved away from the decentralized system established during the 1960s and 1970s to facilitate that era's frantic legislative activity. A knowledgeable British scholar puts it this way: "There can be little doubt that the Congress of the mid-1980s differed from that of the late 1970s in terms of its emphasis on parliamentary reform, legislative activity, constituency attentiveness and distribution of power." In sum, "the reform orientation of the New [or reform-era] Congress [was] left far behind."[42]

Consider the kinds of institutional innovations made by the postreform Congress. Beginning in the late 1970s, Congress confronted an altered set of demands for legislative action. The political agenda shrank, narrowing the prospects for new programs or spending priorities. While many of the structural innovations of the earlier reform era remained intact, procedures were adjusted to cope with the altered environment. Committee and floor agendas contracted. Important decisions were more apt to be folded into lengthy omnibus vehicles, often processed by more than one committee and increasingly superintended by party leaders. Members and committees explored new categories of policy making, or rather they exploited existing categories—for example, oversight, commemorative, indexing, and symbolic measures—that were well suited to the uncertain policy environment.

CONSERVATIVE PARTY GOVERNMENT (1995–2006)

The early 1990s brought a new mix of challenges to governmental institutions—some continuations of long-term trends, others startlingly new. Prolonged economic uncertainty—manifested in sluggish growth, heightened foreign competition, and widely reported job layoffs—weakened citizens' self-confidence and optimism. Widening racial, ethnic, religious, and even sexual fissures, along with a seemingly permanent disadvantaged underclass, fueled growing suspicions that the nation had become uncontrollable and perhaps ungovernable. The public services that most people came in contact with—public schools, police, courts, welfare offices—seemed especially flawed. The end of the Cold War brought only fleeting satisfaction: losing the menace of the Soviet "evil empire" also meant losing a certain sense of national purpose.

Public unrest deepened into what can only be called a crisis of governance. One member of Congress called it a massive "civic temper tantrum."[43] Few institutions escaped public censure. Scarcely more than a year after celebrating the Persian Gulf War in a burst of civic pride, citizens turned President George H. W. Bush out of office in 1992. With a plurality of only 43 percent, successor Bill Clinton's public-opinion honeymoon hardly survived the wedding night; his job ratings remained precarious. Although surveys uncovered public disgust with partisanship and "gridlock," the Democrats' victories that year ended divided government only in a formal sense; two years later, the Republicans captured the House and Senate, dissolving even that deceptive unity.

President Clinton's first two years, with a Democratic Congress, brought mixed results. Having campaigned as a "new" centrist Democrat, Clinton tried to distinguish himself from the increasingly liberal ranks of his party on Capitol Hill—a strategy that came to be known as triangulation.[44] His greatest achievement, however, attracted not a single Republican vote, and was enacted only when Vice President Al Gore cast the tie-breaking vote in the Senate. This was the Omnibus Budget Reconciliation Act of 1993, which raised taxes on upper-income citizens and—affixed to the booming economy of the later 1990s—helped wipe out the federal government's deficits by the 1998 fiscal year. On other matters, the centrist strategy dictated cross-party alliances with Republicans. Their support ensured passage of 1993 legislation implementing the North American Free Trade Agreement (NAFTA); only 40

percent of House Democrats voted for it. Other cross-partisan efforts brought
forth the Brady Handgun Violence Act, the Family and Medical Leave Act,
the Motor Voter Act, a national service law (called Americorps), and a crime
law. But the Clinton administration is remembered as a time of fumbling initiatives: for example, the failed health care reform plan and the clumsy "don't
ask, don't tell" policy for dealing with gays serving in the military.

Of all public institutions, however, Congress bore the largest measure of
public scorn. On top of the generalized public discontent, a series of scandals
on Capitol Hill targeted five senators who had championed a failed savings
and loan magnate, forced closure of the House "bank" (payroll office), and
cast doubt on the personal ethics of numerous members. By the spring of
1992, only 17 percent of those questioned in a national survey approved of
the way Congress was doing its job, whereas 54 percent approved of their
own representative's performance. Both figures were all-time lows.[45] Such
anger exceeded the usual level of Congress bashing and recalled the public
unrest that preceded the reforms adopted in the early 1970s.

Civic unrest caused a dramatic changing of the guard on Capitol Hill. The
1992 elections brought 110 new House members (87 of whom returned two
years later) and 14 new senators. The 1994 contests added 86 new representatives and 11 new senators. When the House convened in January 1995, nearly
a majority of its members had arrived in the 1990s. Although the Senate
changed more slowly, 29 of its members were 1990s arrivals.

Most important, the 1994 elections brought Republican control to Capitol
Hill—in the House, for the first time in forty years, in the Senate after an
eight-year hiatus. The party balance of nearly two generations was overturned. The public policy agenda was transformed. Long-simmering issues
suddenly boiled over: downsizing the federal establishment, devolution of
power to states and localities, welfare reform, budget stringency, and a regulatory cease-fire. Facing the Clinton's struggling presidency, the resurgent
Republicans seized command of policy initiatives, media attention, and public expectations.

On the Hill, GOP leaders flexed their muscles, activity levels initially
soared, and innovative procedures were explored, tested, and adopted. House
Speaker Newt Gingrich (R-GA), backed by an unusually cohesive party dominated by conservative newcomers, pushed wide-ranging changes in structures and procedures. Cuts were made in the number of committees, committee assignments, and committee staffs; committee and floor procedures were
altered; administrative arrangements were streamlined; and most of all, the
Speaker and other party leaders gained greater leverage over committee assignments, committee scheduling, floor scheduling, and administrative management. House leaders used all these tools to win committee approval and

floor votes for all ten items of their campaign platform, the so-called Contract with America, within the first hundred days of the 104th Congress (1995). But political stalemate, manifested by the White House and a more contentious Senate, kept most of these proposals out of the statute books—with the exception of congressional accountability (1995) and welfare reform (1996) and a line-item veto (1996) that was subsequently invalidated by the Supreme Court.

Clinton's last six years, and arguably George W. Bush's first year in office, were clouded by persistent partisan competition and the absence of secure GOP majorities. Indeed, House Republicans lost ground in the three elections following their 1994 triumphs. Leadership miscalculations can be blamed for much of this erosion. The GOP was blamed for shutting down the federal government in the winter of 1995–1996, in the midst of fierce battles between budget slashers on the Hill and the veto-wielding president. Even more dramatic was the 1998–1999 impeachment of President Clinton—a project launched by House Judiciary Committee Republicans and supported by party leaders. The whole affair played poorly with the public, who deplored the president's sexual dalliance but who approved of his second-term performance on the job.[46] Midterm election media ads highlighting the impeachment served only to remind voters that it was the GOP leadership that had targeted the president. After the midterm elections, the Senate failed to muster the two-thirds majority needed to convict the president or remove him from office.

The Clinton-era partisan warfare went far beyond clashes over the president's personal life or even federal spending levels. They reflected a bitter struggle between Capitol Hill Republicans and the White House over control of the policy agenda. Most key votes were along party lines: the various impeachment floor votes of both chambers found more than nine out of ten representatives and senators voting with their respective parties—Republicans opposing the president, Democrats supporting him.[47]

Speaker Newt Gingrich, who had engineered the GOP takeover of the House in 1994, met increasing opposition—including an abortive internal effort to oust him, the 1998 midterm election fiasco, and finally, reports of his own sexual dalliance. He and his heir apparent, Robert Livingston, both stepped aside in late 1998. The agreed-upon successor, Dennis Hastert of Illinois, inherited a fractured and disheartened GOP conference. Eventually he became a master of the House, first by ceding more powers to the committee chairmen and then by consulting widely and making binding decisions. Yet the partisan rule of the leadership cannot be denied: often minority Democrats were excluded from committee markups of bills and leadership decisions on the bills' final contents.

If the Republicans reigned but did not yet rule in 1995–2001, the terrorists' attacks of September 11, 2001, changed the environment of congressional decision making. First, it revitalized the presidency of George W. Bush as a wartime enterprise —a metaphor designed to enhance presidential leadership.[48] For another, it immediately consigned the Congress into a reactive, more compliant institution: initially, at least, it hastily approved the use of force against 9/11 perpetrators and the problematic USA PATRIOT Act (both 2001), the resolution authorizing the use of force against Iraq (2002), and the Military Commissions Act for prosecuting wartime prisoners (2006).

The congressional workload rebounded somewhat during the Republican years—in terms of bills and resolutions introduced, bills per member, and even enactments of public laws. The average page length of public laws continued to rise, reflecting the continuing popularity of large-scale omnibus measures. Although committee meetings tended to subside, hours of floor sessions continued to rise.[49]

AND NOW, HOPE VERSUS ECONOMIC DISASTER

Post-9/11 developments, including the 2004 elections, appeared to strengthen the Republicans as the dominant party. President George W. Bush's reelection that year, far from a landslide, could be credited to his image as a wartime leader who could protect the nation from terrorists. But his job rating stood at only 51 percent; by the end of the year, a clear majority of citizens (56 percent) believed that the Iraq War's costs outweighed its benefits. During his second term, his job ratings continued a steady downward slide, as the war dragged on and the administration's response to the devastation of Hurricane Katrina—the costliest national disaster in the nation's history—was judged as inept and unfeeling. On the eve of the 2008 election, Bush's quarterly Gallup Poll ratings stood at 29 percent. However, the period included two surveys in which his approval level was 25 percent—"the worst of his presidency to date, and just three percentage points higher than the all-time low 22 percent approval rating Harry Truman received in 1951."[50]

Public worries about the state of the nation, coupled with disdain for the Bush administration, led to a measurable shift in partisan loyalties favoring the Democrats. When Bush was reelected in 2005, Democrats claimed only a 2-percent margin over the GOP (35 to 33 percent). By October 2008, however, that margin had climbed to 12 percent. Nearly four in ten voters identified with the Democrats, according to the Pew Research Center's surveys (independents accounted for 34 percent of the electorate, leaving Republicans in third place with 28 percent).[51] The Pew Center's surveys of Americans' political values and core attitudes also revealed a landscape more favorable to the Democrats. The reason was "[i]ncreased public support for the social safety net, signs of rising public concern about income inequality, and a diminished appetite for assertive national security policies."[52]

The 2008 elections extended the Democrats' gains of two years earlier. The top story was the triumph of Barack Obama, their presidential choice. But the party also gained ground in both chambers of Congress. House Democrats gained 24 seats, for a total of 257 (to the Republicans' 178)—approaching the 259 seats the party held in 1994, just before the GOP took over control. In the Senate, eight additional Democrats were elected, which—with one GOP switch (Pennsylvania's Arlen Specter)—gave them a total of 58.[53] Five GOP senators were turned out of office, including Ted Stevens of Alaska—whose forty-year career made him the longest-serving Republican in Senate history. More than a dozen GOP House members were defeated, including the sole remaining New England Republican, Christopher Shays of Connecticut.

Is there a new liberal regime on Capitol Hill? That remains to be seen. President Obama ran on a platform of change—including postpartisan cooperation—but he was elected because of an economic crisis blamed on the Bush administration (and, by association, his party in Congress). His election as an African American was a triumph; but the irony was that he inherited an economic quagmire. (The Onion, a blog, headlined his election as follows: "Black Man Elected to Nation's Worst Job.") Although he reached out to the minority Republicans, his early goal—a gigantic stimulus spending package—was supported by only three senators and no representatives from the Republican Party. The challenge for liberals in the White House and Capitol Hill is twofold: to prevail against the minority Republicans—whose cohesiveness has surged with the virtual disappearance of their moderate lawmakers, while at the same time mobilizing the Democrats' increasingly diverse members (including centrists who had defeated GOP moderates on their own turf).

No one—including the renowned economists Obama recruited to help him—could predict whether the unprecedented spending would jump-start the economy and produce the needed jobs and capital. The Democratic regime's future, for better or worse, will rest on the perceived success or failure of these unprecedented economic measures. House GOP whip Eric Cantor of Virginia remarked that the Democrats have decided to "assume ownership of the era of the bailout." He continued that the 2010 elections would be "a test for the mandate of change that this administration was elected with. I do think there will be a price to pay."[54]

CONCLUSION

Shifting the viewpoint from the Oval Office to Capitol Hill radically changes one's perspective on congressional-executive relations. Rather than measuring political time in terms of successive presidencies, we have sought to identify congressional equivalents. By tracking several variables—leadership, partisanship, workload, and productivity—we have identified four distinctive congressional eras or regimes. Examining legislative attributes within each era, and between succeeding eras, casts new light on interbranch policy making since the New Deal and even helps resolve some puzzling historical anomalies (for example, Franklin Roosevelt's mixed legislative record and the unexpected productivity of the Nixon-Ford period).

Our foray into the thicket of legislative activity and productivity reveals two general truths about modern-day politics and policy making. First, legislative regimes do not necessarily coincide with the tenure of individual presidents. Second, legislative productivity is less determined by party control that one would think.

Presidencies and Legislative Regimes

The bipartisan conservative era outlasted several presidents of widely varying goals and skills. Roosevelt failed after 1936 to keep Capitol Hill safe for New Deal initiatives and, after 1940, was preoccupied with the war effort. Truman repeatedly broke his lance in efforts to push legislation through conservative congresses—most memorably in housing, labor-management relations, civil rights, and medical care. Eisenhower's modest, moderately right-of-center legislative instincts were a better fit with the objectives of the conservative coalition that ruled Capitol Hill. More aggressive than Eisenhower, Kennedy enjoyed considerable success in a transitional period when the old order in Congress was crumbling.

The liberal activist era, with its huge Democratic majorities in both chambers of Congress, spanned the presidencies of Lyndon Johnson, Richard Nixon, Gerald Ford, and (in part) Jimmy Carter. Johnson's presidency was arguably the most productive in history, legislatively speaking. Yet the most telling point is that the flow of legislation continued unabated during the Republican presidencies of Nixon and Ford. A recitation of the legislative high points from the Nixon years suggests that the mutual hostility between the GOP president and the Democratic Congress did not stand in the way of significant legislative achievements. These laws included a comprehensive tax code revision, the National Environmental Policy Act of 1969, major air and water pollution control measures, endangered species protection, a comprehensive organized crime bill, postal reorganization, urban mass transit and reorganization plans, the Occupational Safety and Health Act of 1970 (OSHA), the Consumer Product Safety Act, the Comprehensive Employment and Training Act (CETA), the Federal Election Campaign Act, coastal zone management, the trans-Alaska pipeline, the War Powers Resolution, and the Congressional Budget and Impoundment Control Act of 1974—not to mention the Twenty-sixth Amendment giving eighteen-year-olds the right to vote and a proposed amendment (the Equal Rights Amendment) on women's rights.

The liberal juggernaut continued during these conservative presidencies for at least two reasons. First, the Nixon and Ford presidencies were under relentless siege from Capitol Hill's liberal majorities, composed of Democrats and a scattering of moderate or liberal Republicans. Between 1973 and 1976, wrote Ornstein and his colleagues, these forces "attempted a much higher number of veto overrides than any of the other congresses in the previous thirty years, and a large number of their attempts were successful."[55] Second, Nixon saw his primary mission to be in foreign affairs and diplomacy, which left his aides in the domestic departments relatively free to negotiate as best they could with Capitol Hill majorities. Nixon may have been a conservative president, but the legislative record compiled during his administration was expansive and liberal. This historical irony deserves more careful and dispassionate reassessment by historians and political scientists than it has yet received.

The next legislative regime, the postreform era, spanned part or all of the presidencies of Jimmy Carter, Ronald Reagan, and George H. W. Bush. The advent of zero-sum, stalemate politics was popularly associated with the Reagan administration, which took office in 1981 pledging to cut taxes, domestic aid, and welfare programs. To be sure, his election was interpreted at the time as a sea change in American politics; some of Reagan's initiatives—especially the 1981 revenue cuts and repeated threats to veto new domestic spending or taxes—helped to curtail the legislative agenda. However, deteriorating economic conditions and shifting attitudes had already caused President Carter to begin to trim his legislative agenda.[56] By the 96th Congress (1979–1981) the altered environment had led to a decline in the legislative workload.

Party Control and Legislative Regimes

Party control influences legislative outputs. Many observers further contend that "things go better" when the same party controls both the executive and legislative branches and that divided government is a prescription for confusion, delay, and deadlock. Legislative productivity is, without a doubt, affected by party control. And certainly presidents are more apt to achieve their legislative goals if their partisans comfortably control both chambers.

Equally to the point, shifts in Capitol Hill partisan ratios can yield meaningful changes in policy outputs, quite apart from any questions of party control or alignment. The recession-driven Democrats in 1959–1961, the Johnson landslide class of 1964, the Watergate class of 1974, and the GOP shift in 1981 and again in 1995 were dramatic changes in partisan strength on Capitol Hill that led in turn to policy redirections and procedural innovations. Probably these changes far exceeded any underlying shifts in attitudes or voting habits within the electorate as a whole, not to mention long-term partisan realignments.

Yet party control is an incomplete guide to legislative activity and productivity. The administrations of Roosevelt, Truman, and Carter testify to the fact that party control of both branches is no guarantee of legislative productivity. By the same token, the Nixon-Ford period and the Reagan administration (in its first year and last two years) saw productivity far beyond what would be expected from divided government. The correlation between party control and legislative productivity seems even more tenuous when we consider Mayhew's most intriguing piece of evidence: during what we term the liberal activist era, annual productivity under split party control actually exceeded that under unified control.[57]

Legislative productivity and workload, in short, fit imperfectly with conventional political thinking that stresses presidential leadership or the locus of party control of the two branches. The record of the recent past, moreover, casts doubt on the assumption of many observers that unified party control raises legislative productivity and that divided government necessarily leads to stalemate.

Nonetheless, recent events show that Congress's evolution has by no means run its full course, and that is influenced but not determined by the White House. Continuing changes in Congress's political environment will produce further alterations in the membership, organization, procedures, and policy-making capacities of the House and Senate. As in the past, these alterations will require leadership, ingenuity, and legislative professionalism if Congress is to make its way successfully through the twenty-first century. Will Congress be able to reassert its constitutional prerogatives in a time of party government and a quasi-wartime setting? Only history will judge the outcome.

NOTES

1. Woodrow Wilson, *Congressional Government* (1885; repr., Baltimore: Johns Hopkins University Press, 1981), 56; See also Charles O. Jones, "A Way of Life and Law," *American Political Science Review* 89 (March 1995): 1–9.

2. Robert A. Katzmann, *Courts and Congress* (Washington, DC: The Brookings Institution/Governance Institute, 1997), 33–34.

3. See Michael G. Kammen, *A Machine that Would Go of Itself: The Constitution in American Culture* (New York: Alfred A. Knopf, 1986).

4. See Roger H. Davidson and Walter J. Oleszek, *Congress and Its Members*, 11th ed. (Washington, DC: CQ Press, 2008), table 2-1.

5. For an account of the post-9/11 changes, see James P. Pfiffner, "The Transformation of the Bush Presidency," in *Understanding the Presidency*, 4th ed., Pfiffner and Roger H. Davidson (New York: Pearson Longman, 2006), 474–94.

6. The *locus classicus* of party alignment theory is V. O. Key Jr., "A Theory of Critical Elections," *Journal of Politics* 17 (February 1955): 3–18. More detailed analyses are found in William N. Chambers and Walter Dean Burnham, eds., *The American Party Systems: Stages of Political Development* (New York: Oxford University Press, 1967); Walter Dean Burnham, *Critical Elections and the Mainsprings of American Politics* (New York: W.W. Norton, 1970); James L. Sundquist, *Dynamics of the Party System*, rev. ed. (Washington, DC: The Brookings Institution, 1983), esp. chaps. 1–3; and David R. Mayhew, *Electoral Realignments* (New Haven, CT: Yale University Press, 2002).

7. See, for example, David W. Brady, "Electoral Realignment in the U.S. House of Representatives," in *Congress and Policy Change*, eds. Gerald C. Wright Jr., Leroy N. Rieselbach, and Lawrence C. Dodd (New York: Agathon Press, 1986), 46–69.

8. Stephen Skowronek, *The Politics Presidents Make* (Cambridge, MA: Harvard University Press, 1993), 29–58.

9. Skowronek, *The Politics Presidents Make*, 50.

10. Joseph Cooper, "Organization and Innovation in the House of Representatives," in *The House at Work*, eds. Joseph Cooper and G. Calvin Mackenzie (Austin: University of Texas Press, 1980), 332. This essay draws upon statistical data originally compiled by the author, his former colleagues at the Congressional Research Service, and other investigators. The most relevant data are summarized in Norman J. Ornstein, Thomas E. Mann, and Michael J. Malbin, *Vital Statistics on Congress 2001–2002* (Washington, DC: AEI Press, 2002), 145–54.

11. Ornstein, Mann, and Malbin, 146–47.

12. Richard F. Fenno Jr., *Congressmen in Committees* (Boston: Little, Brown, 1973), 280.

13. Kenneth A. Shepsle, "The Changing Textbook Congress," in *Can the Government Govern?* eds. John E. Chubb and Paul E. Peterson (Washington, DC: The Brookings Institution, 1989), 238–66.

14. See Roger H. Davidson, ed., *The Postreform Congress* (New York: St. Martin's Press, 1992).

15. The seminal work concerning this conceptualization is John H. Aldrich, *Why Parties? The Origin and Transformation of Party Politics in America* (Chicago: University of Chicago Press, 1995).

16. Lawrence H. Chamberlain, *The President, Congress, and Legislation* (New York: Columbia University Press, 1946), 450–53.

17. James MacGregor Burns, *Roosevelt: The Lion and the Fox* (New York: Harcourt, Brace, 1956), 337, 339.

18. Robert J. Donovan, *Conflict and Crisis: The Presidency of Harry S Truman* (New York: W.W. Norton, 1977), 260.

19. Alonzo L. Hamby, "The Mind and Character of Harry S Truman" in *The Truman Presidency*, ed. Michael J. Lacey (Washington, DC: Woodrow Wilson International Center for Scholars; Cambridge: Cambridge University Press, 1989), 46.

20. Fenno, *Congressmen in Committees*, 279.

21. William S. White, *Citadel: The Story of the U.S. Senate* (New York: Harper and Brothers, 1956); and Donald R. Matthews, *U.S. Senators and Their World* (Chapel Hill: University of North Carolina Press, 1960).

22. Fenno, *Congressmen in Committees*; Richard F. Fenno Jr., *The Power of the Purse: The Appropriations Process in Congress* (Boston: Little, Brown, 1966).

23. Shepsle, "The Changing Textbook Congress."

24. Hedrick Smith, *The Power Game: How Washington Works* (New York: Random House, 1988), chap. 2.

25. James L. Sundquist, *Politics and Policy: The Eisenhower, Kennedy, and Johnson Years* (Washington, DC: The Brookings Institution), chap. 10.

26. David R. Mayhew, *Divided We Govern: Party Control, Lawmaking, and Investigations, 1946–1990* (New Haven, CT: Yale University Press, 1991), 76.

27. Allen Schick, *Congress and Money: Budgeting, Spending, and Taxing* (Washington, DC: The Urban Institute Press, 1980), 424–36.

28. John W. Ellwood, "The Great Exception: The Congressional Budget Process in an Age of Decentralization," in *Congress Reconsidered*, 3d ed., eds. Lawrence C. Dodd and Bruce J. Oppenheimer (Washington, DC: CQ Press, 1985), 315–42.

29. Abner J. Mikva and Patti B. Sarris, *The American Congress: The First Branch* (New York: Franklin Watts, 1983), 292.

30. See, for example, Roger H. Davidson and Walter J. Oleszek, *Congress against Itself* (Bloomington: Indiana University Press, 1977); James L. Sundquist, *The Decline and Resurgence of Congress* (Washington, DC: The Brookings Institution, 1981); and Leroy N. Rieselbach, *Congressional Reform: The Changing Modern Congress* (Washington, DC: CQ Press, 1994), esp. chap. 3.

31. David R. Mayhew, *Congress: The Electoral Connection* (New Haven, CT: Yale University Press, 1974).

32. Lester Thurow, *The Zero-Sum Society* (New York: Basic Books, 1980).

33. Paul Krugman, "We're No. 3—So What?" *Washington Post*, March 24, 1990, C1-2.

34. Quoted in Helen Dewar, "Congress Off to Slowest Start in Years," *Washington Post*, November 21, 1989, A18.

35. Gary C. Jacobson, *The Electoral Origins of Divided Government: Competition in U.S. House Elections, 1946–1988* (Boulder, CO: Westview Press, 1990), 112.

36. Barbara Sinclair, *Legislators, Leaders, and Lawmaking: The U.S. House of Representatives in the Postreform Era* (Baltimore: Johns Hopkins University Press, 1995), 48–57.

37. Randall Strahan, "Agenda Change and Committee Politics in the Postreform House," *Legislative Studies Quarterly* 13 (May 1988): 185–94.

38. Allen Schick, "The Ways and Means of Leading Ways and Means," *Brookings Review* 7 (Fall 1989): 17.

39. U.S. House of Representatives, *The Committee on Ways and Means: A Bicentennial History, 1789–1989* (Washington, DC: U.S. Government Printing Office, 1989), 369.

40. U.S. House of Representatives, *The Committee on Ways and Means*, 370–72.

41. Schick, "Ways and Means," 21.

42. Christopher J. Bailey, "Beyond the New Congress: Aspects of Congressional Development in the 1980s," *Parliamentary Affairs* 41 (April 1988): 246.

43. Quoted in Lawrence N. Hansen, "Our Turn: Politicians Talk about Themselves, Politics, the Public, the Press, and Reform," Centel Public Accountability Project (March 1992), 5.

44. The term was invented by Dick Morris, at the time one of Clinton's chief advisers. See Paul J. Quirk and William Cunion, "Clinton's Domestic Policy: The Lessons of a 'New Democrat,'" in *The Clinton Legacy,* eds., Colin Campbell and Bert A. Rockman (New York: Chatham House, 2000), 200–25.

45. Richard Morin and Helen Dewar, "Approval of Congress Hits All-Time Low, Poll Finds," *Washington Post*, March 20, 1992, A16.

46. An analysis from the Capitol Hill perspective is offered by Nicol C. Rae and Colton C. Campbell, *Impeaching Clinton: Partisan Strife on Capitol Hill* (Lawrence: University Press of Kansas, 2004).

47. Roger H. Davidson, "Congressional Parties, Leaders, and Committees: 1900, 2000, and Beyond," in *American Political Parties: Decline or Resurgence?* eds. Jeffrey E. Cohen, Richard Fleisher, and Paul Kantor (Washington, DC: CQ Press, 2001), 284–85.

48. See Kathleen Hall Jamieson and Paul Waldman, *The Press Effect: Politicians, Journalists, and the Stories that Shape the Political World* (New York: Oxford University Press, 2003), 150–52.

49. Norman J. Ornstein, Thomas E. Mann, and Michael J. Malbin, *Vital Statistics on Congress, 1999–2000* (Washington, DC: AEI Press, 2000), 146–50.

50. The Gallup Poll, "Bush Approval Rating Doldrums Continue," October 20, 2008, at Gallup.com.

51. Pew Research Center, "Democrats Hold Party ID Edge Across Political Battleground," October 30, 2008, at Pewresearch.org/pubs/1015.

52. Pew Research Center for the People and the Press, "Trends in Political Values and Core Attitudes, 1987–2007," March 22, 2007, at people-press.org/report/?reportid=312.

53. One race remained undecided: in Minnesota, the Senate candidates—Democrat Al Franken and Republican incumbent Norm Coleman—fought to a virtual tie. After a hand recount, Franken appeared to have won by 225 votes, but the final outcome may be determined in the courts, or even the Senate itself.

54. Quoted by Michael D. Shear and Paul Kane, "Politically, Stimulus Battle Has Just Begun," *Washington Post*, February 16, 2009, A1.

55. Norman J. Ornstein, Thomas E. Mann, and Michael J. Malbin, *Vital Statistics on Congress 1993–1994* (Washington, D.C.: CQ Press, 1994), 151.

56. Charles O. Jones, *The Trusteeship Presidency: Jimmy Carter and the U.S. Congress* (Baton Rouge: Louisiana State University Press, 1988), chap. 7.

57. Mayhew, *Divided We Govern*, 7.

Chapter Seven

The Legislative Presidency in Political Time: Unified Government, Divided Government, and Presidential Leverage in Congress

Richard S. Conley

George W. Bush's trials and tribulations over the course of his two terms are axiomatic for scholars who contend that presidential legislative success pivots on party control of Congress. On May 21, 2001, just four months into his presidency, maverick Senator Jim Jeffords of Vermont made a shocking announcement that rocked the Washington establishment: He was leaving the Republican Party over putative budget disagreements with the administration.[1] Jeffords's decision to throw his support to the Democrats robbed Bush and Republicans of organizational control of the upper chamber. The consequences for the president's agenda were immediate and far-reaching. Changes in key committee chairmanships, including Finance, Education, and Judiciary, presaged turbulent relations between the White House and the Senate. Bush's judicial nominees were blocked, as was the president's sweeping plan to undertake the largest reorganization of the federal government since the 1940s. Bush ultimately made stalled court appointments and differences with Senate Democrats over the creation of the new Department of Homeland Security the centerpieces in his indefatigable, and ultimately successful, midterm campaign for Republicans to regain control of the Senate in 2002.[2] By 2006, however, Democrats recaptured control not only of the Senate but also of the House of Representatives. Opposition party control of Capitol Hill in Bush's closing two years in office, combined with his abysmal popular approval, foreshadowed the singularly worst presidential success rate in Congress since records have been kept—and recourse to the veto power in an attempt to halt congressional initiatives.

Other presidents' bouts with opposition congresses were as, if not more, arduous than Bush's confrontations with Democrats. Bill Clinton waged protracted veto battles with Republican majorities for six of his eight years in office, endured a government shutdown, and faced the ultimate sanction, impeachment. In his second term Richard Nixon frequently found himself at odds with congressional spending, used impoundment in an attempt to halt profligacy, and was finally chased from office by Watergate. And Republicans Gerald Ford and George H. W. Bush, who faced opposition congresses for the duration of their presidencies, made extensive use of the veto power to halt Democratic activism in Congress. From this vantage point, divided government—when an opposition majority controls one or both chambers on Capitol Hill—can place the president's agenda at a sharp disadvantage and is a recipe for institutional combat, if not gridlock.[3]

Critics are quick to point out, however, that such conclusions are incongruous with select periods in the post–World War II political landscape. Divided government seemed to matter less to Dwight Eisenhower, who got along relatively well with Democrats during six years of split-party control of the White House and Capitol Hill from 1955 to 1960. Richard Nixon had a surprisingly high "batting average" in Congress on his position votes during his first term (1969–1972). And in the contemporary period, Ronald Reagan was remarkably successful in convincing the Democratic House to approve his first year agenda in 1981.

Further, divided government does *not* necessarily impede legislative output. As David Mayhew has shown, party control of the presidency and Congress does not affect the production of "significant" laws with lasting impacts on public policy.[4] And unified government has not necessarily been a boon to presidential legislative leadership. The legislative records of Presidents Carter (1977–1980) and Clinton (1993–1994), in particular, were less than illustrious to many. Such examples suggest that unified government in the American context scarcely approximates "responsible party government" of the British parliamentary variety.

This chapter attempts to reconcile elements of this long-standing debate about party control of national institutions by focusing on the ways in which unified or divided government *does matter* for presidential legislative leadership.[5] Single-party control facilitates positive presidential engagement of Congress and furnishes more opportunities for credit claiming, even if unified government does not consistently prove a panacea for the White House. Presidents prevail more often on congressional votes on which they express a position, and agenda synergy with Congress is consistently stronger. They are sometimes able to steer the congressional agenda. At other times, their role has been to cultivate support for continuing party objectives in Congress. Scholars focused solely on congressional lawmaking have overlooked these advantageous features of unified government for the legislative presidency.

Split-party control has had a much more variable impact on presidents' success in Congress, agenda leadership, and legislative strategy. In the early postwar period, presidents were often able to reach across the aisle to the opposition majority and its leadership to cobble together winning coalitions on floor votes. It is in the last several decades that assertive opposition majorities have set more of the policy agenda and have forced presidents to preempt Congress or take a more defensive role in the legislative game. Heightened partisanship and organizational reforms in Congress have hampered presidents' efforts to construct cross-party coalitions. These factors have plummeted presidents' legislative success rates and complicated agenda control. But they have also provided contemporary presidents with a powerful, if different, form of *leverage* over Congress. In this era of party unity and narrow seat margins on Capitol Hill, presidents have turned increasingly to vetoes and veto threats to gain influence over lawmaking. Opposition majorities in Congress have little hope of finding two-thirds majorities capable of overriding chief executives' objections, enhancing the potency of even a mere veto threat by the president to win legislative compromise.

This chapter approaches the question of party control and presidential relations with Congress from a historical perspective. The task is to outline a theory capable of explaining the conditions that subtend different forms of presidential leadership of Congress. The objective of the framework elaborated in the next section is to consider how the intersection of broad electoral dynamics and organizational features and voting patterns in Congress shapes types of leadership opportunities presidents have had under unified and divided government across the post–World War II era. The subsequent section examines longitudinal data on presidential success on floor votes in Congress as well as presidents' involvement in significant legislation—from agenda leadership to veto threats—to substantiate the central argument about the pivotal impact of shifting governing contexts and party control of Congress for the legislative presidency. The chapter concludes with thoughts about how the institutional context following the 2008 presidential and congressional elections may shape Barack Obama's potential for legislative leadership.

PRESIDENTIAL LEVERAGE AND THE ERAS OF CONGRESS

Presidential influence, or leverage, over Congress is best conceptualized by degree along a bounded scale. At one end of the spectrum is "positive leverage" ranging from assertive presidential direction of congressional lawmaking to lending support for a shared agenda with Congress. On the other pole there is "veto leverage," a defensive strategy of partisan coalition building, veto threats, and vetoes to forestall congressional activism when the legislative agenda is sharply contested between the White House and the majority on Capitol Hill.

The broader electoral and institutional setting presidents have confronted has determined the type of leadership they are able to exercise along this continuum. The theoretical approach borrows from the "new institutionalism" perspective.[6] The notion of presidential influence in "political time"[7] hinges on the ways in which party control of Congress has merged with presidents' electoral resources and internal dynamics on Capitol Hill to mold presidential legislative strategy and success in predictable ways in the last fifty years.

The Electoral Realm

One key factor in the president's influence in Congress is his electoral resources. Bringing more members of his own party into Congress upon his election legitimizes the president's agenda in the eyes of the press and the public. The president's electoral popularity in members' constituencies is also an important component of his "political capital."[8]

When members of Congress feel they owe their electoral victory to the president, coattail effects enhance the chief executive's potential for influence over members generally. A president's strong electoral linkage to copartisans may bolster his ability to set and lead the congressional agenda. "Candidates receiving coattail votes," James Campbell and Joe Sumners note, "may be a bit more positively disposed, out of gratitude, to side with a president who had helped in their election."[9] For their part, opposition members may fear electoral retaliation for failing to support a president who ran strong in their district. Legislators on both sides of the aisle must be concerned with their support of an electorally popular president because they believe that their constituents pay attention to their voting records.

The problem for presidents in the latter period of the postwar era is that coattails, however measured, have declined considerably. Gone are the days when presidents were once able to realize significant seat gains in Congress and catapult members of their own party to victory. Greater electoral competition between the two parties in the electorate for the presidency, and the growth of congressional members' incumbency advantage, are complementary explanations for the phenomenon.

The House of Representatives is typically the reference point in analyses of coattails since all 435 seats are contested every two years. Reagan's election in 1980 is the high-water mark for coattails in the last three decades. The Great Communicator brought 33 Republicans to the House, but not enough to overturn Democratic control. Further, "negative coattails" have become routine. John F. Kennedy was the first president in the post–World War II era to suffer a net *loss* of members of his own party in the House of Representatives (20). The losses for George H. W. Bush in 1988 (3), Bill Clinton in 1992 (10), and George W. Bush in 2000 (3) did little to legitimize claims to a mandate for their agendas, however different they were.

Presidents' electoral popularity at the congressional constituency level has also declined vis-à-vis members' own margin of victory. Notwithstanding Eisenhower and Johnson in an earlier period, most presidents in recent decades have "run ahead" of few members of their own party or of the opposition party. Jimmy Carter (1976) ran ahead of less than a tenth of Democrats, and hardly any Republicans. In the contemporary era of frequent divided government, Ronald Reagan (1980, 1984), George H. W. Bush (1988), Bill Clinton (1992, 1996), and George W. Bush (2000, 2004) ran ahead of no more than approximately a third of their copartisans and typically less than a sixth of opposition members.

Presidents today confront members on both sides of the aisle whose electoral victories owe little to the campaign for the White House. As an aide to President Kennedy noted, "If the President runs behind in your district, he becomes a liability. If the President can't help you, why help him?"[10] It is little wonder, then, that under unified conditions presidents like Carter or Clinton had a more fragile basis from which to set the legislative agenda and pursue their own independent policy goals compared to Johnson. They have frequently had to resolve themselves to lend support for congressional priorities, with much more narrow windows of opportunity opening for the pursuit of their own agenda objectives. Under divided party control, members of the opposition party have few incentives to follow the president's lead, and the construction of cross-party coalitions has eroded substantially.

The Internal Configuration of Congress

Another critical factor in the president's influence in Congress is the internal configuration of Congress. The relative levels of centralization of the leadership structure on Capitol Hill and intraparty cohesion on floor votes operate together with chief executives' electoral resources to condition the degree to which any president can steer the congressional agenda and construct partisan or cross-partisan coalitions for his positions, whether under single- or split-party government. Unified or divided government has occurred within distinguishable "eras" of Congress, as Roger Davidson calls them, marked by decisive turning points in leadership organization and voting alignments.[11] Grasping the essential features of these eras in the post–World War II period clarifies the nexus between party control, institutional dynamics in Congress, and presidential influence across time.

The Bipartisan Conservative Era, 1947–1964

The policy-making context on Capitol Hill from 1947 through the mid-1960s enabled presidents—especially those with longer coattails—to lobby individual members and party leaders on both sides of the aisle. Presidents found that members often looked to them for issue leadership. Weaker leadership coordination and lower levels of party unity defined dynamics in Congress. The diffusion of power among senior committee members robbed the Speaker and majority leader of the tools for enforcing party cohesion in the House of Representatives. In the halcyon days of the "textbook Congress" of smoky, backroom bartering and "logrolling," fewer votes pitted a majority of one party against a majority of the other. Cross-party coalitions were frequent because both Democrats and Republicans were internally divided. Moderate members often held the balance over legislative outcomes on the floor of the House. James MacGregor Burns's notion of "four-party" politics captured the essence of the period, as liberal Democrats and conservative Republicans in Congress faced a large contingent of their copartisans whose ideological stances were closer to the opposing party.[12] The influence of these *cross-pressured* legislators resulted in shifting voting alignments and de facto policy majorities that often changed according to the issue, no matter which party had the nominal majority in Congress.[13] The *conservative coalition* of southern Democrats and conservative Republicans often carried the day on economic, defense, and social issues. In other cases liberal Democrats and moderate Republicans could join together on select bills such as civil rights and prevail.

The conservative coalition did often frustrate the agendas of Democratic Presidents Truman and Kennedy under unified government. Yet cobbling together winning cross-party coalitions was not impossible. Kennedy was successful in brokering intra- and cross-party support for important elements of his New Frontier domestic agenda, including housing, manpower training, and urban development, by highlighting constituency benefits to legislators on both sides of the aisle.[14] And through his perseverant leadership Lyndon Johnson was able to overcome staunch southern Democratic opposition to the 1964 Civil Rights Act by unifying liberal Democrats and moderate Republicans.[15]

Under divided government from 1955 to 1960 Republican President Dwight Eisenhower proved skilled at reading the congressional landscape and manipulating voting alignments on Capitol Hill to his advantage. Eisenhower successfully married southern Democratic and Republican support for his stands against domestic spending, including veto overrides occasionally attempted by the Democratic leadership. In other cases, such as civil rights and foreign affairs, he reached across the aisle and marshaled the support of moderates in both parties.[16]

It is little wonder that in this bipartisan conservative era from the 1940s to the 1960s party control of Congress seemingly mattered less to the legislative presidency. The conservative coalition was the dominant voting alignment, whatever the partisan configuration of the White House and Capitol Hill. Unified government for Democratic presidents was a tenuous arrangement marked by internal divisions between northern and southern Democrats. Under divided government the ever-popular Eisenhower played those divisions in Congress like a fine-tuned instrument by negotiating behind the scenes in what Fred Greenstein typecasts the "hidden-hand" presidency.[17] He enjoyed more than a modicum of success in the legislative arena.

The Liberal Activist Era, 1965–1979

The lack of strong intraparty cohesion and a decentralized setting in Congress continued into the early 1970s. Lyndon Johnson's electoral landslide in 1964 momentarily broke the hold of the conservative coalition in Congress. Johnson's coattails provided a *working* legislative majority of liberal Democrats that enabled him to direct the contours of lawmaking around his Great Society agenda. The "surge" in lawmaking continued into Nixon's presidency. Much of the far-reaching legislation adopted in 1965–1972 passed by large bipartisan coalitions, which were a reflection of broad congressional agreement on public policies proposed or backed by the president.

Nixon was caught up in the momentum of the consolidation of the Great Society agenda and was initially unwilling to challenge the large Democratic majorities he confronted. Shifting policy coalitions sometimes permitted him to ally his administration with select policy endeavors, exercise some influence over the substance of legislation, and share credit with Congress for policy accomplishments as he eyed reelection. Positive institutional competition developed between the president and Congress to minimize protracted conflict.[18] Cooperation turned to conflict largely after Nixon's reelection in 1972. His extensive impoundment of funds for domestic programs and vetoes of congressional bills, followed by the Watergate scandal, set in motion an irreversible tide in Congress that brought about stronger party leadership and greater intraparty cohesion among Democrats. The post-Watergate environment on Capitol Hill presaged the twilight of the fluid legislative coalitions of yesteryear.

Democrats judged structural reforms essential to fend off Nixon's threat to the party's agenda. They revamped the committee system to loosen conservatives' grip.[19] The House speakership was strengthened to allow the Speaker greater control over committee appointments and the referral of legislation to committees.[20] The party whip system was also extended to co-opt members into the leadership structure and guarantee stronger party loyalty.[21] The objective was to reinforce Congress's *autonomous policy-making capacity*.

The sum total of these reforms produced an environment scarcely conducive to President Ford for building cross-party coalitions under divided government. Ford, who had been elected neither to the vice presidency nor the presidency, had no electoral leverage over Congress. He faced an uphill battle in attempting to marshal Democratic support among leaders, committee chairs, or rank-and-file members upon assuming the presidency after Nixon's resignation. He resorted frequently to the veto to halt domestic spending, casting a total of forty-eight vetoes in just over two years.

The ramifications for Carter's presidency also became clear. Carter was the first president to come to office following the McGovern-Fraser reforms, which marginalized the role of party and congressional leaders in the presidential nomination process. His "outsider" and "anti-Washington" candidacy for the White House may have been in step with public sentiment following Watergate, but it compounded a breach in comity between him and an increasingly independent Democratic majority in Congress.[22] As Charles O. Jones argues, "Democrats (and some Republicans) came to think of themselves as an alternative government during Nixon's second administration."[23] Though Nixon had departed, the mind-set remained. Carter's travails were connected to changes in congressional policy-making ability, which curtailed members' need to look to him for policy leadership. In addition, Carter's own agenda—the "politics of the public good" and an emphasis on deregulation—fit uncomfortably with his copartisans' aspirations. Congress often (and belatedly) passed scaled-down versions of his proposals, such as the energy plan. Finally, his vetoes "on principle" of Democratic constituency projects provoked a significant backlash and embarrassing overrides.

Carter was arguably most successful when he identified continuing legislative proposals or "promising issues"[24] in Congress that were aimed at calibrating government policy with the new and difficult economic context of the mid to late 1970s, such as banking regulation, Social Security taxes, and minimum wage legislation. Unified government *did* matter, even if Carter's term hardly reflected the lionized FDR or LBJ models of strong presidential leadership of Congress. The electoral and institutional contexts surrounding Carter's term were simply not commensurate with these Democratic predecessors.

The Postreform/Party-Unity Era, 1980–

More than any other single factor, Ronald Reagan's stunning legislative successes in 1981 marked another pivotal turning point in congressional organization and stability in voting alignments in Congress. This defining moment in political time has continued to shape many of the contours of executive-legislative relations into the new millennium. The Democratic majority's reaction against Reagan foreshadowed trends that would dominate two decades of nearly constant divided government—and would outlive the Democratic majority itself as the 1994 elections dramatically ushered in the first Republican majority in the House in forty years. Republicans only bolstered the trend toward "conditional party government" in Congress that Democrats began a decade and a half earlier.[25]

Reagan's early agenda to cut domestic spending and taxes while increasing defense expenditures polarized Congress. His ephemeral legislative successes in 1981 owed to strong unity in the ranks of congressional Republicans and critical support from a waning contingent of cross-pressured southern Democrats whose ideological positions were closer to the median GOP member—and in whose districts Reagan had been particularly popular in 1980. Cross-party voting alliances in the early 97th Congress (1981–1982) represented a sort of "last hurrah" for the conservative coalition, which, in Reagan's first year, was instrumental in pushing his agenda across the threshold of victory.

Just as their leadership reforms in the early 1970s had been a reaction against Nixon, Democrats in the early 1980s embarked on an institutional reform program that was aimed at thwarting Reagan's ability to make the majority's preferred legislation vulnerable to the combination of Republican challenges and southern Democrats' defections from the party line. Reagan's early legislative successes provoked a sense of urgency for leadership reforms because the more steadfastly liberal Democratic membership in the 1980s resented the ability of a shrinking number of conservatives to thwart the majority's policy aspirations. Progressive Democrats redoubled efforts to centralize power and authority in the leadership and reinvigorated the party whip organization. They bolstered the Speaker's ability to control the referral of legislation to committees and to implement restrictive rules on floor amendments to bills. The objective was to insure greater intraparty cohesion and enable a growing liberal core in the Democratic majority to control more fully policy outcomes.[26] Rank-and-file Democrats found the benefits of centralizing power and authority in a stronger leadership organization a necessary and desirable practice in order to enhance the party's agenda-setting capacity and safeguard constituents' interests.[27] Moreover, membership turnover and generational replacement of retiring senior Democrats with new Republicans in the South, as well as redistricting in the 1980s and 1990s, helped to evaporate the traditional ideological rift between northern liberal and southern conservative Democrats. By the 1990s the few Democrats elected from the South were typically African Americans whose ideological positions mirrored those of their colleagues across the nation. Thus, the "geographic realignment" of the southern electorate was a complementary factor in precipitating reforms as party competition increased with Republican gains in the Sunbelt.

As the conservative coalition all but disappeared in the House, Reagan's legislative fortunes declined considerably. The president's successive annual budgets were declared "dead on arrival" in Congress and House leaders put forth their own alternatives. Reagan increasingly turned to the veto to halt Democratic legislation that threatened his early policy accomplishments. His successor, George Herbert Walker Bush, inherited this highly structured policy-making environment on Capitol Hill after winning a bitter campaign in 1988 that left Democrats in charge of both chambers of Congress. Without much of a domestic agenda of his own, Bush focused instead on maintaining "veto strength" against the Democratic legislation he most vehemently opposed. Aided by party-unity voting in the House, Bush sought to ensure enough Republican votes ($\geq 33\%$) to sustain any override challenge to his vetoes. In this way he managed much legislative business through reactive veto threats aimed at forcing Democrats to drop objectionable provisions on bills ranging from the budget to social services. His threats were buttressed by a nearly perfect veto record.[28]

House Republicans bolstered the trend toward stronger party government. In the 1994 midterm elections all House GOP candidates signed the Contract with America, campaigned on the policy goals in the platform, and felt compelled to make good on their promises.[29] The principles of the contract served as a basis for Republican unity in much the same way that Democratic rules of the 1980s and 1990s "bonded" members and conditioned their legislative support.[30] As Barbara Sinclair notes, Republicans were eager to give their leaders "many of the same tools that Democrats utilized when they were in the majority."[31] In the 104th Congress party unity reached heights not seen for over a century.

The policy-making context on Capitol Hill following the 1994 elections redefined Bill Clinton's legislative presidency. In his first two years in office Clinton had struggled to mount a legislative *offensive* on health care reform, the federal budget, and crime. After 1994 the GOP contract supplanted Clinton's agenda as the focus of policy debate in Congress and relegated him to a *defensive* strategy centering on veto leverage. His warning to the Republican majority that the president was still "relevant" to the legislative process because of his veto power was a harbinger of the intense policy battles that would follow.[32] Clinton maximized party unity to sustain his ability to threaten vetoes and force the GOP majority to compromise on policy specifics.[33] And like his predecessor, George H. W. Bush, Clinton had a nearly perfect veto record. Of the thirty-seven regular vetoes he cast from 1995 to 2000, he suffered only a single override.

George W. Bush's strategic use of veto leverage is somewhat more complicated, and his record under divided government from 2007 to 2008 more variable. In the first five and a half years of his presidency George W. Bush did not veto a single bill under unified government. He became the first president since John Quincy Adams not to veto a single bill over the course of a four-year term. Critics—particularly fiscally conservative Republicans—derided Bush's reticence to wield the veto pen.[34] Yet Bush did not find grounds to revert to veto leverage until summer 2006. Presidents are typically loath to cast vetoes with a majority of their partisans in control on Capitol Hill. To do so may suggest to voters and the media a lack of responsible governance. Instead, Bush engaged in "a blend of compromise, careful selection of battles and tactical shifts,"[35] including veto threats, to keep Congress in check under "mixed party control" from 2001 to 2006.

Republican majorities in the House (2002–2006) and in the Senate (2003–2006) responded well to Bush's early warnings. Bush issued sixty-three veto threats from 2001 to 2006. Eight-seven percent of threatened bills were halted in their tracks. Of the remaining bills that were threatened and did pass, Congress most often moved to the president's position. And on bills that were threatened and passed in a different form, Bush and Congress frequently found compromise.[36]

Bush's veto record was mixed. Of the twelve vetoes he issued from 2006 to 2008 the Democratic majority challenged eight. He was ultimately overridden on four bills (including twice on a farm bill for technical reasons). The other overrides were on water projects and Medicare spending. Bush objected to the price tag in each case, but spending on the programs proved popular among members of Congress on both sides of the aisle.[37] In retrospect Bush may well have waited too long to exercise the veto on spending matters to bolster this form of leverage with the return of divided government in the 110th Congress. Still, his 75 percent success rate in sustaining vetoed bills overall, and his power to say no on issues spanning embryonic stem cell research and Democrats' efforts to "de-fund" the war in Iraq, are consistent with the thesis that more partisan voting alignments in the postreform/party-unity era give the White House a decided advantage in veto leverage under divided government.

From this brief narrative spanning the last fifty years, it is obvious that the postreform/party-unity era has been the most salient for executive-legislative relations during times of divided government. Stronger party cohesion in Congress has transformed presidential strategy. With few coattails vis-à-vis the opposition party and unable to build cross-party coalitions, presidents have had to turn to veto leverage to gain influence over lawmaking dynamics. It is not simply a question of presidents enduring low "batting averages"

for their legislative positions in Congress. Rather, as the next section eluci-
dates, divided party control in the postreform/party-unity era has complicated
presidents' agenda-setting efforts and ability to claim credit for significant
policy outcomes, which are more frequently driven by assertive opposition
majorities.

The other lesson is that unified government does not always yield the basis
for strong autonomous policy successes. Presidents like Carter or Clinton
sometimes had to content themselves to further long-standing party objectives. Others, like George W. Bush, may have had a more circumscribed domestic policy agenda. Regardless, agenda congruence between the branches
is unmistakable under unified conditions, and presidents have historically
garnered a much more consistent record of roll-call success in Congress for
their policy stances.

PRESIDENTIAL SUCCESS AND
SIGNIFICANT LEGISLATION ACROSS ERAS

Data on presidents' floor success in Congress and their involvement in significant domestic legislation substantiate the "eras" framework for grasping
how executive-legislative relationships have changed with party control of
national institutions over time. The much more variable impact of divided
government on presidential success and legislative strategy contrasts significantly with the consistently higher presidential floor success rates and agenda
synergy with Congress under unified conditions. Let us now examine key
empirical indicators in greater detail.

Presidential "Batting Averages" in Congress across the Eras

One benchmark for testing the effect of party control of Congress for the
legislative presidency is the rate of presidential-congressional *concurrence*,[38]
or the percentage of times floor outcomes correspond to presidents' positions.
Figure 7.1 shows this measure of annual presidential success in the House of
Representatives in times of unified and divided government.[39]

Consistently higher levels of presidential-congressional agreement during
periods of unified control are unmistakable. Eisenhower (1953) and Johnson
(1965) top the chart with success rates of over 90 percent. Similarly, Clinton (1993) and George W. Bush (2001–2006) enjoyed success rates of over
80 percent on their legislative stands. Carter's (1978) batting average is the
lowest among presidents under unified government, but never fell below 70
percent.

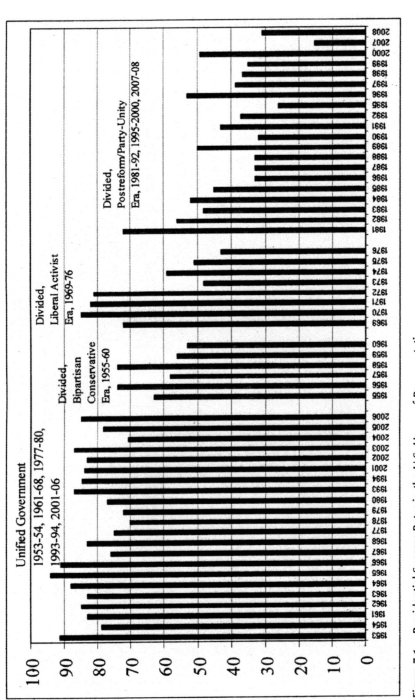

Figure 7.1.   Presidential Success Rates in the U.S. House of Representatives

There is far more inconsistency in presidential success rates during divided government. In the bipartisan conservative era, Eisenhower's (1955–1960) success rate never dipped below 50 percent. In the liberal activist era Nixon's first-term success rate is stunning. Executive-legislative concurrence never dropped below 70 percent. The data allude to Nixon's strategic position-taking in favor of popular legislation during his first term as he eyed reelection. Following his successful 1972 campaign, Nixon's success rate fell by almost half as he began to oppose congressional action much more frequently.

It is during the postreform/party-unity era that the effects of divided government on presidential-congressional concurrence have been most dramatic. Reagan's success rate of over 70 percent in 1981 marks a clear dividing line. Following Democrats' reorganization efforts his success rate fell steadily over time. In his last three years in office Reagan's positions carried the day no more than a third of the time. With few exceptions, divided government for Reagan's successors—George H. W. Bush, Bill Clinton, and George W. Bush—pushed presidential success rates below 50 percent. George W. Bush's success rate of just 18 percent in 2007 is the historical nadir for presidential success in Congress since record keeping began in 1953.

Time-series regression confirms how congressional eras in the postwar period have differentially affected presidential floor success rates. Details on the analysis are in notes.[40] Regardless of party control of Congress, time in office clearly takes an inevitable toll for all presidents. In the House, executive-legislative concurrence declines by about 2 percent for every year of a president's term, regardless of party control. But all things being equal, under unified government presidents can expect success rates of approximately 87 percent. Divided government causes a variable drop in the president's batting average. In the bipartisan conservative era Eisenhower could expect a success rate between 57 and 74 percent, with the higher score coming in his first term. In the liberal activist era the model forecasts average presidential success rates to fall between 60 and 69 percent, controlling for time in office. In the postreform/party-unity era, however, the model forecasts success rates no higher than 50 percent—and as low as 36 percent for two-term presidents like Reagan, Clinton, and George W. Bush. Presidential batting averages in the Senate are similar to the House, despite important contrasts in structural features between the chambers.[41]

The greater impact of divided government on presidential success is intrinsically linked to more stable, partisan voting coalitions in Congress, ideological conflict between presidents and opposition majorities, and party leaders' authoritative control of the legislative agenda. In the postreform/party-unity era of divided government presidents now oppose bills reaching the floor far more than they support them. And they lack essential electoral resources to persuade opposition majorities to take voting stances against their majority leadership. By the end of Reagan's second term he *opposed* nearly three-quarters of the congressional bills on which he took a position. Clinton (1995–2000) and Bush (2007–2008) opposed approximately two-thirds or more of all bills that reached the floor. The current context stands in stark contrast to President Eisenhower, who had more opportunities to maneuver across party lines in Congress or President Nixon, who chose to ally himself to elements of the congressional agenda.

Significant Domestic Legislation, Presidential and Congressional Agendas, and Veto Politics

The foregoing analysis of presidential success rates accentuates that in recent decades divided government has had a profoundly negative impact on one important benchmark measure of presidential influence in Congress. But the story does not end there. The disproportionate impact of divided government on presidential legislative strategy, as well as subtle differences in presidential leadership in periods of unified control is visible in an analysis of presidential involvement in significant or "landmark" bills.

Mayhew's Landmark Bills

A reexamination of David Mayhew's "significant" legislation in the postwar period highlights differences in presidential legislative leadership across time and by party control.[42] Using historical "sweeps" of media and scholarly accounts of legislation that observers regard as having an enduring impact on American public policy, Mayhew assembled more than three hundred laws passed between 1947 and 2006.[43] He is most interested in providing evidence that divided government does not produce legislative gridlock. The proportion of laws produced under unified and divided government, he shows, does not differ greatly. Yet Mayhew fails to answer a critical question for scholars of the presidency: are such laws the product of presidential or congressional agendas, and how does presidential strategy and engagement on such laws vary by party control across time?

Tables 7.1 and 7.2 recategorize Mayhew's significant laws by divided and unified government, respectively, for biennial congressional periods across the three eras. Landmark foreign policy laws were purged to leave a focus on the 287 domestic bills passed from 1953 to 2006. Detailed research of presidents' State of the Union addresses, statements, and legislative histories was undertaken to test the degree to which significant legislation had at least some correspondence to the president's stated policy objectives—and if not, whether the president supported, opposed bills, or "stayed quiet" and took no position on bills inspired by Congress. Bill histories were also utilized to determine whether each bill was subject to "veto politics," including threats, prior vetoes, and veto overrides. This approach paints a vastly more intricate picture of presidential-congressional engagement in the legislative realm.

Table 7.1 shows that during divided government in the bipartisan conservative era the lion's share of significant legislation passed emanated from Eisenhower's priorities. Bills included the federal highway bill of 1956, the National Defense Education Act in 1958, and the civil rights bills of 1957 and 1960. No other period of divided government shows a similar linkage between significant legislation and the president's agenda, even if legislative "output" was rather modest overall. On bills that percolated up from Congress, the president generally took favorable positions. Eisenhower utilized the veto as a last resort on congressional bills. He vetoed a farm bill and a housing bill under divided control but managed legislative coalitions in Congress to block override attempts by the Democratic majority and won compromise on later renditions of the bills.[44]

The liberal activist era marks a qualitative change in presidential management of divided government. President Nixon was *not* the driving force behind many of the significant bills of the day.[45] The evidence shows that Nixon was co-opted to a large degree by the continuing Democratic Great Society agenda in Congress that carried over from Lyndon Johnson's term. This was not his preferred agenda, though he tried to portray himself as a conservative reformer while claiming credit for popular legislation as he postured for reelection. His clear policy victories may have been few, but include revenue sharing with the states, the extension of unemployment insurance coverage, and funds to improve the nation's air transit system. Yet in three cases *he threatened to veto his very own proposals* when the Democratic majority failed to follow his lead. As one example, he proposed a 10 percent increase in Old Age, Survivor, and Disability Insurance (OASDI) benefits as part of the Social Security increase of 1969. In a move to upstage the president, House Democrats adopted a 15 percent increase. Nixon backed down from his veto threat over the costs given the program's widespread popularity.[46] The bulk of other legislation from 1969 to 1974 (91st, 92d, and 93d Congresses) was the product of congressional action. Nixon took *no position* on a third of the bills passed from 1971 to 1974, including Supplemental Security Income (1972), the Higher Education Act of 1972, and the Housing and Community Development Act of 1974. In other cases, he publicly supported bills that originated in Congress in order to take a bit of credit—as he did on so many roll-call votes—including the Equal Employment Opportunity Act of 1972, the Agricultural and Consumer Protection Act of 1973, and federal

Table 7.1. Significant Legislation and Presidential-Congressional Agendas and Interaction, Divided Government, 1953–2002*

Bipartisan Conservative Era

Congress, Number of Laws	President	Agenda Connection and Presidential Position				Vetoes and Veto Threats			
		Presidential Priority	Congressional Agenda—Supported	Congressional Agenda—No Position	Congressional Agenda—Oppose	Presidential Priority—Veto Threat	Congressional Agenda—Veto Threat	Congressional Agenda—Prior Veto	Congressional Agenda—Vetoed/Overridden
84th [n=4]	Eisenhower	3 (75%)	0	0	0	0	0	1 (25%)	0
85th [n=9]	Eisenhower	6 (67%)	1 (11%)	1 (11%)	1 (11%) 0	0	0	0	0
86th [n=5]	Eisenhower	2 (40%)	1 (20%)	1 (20%)	0	0	0	1[b] (20%)	0

Liberal Activist Era

Congress, Number of Laws	President	Agenda Connection and Presidential Position				Vetoes and Veto Threats			
		Presidential Priority	Congressional Agenda—Supported	Congressional Agenda—No Position	Congressional Agenda—Oppose	Presidential Priority—Veto Threat	Congressional Agenda—Veto Threat	Congressional Agenda—Prior Veto	Congressional Agenda—Vetoed/Overridden
91s [n=20]	Nixon	8 (40%)	2 (10%)	3 (15%)	3 (15%)	3 (15%)	1 (5%)	0	0
92nd [n=15]	Nixon	3 (20%)	3 (20%)	5 (33%)	2 (13%)	1 (7%)	0	0	1 (7%)
93rd [n=19]	Nixon/Ford	4 (21%)	6 (32%)	6 (32%)	0	0	2 (11%)	0	1 (5%)
94th [n=14]	Ford	7 (50%)	0	6 (43%)	0	0	1 (7%)	0	0

(continued)

Table 7.1. (continued)

		Postreform/Party Unity Era							
		Agenda Connection and Presidential Position				Vetoes and Veto Threats			
Congress, Number of Laws	President	Presidential Priority	Congressional Agenda—Supported	Congressional Agenda—No Position	Congressional Agenda—Oppose	Presidential Priority—Veto Threat	Congressional Agenda—Veto Threat	Congressional Agenda—Prior Veto	Congressional Agenda—Vetoed/Overridden
97th [n=9]	Reagan	3 (33%)	3 (33%)	1 (11%)	0	0	2 (22%)	0	0
98th [n=6]	Reagan	2 (33%)	0	2 (33%)	0	2 (33%)	0	0	0
99th [n=7]	Reagan	2 (29%)	0	2 (29%)	0	0	3 (43%)	0	0
100th [n=10]	Reagan	3 (30%)	0	1 (10%)	1 (10%)	0	2 (20%)	0	3 (30%)
101st [n=9]	Bush (41)	2 (22%)	2 (22%)	2 (22%)	0	1 (11%)	0	2 (22%)	0
102nd [n=5]	Bush (41)	1 (20%)	0	1 (20%)	0	1 (20%)	0	1 (20%)	1 (20%)
104th [n=14]	Clinton	5c (36%)	5 (36%)	3 (21%)	0	0	0	0	1 (7%)
105th [n=7]	Clinton	1 (14%)	2 (29%)	3 (43%)	0	1 (14%)	0	0	0
106th [n=5]	Clinton	0	0	4 (80%)	0	0	1 (20%)	0	0
107th [n=13]	Bush (43)	3 (23%)	4 (31%)	3 (23%)	1 (8%)	2 (15%)	0	0	0

* Row percentages do not always equal 100% due to rounding.
a Congressional Quarterly did not begin recordkeeping of presidential positions until 1953; see text for discussion.
b Eisenhower vetoed the Housing Act of 1959 twice.
c Clinton vetoed welfare reform twice in the 104th Congress; he also issued prior vetoes on the budget.

Table 7.2. Significant Legislation and Presidential-Congressional Agendas and Interaction, Unified Government, 1953–1994*

Era	Congress, Number of laws	President	Presidential Priority	Congressional Agenda—Supported	Presidential Priority— Veto Threat	Congressional Agenda— Veto Threat
Bipartisan Conservative	83rd [n=8]	Eisenhower	7 (88%)	1 (13%)	0	0
	87th [n=10]	Kennedy	10 (100%)	0	0	0
	88th [n=11]	Kennedy- Johnson	10 (91%)	1 (9%)	0	0
Liberal Activist	89th [n=22]	Johnson	22 (100%)	0	0	0
	90th [n=15]	Johnson	15 (100%)	0	0	0
Postreform/ Party-Unity	95th [n=11]	Carter	8 (73%)	3 (27%)	0	0
	96th [n=9]	Carter	8 (89%)	1 (11%)	0	0
	103rd [n=11]	Clinton	10 (91%)	1 (9%)	0	0
	108th [n=8]	Bush (43)	6 (75%)	2 (25%)	0	0
	109th [n=11]	Bush (43)	6 (55%)	3 (27%)	1 (9%)	1 (9%)

* Row percentages do not always equal 100% due to rounding.

aid to health maintenance organizations (HMOs). Nixon also sometimes accepted legislation he had neither asked for nor wanted. The best example is the passage of price control legislation in 1970. The legislation enabled the president to control inflation by imposing wage and price freezes. Nixon signed the bill reluctantly, contending that he would have rather vetoed it.[47]

The effect of stronger parties on presidential leadership of significant lawmaking under divided government is unambiguous in the postreform/party-unity era. The data accentuate three critical trends. First, few landmark bills are consistently connected with presidents' stated policy objectives. No more than approximately a third of the bills are linked to the president's stated agenda. Second, presidents "stay quiet" and take no position on congressional legislation approximately a third of the time on average. They either disagree with the legislation but choose not to challenge it, or they seek to avoid calling attention to policy accomplishments spearheaded by the opposition. Bill Clinton is the exception. He frequently went out of his way to support congressional legislation in the 104th Congress. As Clinton eyed reelection in 1996 he sought to steal some of the thunder from popular elements in the Republican's Contract with America, including congressional accountability, regulatory matters, and immigration reform. Finally, the veto power plays a considerably larger role in presidents' negotiation with opposition majorities in the current era. A little more than one-third of all landmark bills involved the presidential veto in some form—either implied or applied.

Presidents' increased use of veto threats underscores their adaptation to the highly partisan landscape on Capitol Hill. "Often the purpose of a veto threat is not to kill the legislation," Barbara Sinclair posits, "but to extract concessions from an opposition majority that has major policy differences with the president but lacks the strength to override his vetoes."[48] Reagan, for example, threatened to veto agricultural and job training bills in the 97th Congress in order to coax Democrats to reduce spending levels. Similarly, in the 106th Congress Bill Clinton threatened to veto the "Ed-flex" education bill in order to force Republicans to drop an amendment that would have shifted money to existing special needs students rather than to his objective of hiring new teachers.

In many other cases presidents use veto threats in the bid to reframe the policy debate and preempt congressional action with their own proposal. The institutional context of divided government has bolstered successful veto leverage. For example, George H. W. Bush threatened to veto his proposal for the savings and loan industry bailout in 1989 if Congress did not accord the Treasury Department greater latitude in the bill's implementation. In the 105th Congress Bill Clinton preempted congressional Republicans' long-standing calls for a balanced budget, issuing multiple veto threats to indicate which domestic program cuts were off the table. In the 108th Congress George W. Bush threatened to veto the USA PATRIOT Act if Congress refused to accord provisions for broader law enforcement leeway concerning suspected terrorists.

In a much more dramatic battle with Senate Democrats over homeland security, Bush saw momentum building in Congress to reorganize the federal government in the war on terrorism. After months of eschewing talk of reorganization, Bush launched his own proposal for reorganizing twenty-two existing agencies into a new Department of Homeland Security. When Senate Democrats refused to grant him the broad license he sought concerning hiring, firing, and appointments in the new entity, Bush threatened to veto the bill and it stalled. The president ultimately waged a successful electoral campaign on the issue, which brought about a Republican majority in the Senate and prompted the lame-duck Democratic majority in 2002 to pass the bill on the president's terms.[49]

Veto politics in the postreform/party-unity era stand in sharp contrast with *all* periods of unified government across time. Seventy-three to 100 percent of landmark bills during periods of unified control, however brief historically and whatever the congressional era, are connected to presidents' agenda. Moreover, presidents almost universally *supported* whatever proportion of significant legislation was spearheaded by their congressional majorities. The data are a testimony to the consistently stronger agenda synergy between the branches that is fostered by unified party control. It would surely be a mistake to conclude that each president had equivalent leverage over Congress and was able to *direct* significant lawmaking across time. Lyndon Johnson's presidency marks the exception. Johnson's landslide election in 1964 legitimized his Great Society agenda in a way that neither Carter's narrow victory over Ford nor Clinton's plurality over George H. W. Bush in 1992 did for their campaigns. Moreover, Johnson's coattails produced a largely deferential majority in Congress, which stood poised and willing to pass his policy priorities—a key ingredient missing for Carter and Clinton. The data bear out the notion that Carter and Clinton were better situated to *facilitate* continuing party objectives in Congress, some of which were blocked by their Republican predecessors under divided government.[50]

Much of the domestic legislation adopted from 1965 to 1968 was Johnson's initiative, from voting rights and bills connected to the war on poverty to environmental and regulatory legislation. The pace of legislation is nothing less than extraordinary. More landmark domestic bills passed in Johnson's term than the Carter and Clinton single-party experiences combined. Many of the laws represented new programs targeted at urgent social issues, including the Elementary and Secondary Education Act (1965), the establishment of the Department of Housing and Urban Development (1965), and the Appalachian Regional Development Act (1965). Others represented continuing issues that carried over from Kennedy's presidency and had been blocked by southern conservatives in the Democratic majority, such as Medicare and the minimum wage.

Jimmy Carter, like Bill Clinton, had much weaker leverage over Congress. Several landmark bills were linked to Carter's independent agenda, including trucking, airline, and railroad deregulation. Carter also lent his explicit support to several bills earlier blocked by President Ford that were clearly part of a continuing agenda on Capitol Hill, such as surface mining legislation in 1977, which Ford had vetoed twice. He also lent his support to rework Ford's stalled proposal on Social Security taxes and urged passage of the Clean Air Act amendments.[51] Similarly, Bill Clinton expended much effort lending support for the carryover agenda in Congress and making incremental adjustments to existing domestic programs. Clinton's potential to advance his independent agenda was more circumscribed. The Omnibus Deficit Reduction Act of 1993, national service (Americorps), education goals (Goals 2000), and reforming college loan financing policies were among his greatest agenda victories. As many priority bills were linked to the continuing agenda in Congress, Clinton's predecessor, George H. W. Bush, had vetoed Democrats' efforts to pass gun control, family leave, and motor voter bills. Clinton unequivocally supported the Family Leave and Medical Act, the Motor Voter Act, and the Brady Bill and Omnibus Crime Act as a means of advancing the party agenda and sharing credit with Democrats in Congress for the passage of long-standing party objectives.

Although the military campaigns in Afghanistan and Iraq may have oriented George W. Bush toward foreign affairs from 2003 to 2006, his imprint on domestic policy output in these years of unified government is unmistakable. The bills represent a mix of presidential innovation and support of continuing GOP policy priorities that were blocked by Democratic President Bill Clinton in the 1990s. The 108th Congress (2003–2004) passed sweeping Medicare reform (including prescription drug coverage for seniors), a ban on partial-birth abortions, and comprehensive intelligence reform (including the creation of a director of national intelligence)—all of which were components of the president's agenda. In the 109th Congress Bush eventually prevailed on port security, though he threatened to veto the measure, and persuaded Congress to pass legislation for military commissions to try "enemy combatants" captured in Afghanistan and held at Guantanamo Bay, Cuba.[52]

REPRISE AND PROSPECTS FOR BARACK OBAMA

This chapter has provided evidence to show why party control of national institutions *does matter* to the legislative presidency. Under unified conditions recent presidents have not have profited from the type of leverage over Congress that a single president—Lyndon Johnson—did in an earlier era. Carter and Clinton struggled with a more autonomous membership and because of their lack of coattails. George W. Bush's narrow victory in 2000 scarcely aided his task. Still, deficit of coattails in more recent times has been mitigated by party unity and comity between the branches under unified conditions. Presidents have often been able to facilitate the passage of many bills that had been blocked under previous administrations, and such successes were often made possible by the president's ability to marshal partisan support. Higher levels of executive-legislative concurrence on floor outcomes testify to the greater agenda synergy between the branches. Single-party control has extended opportunities for joint credit claiming and the attainment of shared partisan policy goals across time.

Split-party control today bears little resemblance to the 1950s. Assertive, policy-focused opposition majorities look less to the president for policy leadership and have steered the lawmaking agenda away from the president's preferred direction. Organizational change and party cohesion have rendered presidents' influence over individual legislators in the opposition much more difficult. Executive-legislative concurrence has fallen to historical lows for the post–World War II period. Presidents spend more time fending off the majority's agenda and attempting to recast the national policy debate through vetoes and veto threats. Preemptive politics place a premium on presidents' rhetorical skills and the manipulation of the public presidency to reframe policy choices in order to claim a modicum of credit. Bill Clinton was arguably among the most adroit presidents in this regard, while George H. W. Bush was less adept in making a convincing public case for his frequent use of veto leverage.

The institutional and electoral politics surrounding George W. Bush's legislative presidency accent the importance of party control of national institutions in the contemporary era. Unified government aided his early agenda and the passage of sweeping tax cuts and education reform (No Child Left Behind). With his agenda stifled after losing Republican control of the Senate just a year into his term, Bush used veto threats and "strategic disagreement" with Democrats over the establishment of the Department of Homeland Security to campaign successfully for a GOP Senate in the 2002 midterm elections. From 2003 to 2006, Bush may have failed to find the majorities necessary to pass comprehensive immigration reform, but Republican control of Capitol Hill undeniably aided a moderate-sized domestic agenda that included tax cuts as well as the expansion of programs such as Medicare. Yet, as a lame-duck facing Democratic control of both chambers of Congress in 2007–2008, Bush suffered the lowest success rate in Congress on record—though he often had the last word thanks to the veto power.

The electoral and institutional context of unified government, by contrast, augurs well for Barack Obama's potential for legislative leadership. Aided by an ailing economy, Obama carried the 2008 election by nine and a half million votes and 53 percent of the popular vote—the largest popular margin since George H. W. Bush in 1988. Unlike the elder Bush, however, Obama's strong showing yielded single-party control of national institutions and ample coattails. Democrats deepened their firm control of Congress, gaining twenty-one seats in the House and eight seats in the Senate. Obama's copartisans outnumber Republicans 257–178 in the House and 59–41 in the Senate. Early estimates suggest that Obama carried approximately 80 percent of Democratic districts in the House, providing a solid basis for party unity around his agenda. Obama also carried nearly a third of the districts that elected Republicans, suggesting that at least some Republicans are likely to be pressured to follow his lead.[53]

Still, Democrats do not enjoy a filibuster-proof majority in the Senate. Obama's coattails in the upper chamber may assure solid unity, particularly among newly elected senators from Alabama, North Carolina, and Virginia who feel beholden to him for their victories. But his agenda success may pivot on Majority Leader Harry Reid's ability to convert moderate Republicans from states Obama carried by significant margins. Maine's two Republican senators, Susan Collins and Olympia Snowe, are prime examples, as both have played critical roles in past filibuster votes over the course of their careers—and did so in the passage of the February 2009 stimulus package for which not a single House Republican voted. It seems clear that a handful of moderate Republicans and Democrats will hold the balance over policy outcomes in the upper chamber. The dilemma for Reid is to hold together more fiscally conservative members of his own conference concerned about spiraling deficits. On the GOP side of the aisle, all eyes will naturally focus on Minority Leader Mitch McConnell and his ability to persuade Republicans to toe the line. A generally soft-spoken veteran of the upper chamber known for pragmatic bipartisanship, McConnell is nevertheless an astute master of parliamentary procedure who pledged cooperation from Senate Republicans—so long as Obama governs from the center.[54]

Locating the political center in the midst of the worst economic conditions in decades is the daunting challenge that lies before President Obama. Attempts by the lame-duck congressional session in 2008 to address an economy ravaged by 7 percent unemployment, home foreclosures, and financial services and auto industries teetering on the brink of collapse met with substantial constituency ire over a government bailout of $700 million—half of which seemingly had little impact before the 2008 election. Whether and how President Obama closes the gap between inflated public expectations of his leadership and the harsh realities of economic crisis that will entail difficult policy decisions will either vindicate his rhetorical acumen on the campaign trail or prove his Achilles' heel in the context of governance. Grasping the particular limits and opportunities Obama confronts is key to appreciating the varied impact of party control of the White House and Capitol Hill, and the remarkably shifting fortunes American chief legislators may endure.

NOTES

1. Douglas Waller, "Why Jeffords Bolted from the GOP," *Time Magazine*, May 27, 2001, at www.time.com/time/columnist/waller/article/0,9565,128099,00.html (accessed September 7, 2004).

2. Andrew E. Busch, "National Security and the Midterm Elections," in *Transforming the American Polity: The Presidency of George W. Bush and the War on Terrorism*, Real Politics in America Series, ed. Richard S. Conley (Upper Saddle River, NJ: Prentice-Hall, 2005).

3. James L. Sundquist, *Constitutional Reform and Effective Government* (Washington, DC: The Brookings Institution, 1986) and Sundquist, "Needed: A Political Theory for the New Era of Coalition Government in the United States," *Political Science Quarterly* 10 (1988): 613–35; Lloyd N. Cutler, "To Form a Government," *Foreign Affairs* 59 (1988): 126–43; Benjamin Ginsberg and Martin Shefter, *Politics by Other Means: Politicians, Prosecutors, and the Press from Watergate to Whitewater* (New York: W.W. Norton, 1999); James P. Pfiffner, "Divided Government and the Problem of Governance," in *Cooperation and Conflict Between the President and Congress*, ed. James A. Thurber (Washington, DC: Congressional Quarterly, 1991).

4. David R. Mayhew, *Divided We Govern: Party Control, Lawmaking, and Investigations 1946–1990* (New Haven, CT: Yale University Press, 1991) and "The Return to Unified Party Control under Clinton: How Much of a Difference in Lawmaking?" in *The New American Politics: Reflections on Political Change and the Clinton Administration*, ed. Bryan D. Jones (Boulder, CO: Westview Press, 1995).

5. The more detailed argument and analysis is in Richard S. Conley, *The Presidency, Congress, and Divided Government: A Postwar Assessment* (College Station: Texas A&M University Press, 2002).

6. James G. March and Johan P. Olsen, "The New Institutionalism: Organizational Factors in Political Life," *American Political Science Review* 78 (1984): 734–49.

7. The concept is borrowed from Stephen Skowronek, *The Politics Presidents Make: Leadership from John Adams to George Bush* (Cambridge, MA: Harvard University Press, 1993).

8. Paul C. Light, *The President's Agenda: Domestic Policy Choice from Kennedy to Carter* (Baltimore: Johns Hopkins University Press, 1982).

9. James E. Campbell and Joe A. Sumners, "Presidential Coattails in Senate Elections," *American Political Science Review* 84 (1990): 521.

10. Quoted in Light, *The President's Agenda*, 28.

11. Roger H. Davidson, "The Presidency in Congressional Time," in *Rivals for Power: Presidential-Congressional Relations*, ed. James A. Thurber (Washington, DC: Congressional Quarterly, 1996).

12. James MacGregor Burns, *The Deadlock of Democracy: Four-Party Politics in America* (Englewood Cliffs, NJ: Prentice-Hall, 1963).

13. The term *cross-pressured* is borrowed from Jon R. Bond and Richard Fleisher, *The President in the Legislative Arena* (Chicago: University of Chicago Press, 1990).

14. Conley, *The Presidency, Congress, and Divided Government*, 170–73.

15. Robert D. Loevy, "The Presidency and Domestic Policy: The Civil Rights Act of 1964," in *Understanding the Presidency*, eds. James P. Pfiffner and Roger H. Davidson (New York: Longman, 1997).

16. Loevy, *The Presidency and Domestic Policy*, 96–102.

17. Fred I. Greenstein, *The Hidden-Hand Presidency: Eisenhower as Leader* (Baltimore: Johns Hopkins University Press, 1982).

18. On this point, see Paul J. Quirk, "Domestic Policy: Divided Government and Cooperative Presidential Leadership," in *The Bush Presidency: First Appraisals*, eds. Colin Campbell, S. J. Rockman, and Bert A. Rockman (Chatham, NJ: Chatham House, 1991); see also John C. Whitaker, "Nixon's Domestic Policy: Both Liberal and Bold in Retrospect," *Presidential Studies Quarterly* 26 (1996): 131–53.

19. Fiona M. Wright, "The Caucus Reelection Requirement and the Transformation of House Committee Chairs, 1959–94," *Legislative Studies Quarterly* 15 (2000): 469–80.

20. David W. Rohde, *Parties and Leaders in the Postreform House* (Chicago: University of Chicago Press, 1991), 20–23.

21. Lawrence C. Dodd, "The Expanded Roles of the House Democratic Whip System: The 93rd and 94th Congresses," *Congressional Studies* 7 (1979): 27–56.

22. Tinsley E. Yarbrough, "Carter and the Congress," in *The Carter Years: The President and Policy Making*, eds. M. Glenn Abernathy, Dilys M. Hill, and Phil Williams (New York: St. Martin's Press, 1984).

23. Charles O. Jones, *The Trusteeship Presidency: Jimmy Carter and the United States Congress* (Baton Rouge: Louisiana State University Press, 1988), 59.

24. William W. Lammers and Michael A. Genovese, *The Presidency and Domestic Policy: Comparing Leadership Styles, FDR to Clinton* (Washington, DC: Congressional Quarterly, 2000).

25. John H. Aldrich and David W. Rohde, "The Logic of Conditional Party Government," in *Congress Reconsidered*, ed. Lawrence C. Dodd (Washington, DC: Congressional Quarterly, 2001).

26. Rohde, *Parties and Leaders in the Postreform House*, 83–118; Roger H. Davidson, Walter J. Oleszek, and Thomas Kephart, "One Bill, Many Committees: Multiple Referrals in the U.S. House of Representatives," *Legislative Studies Quarterly* 13 (1988): 3–28; Paul S. Herrnson and Kelly D. Patterson, "Toward a More Programmatic Democratic Party? Agenda Setting and Coalition Building in the House of Representatives," *Polity* 27 (1995): 607–28.

27. On this latter point, see also Bruce I. Oppenheimer, "The Importance of Elections in a Strong Congressional Party Era: The Effect of Unified vs. Divided Government," in *Do Elections Matter?* 3d ed., eds. Benjamin Ginsburg and Alan Stone (Armonk, NY: M. E. Sharpe, 1996).

28. Richard S. Conley, "A Revisionist View of George Bush and Congress, 1989: Congressional Support, 'Veto Strength,' and Legislative Strategy," *White House Studies* 2 (Winter 2002): 359–74.

29. James G. Gimpel, *Legislating the Revolution: The Contract with America in Its First 100 Days* (Boston: Allyn and Bacon, 1996).

30. Gary W. Cox and Matthew D. McCubbins, "Bonding, Structure, and the Stability of Political Parties: Party Government in the House," *Legislative Studies Quarterly* 19 (1994): 215–31.

31. Barbara Sinclair, "Trying to Govern Positively in a Negative Era: Clinton and the 103rd Congress," in *The Clinton Presidency: First Appraisals*, eds. Colin Campbell, S. J. Rockman, and Bert A. Rockman (Chatham, NJ: Chatham House, 1996), 113.

32. In an April 13, 1995, interview with CNN's Wolf Blitzer and Judy Woodruff, President Clinton commented on the Republicans' 100 days: "Well, they had an exciting 100 days, and they dealt with a lot of issues that were in their contract. But let's look at what happens now. The bills all go to the United States Senate, where they have to pass, and then I have to decide whether to sign or **veto** them. So now you will see the process unfolding. And I will have my opportunity to say where I stand on these bills and what I intend to do with the rest of our agenda. I have enjoyed watching this last 100 days, and have enjoyed giving them the chance to do what they were elected to do. And also I made it clear what I would not go along with." *Public Papers of the President 1995* (Washington, DC: GPO, 1995), 527–28).

33. Richard S. Conley, "President Clinton and the Republican Congress, 1995–2000: Political and Policy Dimensions of Veto Politics in Divided Government," *Congress and the Presidency* 33 (2004): 133–60.

34. Sheryl Stolberg, "Bush's Record: One Veto, Many No's," *New York Times*, July 23, 2006, 4.

35. Jill Barshay, "Bush Starts a Strong Record of Success with the Hill," *Congressional Quarterly Weekly Report*, January 12, 2002, 110.

36. Richard S. Conley and Richard M. Yon, "In the Shadow or the Sunshine of the Father? Veto Threats in the Administration of George W. Bush, 2001–2006," *White House Studies* 7 (2007): 125–39.

37. See Avery Palmer, "Congress Overrides Water Projects Veto," *Congressional Quarterly Weekly Report*, November 12, 2007, 3411; Aliya Sternstein, "2008 Legislative Summary: Farm Programs Reauthorization," *Congressional Quarterly Weekly*

Report, December 8, 2008, 3256; Drew Armstrong, "Democrats Prevail on Medicare Bill," *Congressional Quarterly Weekly Report*, July 14, 2008, 1907.

38. Lyn Ragsdale, *Vital Statistics on the Presidency: Washington to Clinton* (Washington, DC: Congressional Quarterly, 1996). Ragsdale prefers the term *concurrence* to better reflect that presidents take positions on votes not only concerning their agenda but also legislation generated in Congress.

39. Data are from yearly *Congressional Quarterly Almanacs* (1953–2006) and *Congressional Quarterly Weekly Almanacs* (2007–2008) of all presidential position votes.

40. To correct for serial correlation, estimates for the House model were generated using the Prais-Winsten (AR 1) technique in STATA 8.0. The dependent variable is the president's annual success rate. The variable for time in office ranged 1–8 years. The variables for each era are dummy variables for the respective period, and as such, provide a "stylized" account of the effect of divided government across time. The equation yields the following coefficients, all of which are significant at $p < .05$ or better:

Presidential support = 87.53 – 2.02 (time in office) – 13.58 (bipartisan conservative era) – 18.48 (liberal activist era) – 37.39 (postreform/party unity era) N = 56; adjusted R^2=.74; rho = .22; Durbin-Watson = 1.56; Durbin *h* (transformed) = 2.04

41. To correct for serial correlation, estimates for the Senate model were generated using the Prais-Winsten (AR 1) technique in STATA 8.0. The dependent variable is the president's annual success rate. The variable for time in office ranged 1–8 years. The variables for each era are dummy variables for the respective period, and as such, provide a stylized account of the effect of divided government across time. The equation yields the following coefficients, all of which are significant at $p < .05$ or better, except the coefficient for the bipartisan conservative era, which is statistically insignificant:

Presidential support = 87.61 – 3.01 (time in office) – 2.70 (bipartisan conservative era) – 14.66 (liberal activist era) – 11.39 (postreform/party unity era) N = 55; adjusted R^2= .48; rho = .17; Durbin-Watson = 1.64; Durbin *h* (transformed) = 1.96

42. David Mayhew, *Divided We Govern*.

43. At the time of writing, Mayhew had not yet compiled significant laws for the 110th Congress (2007–2008).

44. *Congressional Quarterly Almanac* 1956, 375–92; *Congressional Quarterly Almanac* 1959, 245–56.

45. For an opposite perspective that credits Nixon with many of the policy accomplishments of the 91st–93d Congresses, see Joan Hoff, *Nixon Reconsidered* (New York: Basic Books, 1994).

46. *Congressional Quarterly Almanac* 1969, 833–40.

47. *Congressional Quarterly Almanac* 1970, 433.

48. Barbara Sinclair, "Hostile Partners: The President, Congress, and Lawmaking in the Partisan 1990s," in *Polarized Politics: Congress and the President in a Par-*

tisan Era, eds. Jon R. Bond and Richard Fleisher (Washington, DC: Congressional Quarterly, 2000), 145.

49. For details, see Richard S. Conley, "Presidential and Congressional Struggles over the Formation of the Department of Homeland Security," in *Transforming the American Polity: The Presidency of George W. Bush and the War on Terrorism*, Real Politics in America Series, ed. Richard S. Conley (Upper Saddle River, NJ: Prentice-Hall, 2005).

50. The distinction between direction and facilitation is owed to George C. Edwards III, *At the Margins: Presidential Leadership of Congress* (New Haven, CT: Yale University Press, 1989).

51. *Congressional Quarterly Almanac* 1977, 161–72 and 627–46.

52. The Supreme Court ruled in *Boumediene v. Bush* (2008) that the military commissions were unconstitutional.

53. www.swingstate.com (accessed January 20, 2009).

54. David R. Sands, "McConnell Rallies GOP," *Washington Times*, November 23, 2008, M10.

Chapter Eight

The Imperial Presidency vs. the Hill

Andrew Rudalevige

"Congress meets—too bad, too," Harry Truman told his diary, as the legislators he would soon malign as "do-nothing" came into session in early 1948. "They'll do nothing but wrangle, pull phony investigations, and generally upset the affairs of the Nation."[1]

It is fair to say that every president has felt this way, at least sometimes. Despite iconic images of presidential authoritativeness—from Lyndon Johnson's famous "treatment" of recalcitrant lawmakers to George W. Bush's address by bullhorn from the rubble of the World Trade Center—the chief executive's sway over Congress is normally more a matter of entreaty than edict. Indeed, political scientist Michael Genovese's *Memo to a New President* advises its recipient that "there is no way to convey to you at this point the utter frustration and anger to which the Congress will drive you." Longtime senator John Warner (R-VA) put it well: "Every president, as he leaves the Capitol steps and gets into his limo [after his inauguration], is calculating, 'how soon can I put that place behind me?'"[2]

It doesn't help that over time the president's relations with Congress have become key to assessing his overall success—as was clear in Barack Obama's early efforts to pass a huge fiscal stimulus package.[3] Dependence, like any familiarity, may breed contempt. But presidents have not always accepted that the creation of policy by legislative means should trump their own abilities to do the same by executive action. In 2004, for example, George W. Bush told a group about trying to change the law to facilitate government contracting with religious organizations. "I got a little frustrated in Washington because I couldn't get the bill passed out of the Congress," the president said. "They were arguing *process*."

Bush, though, had an answer to the tedious "process" that meant "Congress wouldn't act." He had gone around legislators by issuing an executive order. In short, he said, he could "do it on my own."[4]

It would not be the only time: certainly not for Bush, but not for the presidency, either. Over time, the "foetus of monarchy" warned of by Virginia's Edmund Randolph at the Constitutional Convention had matured into something less than monarch but more than mere "presider." And in the twenty-first century, as the nation reacted to the terrorist attacks of September 11 and the subsequent wars in Afghanistan and Iraq, one hallmark of that reaction was a renewed and aggressive use of unilateral presidential authority. As Jonathan Mahler argues, "The assertion and expansion of presidential power [was] arguably the defining feature of the Bush years." Enough so that some warned the office had pushed past its natural boundaries, colonizing new authorities, and returning to the "imperial presidency" of the Vietnam/Watergate era.[5]

That expansion, however, was ultimately mirrored by—indeed, made possible by—both passive and active congressional acceptance of presidential claims. There seems some truth, as well as sour grapes, in one senior Democratic congressman's bitter complaint that "this administration thinks that Article I of the Constitution was a fundamental mistake."[6] The theory of the "unitary executive" became an important justification for disregarding the very relevance of the legislative branch. But at the same time, as four Brookings Institution scholars recently concluded, "It is hard to find an era to match 2001 through 2006, when the Bush presidency asserted breathtaking executive authority with virtually no challenge or pushback from Congress."[7] An imperial presidency, in other words, requires for its activation an invisible Congress. And in the early rounds of the matchup—the imperial presidency versus the Hill—there was no contest.

The remainder of this chapter explores that assessment, in theory and practice, with an eye on future rounds as well. In the long term, each protagonist has tools for ensuring, in James Madison's famous phrase, that ambition can counteract ambition, turning insular institutional interest toward the public weal. It is crucial that they use them. The risks that face the United States are real, the temptation to take shortcuts correspondingly strong, and, in the short term, always justifiable. The tragedies of September 11 made it clear that strong presidential leadership is essential to the nation. But, perhaps counterintuitively, they made it equally clear that Congress has a critical role to play in determining policy in times of crisis. If government must efficiently carry out national priorities, those priorities must themselves be arrived at through a deliberative process grounded in coalition and consensus, not command. As Justice Robert Jackson said a half century ago, in an equally dangerous world, "with all its defects, delays and inconveniences, men have discovered no technique for long preserving free government except that the Executive be under the law, and that the law be made by parliamentary deliberations." Or, as President Dwight Eisenhower put the point: "to defend freedom in ways that themselves destroy freedom is suicide—perhaps slow, but certainly sure."[8]

ON THEIR OWN: TRACKING EXECUTIVE POWER

Given the institutional constraints that limit presidential power—not least, a Constitution that gives the president few explicit grants of unchecked authority—presidents have long sought to build up resources that enable them to make policy "on [their] own" and bypass Capitol Hill. Over time, through aggressive (and sometimes creative) interpretations of article II's vesting clause and their duties as commander in chief of the armed forces, through extending their charges to "faithfully execute" the laws and defend the Constitution, through their ability to pound the bully pulpit and set the national agenda, presidents have stocked the White House toolbox with unilateral powers, piece by piece.

So far, so good? Few would argue that presidents do not or should not have some discretionary authority to administer laws and carry out executive functions. There are practical considerations as well. Congress is a plural body, fragmented structurally and along party lines; it is wordy, slow, indiscreet. In times of crisis, particularly, the singular nature of the presidential office illuminates the contrasting virtues (cf. Alexander Hamilton's paean to "energy in the executive") of "decision, activity, secrecy, and dispatch."[9] Indeed, as the presidential office grew in power in conjunction with the growth of the American administrative state at home and its enhanced role abroad, most observers thought this not only necessary but beneficial. If the history of presidential power through the middle of the crisis-ridden twentieth century was "a history of aggrandizement," it was one that received good reviews most of the time.[10]

But in the confluence of Vietnam and Watergate presidents pushed their prerogative too far—sometimes criminally so. The historian Arthur M. Schlesinger Jr. would famously set a new tone, labelling the assertiveness of Presidents Johnson and especially Nixon symptomatic of an "imperial presidency." Congress, too, would push back against those administrations' unilateral use of the war powers, of secrecy, of spending, of covert surveillance and use of force both abroad and at home. Even an abridged listing of the many enactments that sought to reshape key policy processes and rein in presidential discretion gives a flavor of the resurgence: the War Powers Resolution and Intelligence Oversight Act, the Congressional Budget and Impoundment Control Act, the Foreign Intelligence Surveillance Act (FISA), the Freedom of Information Act, the Ethics in Government Act (and its Independent Counsel Act), and so on.[11]

Twenty years later George W. Bush and his vice president, Richard Cheney, came into office with aggressive attitudes toward executive authority. Cheney, whose long resume included formative stints in the Nixon and Ford White Houses, was blunt: "For the 35 years that I've been in this town, there's been a constant, steady erosion of the prerogatives and the powers of the president of the United States, and I don't want to be a part of that." Bush took up the challenge. "I have an obligation to make sure that the Presidency remains robust," the president noted in 2002. "I'm not going to let Congress erode the power of the executive branch."[12]

This assessment was appealing, especially to those angered by the combination of poor judgments that prompted the House to impeach Bill Clinton, but far too simplistic. In fact, by the time Bush took office in 2001, most of the limits imposed by Congress's "resurgence regime" had crumbled, either by presidential action or legislative inaction. For that matter, Clinton himself forcefully asserted presidential prerogative, ordering an extensive air war over Kosovo and firing cruise missiles at the Sudan and Afghanistan even as the House debated his fate. Even his impeachment would backfire on Congress, discrediting its strongest power over the presidency and effectively killing the Independent Counsel Act.[13]

However, while the Bush-Cheney administration used existing tools established or regained by their predecessors, its term also marked an expansion and refinement of the presidential toolkit. As early as 2001, presidential historian Michael Beschloss announced that "the imperial presidency is back!" and by the time Bush left office Schlesinger's phrase was again in common currency.[14]

Part of the shift rested in new and rather grandiose theoretical assumptions about presidential power. These had important implications for the practical actions taken by the president and for the presidency's relationship to the other branches of government—especially the legislative. Indeed, the theory tended to reject the very need for such a relationship. While asserted by a conservative administration, one core aspect of the imperial presidency as redefined in the 2000s was revolutionary, rejecting a key tenet of the argument for shared powers laid out by James Madison in "Federalist No. 49": "The several departments being perfectly co-ordinate . . . neither of them . . . can pretend to an exclusive or superior right of settling the boundaries between their respective powers." But in the new theory of the "unitary executive," the president aspired to just that, beating the bounds of his own authority.

ZONES OF AUTONOMY:
THE "UNITARY EXECUTIVE" IN THEORY

Numerous documents from the Bush administration reference a "unitary executive" and "the President's constitutional authority to supervise the unitary executive branch."[15] The phrase was not new in itself, but received a new exegesis that formed a theoretical foundation girding new expansions of executive power.

Little at the Constitutional Convention had provoked more debate than the shape and scope of the executive branch. Some of the framers were unconvinced of the need for an executive branch at all; others felt executive power must be strictly divided to impede future tyranny, that a single executive would evolve to replace the very monarchy they sought to overthrow. But driven by concerns of accountability and executive "energy," the Constitution did create one president, independent of the legislature (thanks to the conveniently vague mechanism of the electoral college, a fixed term, "adequate support" and "competent powers"), and originally, eligible for indefinite service.[16]

The theory of the unitary executive flows from that decision, and the simple declarative statement that begins article II of the Constitution: "The executive power shall be vested in a President of the United States of America."

On its face this delegation of power seems a clear assignment of authority in the Constitution's congested system of checks and balances. It "does not mean *some* of the executive power," as Supreme Court Justice Antonin Scalia wrote in 1988, "but *all* of the executive power." As such, Scalia concluded, any statute denying the president "exclusive control" over a "purely executive" power was necessarily invalid as a violation of "fundamental separation of powers principles."[17]

If so, Congress (or for that matter the courts) cannot regulate or limit something like the pardon power, which is clearly granted solely to the president. Likewise, since the president is given discretion to judge the specifics of the measures he deems are "necessary and expedient" for legislative action, he might well argue he cannot be forced to submit legislation by act of Congress.

However, the formulation thus far dodges a key question: what is "the executive power," anyway? It is, after all, nowhere defined in the Constitution. Depending on its scope, the "unitary executive" could be either a descriptive fact without much import or a means of enshrining vast unilateral authority in the executive establishment. A good deal of debate has thus gone into establishing a definition: on what, for instance, might be gleaned from the difference between the vesting clause in article II and the parallel language in article I, or from the president's oath of office, or duty to "faithfully execute" the laws of the land.[18]

On the domestic side, the focus tends to be on presidential control of executive personnel. In a magisterial body of work on this front, law professor Steven Calabresi and his colleagues argue that history favors unimpeded presidential authority over the administration of the executive branch, especially as it extends to the ability of presidents to control their subordinates: "The text and structure of Article II compel the conclusion that the President retains supervisory control over all officers exercising executive power."[19] If so, efforts by Congress to constrain that power—by creating an independent counsel, for instance, or even commissions with members serving fixed terms—are improper. Nor can legislators compel executive branch personnel to appear before Congress, even under subpoena.

Pushed further, this line of reasoning implies that large areas of American government—comprising the regulatory state that arose in the Progressive era and grew exponentially through the twentieth (and twenty-first) century—are illegitimate, since the agencies created over time were frequently structured in ways that insulated them from presidential reach.[20] Secrecy was also a fundamental right, not merely an executive privilege. Congress (or anyone else) had no power to get information from any part of the executive establishment. Attorney General Richard Kleindienst put it this way to the Senate in 1973: "Your power to get what the President knows, is in the President's hands."[21]

That logic also carried over to the world of foreign policy, especially as it was linked to the president's constitutional role as commander in chief. The power to annul treaties was one—if presidents can remove appointees the Senate has confirmed, should they not be able to "remove" treaties the Senate has ratified? (Presidents as different as Jimmy Carter and George W. Bush would do just that.) Further, scholars such as John Yoo argue the war powers were vested nearly entirely in the president—even the power to go to war in the first place. In this view the congressional power to declare war was a matter of eighteenth-century etiquette, meant to deliver formal notification of a state of affairs that already existed, not to provide a substantive grant of authority.[22] And once war began, legislators could not limit presidential authority at all, except by use of the power of the purse to cut off military funding.

The new approach to the unitary executive was laid out clearly in a series of opinions issued by the Department of Justice (DOJ) starting in 2001 interpreting the law on behalf of the executive branch. They may be summed up as an effort to define and extend what the Bush administration termed the president's "zone of autonomy"—a region that clearly lay in newly occupied interbranch territory.[23]

For instance, within weeks of the terrorist attacks of September 11, 2001, the DOJ's Office of Legal Counsel advised the president that no statute could "place any limits on the President's determinations as to any terrorist threat, the amount of military force to be used in response, or the method, timing, and nature of the response. These decisions, under our Constitution, are for the President alone to make." Indeed, even "Congress's power to declare war does not constrain the President's independent and plenary constitutional authority over the use of military force."

The administration argued similarly in a 2003 appeals court case:

> Irrespective of any Congressional assent, the President has broad powers . . . under the Constitution that would justify the use of force. . . . The Constitution vests the President with full "executive power" and designates him "Commander in Chief" of the Armed Forces. Together, these provisions are a substantive grant of broad war power that authorizes the President to unilaterally use military force in defense of the United States's national security.[24]

But that "substantive grant" extended yet farther. When dealing with potential limits on the interrogation of prisoners, for example—in plain English, when considering prohibitions against torture—the administration asserted that "Congress can no more interfere with the President's conduct of the interrogation of enemy combatants than it can dictate strategic or tactical decisions on the battlefield."[25] Additionally, who might be designated an "enemy combatant," or what constituted torture itself, for the purposes of American law and international treaty obligations, was at the president's discretion. Courts and Congress had no jurisdiction.[26]

The theoretical basis of the administration's approach was perhaps most extended publicly in justifying an inherent presidential power to order surveillance of Americans' communications with people abroad. This, the Justice Department argued, was a "fundamental incident" of warfare, "supported by the President's well-recognized inherent constitutional authority as Commander in Chief and sole organ for the Nation in foreign affairs to conduct warrantless surveillance of enemy forces for intelligence purposes to detect and disrupt armed attacks on the United States. The President has the chief responsibility under the Constitution to protect America from attack, and the Constitution gives the President the authority necessary to fulfill that solemn responsibility." As before, any statute that sought to limit the president's "core exercise of Commander in Chief control" was simply unconstitutional and did not need to be enforced.[27]

Again, to the extent an exclusive executive power is infringed, this argument is valid. But the boundaries of the "core" of the commander-in-chief authority are highly contested. (Justice Scalia's argument above, remember, received only his vote—with seven against.) Thus the key addition, over time, to the basic notion of a unitary executive—that the executive power was the indivisible purview of the president—was the key proviso that the scope of that executive power was also *defined* entirely by the president. This was truest in wartime—but at the same time the president was allowed to define the parameters of war and peace. If so, the theoretical claim that Congress could not infringe legislatively on the president's unilateral authority had new practical resonance. For if the president was the only actor who could decide what presidential powers comprised, not only could he act when Congress had not spoken on a given topic, but even in the face of congressional opposition. Indeed, that opposition was constitutionally illegitimate.

A UNITARY EXECUTIVE IN PRACTICE

As the examples above already suggest, the tangible issues raised in the context of the Bush theory of presidential power are literally those of life and death. The administration's most salient and controversial actions took place in the national security arena, girded by its claims about the commander-in-chief power. The president designated captured terrorist suspects—even American citizens—as "unlawful enemy combatants," outside the realm of civilian courts and the rules of due process. They were to be tried, if at all, by military tribunals themselves established by presidential order. Suspects were picked up, anywhere in the world, and secretly transported to "black sites" established to detain and interrogate them. That interrogation utilized techniques long renounced by American policy makers and military leaders as uncivilized, contrary to American law and treaty commitments, and anyway counterproductive. It was supported by an immense surveillance infrastructure built and supported by a classified budget. Money and matériel were moved around the globe, from Afghanistan to the Middle East (long before any publicly proclaimed interest in invading Iraq). The administration negotiated pacts with foreign governments, including a status-of-forces agreement with Iraq governing American troop commitments and a variety of basing (and prison-sharing) agreements, without putting them into treaties requiring Senate ratification.[28]

When Congress did seek to regulate, it found it difficult to gain a foothold. In a well-known case, when legislators passed a law banning "cruel, unusual, or degrading treatment or punishment" by U.S. personnel against any "individual in the custody or under the physical control of the United States government," anywhere in the world, the president signed it. But shortly afterward, he issued a statement clarifying that he would implement the section only to the extent it was "consistent with the constitutional authority of the President to oversee the unitary executive branch and as Commander in Chief and as consistent with the constitutional limitations on the judicial power."[29] It would be enforced, in short, as—and if—the president saw fit.

This example brought the practice of signing statements from the fine print of scholarly footnotes to the headlines. However, it was only one manifestation of a remarkably consistent strategy across eight years. Signing statements, while a practice that extended back to the nineteenth century, had been used only occasionally; for the Bush administration they became a systematic means of establishing control over policy implementation. By one count, Bush issued more than all his predecessors combined—objecting to nearly 1,200 provisions in more than 170 laws.[30] These provided a new boilerplate, repeated so frequently as to numb opposition: across every substantive realm, Congress only "purported" to act; the president had, as a matter of fact, "Constitutional authority to supervise the unitary executive branch." In rejecting congressional reporting requirements, standards for the qualifications of appointees, and other bureaucratic procedures, the administration went far beyond the formulaic to impose centralized direction of what the departments and agencies did, what credentials their personnel held, what information they released, with whom they communicated. As with the Detainee Treatment Act, presidential preferences in these regards were intended to override the language of the law he had just signed.

In some cases, as suggested at the outset, the president's claims had merit (though if so, he could have chosen to veto the legislation outright). But the executive bureaucracy is a battlefield of its own. Departments and agencies report to the president, but have conflicting loyalties, since they are created and funded by Congress and subject to constant demands from various constituencies. Thus, presidents' preferences are far from automatically enforced upon the permanent government. Signing statements provided one means of providing presidential direction. As Bush staffer Brad Berenson observed, referring to Cheney aide David Addington and his role in systematizing signing statements, such efforts served to "unite two of Addington's passions. One is executive power. And the other is the inner alleyways of bureaucratic combat. It's a way to advance executive power through those inner alleyways."[31]

How effectively that power was thus advanced awaits further study. After all, signing statements only carve out a claim, rather than achieving the substance of that claim directly. A study by the Government Accountability Office (GAO) in 2008 did find that twenty of twenty-nine selected provisions had been implemented by executive agencies in accordance with the statements.[32]

In any case, such statements were hardly the only tool designed to wrest bureaucratic behavior away from congressional influence. Executive orders and their cousins—proclamations, administrative directives, national security directives, presidential decision memoranda, and the like—have also become important mechanisms for presidents for shaping the implementation of key policies. For example, an early Obama administration memorandum to the secretary of health and human services rescinded two earlier restrictions placed on states' ability to regulate their children's health insurance programs.[33] Executive orders, further, may sometimes serve as substitutes for legislative action, as the example that led off this chapter made clear. As then Clinton aide (and now Obama chief of staff) Rahm Emanuel put it in 1998, "Sometimes we use [an executive order] in reaction to legislative delay or setbacks. Obviously, you'd rather pass legislation that can do X, but you're willing to make whatever progress you can on an agenda item."[34]

Another way to make progress—sometimes, again, by eliding the intended meaning of statutory language—is through the issuance of regulations. To control those, every president since Reagan has utilized a form of "central clearance" providing regulatory review within the Office of Management and Budget (OMB). Since regulations are usually boring (at best), this is a usefully low-salience way to manipulate policy outcomes.[35]

Reagan's original executive order required the "potential benefits to society" of any new regulation to outweigh its potential costs; this was strengthened in 1985, extending OMB's reach to agency "pre-rulemaking activities," and in 2007 by including "significant guidance documents" (advisory opinions that did not reach the formal status of rules) as well.[36] The 2007 order also required a new political appointee to sign off on anything included in an agency's annual rulemaking plan.

In so doing the White House hoped to forestall agency activism before it wandered up to either end of Pennsylvania Avenue. As a backstop, though, presidential staffers energetically monitored, and intervened in, a wide range of bureaucratic activities that threatened to shift policy from presidential preferences. "Science," broadly speaking, was a key target, attracting charges that ideology trumped research in areas ranging from climate change to workplace safety standards to the evaluation of toxic chemicals. Executive Office of the President (EOP) staff even weighed in on a Commerce Department measure seeking to avoid collisions between ships and whales.[37]

The process as it has developed is mainly off-the-record, since Congress normally vests rulemaking power with the agency, not the president. But it is no less effective at shaping outcomes for that. In 2008, for instance, a major regulatory change in how government would treat greenhouse gas emissions was preempted by White House resistance, forcing the Environmental Protection Agency back to the drawing board.[38]

This sort of tight control tends to deny the value of extra-executive (indeed, nonpoliticized) input. And the administration's efforts to control the flow of information within and between the branches went far beyond the regulatory arena. National security was one area, naturally, where access to information was limited, the ability of government officials to classify information as secret greatly expanded, and the information *de*classified often chosen selectively in order to make a particular case. The release of CIA agent Valerie Plame's name drew wide attention; but more troubling, perhaps, was the way intelligence was presented in the lead-up to the Iraq War. In 2002, for example, House Majority Leader Dick Armey (R-TX) was sceptical of the threat posed by Iraq to the United States—until he was briefed by the vice president. According to Armey, Cheney told him that Saddam Hussein had made significant progress toward building a miniature nuclear weapon and, further, that the Al Qaeda network was "working with [Hussein] and his family" to provide a delivery system for those weapons. Neither claim had any grounding in the available evidence. And postwar reporting has unearthed numerous stories detailing the institutional means by which at best uncertain intelligence—about uranium enrichment or missile launch tubes—was smoothed into plausible accusation, as it moved up the White House hierarchy.[39]

The control of information thus meant the control of outcomes. Nor was this limited to national security policy: from the outset, the White House staked out aggressive ground on issues of executive privilege more generally. A telling summary of the administration's attitude toward the other branches of government in this regard comes from what the administration intended as "a demonstrative use of power" involving its refusal to release records pertaining to an energy task force to the GAO, Congress's auditing agency.[40]

The information itself, in this case, was not important (indeed, the GAO was asking for very little). The principle that information could be withheld, however, was crucial. If it could be established, *Washington Post* reporter Barton Gellman noted, it would show that "a president possessed of his rightful powers, untrammelled by Congress, could work great change by regulation and executive order alone." Thus eventually the administration argued in court that Congress had no power to review how information of any sort traveled, "within the unitary structure of the Executive." While the ultimate judicial decision did not endorse the full breadth of this claim, it did give the administration a victory, placing the burden of obtaining information on those seeking it, even before requiring the president to make a formal claim of executive privilege.[41]

In this vein, the president also prevented his staff from testifying before congressional investigators. When a furor arose over partisan hiring and retention of U.S. attorneys, the White House refused to allow officials to appear before Congress to testify, offering only interviews "without the need for oath, transcript, subsequent testimony, or the subsequent issuance of subpoenas." When legislators balked and threatened contempt charges, the administration replied that since Justice Department prosecutors reported hierarchically to the president, he could mandate they not pursue such charges. There was an echo here of the presidential claims advanced in *U.S. v. Nixon*, where Nixon argued he could not be pursued by a prosecutor who, as a presidential subordinate, could be ordered not to pursue him.[42] The result showed less contempt of Congress, than contempt *for* Congress.

These developments, obviously, have important ramifications for the ability of Congress to conduct oversight. Actions kept secret cannot by definition be overseen; information withheld cannot be evaluated.

But that in turn assumes a desire to conduct oversight. And as two long-time observers of the Washington scene have observed, "when George Bush became president, oversight largely disappeared."[43]

THE HILL FIGHTS BACK?

In March 2008, Rep. Gary Ackerman (D-NY) convened a hearing on the proposed status-of-forces agreement with Iraq. A State Department official argued that the agreement was not a treaty and did not need to be one—and thus, it did not require Senate ratification or indeed any congressional approbation at all.

Ackerman exploded, "Does this administration think that anything it wants to do that's not in the Constitution—or that [what] is in the Constitution can be twisted any which way that they want, to come out with the outcome that they want, and ignore what everybody else thinks is a constitutional requirement?"

State's answer—"Certainly not, Mr. Chairman"—did not appease. Ackerman continued to rage: "The Constitution is a document. It's not a hypothetical. This is not a theory that we're discussing. The trouble with the administration is that it thinks that the Constitution is optional. It seems to me that it's already been ratified."[44]

Such a complaint rhetorically recalled the 1970s congressional resurgence. Yet it was the exception, not the rule. Nor did it achieve any substantive result. More commonly, accompanying what conservative columnist George Will called the "executive truculence" of the Bush administration was a long trend of congressional acquiescence. Moreover, legislators did not merely accept presidential claims but delegated additional powers to the presidency.[45]

The immediate context for Will's lament was the massive bank bailout bill passed toward the end of the 110th Congress, but the pattern of empowerment was clear before that.[46] From the PATRIOT Act (twice) to the Military Commissions Act to the Foreign Intelligence Surveillance Act Amendments, Congress was generally ready to give the president the enlarged powers he said he needed, or to legitimate retrospectively those he had exercised unilaterally. The efforts to prohibit torture noted above came a full eighteen months after the infamous photos from Abu Ghraib prison spotlighted the dark side of the war on terror.

And while the Bush administration made broad claims about its war powers, before fully proceeding with its commitments of U.S. forces in Afghanistan and Iraq it did ask for and receive statutory sanction. In September 2001, Congress, finding that "the President has authority under the Constitution to take action to deter and prevent acts of international terrorism against the United States," gave him wide latitude "to use all necessary and appropriate force against those nations, organizations, or persons he determines planned, authorized, committed, or aided the terrorist attacks that occurred on September 11, 2001, or harbored such organizations or persons." In October 2002, legislators likewise declared that "the President is authorized to use the Armed Forces of the United States as he determines to be necessary and appropriate in order to . . . defend the national security of the United States against the continuing threat posed by Iraq." Five years later, they approved an expanded program of covert action against Iran.[47]

If providing less than he had apparently asked for in each case, these delegations nonetheless gave President Bush massive grants of discretionary authority. The administration argued later that its surveillance program was an "incident of war" activated by the 2001 resolution. Certainly the Supreme Court, in its 2004 *Hamdi* decision, would read that authorization's language as sufficient to allow the president to name and detain American citizens as enemy combatants. Some lawmakers said this grant was unintended; but Congress never clarified its intent—and in the Military Commissions Act of 2006 it sought to cement the president's authority into statute. (At least one senator argued that the bill was "patently unconstitutional on its face"—but voted for it anyway.)[48]

And if legislators felt manipulated by the use of intelligence by the administration as it sought war with Iraq, they did not do much to fight back. No more than six senators and a "handful" of House members ever read the full National Intelligence Estimate available to them in 2002.[49] Those that were more widely (if vaguely) briefed on intelligence issues, members of the intelligence committees and the leadership, did nothing to stop the administration moving forward on issues of surveillance, rendition, "black sites," and "enhanced interrogation," even when they had private doubts. Some, even Democrats, strongly supported the president's actions on issues such as domestic surveillance. Others pushed the administration to go further. When four members of the legislative leadership were briefed about interrogation techniques such as waterboarding in 2002, for example, "no objections were raised. Instead, at least two lawmakers in the room asked the CIA to push harder." After Abu Ghraib, the message from senior members to those seeking additional oversight was crystal clear: "No more hearings."[50]

The September 11 attacks were obviously part of the reason for legislative passivity. But they are not the whole story—that comprises a general loss of institutional pride tied to a polarized (and, as it went on, additionally polarizing) political warfare. Legislators did not insist on their prerogatives, whether the power of the purse or of informational oversight. Instead, Norman Ornstein argues, "the Republican leaders in both houses of Congress made the decision that they were going to be field soldiers in the president's army, rather than members of an independent branch of government."[51] This in turn meant that regular legislative process was upended, with an aim toward quick results rather than good policy, shutting out minority input (sometimes by physical exclusion) and actively avoiding lengthy and thoughtful deliberation. Members spent fewer days in session and turned key decisions over to their party leadership ("We're just told how to vote," said Rep. Jim Cooper (D-TN). "We're treated like mushrooms most of the time.") Budgets were produced late, or not at all, making a mockery of the systematic deliberation envisioned by the Congressional Budget Act. Debate turned angry, and personal. The result, as Ornstein and his coauthor Thomas Mann have comprehensively concluded, was a "broken branch."[52]

LOOKING AHEAD

As a new president and new Congress took their places in January 2009, change was in the air. Would it infuse interbranch relations as well?

In part, the rise of presidential unilateralism arises from simple pragmatism. It is difficult to provide direction to an enormous nation, with an enormous bureaucracy, in the face of enormous public expectations, without centralized executive authority. The discursive and dilatory nature of congressional debate will often seem, as John Yoo testified in 2002, "a luxury we cannot afford."[53]

Further, from the president's perspective, seeking congressional legitimation often means (as one Bush aide put it) that "you will never get everything that you want. So, why wait weeks and get eighty-five percent of what you want, if you can get a hundred percent of what you want, and get it immediately, by doing it on your own?"[54]

The temptations to unilateralism, then, are real—even when not backstopped with the expansive theory of inherent authority outlined above or even exigent crisis. Recall again that while the consistency, clarity, and scope of the Bush administration's strategy on this score were new, the capacity for presidential "imperialism" had been largely rebuilt before Bush took office.

Recent campaigns suggest the question for the future, too, remains one of "positionality" more than personality. In 2004 the Democratic nominee, Senator John Kerry, argued that his vote approving the use of force in Iraq was superfluous: "We did not give the president any authority that the president of the United States didn't have."[55] In 2008, Clinton chief of staff Leon Panetta—who would become President Obama's CIA director—observed, "I don't think any president walks into their job and starts thinking about how they can minimize their authority."[56]

Barack Obama walked into that job with a mixed record on such matters. During the campaign, he had spoken out against the detention of American citizens as "enemy combatants." As a U.S. senator, Obama voted against the Military Commissions Act and sponsored a bill specifying that "any offensive military action taken by the United States against Iran must be explicitly authorized by Congress." But he also voted for the reauthorization of the PATRIOT Act, endorsing its major expansion of domestic law enforcement power, as well as for the FISA Amendments Act legalizing (with some limits) the president's surveillance initiative. (Thus, his campaign statements arguing that the president should comply with FISA remained operative—but FISA changed, in the president's favor.) He argued that "no one doubts that it is appropriate to use signing statements to protect a president's constitutional prerogatives," but added that "it is a clear abuse of power to use such statements as a license to evade laws that the president does not like or as an end-run around provisions designed to foster accountability."[57]

Early on, President Obama cut through this ambiguity to signal significant changes to his predecessor's policies. In his inaugural address, he talked of "ideals" that "still light the world" and pledged that "we will not give them up for expedience's sake." He issued a series of orders expanding government transparency; pledging the closure of the Guantanamo Bay detention facility; reviewing "detention policy options" generally and the detention of Ali Al-Marri specifically (as the sole enemy combatant still held in the United

States); and "ensuring legal interrogations."[58] In the last order, most notably, Obama rejected the array of administration legal opinions underpinning the broadest reaches of the theory of the unitary executive described here. This was a major shift, buried in bureaucratic boilerplate: "From this day forward, . . . officers, employees, and other agents of the United States Government . . . may not, in conducting interrogations, rely upon any interpretation of the law governing interrogation . . . issued by the Department of Justice between September 11, 2001, and January 20, 2009."[59]

Even so, it was notable that the new administration's reversal of its predecessor's unilateral actions was conducted unilaterally—executive orders were changed by executive order. In the first two weeks of his term, President Obama issued ten formal orders and another ten memoranda to the executive agencies, on topics ranging from automobile emissions to Gazan refugees. He rejected the substance of past policy, that is, but not the manner of its formulation. And while the meat of the orders mattered, so, potentially, did the ellipses: in the executive order on interrogations noted above, for instance, they contain the proviso "unless the Attorney General with appropriate consultation provides further guidance." Then, in early February, the Obama Justice Department, to shrieks of protest from civil libertarians, endorsed the Bush administration strategy of invoking the "state secrets doctrine" in a court case involving the rendition program. The case, administration attorneys argued, should be dismissed, since even discussing it in court could jeopardize national security.[60]

As this suggests, it will be challenging for the new administration to live up to its stated ideals with regard to enforcing transparency and limiting unilateralism. It will be just as challenging for a Democratic congressional majority, with a vested interest in seeing the president "succeed," to challenge presidential prerogative. Will the majority once more see itself as working for, rather than with, the president? Will oversight wither? Will majority obduracy continue to shut out minority complaints?

It is hard to know. A large economic stimulus package in early 2009 passed on near-perfect party lines, like many a bill before it. But during the debate, Obama visited Capitol Hill twice to meet with the Republican conference. He even brought cookies to legislators visiting the White House. This suggested that outreach was seen as politically beneficial, itself an important development. Presidents bearing cookies do not seem very imperial.

And though the cookies will surely crumble, the image reinforces an important point: that to frame the larger question in terms of the imperial presidency—or the presidency, period—"versus" the Hill is to start with a counterproductive proposition. For public policy is not a zero-sum game. The idea is not for one branch of government to "win," but for all those branches to work for all of us, and with each other. As Justice Jackson noted: "While the Constitution diffuses power the better to secure liberty, it also contemplates that practice will integrate the dispersed powers into a workable government. It enjoins upon its branches separateness but interdependence, autonomy but reciprocity."

That sort of relationship must be long-term. The unilateral action justified by the unitary executive theory achieved impressive short-term results for President Bush. Having entered the Oval Office determined to strengthen its autonomy vis-à-vis legislative constraints—and to extend its control over the behavior of the executive branch more generally—Bush did just that. At the same time, though, his insistence on unilateralism, and on its infallibility, forfeited much comity and credibility. The unitary executive, in practice if not necessarily in theory, rests on the idea that, as a Justice Department attorney told the Senate in 2006, "the President is always right." Yet democracy itself rests on a different assumption: as political scientist E. E. Schattschneider pointed out long ago, it "is a political system for people who are not too sure they are right."[61] Efficiency is one interest among many others, including transparency, inclusion, and the protection of civil liberties. In our separated system, legitimating large-scale change requires bridging its divisions, building coalitions persuaded the president *is* right.

Since the September 11 attacks, the need to make "tough" choices has been frequently invoked. But unilateral authority is the easy way out. It is easier for legislators and voters to delegate powers to the president than to deliberate on their proper scope. It is easier to prevent debate than to allow it, easier to stop opponents from participating than to risk their upsetting your priorities.

Congress's job is not to manage policy implementation on a day-to-day basis. Nor is it always to pass a new law: the failures of the 1970s resurgence regime bear witness to the inadequacy of creating a statutory framework in the absence of political will reinforcing its component parts. But it has a critical task nonetheless. It must use debate and deliberation to distill priorities and set clear standards, to oversee and judge by those standards the decisions and actions taken, to expose both the bad and good efforts of government to public scrutiny, and to revisit its earlier debate in the light of later events. All this is Congress's job; and debate, judgment, and oversight are delegated to other actors in the system at our potential peril. As we accept that executive discretion is increasingly important, it is all the more critical that such discretion is exercised within boundaries arrived at by the democratic process.

And so we must return not only to Justice Jackson but to Justice Scalia. As he wrote in *Hamdi*: "The Founders warned us about the risk—and equipped us with a Constitution designed to deal with it." Accepting, and empowering, that judgment is the truly tough—but imperative—choice.

NOTES

1. Quoted in Robert Schlesinger, *White House Ghosts* (New York: Simon & Schuster, 2008), 48.

2. Michael A. Genovese, *Memo to a New President* (New York: Oxford University Press, 2008), 161; Warner quoted in Jonathan Mahler, "After the Imperial Presidency," *New York Times Magazine*, November 9, 2008.

3. Michael D. Shear, "President's Stimulus Plan Tests Powers of Persuasion," *Washington Post*, February 6, 2009, A8; more generally, see Andrew Rudalevige, "The Executive Branch and the Legislative Process," in *The Executive Branch*, eds. Joel Aberbach and Mark Peterson (New York: Oxford University Press, 2006).

4. "President's Remarks at Faith-Based and Community Initiatives Conference," Office of the White House Press Secretary, March 3, 2004; and see Executive Orders 13199 and 13279.

5. Mahler, "After the Imperial Presidency"; Arthur M. Schlesinger Jr., *The Imperial Presidency* (Boston: Houghton Mifflin, 1973); Andrew Rudalevige, *The New Imperial Presidency: Renewing Presidential Power after Watergate* (Ann Arbor: University of Michigan Press, 2005).

6. Quoted in Lisa Caruso, "You've Got to Know When to Hold 'Em," *National Journal*, July 12, 2003, 2258.

7. Sarah A. Binder, Thomas E. Mann, Norman J. Ornstein, and Molly Reynolds, *Mending the Broken Branch: Assessing the 110th Congress, Anticipating the 111th* (Washington, DC: The Brookings Institution, January 2009), 13.

8. Madison, "Federalist No. 51"; Jackson, concurring opinion to *Youngstown Sheet and Tube Co. v. Sawyer*, 343 U.S. 579 (1952); Eisenhower, Address at the Annual Convention of the National Young Republican Organization, June 11, 1953, available at www.presidency.ucsb.edu/ws/index.php?pid=9603&st=&st1 (accessed February 11, 2009).

9. Hamilton, "Federalist No. 70."

10. Edward S. Corwin, *The President: Office and Powers*, 5th rev. ed. (New York: New York University Press, 1984), 4.

11. Schlesinger, *The Imperial Presidency;* Rudalevige, *New Imperial Presidency,* chap. 3–4; James Sundquist, *The Decline and Resurgence of Congress* (Washington, DC: The Brookings Institution, 1981).

12. George W. Bush, "President Bush Holds Press Conference," Office of the White House Press Secretary, March 13, 2002; Richard Cheney, "Interview of the Vice President by Campbell Brown, NBC News," Office of the White House Press Secretary, January 28, 2002.

13. Rudalevige, *New Imperial Presidency*, 101 and chap. 6.

14. Beschloss quoted in Tom Shales, "From President Bush, a Speech Filled with Assurance and Reassurance," *Washington Post*, September 21, 2001, C1; see, among many others, Rudalevige, *New Imperial Presidency*; Peter Irons, *War Powers: How the Imperial Presidency Hijacked the Constitution* (New York: Metropolitan Books, 2005); Charlie Savage, *Takeover: The Return of the Imperial Presidency and the Subversion of American Democracy* (Boston: Little, Brown, 2007); "The Imperial

Presidency 2.0," *New York Times*, January 7, 2007; and, in rebuttal, Gary J. Schmitt, *The Myth of the (Bush) Imperial Presidency* (Washington, DC: American Enterprise Institute, January 2009).

15. For example, "President's Statement on H.R. 4954, the Security and Accountability for Every Port Act of 2006," Office of the White House Press Secretary, October 13, 2006.

16. Alexander Hamilton, "Federalist No. 70." The Twenty-second Amendment imposing term limits was ratified in 1951.

17. Scalia, dissenting opinion in *Morrison v. Olson*, 487 U.S. 654 (1988).

18. Article I begins, "All legislative powers *herein granted* shall be vested in a Congress of the United States . . ." (emphasis added).

19. Steven G. Calabresi and Kevin H. Rhodes, "The Structural Constitution: Unitary Executive, Plural Judiciary," *Harvard Law Review* 105 (1992): 1215. This work is consolidated in Calabresi and Christopher S. Yoo, *The Unitary Executive: Presidential Power from Washington to Bush* (New Haven, CT: Yale University Press, 2008). But see Robert V. Percival, "Presidential Management of the Administrative State: The Not-So-Unitary Executive," *Duke Law Journal* 51 (2001); Jeremy Bailey, "The New Unitary Executive and Democratic Theory: The Problem of Alexander Hamilton," *American Political Science Review* 102 (November 2008): 453–65.

20. Jess Bravin, "Judge Alito's View of the Presidency: Expansive Powers," *Wall Street Journal*, January 5, 2006, A1; Jeffrey Rosen, "Power of One," *New Republic*, July 24, 2006.

21. Hearings before the Senate Subcommittee on Intergovernmental Relations, "Executive Privilege, Secrecy in Government, Freedom of Information," 93d Congress, 1st session, April 10, 1973, volume I, 20; Barton Gellman, *Angler: The Cheney Vice Presidency* (New York: Penguin Press, 2008), 105.

22. John Yoo, *The Powers of War and Peace* (Chicago: University of Chicago Press, 2005).

23. Solicitor General Theodore B. Olson, et al., Brief for the Petitioners, *Cheney v. U.S. District Court for the District of Columbia*, U.S. Supreme Court case 03-475, April 2004.

24. From brief in *Doe v. Bush*, U.S. Circuit Court of Appeals, 1st Circuit (03-1266).

25. U.S. Department of Justice, "The President's Constitutional Authority to Conduct Military Operations against Terrorists and Nations Supporting Them," Office of Legal Counsel (OLC), September 25, 2001; U.S. Department of Justice, "Re: Standards of Conduct for Interrogation under 18 U.S.C. §§2340-2340A," Office of Legal Counsel, August 1, 2002.

26. See Executive Order 13440, July 2007. Another OLC opinion defining torture was issued on December 30, 2004. It denounced torture but did not argue earlier opinions were substantively incorrect. See Rudalevige, *New Imperial Presidency*, 225–33, 248–53.

27. U.S. Department of Justice, *Legal Authorities Supporting the Activities of the National Security Agency Described by the President*, January 19, 2006, 1–2, 10–11, 17, 30–31.

28. Louis Fisher, *The Constitution and 9/11* (Lawrence: University Press of Kansas, 2008); Jack Goldsmith, *The Terror Presidency* (New York: W.W. Norton, 2007); Jane Mayer, *The Dark Side* (New York: Doubleday, 2008); James P. Pfiffner, *Power Play: The Bush Presidency and the Constitution* (Washington, DC: The Brookings Institution, 2008); John Yoo, *War by Other Means* (New York: Atlantic Monthly Press, 2006).

29. Detainee Treatment Act of 2005, Section 1003; "President's Statement on Signing of H.R. 2863," Office of the White House Press Secretary, December 30, 2005.

30. Christopher Kelley provided this count, updated to October 15, 2008; see www.users.muohio.edu/kelleycs/ (accessed February 27, 2009); see also Kelley and Bryan W. Marshall, "The Last Word: Presidential Power and the Role of Signing Statements," *Presidential Studies Quarterly* 38 (June 2008): 248–67, and Savage, *Takeover*, chap. 10.

31. Quoted in Savage, *Takeover*, 236.

32. *Presidential Signing Statements: Agency Implementation of Selected Provisions of Law*, GAO-08-553T, U.S. Government Accountability Office, March 11, 2008. It is not clear this is a representative sample.

33. See Memorandum on State Children's Health Insurance Program (SCHIP), Office of the White House Press Secretary, February 4, 2009.

34. Quoted in Alexis Simendinger, "The Paper Wars," *National Journal*, July 25, 1998, 1737.

35. Cornelius Kerwin, *Rulemaking: How Government Agencies Write Law and Make Policy*, 3d ed. (Washington, DC: CQ Press, 2003); William F. West, "The Institutionalization of Regulatory Review: Organizational Stability and Neutral Competence at OIRA," *Presidential Studies Quarterly* 35 (March 2005): 76–93.

36. Curtis Copeland, "Executive Order 13422: An Expansion of Presidential Influence in the Rulemaking Process," *Presidential Studies Quarterly* 37 (September 2007): 531–44.

37. Christopher Lee, "Scientists Report Political Interference," *Washington Post*, April 24, 2008; Seth Shulman, *Undermining Science* (Berkeley: University of California Press, 2008); "Toxic Chemicals," testimony of the GAO's John Stephenson before the Senate Committee on Environment and Public Works, April 29, 2008; Rep. Henry Waxman, "Responses to 16 November Questions from White House on Right Whale Ship Strike Reduction Final Rule," at oversight.house.gov/documents/20080430104534.pdf (accessed February 27, 2009).

38. John Shiffman and John Sullivan, "An Eroding Mission at EPA," *Philadelphia Inquirer*, December 7, 2008, A1.

39. Gellman, *Angler*, 215–22; James Pfiffner and Mark Phythian, eds., *Intelligence and National Security Policy Making on Iraq: British and American Views* (Manchester, UK: Manchester University Press, 2008); Paul Pillar, "Intelligence, Policy, and the War in Iraq," *Foreign Affairs* 85 (March/April 2006).

40. John Gribbin, a friend of Cheney's, quoted in Gellman, *Angler*, 93.

41. "Memorandum of Points and Authorities in Support of Defendant's Motion to Dismiss," *Walker v. Cheney*, U.S. District Court for the District of Columbia, 48ff;

Cheney v. U.S. District Court for the District of Columbia, 542 U.S. 367 (2004); and see Gellman, *Angler*, 106–7.

42. Letter from Fred Fielding to Chairman Leahy et al., Office of the White House Press Secretary, March 20, 2007; Dan Eggen and Amy Goldstein, "Broader Privilege Claimed in Firings," *Washington Post*, July 20, 2007, A1; *U.S. v. Nixon*, 418 U.S. 683 (1974). Administration officials preferred to cite "Prosecution for Contempt of Congress of an Executive Branch Official Who Has Asserted a Claim of Executive Privilege," 8 U.S. Opinions of the Office of Legal Counsel 101, 1984 WL 178358.

43. Thomas E. Mann and Norman J. Ornstein, *The Broken Branch*, paperback ed. (New York: Oxford University Press, 2008), 151.

44. House Foreign Affairs Committee subcommittee hearing of March 4, 2008.

45. George F. Will, "Making Congress Moot," *Washington Post*, December 21, 2008, B7.

46. Rudalevige, *New Imperial Presidency*, chap. 2.

47. P.L. 107-40; P.L. 107–243; and see Seymour Hersh, "Preparing the Battlefield," *New Yorker*, July 7, 2008. Note that the Bush OLC asserted that the authorization was not necessary. Its September 25, 2001, opinion cited earlier states: "It [is] beyond question that the President has the plenary constitutional power to take such military actions as he deems necessary and appropriate to respond to the terrorist attacks. . . . Force can be used both to retaliate for those attacks, and to prevent and deter future assaults. . . . Military actions need not be limited to those . . . that participated in the attacks."

48. *Hamdi v. Rumsfeld*, 542 U.S. 507 (2004). Sen. Arlen Specter quoted in Charles Babington and Jonathan Weisman, "Senate Approves Detainee Bill Backed by Bush," *Washington Post*, September 29, 2006. The law *was* unconstitutional: see *Boumediene v. Bush*, 553 U.S. (2008).

49. Dana Priest, "Congressional Oversight of Intelligence Criticized," *Washington Post*, April 27, 2004, A1.

50. "Bush Says Bring It On," *Time*, January 3, 2006; Joby Warrick and Dan Eggen, "Hill Briefed on Waterboarding in 2002," *Washington Post*, December 9, 2007, A1; Mahler, "After the Imperial Presidency," quoting Sen. Ted Stevens (R-AK).

51. Quoted in Mahler, "After the Imperial Presidency."

52. Mann and Ornstein, *Broken Branch*; and see Binder et al., *Mending the Broken Branch*. For Cooper, see politics.nashvillepost.com/2009/02/03/the-coop-is-loose/ (accessed February 11, 2009).

53. Quoted in John E. Owens, "Presidential Power and Congressional Acquiescence in the 'War' on Terrorism," *Politics and Policy* 34 (2006): 270.

54. "Senior administration attorney" quoted in Savage, *Takeover*, 131.

55. Kerry, Democratic primary debate of February 27, 2004, partial transcript at transcripts.cnn.com/TRANSCRIPTS/0402/27/ltm.04.html (accessed February 11, 2009).

56. Panetta quoted in David Nather, "New Handshake, Same Grip," *CQ Weekly*, December 17, 2007, 3702; Keith Perine, "Detainee Rights Pose a Question for '08 Hopefuls," *CQ Weekly*, December 10, 2007, 3636.

57. Charlie Savage, "Barack Obama's Q&A," *Boston Globe*, December 20, 2007, available at www.boston.com/news/politics/2008/specials/CandidateQA/ObamaQA/ (accessed February 11, 2009).

58. See www.whitehouse.gov/briefing_room/PresidentialActions/ (accessed February 27, 2009). Al-Marri's case was moved into the civilian court system in late February 2009.

59. Executive Order 13491, Section 3(c).

60. John Schwartz, "Obama Backs Off a Reversal on Secrets," *New York Times*, February 9, 2009, A12.

61. Dana Milbank, "It's Bush's Way or the Highway on Guantanamo Bay," *Washington Post*, July 12, 2006, A2; E. E. Schattschneider, *Two Hundred Million Americans in Search of a Government* (New York: Holt, Rinehart and Winston, 1969), 53.

Chapter Nine

Executive Privilege and the Unitary Executive Theory in the George W. Bush Administration

Mark J. Rozell and Mitchel A. Sollenberger

A key element of the George W. Bush legacy will be his administration's varied attempts to vastly expand the powers of the presidency. Under the unitary executive theory that espouses the inherent authority of the president to act unilaterally in a number of areas, the president adopted broad-reaching and in some cases unprecedented efforts to expand the powers of the Oval Office. One of these areas, and the focus of this analysis, is the presidential authority to claim executive privilege, or the right to withhold documents and testimony from Congress, the judicial branch, and ultimately the public.

Bush's executive privilege actions had far-reaching consequences for the exercise of presidential powers. He did not act on executive privilege matters merely to legitimize and protect his well-established right to claim this constitutional-based authority under certain circumstances. Rather, the president used the privilege to broaden the scope of executive powers in ways that reached well beyond his predecessors' actions.

To take one example, toward the end of his administration Bush declared executive privilege to conceal from Congress documents regarding an Environmental Protection Agency (EPA) decision to deny the state of California the authorization to regulate the greenhouse gas emissions of vehicles (Bliley 2008). Bush reasoned that because the EPA decision involved White House discussions, he could withhold the documents. This action expanded executive privilege to include not only documents that deal directly with presidential decision making—the normally accepted limit to that power—but also ones concerning decisions made by agency officials. If executive privilege were accepted as so broad in scope, then whenever White House staffers advise an agency, the president can protect any related documents from disclosure. Acceptance of such a broad concept of the privilege would have far-reaching consequences for Congress's ability ever to conduct investigations of executive departments and agencies.

Bush's action in this case thus went well beyond the normal confines of executive privilege. Traditionally departments or agencies have not been able to guard information from Congress by claiming that they were advised by White House staff. Executive privilege in nearly all of its forms can be overcome by a showing of congressional need for information or in cases of alleged wrongdoing. In this situation the Bush administration attempted to pull an agency and its decision-making processes into the Executive Office of the President (EOP) in order to control the release of information to Congress. An understanding that White House assistance in nonpresidential decisions can somehow guard the executive branch from releasing information to Congress not only violates principles of interbranch cooperation, but it also sets a dangerous precedent that future presidents can wall their administrations off from congressional oversight.

This paper describes and analyzes various other significant attempts by the Bush administration to employ the unitary executive theory in its efforts to conceal information from Congress and the public. In what follows, we establish the parameters of an analysis of Bush's legacy by briefly reviewing the principle of executive privilege and the unitary executive theory. We then critique a variety of attempts by the Bush administration to effectively join executive privilege under the broader theory of a unitary executive. We conclude with an analysis of the future implications of Bush's actions and why it is essential that the new administration avoid the pitfalls of overreaching in the use of executive privilege.

EXECUTIVE PRIVILEGE

Executive privilege is the constitutionally based principle that allows the president, or high-level executive branch officials under the direction of the president, to withhold information (usually documents or testimony) from entities with compulsory power. The Supreme Court has legitimized this presidential power while also qualifying that executive privilege is not absolute (*U.S. v. Nixon* 1974). It can be overcome by a showing of possible wrongdoing within the executive branch or by a congressional need for information for its legislative or oversight functions. Executive privilege dates back to the presidency of George Washington, although the phrase was not used until the presidency of Dwight Eisenhower.

The Supreme Court case of *United States v. Nixon*, several post-Watergate circuit court cases, and interchanges between the executive and legislative branches have established the broad contours of executive privilege. Specifically an executive branch claim of privilege is primarily based on four general areas: (1) presidential communications privilege; (2) deliberative process privilege; (3) national security, foreign relations, or military affairs (often referred to as state secrets); and (4) an ongoing law enforcement investigation.

The presidential communications privilege is one of the strongest areas to make an executive privilege claim but is limited by the same fundamental threshold concerns as the other categories. It is based on the constitutional separation of powers principle and the president's unique position in the governing system. The privilege claim applies to a president's decision making when carrying out a "quintessential and non-delegable Presidential power" such as the nomination or pardon powers (*In re Sealed Case* 1997, 752). Such a privilege claim will cover all documents, whether predecisional or postdecisional, but is not an absolute barrier. The claim only protects the communications of those who are personally advising, or preparing to advise, the president (i.e., White House staff). Congress can overcome this privilege with a showing of need and providing evidence that the information sought cannot be found elsewhere. The executive branch has traditionally yielded to the legislative branch when Congress is carrying out its legislative and oversight functions.

As defined by the Federal Circuit Court of the District of Columbia (*In re Sealed Case*, 1997, 746) there is a separate deliberative process privilege that has a much lower threshold to overcome, partially because it is a common law privilege. All executive branch officials are protected generally; however, only predecisional documents are covered and not those that state a policy decision or only contain factual information. In addition, like the presidential communications privilege, a showing of corruption or other wrongdoing will wipe away any protection that results from a claim of deliberative process privilege.

Certain court decisions have acknowledged the national security or state secrets component of executive privilege as a separate field for the protection of executive branch information (*U.S. v. Nixon* 1974, 706; *Harlow v. Fitzgerald* 1982, 812; *Committee on the Judiciary v. Miers et al.* 2008a, 3, 88). Despite the claims of some presidents that they possess exclusive control over military and foreign affairs, Congress has long been able to access executive branch information that legislators deem necessary to carry out their own foreign policy duties.

In the first example of an executive privilege claim by President George Washington, Congress sought information about a failed military expedition. Even though Washington determined that he possessed the authority to withhold information from Congress if doing so were in the national interest, the president determined in this case that he could disclose the information without any harm. Importantly, the president made the distinction between withholding information to protect the public interest and doing so to protect the administration from disclosures that might be embarrassing or politically damaging (Fisher 2004, 10–11; Rozell 2002, 29–30). The president did not conclude that Congress is shut out merely because a matter involved the military or national security. Like the executive communications and deliberative process privileges, national security cannot stand as an absolute shield to protect against allegations of corruption or other wrongdoing in the executive branch.

The final area that is sometimes used to make an executive privilege claim is an ongoing law enforcement investigation. This category is the most difficult for Congress to overcome because of due process concerns and the rule of law. Only after an investigation or when a trial has ended do legislative concerns overtake claims of executive branch autonomy. For example, in 2001 the Bush administration claimed executive privilege over documents relating to a closed Department of Justice (DOJ) investigation into FBI corruption with the Boston mob. There was no justification for withholding information in this case because it did not concern an ongoing investigation but rather one that had been closed for over twenty years (Rozell and Sollenberger 2008a, 3–8).

Presidents sometimes assert executive privilege based upon a combination of the deliberative process exemption and then one or more of the other categories. Doing so allows a president to claim broad protection of information over all aspects of the executive branch—not just presidential or White House concerns. The following analysis, including our critique of George W. Bush's expanded use of the unitary executive theory, should not be taken as a refutation of the core reasons for protecting in some cases predecisional discussions by executive branch officials. Certainly there is a need to ensure communications are not routinely made public. The Supreme Court did well in announcing such a principle in *United States v. Nixon*: there is a "valid need for protection of communications between high Government officials and those who advise and assist them in the performance of their manifold duties; the importance of this confidentiality is too plain to require further discussion. Human experience teaches that those who expect public dissemination of their remarks may well temper candor with a concern for appearances and for their own interests to the detriment of the decisionmaking process" (705). There is constitutional value in the president receiving candid advice from his White House staff with the expectation that subsequent disclosure is highly unlikely.

THE RISE OF THE UNITARY EXECUTIVE MOVEMENT

The danger of guarding information from disclosure is that all too often presidents have done so in order to conceal wrongdoing or as an attempt to expand their powers. Not all presidents have tried to advance their powers in a unitary manner. At times, Congress has pressed its own advantage in battling the executive branch. However, the drive and determination of those who advocate a unitary conception has rarely been matched.

The unitary executive movement is based on the theory that "the president, given 'the executive power' under the Constitution, has virtually all of that power, unchecked by Congress or the courts, especially in critical realms of authority" (MacKenzie 2008, 1). This theory has had many forceful advocates in the academic and political worlds. In 1960, Richard E. Neustadt suggested that the office of the chief executive is essentially divorced from the Constitution and that "presidential power is the power to persuade" (Neustadt 1960, 10). This viewpoint directly countered what had been the dominant view of such presidential scholars as Edward S. Corwin (1957) who believed that presidents could only exercise powers that were outlined in the Constitution. Neustadt thought that such a narrow view did not adequately explain the many dimensions of actual presidential power. After the presidency of Richard M. Nixon some presidential scholars began to rethink the Neustadt model. In his book *The Imperial Presidency*, Arthur M. Schlesinger Jr. argued that the president had gained more power than the Constitution provided. However, even while attacking the increase of executive power, he noted: "The answer to the runaway Presidency is not the messenger-boy Presidency . . . we need a strong Presidency—but a strong Presidency *within the Constitution*" (Schlesinger Jr. 1973, xxviii).

Despite pushing against what he saw as an imperial presidency, Schlesinger nonetheless left open the intellectual justifications that would later be advanced by unitary executive advocates. For example, contemporary scholars who defend a unitary model believe in a strong presidency that is based within the Constitution. The problem is that article II of the Constitution, according to unitary advocates, does not really limit executive power but instead expands it indefinitely through the use of the Vesting, Take Care, Oath, and Commander in Chief clauses. Today leading unitary executive scholars have used these textual arguments and various constitutional theories to press for greater presidential power. In their recent book titled *The Unitary Executive*, unitary proponents Stephen Calabresi and Christopher Yoo contend that "all of our nation's presidents have believed in the theory of the unitary executive." In fact, they say that the "Constitution gives presidents the power to control their subordinates by vesting all of the executive power in one, and only one, person: the president of the United States" (Calabresi and Yoo 2008, 4). "The executive branch's repeated and persistent opposition to any limits on the president's power to control the execution of federal law forecloses," according to them, "the argument that a 'gloss' on the meaning of the words 'the executive Power' has emerged, allowing Congress to create a headless fourth branch of government wielding executive power outside presidential control" (418).

The framework of the imperial presidency and unitary executive set the stage for presidents to use and expand executive privilege in a manner that went well beyond its traditional use. Certainly George W. Bush was not the first president to push the concept of the unitary executive to defend his expansive uses of executive privilege. Since the 1950s several chief executives have taken the position that such a privilege can and should be extended well beyond the White House.

Dwight D. Eisenhower argued that confidential communications are protected even when not made in the White House (Rozell 2002, 40). Richard M. Nixon maintained that executive privilege could be invoked by the president on behalf of all executive branch officials and that he could prevent Congress from calling any staff member to testify, "for their roles are in effect an extension of the president" (U.S. Congress 1973, 308). George H. W. Bush reasoned that senior department officials and policy makers are as well protected, when directed by the president to conceal information (Rozell 2002, 115–16). Even Bill Clinton took the position that Congress has no right to obtain documents and information regarding communications between the White House and various departments or agencies (128–31). In short, there is a history of presidents using what would be considered today a unitary executive model to expand the reach of executive privilege into all areas of the executive branch to protect information from disclosure.

In effect, some presidents have tried to take the higher threshold of protection that the presidential communications privilege gives and graft that onto the deliberative process privilege in order to protect all executive branch information from disclosure. The George W. Bush administration carried on this battle and introduced some of its own novel reasoning in an attempt to expand presidential control and power over all areas of the executive branch. Executive privilege did not escape Bush's sight and from early on in his presidency he sought to expand the capacity of that power to safeguard documents and communications.

PRESIDENTIAL PARDONS AND THE EXPANSION OF
EXECUTIVE BRANCH SECRECY POWERS

President Bush attempted to put his own unitary stamp on the presidential power of secrecy in 2002 when he directed his administration to refuse to release documents related to former president Bill Clinton's last-minute pardons. Although Bush never made a formal claim of executive privilege, the administration did use the codified version of the presidential communications privilege exemption found in the Freedom of Information Act (FOIA) to block access to the pardon files (*Judicial Watch v. Department of Justice* 2004, 1010). This incident parallels closely with the energy task force controversy involving Vice President Richard Cheney where the White House made secrecy claims based indirectly on executive privilege. Although again there was not a formal claim of executive privilege, in protecting the administration from having to release requested information regarding the energy task force hearings, Bush directed the vice president to invoke many of the traditional bases of a formal privilege claim (Rozell and Sollenberger 2009). In both of these cases, the failure to utter the words "executive privilege" did not matter because the administration advanced the same principle with different language.

The problem of withholding these pardon documents was that they were in the possession of the Justice Department's pardon office and they had never been seen by the president or any White House official. The question came down to whether the FOIA privilege exemption could be expanded to include documents that had never been directly associated with the president. The administration seemed to say it could. A Justice Department official remarked that "the pardon power is exclusively granted to the president" and any "information, any advice and any memos would be part of the deliberative process. We want to preserve the integrity of that process" (Bumiller 2002, A17). This understanding of what can be classified as privileged reaches beyond the traditional executive privilege areas of presidential communications and deliberative process. It was a more expansive position from what previous administrations had claimed in that it provided protection to all executive branch officials regardless of their association to the president or to the White House more generally.

In 2003 D.C. district court judge Gladys Kessler accepted the Bush administration's argument noting that the presidential communications privilege claimed in exemption 5 of FOIA "must be viewed in its broader, historical context, allowing presidential advisors to provide the President with the fullest and most candid information and advice regarding decisions to be made in many sensitive areas, including the granting or denial of pardon requests" (*Judicial Watch v. Department of Justice* 2003, 87). In light of this rather expansive reading of the presidential communications privilege, the case was appealed to the D.C. circuit court.

At the circuit court, writing for the majority, Judge Judith Rogers noted the importance of striking "a balance between the twin values of transparency and accountability of the executive branch on the one hand, and on the other hand, protection of the confidentiality of Presidential decisionmaking and the President's ability to obtain candid, informed advice" (*Judicial Watch v. Department of Justice* 2004, 1112). Rogers acknowledged that Congress had placed great emphasis on disclosure in FOIA requests. With that in mind, she declared that the presidential communications privilege only applies to documents "solicited and received" by the president or "his immediate White House advisers who have 'broad and significant responsibility for investigating the advice to be given the President'" (1114). Limiting the definition of executive privilege, the court said, recognized certain "principles underlying the presidential communications privilege" and conceded "the dangers of expanding it too far" (1114–15).

More specifically Rogers believed that an "extension of the privilege to internal Justice Department documents that never make their way to the Office of the President on the basis that the documents were created for the sole purpose of advising the President on a non-delegable duty is unprecedented and unwarranted" (1116–17). She warned that "a bright-line expanding the privilege could have the effect of inviting use of the presidential privilege to shield communications on which the President has no intention of relying in exercising his pardon duties, for the sole purpose of raising the burden for those who seek their disclosure" (1118).

The D.C. circuit court correctly balanced the competing needs for candor in presidential-level discussions and the goal of openness in government that Congress had intended when it established the FOIA provisions. All too often presidents try to modify legislative enactments not through the process of amending existing laws but by announcing a presidential right and expanding power without any constitutional, legal, or historical justification. In this case, the Justice Department tried to expand the definition of presidential communications privilege to reach down into all levels of the executive branch. If such a characterization held then any action by a department or agency would be given a much higher level of protection from disclosure. In a sense what the Justice Department wanted in this case was to make all departments and agencies an extension of the presidency and receive the benefits of constitutional protection of the office of the president. Extending presidential power and control into all levels of government is inherently dangerous. The circuit court was correct to reject this position and the ruling was a clear defeat for President Bush and unitary executive advocates.

EXECUTIVE PRIVILEGE AND ABSOLUTE IMMUNITY

President Bush pushed the bounds of presidential autonomy in another major controversy where he made multiple claims of executive privilege to conceal White House documents and to prevent current and former administration aides from testifying before Congress about the contentious decision to force the resignations of a number of U.S. attorneys. His claims of absolute immunity for current and former presidential aides led Congress to issue several subpoenas, a contempt resolution, and finally a judicial ruling that could force the executive branch to comply with a committee investigation.

At the heart of this controversy was the administration's decision to remove several U.S. attorneys, allegedly for reasons of poor job performance (Rozell and Sollenberger 2008b, 319–20). After reports surfaced in early 2007 that political considerations had come into play, the House and Senate Judiciary Committees launched investigations that remain ongoing as of this writing. After much battling between the branches the president made four executive privilege claims to block the disclosure of testimony and documents (Rozell and Sollenberger 2008b, 320–22). The White House reasoned that Bush made these claims "to protect a fundamental interest of the Presidency" by not revealing internal decision-making processes (Fielding 2007).

After repeated attempts to obtain testimony and documents related to the removals, the House Judiciary Committee held former White House counsel Harriet Miers and White House chief of staff Joshua Bolten in contempt of Congress (Lewis 2007, A13). In early 2008 the House of Representatives voted 223 to 32 to issue contempt citations against Miers and Bolten (Kane 2008, A4). The administration refused to enforce the contempt charges and the House quickly filed a lawsuit in the D.C. district court. The House requested that the court declare that Miers was not immune from testifying before a congressional committee and also sought the disclosure of documents withheld by Bolten (*Committee on the Judiciary v. Miers et al.* 2008a).

A central focus of this suit was the claim of absolute immunity that principal deputy assistant attorney general Stephen Bradbury articulated in his Office of Legal Counsel (OLC) July 10 memorandum. He declared that "since at least the 1940s, Administrations of both political parties have taken the position that 'the President and his immediate advisers are absolutely immune from testimonial compulsion by a Congressional committee . . . [which] may not be overborne by competing congressional interests'" (Bradbury 2007). Bradbury added the rationale that the "separation of powers principle" not only makes the president himself immune to testimony, but it also applies "to senior presidential advisers." Bradbury even broadened the absolute immunity claim to include former presidential aides such as Miers when Congress seeks "testimony about official matters that occurred during their time" in office (Bradbury 2007).

Yet it is inaccurate to claim that absolute immunity has a long history of protecting White House officials from compelled congressional testimony. Not even a claim of executive privilege has been successfully used to block executive branch advisers from appearing before Congress. As the House Judiciary Committee noted: "White House aides, in the past, have appeared before congressional committees in overwhelming numbers—both voluntarily and pursuant to subpoenas. Since World War II, close presidential advisers—including former Counsels and Special Assistants—have appeared before congressional committees to offer their testimony on more than *seventy* occasions" (Plaintiff's Motion 2008, 32). In addition, the argument that absolute immunity protects White House officials from testifying in cases of wrongdoing is misguided because executive privilege does not provide such protection. No theory of executive autonomy protects against corruption or wrongdoing. The D.C. circuit court has recognized the duty to shed light on "government misconduct" and that privilege claims do not overwhelm the vital need to ensure the existence of honest and effective government (*In re Sealed Case* 1997, 737–38).

On July 31, 2008, the D.C. district court rejected the administration's position that current or former presidential aides have absolute immunity. Indeed, in a single sentence, Judge John D. Bates's eviscerated the administration's argument: "The Executive's current claim of absolute immunity from compelled congressional process for senior presidential aides is without any support in the case law" (*Committee on the Judiciary v. Harriet Miers et al.* 2008a, 3).

Later on in this opinion Bates made clear the novelty of Bush's broad interpretation of his powers: the executive branch "cannot identify a single judicial opinion that recognizes absolute immunity for senior presidential advisors in this or any other context. That simple yet critical fact bears repeating: the asserted absolute immunity claim here is entirely unsupported by existing case law" (78).

Citing the Supreme Court decision of *United States v. Bryan*, Bates stated "that compliance with a congressional subpoena is a legal requirement" (78–79). He then discussed the importance of *Harlow v. Fitzgerald*, where White House staffers argued that they had an absolute immunity against civil damages claims arising from their official duties. Bates said that the *Harlow* Court "rejected that position" and declared that there was "no reason to extend greater protection to senior aides based solely on their proximity to the President" (80–81). The "'alter ego' immunity that the Executive requests here due to Ms. Miers's and Mr. Bolten's close proximity to and association with the President has been explicitly and definitively rejected, and there is no basis for reaching a different conclusion here" (81–82).

Bates next addressed the argument that compelled congressional testimony has a chilling effect on the executive branch. He noted that "the historical record" argues against this understanding and added that "senior advisors to the President have often testified before Congress subject to various subpoenas dating back to 1973." Thus, "it would hardly be unprecedented for Ms. Miers to appear before Congress to testify and assert executive privilege where appropriate" (83). The simple fact, as Bates pointed out, is that even the president himself "may not be absolutely immune from compulsory process" (84). Indeed, Congress does not lack authority to investigate the executive branch. "Congress's power of inquiry," Bates described, "is as broad as its power to legislate and lies at the very heart of Congress's constitutional role" which means that "the subpoena power in this case is no less legitimate or important than was the grand jury's in *United States v. Nixon*" (84).

Bates found no legal rationale at all to support a claim of presidential autonomy. He argued that "it is certainly the case that if the President is entitled only to a presumptive privilege, his close advisors cannot hold the superior card of absolute immunity" (84–85). Even if the president possessed a limited autonomy, it "cannot mean that the Executive's actions are totally insulated from scrutiny by Congress." Bates reasoned that "would eviscerate Congress's historical oversight function" (85). He then noted that the executive branch's interest in absolute immunity really is about independence from congressional and judicial checks. Such a "proposition is untenable and cannot be justified by appeals to Presidential autonomy" (86).

Bates's decision was a resounding repudiation of the theory that the president and his advisers could act without regard to Congress or the judiciary. On August 26 Bates dismissed a White House request to delay testimony by Miers and the House Judiciary Committee reacted by scheduling a hearing.

The D.C. Court of Appeals has granted the Bush administration's appeal of Bates's decision and issued a temporary stay in the case. However, the court decided not to grant an expedited briefing and oral argument schedule, which meant that the controversy was left to Bush's successor to resolve (Committee on the Judiciary v. Harriet Miers, et al. 2008b). In early March 2009, the new administration helped to broker an agreement between the House Judiciary Committee and former Bush White House staffers that largely sidestepped the executive privilege questions. As such, the impact of Bush's absolute immunity claim remains unresolved.

THE EPA CASE AND AGENCY LEVEL PRIVILEGE

One of the final examples of the attempt to expand executive privilege to fit within the parameters of the unitary executive concept was the president's refusal to provide Environmental Protection Agency (EPA) documents to the House Oversight and Government Reform Committee. The information sought by the committee pertained to correspondence between the EPA and the Office of Information and Regulatory Affairs in the Office of Management and Budget (OIRA) in the agency's decision to deny the state of California the authorization to regulate the greenhouse gas emissions of motor vehicles (Bliley 2008).

In a June 20, 2008, letter to Chairman Henry Waxman, EPA associate administrator Christopher P. Bliley notified the committee that Bush claimed executive privilege on a number of documents that "identify communications or meetings between senior EPA staff and White House personnel, or otherwise evidence information solicited or received by senior White House advisors." Regretting that the committee still sought information after the release of thousands of pages of documents Bliley noted that "the Committee's subpoenas infringe upon the Executive Branch's strong interest in protecting the confidentiality of communications with and/or information received or solicited by the President and his senior advisors" (Bliley 2008).

Waxman immediately responded: "Today the President has asserted executive privilege to prevent the Committee from learning why he and his staff overruled EPA. There are thousands of internal White House documents that would show whether the President and his staff acted lawfully. But the President has said they must be kept from Congress and the public. . . . This Committee," Waxman continued "has a fundamental obligation to learn the truth about what actually happened on these critical health and environmental decisions. That is why we have been seeking documents in both cases that would provide important details about the President's role" in this matter. Waxman said he wanted to confer with his colleagues "about this new development and consider all our options before deciding how we should proceed" (Waxman 2008). Time quickly ran out on Waxman and Congress adjourned without the committee taking any formal action.

Attorney General Michael Mukasey supplied the legal arguments for Bush's executive privilege claim. Mukasey's analysis suffered from poor citations, bad reasoning, and irrelevant conclusions. His memorandum to the president focused on four primary assertions. First, Mukasey argued that the documents protected were drafted "for the purpose of assisting the President in making a decision" about the ozone regulation (Mukasey 2008a). At several points Mukasey repeatedly asserted this very point as if it were factually accurate. Indeed, although a president's decision making can likely be protected under the presidential communications privilege, such a claim can only be made on a "quintessential and non-delegable Presidential power" (*In re Sealed Case* 1997, 752). Congress directed the EPA administrator to assess whether "the State standards will be, in the aggregate, at least as protective of public health and welfare as applicable Federal standards" (42 USC 7543(b)(1) [2006]). Nothing in the law directs the EPA administrator to confer with the president or provides evidence that agency decision making would fall under the quintessential powers of the president.

Mukasey's second claim dealt with the deliberative process privilege and his statement that "communications that do *not* implicate presidential decisionmaking" are protected from disclosure. He cited as evidence multiple OLC memorandums and he maintained that "based on this principle, the Justice Department under Administrations of both political parties has concluded repeatedly that the privilege may be invoked to protect Executive Branch deliberations against congressional subpoenas" (Mukasey 2008a).

Certainly executive privilege does expand outside of the president and his immediate advisers; however, the deliberative process privilege has a lower threshold of protection for the executive branch. It is misleading merely to note that executive branch officials are protected and then not acknowledge that there is a difference between presidential and agency or department level documents. For support of this assertion Mukasey referenced a number of OLC memorandums. Repeated citations of self-serving executive branch documents do not add up to a valid legal basis for privilege, no more so than, say, the House of Representatives defining its constitutional powers based on references to multiple internal congressional staff memoranda.

At first blush Mukasey's point about protecting certain executive branch deliberations may sound reasonable. However he sidestepped the issue of whether a department or agency—not the president—can withhold information from Congress by just stating the EPA documents needed protection. Then he made repeated assertions, not by citing the Constitution, case law, or historical examples, but by noting that other executive branch officials have said it is so.

Next Mukasey noted that in order for Congress to overcome a claim of executive privilege it must show "that the subpoenaed documents are 'demonstrably critical to the responsible fulfillment of the Committee's functions.'" Based on this requirement he determined that the committee had not met that standard. "Given the overwhelming amount of material and information already provided to the Committee," Mukasey declared, "it is difficult to understand how the subpoenaed information serves any legitimate legislative need." He concluded that the executive branch's strong interest in protecting these documents outweighed the committee's need for disclosure (Mukasey 2008a).

There are two overriding problems with Mukasey's point. First, merely because the executive branch discloses some or even many documents does not mean that the most important or relevant documents were provided. With that argument a future president—if wanting to hide information from Congress—would only have to release boxes after boxes of material that has nothing to do with the congressional investigation in order to meet the fallacy of this non sequitur. Second, that the attorney general is the one who made this determination raises a question of bias. Mukasey is not a neutral decision maker and cannot through executive fiat say certain information should be withheld from Congress.

Finally, after summarizing various documents that he deemed would provide Congress with the same information Mukasey pointed out that during a May 20, 2008, hearing none of the committee members asked the OIRA administrator any questions related to the agency's role in the EPA decision (Mukasey 2008a). The implication being that the committee did not do due diligence in seeking alternative sources for the same information. The problem with this argument is that it does not follow that just by not asking questions at one committee hearing Congress gives up its right to executive branch documents. That is not a valid legal standard by any definition for withholding information.

The overarching goal of Mukasey's legal reasoning was to protect not only presidential decision making from congressional disclosure but all executive branch information. Such an argument would guard communications that were not even connected to a presidential act. Although Congress has been delegating power to agencies since the latter part of the nineteenth century, that does not necessarily mean a president has the responsibility of direct supervision. There are incidences when the enabling legislation is sufficiently unclear as to create a practice where a head of an agency might consult with the president or his White House advisers. Unitary executive advocates argue this point while claiming that the president's duty to see that all "laws be faithfully executed" provides additional evidence for this understanding.

Neither of these arguments gives a president the power to counter the wishes of Congress or use congressionally created agencies and officials in an attempt to withhold information from the legislative branch. In this case, the Clean Air Act empowers the EPA administrator to evaluate state motor vehicle standards (42 USC 7543(b)(1) [2006]). In short, environmental regulations are not core presidential powers. The Supreme Court has weighed in on the question of congressional and presidential powers in this type of situation before. In *Kendall v. United States* the argument had been made that the president could direct and control the postmaster general "with respect to the execution of the duty imposed upon him" by law. That belief was based on the obligation imposed on the president "to take care that the laws be faithfully executed." The Court declared that this "is a doctrine that cannot receive the sanction of this court. It would be vesting in the President a dispensing power which has no countenance for its support in any part of the Constitution, and is asserting a principle, which, if carried out in its results to all cases falling within it, would be clothing the President with a power entirely to control the legislation of Congress and paralyze the administration of justice" (*Kendall v. U.S.* 1838, 612–13).

The Court's decision directly countered the unitary executive argument made in that case but, more important, it refuted the contention that the president has direct control and authority over the EPA administrator in the current situation. There is an expectation of autonomy from presidential control if the congressional delegation of power is given solely to an agency official and it does not interfere with a constitutional power of the president. As the Supreme Court announced in *Kendall*: "To contend that the obligation imposed on the President to see the laws faithfully executed implies a power to forbid their execution is a novel construction of the Constitution, and entirely inadmissible" (*Kendall v. U.S.* 1838, 613). In the case of executive privilege the president cannot force an agency official to withhold information from Congress that has no relationship to the president's core constitutional duties. Even if the decision-making issue at hand were a delegation of presidential authority to the EPA—which it was not—a president cannot properly conceal such documents with a claim of privilege.

VALERIE PLAME AND COVERING UP CLAIMS OF EXECUTIVE BRANCH WRONGDOING

President's Bush claimed executive privilege over a congressional request for an interview transcript with Vice President Cheney and several FBI reports on the leaking of the name of Valerie Plame, who had been a Central Intelligence Agency (CIA) operative. Bush claimed executive privilege over these documents right before the House Oversight and Government Reform Committee was scheduled to vote on a resolution citing Attorney General Mukasey in contempt of Congress. In a July 15, 2008 letter to Chairman Waxman the administration claimed the reports "deal directly with internal White House deliberative communications relating to foreign policy and national security decisions faced by the President and his advisers, communications that lie at the absolute core of executive privilege." Additionally, the congressional inquiry "raises a serious additional separation of powers concern relating to the integrity and effectiveness of future law enforcement investigations by the Department." Disclosing reports that contain voluntary interviews with the vice president and senior White House staff "would significantly impair the Department's ability to conduct future law enforcement investigations where such investigations would benefit from full and voluntary White House cooperation" (Nelson 2008).

The Bush administration had used many court-based and statutorily created categories of executive privilege to withhold information from Congress before. Walling off the executive branch by withholding information through another claim of unitary protection has not been unusual in the Bush presidency. Attorney General Mukasey once again announced the underlying justifications for an assertion of privilege in this case. In a letter to Bush, he said that a claim of privilege would not be about hiding an act of wrongdoing but rather protecting the separation of powers as well as the integrity of future Justice Department investigations of the White House. "I am greatly concerned about the chilling effect that compliance with the committee's subpoena would have on future White House deliberations and White House cooperation with future Justice Department investigations," Mukasey wrote Bush. "I believe it is legally permissible for you to assert executive privilege with respect to the subpoenaed documents, and I respectfully request that you do so" (Mukasey 2008b).

Mukasey claimed that executive privilege "extends to all Executive Branch deliberations, even when the deliberations do not directly implicate presidential decisionmaking" (Mukasey 2008b). He noted that the information requested is protected by the presidential communications privilege, deliberative process privilege, and the law enforcement component of executive privilege. Moreover, the committee "has yet to identify any specific legislative need for the subpoenaed documents, relying instead on a generalized interest in evaluating the White House's involvement in the Plame matter as part of its review of White House procedures governing the handling of classified documents" (Mukasey 2008b).

For much of the letter Mukasey combines the different threshold standards together in a way that is often confusing and is, for the most part, bad reasoning based on faulty analysis. There is a clear distinction between the president and the rest of the executive branch in terms of what can and cannot be protected from a congressional investigation. Arguing in rather befuddled language that there is no difference between the two seems disingenuous. In addition, repeating that Congress has not met the "demonstrably critical" need does not mean it is so. A deliberative process claim, which most of the documents in question fall under, cannot stand up to a showing of government misconduct or wrongdoing (*In re Sealed Case*, 1997, 745). The unlawful release of a CIA agent's name clearly meets this threshold standard. It is also not accurate that the law enforcement privilege protects information from closed investigations.

What the Bush administration tried to do in this case is expand executive privilege to protect the attorney general from disclosing nonpresidential documents to a congressional committee. In its reply to Waxman the administration even declared that if the committee did not move ahead and cite Mukasey for contempt then the Justice Department was "prepared to continue the accommodation approach" (Nelson 2008). This offer borders on a bribe to Congress and even if it is not illegal it is certainly unethical. Moreover there was clearly a conflict of interest on the part of Mukasey in giving executive privilege advice to President Bush on a contempt of Congress vote that applied directly to the attorney general. The resulting executive privilege claim protected Mukasey from having to respond to a contempt citation.

At its heart this executive privilege claim is an attempt to protect the release of an FBI interview by Vice President Cheney to a congressional committee. The information requested by Congress did not involve a discussion between the president and vice president that dealt with a core presidential power. Instead it was an interview of Cheney conducted by a government attorney and FBI agents in the Plame investigation that was not protected by grand jury secrecy requirements or with any expectations that the information given would remain sealed or not be disclosed to Congress at some point (Fitzgerald 2008). The refusal to release the interview and other information to Congress was therefore an attempt to expand the executive privilege to provide greater protection of the vice president and the executive branch. The evolution of case law on executive privilege, as well as its many precedents, does not provide support for such an expansive definition of this power. Congress has the authority to conduct its oversight duties over all areas of the executive branch including the president's and vice president's offices. Nothing in the Constitution, case law, or interbranch practice counters that point.

CONCLUSION

At the end of the Bush era it was well established that the administration acted in a purposeful, and some would say aggressive, way to expand presidential powers. Revealing comments by Vice President Cheney—often seen as the leading architect of the administration's efforts in this regard—early in Bush's first term show the centrality of goal to the Bush presidency. The vice president stated that the administration would be dedicated to restoring the balance of powers in the system of separated powers to ensure that the president was able to fully exercise his rightful authority. Cheney went so far as to suggest that the modern era has been characterized by legislative encroachments on presidential powers combined with presidential acquiescence in the face of such congressional power grabs (ABC 2002).

The unitary executive theory provided the rationale for President Bush's agenda to defend and expand presidential powers in a variety of areas as well as to protect the executive branch from what he and Vice President Cheney perceived as an overly intrusive Congress. And it is no coincidence that the vice president himself was a central character in a number of the most contentious efforts by the administration to achieve these goals.

One of the key areas of contention was the administration's broad rationales for, and exercises of, executive privilege. The administration could have made a valid case that because of the taint of its exercise during the Watergate and Clinton-Lewinsky scandals, executive privilege, a legitimate and sometimes necessary presidential power, had earned an unfair bad reputation and needed to be restored. Yet the Bush era claims of executive privilege and rationales reached far beyond the customary exercises of that power, as defined by the evolution of court law and precedents. The above cases reveal that the administration, under the guidance of the unitary executive theory, sought to vastly expand the traditional categories of executive privilege in ways that, if successful, would have ultimately walled off the executive branch from any system of accountability. Such efforts, had they succeeded, could have had profound long-term consequences for the delicate system of balances built into the Constitution.

Although the Congress and judicial entities held back many of the administration's most far-reaching efforts in this area, the administration picked up a few significant victories along the way, either through the courts (*Cheney v. U.S. Dist. Court for Dist. Of Columbia* 2003) or due to delay tactics (U.S. attorneys' firings case). These administration victories create some temptation for Bush's successor to make similar efforts when doing so might temporarily benefit the agenda of the Barack Obama administration.

If history is an accurate guide, administrations rarely turn back their own powers, and it takes integrity and courage for the new president to pass up opportunities to advance his goals. Nonetheless, it is possible that things could be different beginning in 2009, but only if President Barack Obama truly is committed to the reforms he promised as a candidate, and if those who have compulsory power, especially his own party majority in Congress, challenge him at every turn if he ever tries to conceal documents and testimony in questionable circumstances. As the contentious Bush era reveals so clearly, that is the only way to maintain the delicate system of balanced powers envisioned by the constitutional founders—a system that has survived presidential overreaching many times.

REFERENCES

ABC News. 2002. The Vice President Appears on ABC's *This Week*. January 27, at www.whitehouse.gov/vicepresident/news-speeches/speeches/vp20020127.html (accessed November 24, 2008).

Bliley, Christopher P. 2008. Letter to Henry A. Waxman. June 20, at oversight.house. gov/documents/20080620114653.pdf (accessed November 24, 2008).

Bumiller, Elisabeth. 2002. White House Withholding Documents on Pardons. *New York Times,* August 28.

Bradbury, Stephen G. 2007. Immunity of Former Counsel to the President from Compelled Congressional Testimony. Office of Legal Counsel. July 10, at www. usdoj.gov/olc/2007/miers-immunity-Opinion071007.pdf (accessed November 24, 2008).

Calabresi, Steven G., and Christopher S. Yoo. 2008. *The Unitary Executive: Presidential Power from Washington to Bush*. New Haven, CT: Yale University Press.

Cheney v. U.S. Dist. Court for Dist. Of Columbia. 2003. 540 U.S. 1088.

Committee on the Judiciary v. Miers et al. 2008a. Civil No. 1:08-cv-00409 (D.D.C.).

———. 2008b, No. 08-5357 (D.C. Cir.).

Corwin, Edward S. 1957. *The Presidency: Office and Powers*, 4th ed. New York: New York University Press.

Fielding, Fred F. 2007. Letter to John Conyers and Patrick Leahy. June 28, at www.whitehouse.gov/news/releases/2007/06/LetterfromCounseltothePresident06282007.pdf (accessed November 24, 2008).

Fisher, Louis. 2004. *The Politics of Executive Privilege*. Durham, NC: Carolina Academic Press.

Fitzgerald, Patrick J. 2008. Letter to Henry A. Waxman. July 3, at oversight.house. gov/documents/20080708103231.pdf (accessed November 24, 2008).

Harlow v. Fitzgerald. 1982. 457 U.S. 800.

In re Sealed Case. 1997. 121 F.3d 729 (D.C. Cir.).

Judicial Watch v. Department of Justice. 2003. 259 F. Supp. 2d 86 (D.D.C.).

———. 2004. 365 F.3d 1108 (D.C. Cir.).

Kane, Paul. 2008. West Wing Aides Cited for Contempt. *Washington Post,* February 15.

Kendall v. United States. 1838. 37 U.S. 524.

Lewis, Neil A. 2007. Panel Votes to Hold Two in Contempt of Congress. *New York Times,* July 25.

MacKenzie, John P. 2008. *Absolute Power: How the Unitary Executive Theory Is Undermining the Constitution.* New York: The Century Foundation Press.

Mukasey, Michael B. 2008a. Letter to George W. Bush. June 19, at oversight.house. gov/documents/20080620114653.pdf (accessed November 24, 2008).

———. 2008b. Letter to George W. Bush. July 15, at oversight.house.gov/documents/20080716104027.pdf (accessed November 24, 2008).

Nelson, Keith B. 2008. Letter to Henry A. Waxman. July 16, at oversight.house.gov/documents/20080716104053.pdf (accessed November 24, 2008).

Neustadt, Richard E. 1960. *Presidential Power: The Politics of Leadership.* New York: John Wiley and Sons.

Plaintiff's Motion for Partial Summary Judgment [Plaintiff's Motion]. 2008. *Committee on the Judiciary v. Miers et al.* 2008. Civil No. 1:08-cv-00409 (D.D.C.).

Rozell, Mark J. 2002. *Executive Privilege: Presidential Power, Secrecy and Accountability* (2d ed.). Lawrence: University Press of Kansas.

Rozell, Mark J., and Mitchel A. Sollenberger. 2008a. Executive Privilege and the Bush Administration. *Journal of Law and Politics* 24: 1–47.

———. 2008b. Executive Privilege and the U.S. Attorneys Firings. *Presidential Studies Quarterly* 32: 315–28.

———. 2009. The Unitary Executive and Secrecy in the Bush Presidency: The Case of the Energy Task Force Controversy. In *The Unitary Executive and the Modern Presidency,* eds. Christopher Kelly and Ryan Barilleaux. College Station: Texas A&M University Press.

Schlesinger, Arthur M. 1973. *The Imperial Presidency.* Boston: Houghton Mifflin.

United States v. Nixon. 1974. 418 U.S. 683.

U.S. Congress, *Availability of Information to Congress.* 1973. Hearings before a Subcommittee of the Committee on Government Operations, House of Representatives, 93d Cong., 1st sess. (April 3, 4, 19).

Waxman, Henry. 2008. *Opening Statement of Rep. Henry A. Waxman.* June 20, at oversight.house.gov/documents/20080620121418.pdf (accessed November 24, 2008).

Chapter Ten

The President's Budget vs. Congressional Budgeting: Institutionalizing the Adversarial Presidency?

Joseph White

In the constitutional system of separated institutions sharing powers, the powers to spend and tax are especially important and subject to conflict. Budgeting is at the heart of government, because it is the most direct example of the authoritative allocation of values. The importance of budget decisions and the structural necessity that one subset of those decisions, discretionary appropriations, be made each year puts federal budgeting at the center of much conflict between the president and Congress, as revealed dramatically in the battles during the Reagan administration and during the 104th Congress. But budgeting is also the most fundamental area of cooperation between the two branches, because without cooperation on discretionary appropriations, large sections of federal activity will come to a halt.[1] Budgeting institutions and processes are a major aspect of the modern presidency, just as budgeting is at the heart of governmental decision making.[2]

The constitution, as explained by its framers, clearly intends to give the Congress the largest say in budgeting decisions. Yet it also, both through the president's veto over legislation and his supervision of administration, gave him a major role in the allocation of government funds.[3] Developments in the extraconstitutional political system, such as the emergence of the presidential role as a party leader and his occasional ability to appeal to public opinion, also guarantee that the president, under any circumstances, must have a share of budgeting power.

Under extreme circumstances, such as the warfare between President Clinton and the 104th Congress, the presidential role in budgeting is based almost entirely on those basic resources. Yet federal budgeting is an immensely technical and complicated task, involving many thousands of decisions that are supposed to be integrated into a complex web of legislation and implementation. As a result, both Congress and the presidency include specialized budgeting institutions.

The congressional budget process includes specialized committees for what we now call discretionary spending (the House and Senate Appropriations committees); concentration of authority over revenues also in distinct committees (House Ways and Means and Senate Finance); distinct committees that are required to provide an annual framework for decisions about spending and taxing (the House and Senate Budget Committees, through the annual Congressional Budget Resolution); a wide variety of special rules about consideration of revenue legislation, appropriations, and the class of laws called entitlements (or mandatory spending) that provide budget authority for more than one year (such as for farm price supports and Medicare); and a congressional agency to oversee executive management of budget allocations (the Government Accountability Office).

The executive (or presidential) budget process is managed by the Office of Management and Budget (OMB) within the Executive Office of the President. Although it has undergone various reformulations since its original creation in 1921, the presidential budget bureau[4] has always both managed allocation of funds among agencies, a crucial and occasionally controversial task (budget execution), and packaged agencies' budget requests into an overall bundle subject to presidential approval. It thus asserts presidential power in three ways: influencing information provided to Congress (as agencies are expected to testify in favor of OMB's proposals), influence over implementation (the extent to which bureaus do what legislators expected them to do with the budget, or more what decision makers within the administration prefer), and a basic coordinating function in which individual tax and spending plans are related both to each other and to an argument about desirable totals for taxes, spending, and the federal surplus or deficit.

This chapter addresses the relationship between the presidential process and the congressional process in making budget decisions for the federal government. As budget expert Naomi Caiden wrote, the executive budget process within the United States government is a creature of "paradox, ambiguity, and enigma" that fits awkwardly, at best, with the constitutional design.[5] There are conditions under which it can be the basis for cooperation that serves both branches. That pattern, however, has become much less common over the past three decades. The development of presidential budgeting appears to reflect a broader trend in congressional-presidential relations, which I call the *adversarial presidency* in contrast to the earlier model.

PURPOSES OF BUDGET PROCESSES

Specialized budget processes have a series of functions, or justifications, as part of both democratic politics and competent government. The most commonly cited is to obtain a desirable balance of taxing and spending: "budget balance" broadly defined. Budgeting is also a set of procedures designed to set standards for both bureaucrats and politicians and thereby hold them accountable, is a way to make government transparent and its actions predictable, is a procedure to set social priorities and to pursue efficiency in the operation of public services, and (sometimes) is a process to manage the economy as well as the government.[6]

The fundamental reason for centralized budget processes, however, is to resolve a social choice problem: that preferences about program and tax policy details are highly unlikely to add up to preferences about total spending, total taxes, and the resulting budget balance. Hence processes are needed to *adjust those two preferences to each other*, in such a way that the combination in the end is as satisfactory as possible to the decision-making person or group.

As this problem is normally posed, a set of fragmented decisions about programs and taxes, which is what would happen if agencies simply proposed their own budgets and Congress responded committee by committee, must be resisted by central "guardian" bodies such as the Appropriations or Budget Committees or the Office of Management and Budget. But there is a further problem: there are many ways to obtain the same budget totals.

Most participants in budget making can identify *somebody else's spending* that they would be willing to eliminate, or *somebody else's taxes* that they would be willing to raise, so as to bring details in line with a preferred total. During the budget battles of the 1980s, for example, conservative Republicans could consistently favor a balanced budget because they were willing to slash social programs to achieve the goal, while liberal Democrats could favor balance because they were willing to cut defense spending and raise taxes on corporations and people with higher incomes.[7] Therefore, in reconciling preferences about details and totals, there are three systematic sources of conflict between the presidential and congressional budget processes.

The first is that the median preference within Congress may well be substantively different than the president's budget policy, yet each be equally "responsible," as defined by the amount of government deficit or surplus—which is a recipe for self-righteous conflict. Second, if budget deficits exceed public and elite views of what is proper, that may be because majorities oppose any single set of details that would lower the deficit further. Yet virtually everyone could blame politicians for not lowering the deficit in some way. This exacerbates the fact that budgeting must disappoint a lot of interests so attracts extensive blame anyway, and encourages blame-shedding tactics. Third, the budget bureau asks, "What will fit the president's policies?" Within Congress, however, the basic question is, "How will we pass the bill?" This difference leads to a basic conflict of worldviews, with OMB seeing legislative budgeters as too "political," and their counterparts viewing

OMB's claim to "rationality" as easy for OMB to say because it is only making a proposal to satisfy one hierarchical overseer.

The role of the president's budget in federal budgeting has moved from one (mainly theoretical) model, through a model that roughly was the status quo from the 1940s into the late 1960s, toward the model that best describes the budgeting system today. We can call these the *executive dominance, clerk/ broker*, and *adversarial* models. The executive dominance model essentially assumes that only the president's preferences should matter, which would eliminate the first two conflicts but give him all the blame. In the clerk/broker model, the president would take the lead in finding a middle ground between branch preferences, thereby sharing blame. In the adversarial model, the two sides fight over preferences while trying to stick each other with the blame.

ORIGINS OF THE PRESIDENTIAL BUDGET

The core institutions of the presidential budget were created in the Budget and Accounting Act of 1921, emerging from an elite executive budget movement. As Irene Rubin explained, this movement developed in directions encouraged by President Taft. The "Taft conservatives" distrusted both the legislature and the public, and believed the chief executive and administrators should be free to make decisions that served their view of the public interest.[8] Many subsequent reformist analyses have followed in the Taft tradition, of which the most prominent was the 1937 Brownlow report's analysis of budgeting.[9]

As Naomi Caiden argues, this view was (and is) "at odds both with contemporary practice and the separation of powers." Yet the presidential process as created worked fairly well for decades. It retained "legislative initiative in appropriations" and stressed "the executive budget as a means of gaining executive responsibility and strengthening legislative budgetary control."[10] But how could the same process both make the executive more responsible and strengthen legislative control? The short answer is, the executive budget could serve Congress by helping *both* president and Congress control the executive agencies.

DEVELOPMENT OF THE CLERK/BROKER PATTERN

The executive process could be useful to both by performing a series of functions. The most basic was preventing the agencies from creating "coercive deficiencies." Neither president nor Congress gains if agencies run out of appropriated funds before the end of the fiscal year, for reasons that the agencies could have controlled. Congress will desire neither to appropriate more nor to suffer the political pain of closing down an agency; and the president has no more reason to desire either result. The process created by the 1921 act, in which the budget bureau apportions funds to agencies, greatly reduced this problem.[11]

A second vital contribution was to search for efficiencies within individual agency spending plans. Efficiency is not politically biased because, though it could be used to reduce total spending, it can also be used to obtain more social good for the same spending or to free up funds for different spending. Over time, the budget bureau adopted this broad definition of efficiency, rather than a narrow focus on economy.[12] As one senior OMB career official put it in an interview, "The idea I grew up with was to be a neutral competent budget analyst. As I told my staff, that meant *if it was a Republican administration trying to minimize cost; if it was a Democratic administration, how to maximize value for the money we had.*"

Both branches might benefit from a degree of coordination across programs, both by revealing if agencies were working at cross-purposes and by uncovering the "wasteful" opposite, redundancy or overlap of functions. Congress might choose not to use such information, but providing it would improve Congress's options.[13] The executive process also prevented agencies from submitting "blue sky" requests to Congress, and could provide a first "scrub" to identify technical issues.

The budget bureau developed a somewhat controversial and unstable role in administrative management. Congress has been conflicted on this topic, with some legislators at any given time hoping that better management will yield economies, and others objecting to central (e.g., budget bureau) interference with their own influence over the agencies. Nevertheless, there have been periods when the management wing of the budget bureau played a positive role. By multiple accounts, the Division of Administrative Management established within the budget bureau by Director Harold Smith in 1939 contributed in ways that are still recalled as a kind of "golden age" of the budget bureau.[14]

Most significant, a presidential budget can serve Congress by dispersing blame. If the president proposed restraints that Congress was willing to accept, legislators could accept the proposal and give him some of the blame. If Congress rejected a presidential proposal, so had to replace it with another, legislators could get some credit from the interest they protected. Sharing blame with the president helped with both guardianship and coalition building. The president, however, also benefited, at least in policy terms. If there was agreement that hard choices must be made, the initiative and agenda-setting role given to the president through his budget process, as well as legislators' desire to avoid blame, gave him substantial influence on budget results.

In these ways, the presidential process helped both president and Congress match details to totals, and the budget system developed into a rough equilibrium of shared expectations and mutual adjustment.[15] It fit into the presidential role that Richard Neustadt describes as "clerkship." A better term might be *brokerage*: the president sits at a key point within a complex system of bargaining. In return for facilitating transactions, he collects resources that he uses for his own purposes. Neustadt describes the budget as "among the cardinal services the president-as-clerk performs for Congressmen and bureaucrats and lobbyists."[16] Because it was created by an intensive process within the executive branch; because it represented commitment in its most concrete form, money; and because the nature of appropriations meant that Congress had to respond to those proposals, the budget became the year's premier initiator.

Budgeting in this period was hardly a nonpartisan lovefest. Nevertheless, what Allen Schick termed the "Seven Year Budget War" from 1966 to 1973 initiated a transition to a much more adversarial role for the president's budget.[17] The clerk/broker role depended on conditions that faded away in the late 1960s and would disappear by the 1980s.

TOWARD ADVERSARIAL BUDGETING

One condition was that Congress and the president have roughly similar goals for budget totals. Liberal Democrats and conservative Republicans had very different fiscal policy views, but the conservative coalition that dominated Congress in the 1950s largely agreed with President Eisenhower, and disagreement only became systematic when President Nixon faced a more liberal Congress. At that point, the fact that only the president had economists and a process for saying what the fiscal totals should be became a major problem for Congress.

A second condition was that the instruments available within the budget process be adequate to the task of making details fit the totals. The process that had emerged only guaranteed action on annually appropriated programs, what would later be called "discretionary" spending. In the 1960s the growth of entitlements such as Social Security and Medicare reduced the portion of spending that the traditional process could manipulate.

A third condition was that the president and congressional majority be in rough agreement on program details or priorities. Again, this disagreement appears to have widened during the Nixon presidency. A fourth condition was that the apportionment power be used in a way that was remotely acceptable to Congress. Instead, President Nixon used it to impound (refuse to spend) appropriations for purposes that he did not approve and had not been able to veto. A constitutional crisis over budget powers was avoided only because another, culminating in Nixon's resignation, took its place.

Congress responded by passing the Congressional Budget and Impoundment Control Act of 1974. The Budget Act created the Budget Resolution process, through which Congress, before passing other spending and tax legislation, would lay out targets for spending and revenue totals and priorities. This process would be reformed and strengthened in 1980 by implementation of reconciliation, a process through which legislative committees would be given targets for spending cuts or revenue increases in the Budget Resolution. Reconciliation had strong procedural protections against filibuster in the Senate. This provided a vehicle through which Congress was much more likely to respond to presidential proposals to alter entitlement programs such as Medicare and Medicaid, or to change tax law, than had been the case before reconciliation was put into full effect in 1980. This extended the potential influence of the president's budget through both agenda setting and blame sharing, and the Budget Act therefore gave President Reagan greater influence than he would otherwise have had in 1981.[18]

But the Budget Act also reduced Congress's dependence on the president for information, through creation of the Congressional Budget Office (CBO) and the Budget Committee staffs. It eliminated the president's monopoly of fiscal policy arguments, and so enabled Congress to challenge him more directly about the totals. It further forced Congress to make a statement for or against the president's proposed totals and priorities through the Budget Resolution, and therefore highlighted conflict. The resolution could replace the president's budget as an organizing framework for decisions about budget details.

The combination after 1981 of deficits unprecedented during peacetime with intense disagreement between the president and much of Congress (including moderate Republicans) about other budgetary values led, therefore, to battles about budget resolutions and diminishing attention to the president's framework. Either Congress took the lead, as in 1982 and 1984, or leaders maneuvered to create some form of "budget summit," as in 1987 and 1990.

Around 1985, federal budgeting degenerated into a period of competitive blame avoidance and hostage taking, epitomized by the Gramm-Rudman Act, which was described by House Majority Whip Tom Foley as "about the kidnapping of the only child of the President's official family that he loves [defense], holding it in a dark basement and sending the President its ear."[19] As one OMB senior career official described the situation, budgeting became a game of "deficit-reduction roulette." The only ways OMB could look like it was proposing doing "enough" on the deficit were to submit proposals that were obviously unacceptable (so in no sense constituted an "agenda"); to submit or even enact pure gimmicks, such as the 1989 "summit agreement" between the president and Congress that included about $39 billion in smoke and mirrors out of a $47 billion total;[20] or not to submit serious proposals at all. As one agency budget officer expressed it, some proposals did not pass the "laugh test . . . , the committees regard it with utter disdain, with laughter. Even around this table we laugh."

OMB was transformed both in workload and orientation by the pervasive adversarial relationship between the branches. The professional staff were redeployed to support the budget director and his political staff in their negotiations with the many faces of Congress. One of Director David Stockman's top aides described the change as "OMB's adaptation from the budget as a ministerial, executive process to a pluralistic, legislative process." Rationales for cuts were sought as weapons; "the notion was . . . one could find reasons to fit whatever our goal might be." Examiners, once "the center, the institutional weight of the agency," became more like "research assistants" as "we brought that system to an end in our search for centralized control." The cost of this approach was in organizational capacity to identify efficiencies: to understand programs well enough to tell how they could do as much with less. Rationales for cuts are not the same as understanding "the law and the program." This does not mean that no analysis occurred, or that all proposals were unreasonable. If the president proposed an increase within the budgetary environment of the 1980s, it would get more attention than if it came from anyone else. OMB might still find what one senior OMB civil servant called "the least provocative minuses"—proposals Congress could accept. But this became both less common and less of a focus for the process.[21]

In the circumstances of the 1980s intense disagreement about preferences meant that policy gains for one were more likely to look like losses for the other; while the intense pressure to do more about the deficit meant that there was far too much blame to share.[22] During the 1980s, the president's budget was so commonly termed "dead on arrival" that the Office of Management and Budget released the fiscal year 1987 plan by sending it to Congress in an ambulance, in the form of a staffer on a stretcher. He jumped up to reveal a shirt proclaiming, "The FY87 Budget Lives." The George H. W. Bush administration's revisions to the Reagan administration's FY90 plan only specified increases. In the words of one House Appropriations Committee aide, it was "the strangest year I've ever seen. We didn't really feel we ever had a President's Budget." By 1990, the president's men were blaming Congress for not changing his budget enough.[23]

These developments led budget scholars to ask whether the presidential process had outlived its usefulness. Bernard Pitsvada, for example, argued that the president's budget "has passed from a paradox to an enigma and now into an anachronism."[24]

PRESIDENT AND CONGRESS IN THE 1990S

During the first two years of the George H. W. Bush administration, the executive budget was not even a significant part of the president's budget maneuvers. The administration's first two proposals appear to have been placeholders for eventual negotiations, at best. Nevertheless, in 1990 OMB director Richard Darman managed to negotiate both significant deficit reduction and procedural rules—the Budget Enforcement Act—that eliminated the absurdities of Gramm-Rudman and provided totals with which it was possible to budget somewhat more regularly for the rest of the term. In order to do this, however, President Bush had to court blame by abandoning his 1988 campaign pledge of "no new taxes." Then his first package was rejected by his own party in the House, leaving him out on a limb where he had to accept terms that were much more acceptable to congressional Democrats. The process changes that eliminated the most damaging aspects of Gramm-Rudman were done in an obscure way so the president and Congress would not be accused of "weakening" that law's ostensible commitment to deficit reduction. The law included a clearly optimistic economic forecast in order to make its results look better. After years of tight restraint on domestic discretionary spending, negotiators agreed that it was time for those accounts to at least be held harmless, and maybe get a bit of an increase. But they wouldn't say that, either, so the final deal hid this agreement through manipulating the baselines.[25]

President Bush thereby took on blame and helped protect the congressional majority, and the final package in the long run significantly improved budget totals. He then ran for reelection against a Democrat who accused him of not being in touch with economic problems (that he had tried to fix through the conventional wisdom nostrum of deficit reduction), with a third-party candidate (Ross Perot) attacking both parties for not caring about the deficit that Bush had sacrificed political standing to reduce, and with an unenthusiastic base that objected to his raising taxes. His son, if one can judge from behavior, drew a perhaps too obvious conclusion: compromise with your rivals just to improve the budget situation does not serve presidential interests.

Compared to 1990, 1993 was much more clearly a case of presidential leadership, in that the Clinton administration laid out a direction and some details that were largely followed—unlike the bargaining process for the 1990 deal. In its first two years, the Clinton administration's budgets related details to preferences about totals in a way that was careful and considered both short- and long-term effects. However, this was made possible by the presence of a newly united government; the legislation passed by one vote in both the House and Senate, and in the 1994 election congressional Democrats paid the price by losing control of both houses of Congress for the first time in forty years. Apparently united government helps focus partisan blame.

The Republican takeover of Congress in 1994, and especially the capture of the House by Republicans led by Speaker Newt Gingrich who sought to revolutionize American government, created extreme disagreement that left little room for the clerk/broker role. The budgetary relationship between Clinton and the Republican Congress was among the worst in American history, with the logical result that, as two budget process experts expressed, "it often seemed that policy proposals were designed more for partisan posturing than for effectiveness and efficiency."[26]

OMB returned to the Reagan era role of serving the president in continual pitched battles and negotiations with Congress. In both chambers, the leadership wanted the president to make proposals that would reduce the blame they could get for slashing programs, and would take almost any savings he could find so long as they weren't in defense, but this was not a matter of seeking clerical or analytic services. As the FY96 budget debacle stretched into calendar 1996, "there was no way to put together a budget that started from a knowable point," so the administration "submitted . . . a thin set of numbers that were placeholders, and we did the real budget later that year. . . . Anything would be flawed, so we punted."

After Clinton's reelection and the turn of events that allowed the passage of the Balanced Budget Act of 1997 (BBA)—including, to general surprise, a balanced budget—one might have expected that extra money in a budget surplus would lubricate compromise. It did not for two reasons. First, the preferences of the president and of the congressional majority leadership differed too greatly. Second, built into the deficit reduction legislation of 1997 were terms that made a responsible relationship of details to totals extremely difficult.

Clinton sought new spending and congressional Republicans sought new tax cuts. The president, however, appears not to have wanted to spend as much as the congressional Republicans wanted to cut taxes. Moreover, the administration was concerned about the long-term financing of Social Security, and concluded future pensions could be made more affordable by reducing the federal debt and thereby future interest expenses. Therefore the Clinton administration promoted a standard of "saving Social Security first," by which it meant balance the budget without counting the Social Security surpluses. The policy made sense but the politics, which included much posturing about "lockboxes," was viewed as ludicrous even by conservative budget professionals such as former CBO director Rudolf Penner and Senator Pete Domenici (R-NM), the longtime chair of the Senate Budget Committee.[27] But it served to artificially heighten budget constraints as part of partisan and institutional rivalry.

The BBA also enacted "caps" on discretionary spending, as part of its path to budget balance. These caps required that outlays be cut by about 3 percent relative to their real value in FY98 for FY99, and then be flat from FY99 through FY2002.[28] There was no evident policy reason for these figures; for example, they did not consider predictable events such as the decennial census. The 1990 budget deal had also created five-year caps, but they were based on a quiet agreement to create a bit of room for a compromise level of spending. Those caps were revised and extended in 1993 as part of a strong push within Congress for savings from discretionary spending, with much less attention to the details that would result.[29] These targets were met only with assistance from the Gingrich Congress that the Clinton administration did not seem to appreciate at the time.

The caps enacted in the BBA were especially stringent after the restraint in previous years. They were also, by normal budget logic, entirely unnecessary given that the budget went into surplus in 1997. The Clinton administration therefore immediately began to propose spending more than the caps. From the administration's perspective it was being responsible because it offset the extra spending with proposals such as increased tobacco taxes and user fees. From the congressional perspective the administration was welshing on a deal to constrain domestic spending, and its offsets were generally politically unacceptable. The trouble was that majorities in Congress neither wanted to violate conservative principles by raising the caps, nor fulfill them by spending as little as the caps required, nor enact the offsets.

To some extent this was a problem the Republican Congress brought on itself, but the Clinton administration was not about to risk blame by admitting the caps were nonsensical. So, each year, the administration insisted on its spending; appropriations were delayed by intense conflict; congressional Republicans largely gave in; and the caps were evaded with maneuvers that mainstream observers viewed as "gimmicks," such as shifts of payment dates from one year to another, declaring census spending an "emergency," and declaring somewhat predictable spending for military deployments in Bosnia an "emergency." By the end of 2000, discretionary spending was nearly $100 billion above the cap set in the BBA.[30]

Clinton's budgets could be justified on the grounds that the offsets were good policy, that budget surpluses grew in spite of the higher discretionary spending, or that some "gimmicks" were better policy than the alternatives. If enacting caps without considering the census was irresponsible, it would be more irresponsible to just slash the census to meet the caps. Nevertheless, the combination of deep disagreement with the political need to meet unprecedented stringent goals for totals led OMB to make many proposals that its personnel knew were not going to pass. One explained, "You do what you can to legitimately and sensibly come up with a total that is consistent with the overall decision of the president about what level of spending he wants to propose for the next year, and then turn it over to the appropriations process to change. Sometimes you propose things that you know aren't going to be enacted; it's a feature of the process." Naturally this looked less defensible to the appropriators, who were placed between a rock (the administration's demands) and a hard place (their party leaders' positions about totals) and couldn't solve the problem by adopting "offsets" such as user fees and new taxes that were not likely to be passed by any Congress, never mind a highly conservative Republican one. No Congress is likely to raise revenues when the budget is in surplus!

BUDGETING DURING THE
GEORGE W. BUSH ADMINISTRATION

The George W. Bush administration inherited a massive budget surplus and had, for most of its time in office, a supportive Congress. One might have expected not just presidential leadership on the budget, but a presidential budget process that could meet common views about what a good process would do. Instead, events demonstrated that an administration's own preferences control how the presidential process fits into federal budgeting. The second Bush administration had little interest in a clerk/broker role based on functions such as coordination and the search for programmatic efficiencies. But it had no more interest in leading Congress to match details to totals, mainly because it had little interest in totals as conventionally defined (the budget balance), and not much more in many details (particularly for discretionary domestic spending).

Process breakdowns approached levels seen at the height of conflict toward the end of the Reagan administration and from 1995 to 1996. Congress was unable to pass a budget resolution for fiscal years 2003, 2005, or 2007. In 2004 nine of the thirteen appropriations bills did not pass until they were packaged together in an omnibus bill after the election, on November 20. In 2006, the Republican Congress not only failed to agree with the Republican president to pass nine of the bills before the election, but then passed only a short-term continuing resolution, leaving the new Democratic Congress to deal with those bills in 2007. The Bush administration expressed its disappointment, but had done nothing to make agreement more likely.

Congressional Democrats, who had to get to work on the bills for 2008, then enacted the remaining 2007 bills in a full-year continuing resolution for the first time since 1986. The new Democratic majorities did pass budget resolutions, but only passed appropriations for all of the government except the Pentagon in an omnibus bill on December 19. Such a sweeping bill had not been necessary since 1987. In 2008, Congress, faced with certain vetoes and the possibility of a different president if it waited long enough, passed only the three bills that covered security-related spending (for defense, homeland security, and military construction/veterans affairs), and didn't even bother bringing other bills to the floor of the House and Senate. The new president and Congress were left, again, to deal with the problem after the inauguration.

The second President Bush and his congressional allies engaged in a series of maneuvers to obscure their policy choices and their consequences. These included suppressing the administration's own cost estimates for its Medicare prescription drug legislation, complicated maneuvers with sunset dates of tax legislation, continual failures to honestly address the alternative minimum tax, systematic funding of an ongoing war through supplemental appropriations, and direct defiance of the law through signing statements. Although deficits were not large by historical standards, they appeared larger given the preceding surpluses and previous conservative rhetoric about the threat of higher entitlement spending as baby boomers reached eligibility for benefits.

Previous administrations would have felt compelled to propose measures to improve the budget balance. The Bush 43 administration, however, did not think of budgets in these terms. In its view lower taxes per se were good, lower spending on domestic programs per se was good, defense spending was not to be constrained by budget concerns, and the overall balance mattered much less than the results on the component parts.[31] Within its value structure privatization was more important than budget balance, so it was perfectly reasonable to propose privatizing Social Security without specifying the transition costs, as in 2005; or to enact Medicare legislation that added extra spending to entice people to shift from traditional Medicare to private insurance plans, as in 2003.[32]

The G. W. Bush administration does not appear to have constructed its budgets by making some sort of judgment about the proper balance of spending and revenues. A senior political official reported that they focused on "what is appropriate, needed and fair for nonsecurity. . . . We ended up with some increase, just below inflation, and building from that. So then you ask what is the increase on the security side, you build in that. Then there is DOD, and you can imagine there were discussions on that. *There was no magic on the top line, it's just the sum of the parts.*" This is remarkably different from standard ways of thinking about the budgeting task. Yet career OMB staff broadly supported this description. One, for example, reported that "in recent years it's basically been the Bush administration calling for a dollar freeze on nondefense discretionary spending. Not a whole lot of macroeconomic analysis underlies that." Nor was there much thought for how totals affected details; as another reported, "we have less and less input about the details before the top line is set. The BEA in 1990 really changed how we do our job. . . . We're given a dollar level and have to fit within our number."

How cabinet secretaries allocated their budgets was basically their problem, as one OMB veteran reported, "so long as it meets the totals." The administration took much the same view in its negotiations with Congress. In a July 11, 2007, press conference, outgoing budget director Rob Portman declared, "I think the position of the administration has been clear, which is, $933 billion is the top line, and the flexibility occurs under that top line."[33] A congressional source commented that "for the most part this administration cared about the top line and didn't care much about the detail under that top line . . . [in 2007] we got down to the President's number by cutting $10 billion out of our bills, and we did it without them in the room. There was literally no involvement, which was completely different from the Clinton years."

Even if the administration had wanted to take leadership on the details, institutional developments had left it with less ability to do the work of the clerk/broker model. OMB analysts spent much less time monitoring the appropriations process, because of the administration's disengagement from the details. But OMB's capacity had been reduced through staff cuts under both Clinton and Bush, and the remaining staff was buried under new "management" work, especially the Bush administration's PART (Program Assessment and Rating Tool) process.[34] As one senior career official put it, "you've got fewer people and you're engaged in doing more things."

"There has been a gradual expansion of legislated tasks," another added, "and the result is that there is a substantial amount of examiners' time that gets consumed with responding to requirements that are either mandated or legislated on the institution. During the Bush administration the president's management agenda and interacting with that agenda has been a major change." PART analyses occasionally generated new information that somewhat changed OMB's impressions of programs. But the most common report was that, in one senior career official's words, PART "really ate a lot of time." Another said that "one thing I used to do was sit down with examiners and identify two or three things we would need to learn more about from March to September. . . . We could no longer do that, because PART sucked up every moment between February and September." One put the concern most strongly. He worried that "when examiners can't tell if an agency is lying because they've never been out there to check things, the whole relationship has fundamentally changed. They say whatever they need to say to OMB, because the examiners can't tell. To me that's been one of the problems with the President's Management Agenda. There's a whole lot of paper there, but we don't have the time to see if any of it is actually representative of anything."

The Bush 43 budgets were viewed as having much the same problems as the late Reagan budgets. Some of these controversies involved traditional worldview differences between OMB and the agencies, such as whether agencies could find savings to offset pay increases (OMB finds that more reasonable). One should not imagine, either, that legislative budgeters are less likely than executive budgeters to resort to gimmicks to square budgetary circles. In some cases they will take an OMB "trick" and improve on it. But my congressional respondents made the same kind of comments that had been made in the late 1980s. PART didn't help in part because of distrust: in one's words, "the sense was that the program evaluation process was established for the purpose of destroying programs, so there wasn't a great deal of respect for those evaluations." But they also complained that PART didn't provide real budget analysis; in one appropriations veteran's words, "a sense of how our agencies are doing."

The most fundamental problem with PART, for Congress, was that it involved OMB making value judgments while pretending that they were efficiency judgments. There are clear cases of PART judgments being based on opinions of program content, such as the fact that Medicare does not offer stop-loss coverage; or dislike of block grants as a program design; or even setting standards that contradict the law.[35] In all these cases OMB was saying it did not like the program designs that the political system has created. That's not a position that Congress can be expected to approve.

Even at the height of conflict, appropriations staff suspected that the president's budget could be helpful by providing some constraints on agency requests and vetting of their details. One pointed to the example of the National Cancer Institute's "bypass budget," the list of what the institute wants separate from the constraints of the president's process, which "is just too expensive. No one can use it." So Congress wants information about how to increase the efficiency of individual programs. Yet what PART offered was program comparisons, and because each program is motivated by different values comparative "efficiency" judgments are inherently value judgments.

Hence the president's budget process in the second Bush presidency was a strange amalgam of relevance and irrelevance from an adversarial stance. Both because of his veto and his party's control of Congress for most of the period, President Bush largely got his way on both totals and details he cared about. Discretionary domestic "nonsecurity" spending was substantially constrained, military spending was not, and two large tax cuts were passed along with a major expansion and "reform" of Medicare. But this level of success appears to have had little to do with the apparatus of presidential budgeting. Some observers have even wondered in what sense the Bush administration took its own budgets seriously. Press coverage of the president's budget declined substantially; whether because of the administration not wanting attention or because of changes in the structure and interest of the media is hard to say.[36]

Disinterest in the usual activities of the clerk/broker role makes "adversarial" the default description of Bush 43 presidential budgeting. So does that administration's complicity in process breakdowns even during united government. An alternative interpretation, however, would be that both the Bush administration and congressional Republican leadership were more interested in attacking the federal government than in making budgets. In this sense they were allies, not adversaries.

A WAY FORWARD?

In spite of the substantial influence of the president on budget policies, there has been little recent advocacy for change in the presidential process. Perhaps that is because the adversarial nature of the president's budget is now taken for granted. It's his budget process. He will do with it what he wishes. Hardly anyone appears to expect executive dominance (if they did, they would call for executive responsibility). But even fewer observers appear to expect the process to serve the rest of the political system.

Intense disagreement between particular congresses and presidents is the most obvious reason for this development. More subtle but almost as pervasive is the failure of budget commentators to recognize that policies about details are as legitimate as policies about totals. The focus on totals far more than details during the 1980s and 1990s created a bizarre dynamic of blame avoidance by both Congress and president, which further intensified conflict. The extreme results were the hostage game of Gramm-Rudman and then the failure to repeal the BBA spending caps even when they were clearly not necessary. A third evident factor is actual presidential preferences, both about how to relate to Congress and what budgeting should do. The George

W. Bush administration simply wanted more of what it liked and less of what it disliked. Starting from this point of view, there could not be any functions that the president's budget could serve for Congress or the agencies.

A fourth, more subtle, factor is the current understanding of the presidency among politicians, the public, and scholars. Richard Neustadt's view of how presidents can benefit from serving as clerks or brokers is no longer dominant among political scientists. Barbara Sinclair begins her chapter in this volume by expressing the more recent public expectations when she states, "A good president, most voters will tell you, is one who keeps his promises, and that requires, at minimum, enacting his agenda." One suspects that FDR, in contrast, thought he would be judged by how well the government performed. In that view, the president has many reasons to pursue power, but also incentives to think about how he can make Congress's job easier so the government as a whole performs better.

Both presidents and recent political scientists appear to lean toward the view of the president's situation articulated by Terry Moe.[37] Moe describes presidents as surrounded by political rivals outside the executive branch and within it by bureaucrats, even within the Executive Office, who cannot be trusted to follow their lead. Yet, he argues, expectations for visible leadership from the public and media, as well as the desires of activist presidents of both the left and right, require that presidents accumulate power more directly than by the Neustadt methods, in particular by dominating the bureaucracy through ensuring its political loyalty. From this view, the concept that Congress and the president share some agenda in relating to the agencies is counterintuitive; the basic subject of their rivalry is control of the agencies that do the government's work.

From a different perspective, the expectation of rivalry could be viewed as part of the "resurgence" of Congress, and the period of brokerage viewed as one of congressional submission to the presidency. While there is certainly a case that the executive had far more initiative in the era before expansion of both congressional staff and interest groups, it is interesting that neither the budget literature nor the traditional presidency literature views budgeting in the time Neustadt and Wildavsky described as dominated by the president.

So it seems worthwhile to ask what, if both president and Congress believed they could work together in federal budgeting, they might do.

Congress could begin by removing some of the management mandates that were created during the 1990s. Second, it could encourage and support increases in both the size and stability of OMB staff. Each of these measures might seem counterintuitive to supporters of Congress. Yet the shrinking OMB under first Bill Clinton and then George W. Bush did not make presidential budget moves less obnoxious to Congress; and if OMB has performed all its new management functions in a helpful manner, that does not appear to have been noticed.

Presidents could contribute by, at a minimum, avoiding the kinds of egregious challenges to Congress issued by the second President Bush, such as signing statements declaring he would not follow the terms of laws. Most important, presidents could seek agreement rather than confrontation. Partisan divides may make that impossible, but better analysis can help a bit whether the president wants more or less spending than Congress.

Commentators in the public sphere could help by not succumbing to the misleading belief that the problem is simply "guardianship," a view that leads to promotion of budget constraint with little regard for the consequences to the details, and so fails to recognize the legitimacy of disagreement about the details. Unrealistic standards for the totals make the job of budgeting harder than it has to be. Elite panic about the deficit in the 1980s, about supposed long-term budget crises in the 1990s and at present, force adversarial budgeting by creating too much blame to be shared.

There may well be periods of united government when the president and Congress have a relationship that allows the clerk/broker role, even if totals are challenging. This occurred in 1993, and could have occurred during the George W. Bush administration. So some of how the president's budget fits into American governance will be chosen by the president.

Yet it seems reasonable to assume that there will be many periods in the future, as during the past four decades, when Congress and the president disagree seriously enough that they define their political interests in an adversarial manner. That seems especially likely given how common views of the president's interests have developed. The adversarial model, therefore, is likely to be common going forward.

NOTES

I would like to thank John Gilmour, Tom Lauth, Roy Meyers, and Jim Savage for their comments on various iterations of this manuscript; none bear any responsibility for any errors or infelicities herein. In addition to the literature cited below, this article is derived from interviews conducted over twenty-five years of research, and most especially thirty-three interviews on the executive process in 1990 and twenty-three on the executive process in the summer of 2008. A more extensive report based on the 1990 interviews is Joseph White, "Presidential Power and the Budget," in *Federal Budget & Financial Management Reform*, ed. Thomas D. Lynch (New York: Quorum Books, 1991).

1. For accounts of conflict, see Elizabeth Drew, *Showdown: The Struggle between the Gingrich Congress and the Clinton White House* (New York: Simon & Schuster, 1996); David Maraniss and Michael Weiskopf, *Tell Newt to Shut Up! Prize-winning*

Washington Post *Journalists Reveal How Reality Gagged the Gingrich Revolution* (New York: Simon & Schuster, 1996); Joseph White and Aaron Wildavsky, *The Deficit and the Public Interest: The Search for Responsible Budgeting in the 1980s* (Berkeley and New York: University of California Press and Russell Sage Foundation, 1991).

2. Larry Berman, *The Office of Management and Budget and the Presidency* (Princeton, NJ: Princeton University Press, 1979); Richard E. Neustadt, *Presidential Power: The Politics of Leadership from FDR to Carter* (New York: John Wiley and Sons, 1980); Aaron Wildavsky, *The Politics of the Budgetary Process* (Boston: Little, Brown, 1964).

3. The basic statement of both the need to combine authority and the expected greater role of the Congress over spending matters is Alexander Hamilton, James Madison, and John Jay, *The Federalist Papers*, for example, the Bantam Classic Edition (New York: Random House, 2003), especially papers 47 and 48, by Madison.

4. The term *budget bureau* will be used in this chapter when I refer to either the Bureau of the Budget (pre-1971) or Office of Management and Budget (1971 and after) in general; I will use the formal names of the agency in question when the use of the term is clearly time bound.

5. Naomi Caiden, "Paradox, Ambiguity, and Enigma: The Strange Case of the Executive Budget and the United States Constitution." *Public Administration Review* 47, no. 1 (Jan/Feb 1987).

6. Typical lists of functions are in Donald Axelrod, *Budgeting for Modern Government* (New York: St. Martin's Press, 1988); Irene Rubin, *The Politics of Public Budgeting: Getting and Spending, Borrowing and Balancing*, 3d ed. (Chatham, NJ: Chatham House, 1997); Allen Schick, "Twenty-five Years of Budgeting Reform," *OECD Journal on Budgeting* 4, no. 1 (2004); and White and Wildavsky, *The Deficit and the Public Interest.*

7. The classic statement of this problem is Anthony Downs, "Why the Government Budget Is Too Small in a Democracy," *World Politics* 12, no. 4 (1962): 541–63; also see Joseph White, "Making 'Common Sense' of Federal Budgeting," *Public Administration Review* 58, no. 2 (1998).

8. Irene Rubin, "Early Budget Reformers: Democracy, Efficiency, and Budget Reforms," *American Review of Public Administration* 24, no. 3 (1994), 246.

9. Paul Posner, "The Continuity of Change: Public Budgeting and Finance Reforms over 70 Years," *Public Administration Review* 67 (Nov/Dec 2007): 1023.

10. Caiden, "Paradox, Ambiguity, and Enigma," 84.

11. United States Senate Committee on Appropriations, *Committee on Appropriations U.S. Senate: 1867–2008.* 110th Congress, 2d Session, Document no. 14. Washington, DC: U.S. Government Printing Office, 2008.

12. Allen Schick, "The Road to PPB," *Public Administration Review* 26, no. 4 (1966); Aaron Wildavsky, "The Political Economy of Efficiency: Cost-Benefit Analysis, Systems Analysis, and Program Budgeting," *Public Administration Review* 26, no. 4 (1966).

13. The coordinating function expanded to legislation, and even that can have benefits to Congress by revealing problems before extensive investment in an initiative.

Richard E. Neustadt, "Presidency and Legislation: The Growth of Central Clearance," *American Political Science Review* 48, no. 3 (1954).

14. Mathew J. Dickinson and Andrew Rudalevige, "Worked Out in Fractions: Neutral Competence, FDR, and the Bureau of the Budget," *Congress & the Presidency* 34, no. 1 (2007); Frederick C. Mosher, *A Tale of Two Agencies: A Comparative Analysis of the General Accounting Office and the Office of Management and Budget* (Baton Rouge: Louisiana State University Press, 1984); Donald Stone, "Administrative Management: Reflections on Origins and Accomplishments," *Public Administration Review* 50, no. 1 (1990).

15. Wildavsky, *The Politics of the Budget Process*; for a useful corrective that emphasizes the budget bureau's role, see John P. Crecine, M. S. Kamlet, D. C. Mowery, and M. Winer, "The Role of the Office of Management and Budget in Executive Branch Budgetary Decision-Making," in *Proceedings of the First Annual Research Conference on Public Policy and Management*, ed. J. P. Crecine (Greenwich, CT: JAI Press, 1980).

16. Neustadt, *Presidential Power*, 83.

17. Allen Schick, *Congress and Money* (Washington, DC: Urban Institute Press, 1980).

18. How reconciliation worked in practice is a very complicated story. I have argued (White and Wildavsky, *The Deficit and the Public Interest*) that the Ways and Means and Finance committees remained the key players; and certainly they took the lead in ways the president did not after 1981. For other accounts, see John B. Gilmour, *Reconcilable Differences? Congress, the Budget Process, and the Deficit* (Berkeley: University of California Press, 1990); and Allen Schick, *Reconciliation and the Congressional Budget Process* (Washington, DC: AEI Press, 1982).

19. This development is documented in White and Wildavsky, *The Deficit and the Public Interest,* quoted on 431–32. The president thought he was taking domestic programs hostage.

20. See the statement of Rep. Lee Hamilton in the *Congressional Record* for May 3, 1989, pp. H1553–56.

21. A longer account with citations is in White, "Presidential Power and the Budget."

22. Joseph White and Aaron Wildavsky, "Public Authority and the Public Interest: What the 1980s Budget Battles Tell Us about the American State," *Journal of Theoretical Politics* 1, no. 1 (1989).

23. White, "Presidential Power and the Budget."

24. Bernard T. Pitsvada, "A Call for Budget Reform," and see also Fred Thompson, "Reforming the Federal Budget Process: A Symposium Commemorating the 75th Anniversary of the Executive Budget," both in *Policy Sciences* 29 (1996); quote p. 225.

25. See the postscript to White and Wildavsky 1991 op.cit., *The Deficit and the Public Interest*, as well as Shelley Lynne Tomkin, *Inside OMB: Politics and Process in the President's Budget Office* (Armonk, NY: M. E. Sharpe, 1980).

26. Philip G. Joyce and Roy T. Meyers, "Budgeting during the Clinton Presidency," *Public Budgeting & Finance* (Spring 2001), 2; also Drew, *Showdown*, and Maraniss and Weiskopf, *Tell Newt to Shut Up!*

27. The quotes are from Daniel J. Parks, "Between the Lockbox and a Hard Place," *CQ Weekly Online*, September 8, 2001, at library.cqpress.com/cqweekly/weeklyreport107-0000003061-17 (accessed June 11, 2008). For an explanation of the arguments about Social Security, see Joseph White, *False Alarm: Why the Greatest Threat to Social Security and Medicare Is the Campaign to "Save" Them* (Baltimore: Johns Hopkins University Press, 2003).

28. See United States Congressional Budget Office, *The Economic and Budget Outlook: Fiscal Years 1999–2008* (Washington, DC: Congressional Budget Office, 1998), 67.

29. The administration was divided about the 1993 caps; Tomkin, *Inside* OMB, op.cit.

30. On process, see Joyce and Meyers, "Budgeting during the Clinton Presidency"; for numbers, U.S. Congressional Budget Office, *The Budget and Economic Outlook: Fiscal Years 2004–2013* (Washington, DC: Congressional Budget Office, 2003).

31. For a good example of the fundamentalist view about the evils of taxes, in an unlikely place, see White House Office of Homeland Security, *National Strategy for Homeland Security* (July 2002), 65.

32. Jonathan Oberlander, "Through the Looking Glass: The Politics of the Medicare Prescription Drug, Improvement, and Modernization Act," *Journal of Health Politics, Policy, and Law* 32, no. 2 (2007).

33. Brian Friel, "Spending: The Power of the Purse Strings." *NationalJournal.com*, July 28, 2007, at www.nationaljournal.com/njmagazine/print_friendly. php?ID=nj_20070728_7 (accessed June 11, 2008).

34. For a variety of views of PART, see F. Stevens Redburn, Robert J. Shea, and Terry F. Buss, eds., *Performance Management and Budgeting: How Governments Learn from Experience* (Armonk, N.Y.: M. E. Sharpe, 2008). For a summary of other management initiatives during the 1990s, see Posner, "The Continuity of Change."

35. For examples of the latter, see Beryl A. Radin, "The Legacy of Federal Management Change: PART Repeats Familiar Problems," in *Performance Management and Budgeting*, eds. Redburn et al.

36. Administration officials virtually disappeared from the Sunday morning talk shows when the budget was released. Two sources in my interviews said that was more because the major networks were not interested, but that in itself says something negative about the stature of the president's budget. Stan Collender, "Ego Interrupted," *NationalJournal.com*, February 28, 2007, at www.nationaljournal.com/scripts/printpage/cgi?/members/buzz/budget/022707 (accessed June 12, 2008).

37. Terry M. Moe, "The Politicized Presidency," in John E. Chubb and Paul E. Peterson, eds., *The New Direction in American Politics*, eds. in John E. Chubb and Paul E. Peterson (Washington, DC: The Brookings Institution, 1985). On the contrast, see Dickinson and Rudalevige, "Worked Out in Fractions" and William F. West, "Neutral Competence and Political Responsiveness: An Uneasy Relationship," *Policy Studies Journal* 33, no. 2 (2005).

Chapter Eleven

Congress and the President: "Yes We Can!" or "Can We?"

Mark J. Oleszek and Walter J. Oleszek

During the November 2008 presidential campaign, Barack Obama successfully employed several rhetorical expressions, such as "change," "Yes we can," and "postpartisanship." His themes suggested to Congress and the country that an Obama presidency would be a watershed event for at least two reasons—he would be the first African American elected as president and one who could usher in a bipartisan era in legislative-executive relations. As Obama once said, I don't "look like all those other presidents" on our currency. That reality is truly a momentous and historical American development. What remains outstanding is whether President Obama will be able to ease the bitter partisanship that has suffused congressional Democratic and Republican relationships for more than a decade to win enactment of his policy priorities. Can he bring a "new politics" of unity, compromise, and conciliation to national governance? How much change, and what kind, will he be able to deliver? What factors might strengthen his chances of being a successful chief executive and legislator?

The Democratic 111th Congress (2009–2011) and President Obama face a multiplicity of major and overlapping domestic and international challenges. Domestically, the nation confronts a number of critical issues, such as a heavy dependence on oil; an escalation of health care costs and the number of uninsured; a transportation system that requires modernization; and the financial meltdown on Wall Street triggered by the subprime mortgage debacle, an event that has led to the most dramatic governmental intervention in the marketplace since the Great Depression. Internationally, Iraq and Afghanistan remain urgent and long-term issues. The international agenda also includes global warming, the fight against terrorists, the impact of global economic integration on American workers, and the challenge of encouraging global economic cooperation among nations. When asked about fiscal deficits estimated to exceed $1 trillion in fiscal year 2009, Representative David Obey (D-WI), the chair of the Appropriations Committee, highlighted numerous "deficits" facing the 111th Congress and the Obama administration:

> In fact, we've got a hell of a lot of deficits. We've got a budget deficit. We've got an education deficit. We've got a healthcare coverage deficit. We've got a scientific research deficit. We've got an infrastructure deficit. This country has neglected for a long time so many of the basic investments that we need to make this country strong. And we also have an equity deficit, a fairness deficit.[1]

This chapter will shed analytical light on the prospects for major policy change during the Obama administration. First, we identify several major structural elements of American politics and policy making that make it difficult for the House, the Senate, and the president to act collectively to forge the winning coalitions required to make tough governing decisions. Second, we consider key characteristics that shape legislative-executive relationships based on the experiences of three previous presidents who won congressional approval of their policy priorities during their first year in office—Franklin Delano Roosevelt (FDR), Lyndon Baines Johnson (LBJ), and Ronald Reagan. Finally, we assess these characteristics as they relate to President Obama and conclude with our view of what might facilitate a legislative-executive relationship of "yes we can" governance.

THE STRUCTURAL ELEMENTS OF NATIONAL GOVERNANCE

Policy making in decentralized political systems tends to occur incrementally through a process of "partisan mutual adjustment" among competing organized interests.[2] Politicians are said to "referee the group struggle" by assigning winners and losers in statutory form.[3] Incremental policy making also has a strong political appeal, because incremental change is usually the path of least resistance for lawmakers when a pluralistic distribution of power exists among groups. In this way, the current state of policy generally reflects the distribution of political influence within society and major policy departures can be met with heated opposition from affected groups.

It is one thing for President Obama to say on the campaign trail that he can deliver "change we can believe in"; it is quite another to fulfill his campaign promises after being sworn into office. Voters often have high hopes and expectations that simply cannot be met by an incoming president and Congress. Dashed expectations can foster voter frustration with their government and its leaders, especially the president. Leaders are expected to devise strategies that simultaneously promote broad public support for major policy priorities and muster, concomitantly, the winning coalitions required to get them through the House, the Senate, and to the White House. Whether lawmakers and the president are able to resolve many of today's critical issues will depend on the coalition-building skills of influential actors who understand the complex interplay of three bedrock features of national governance: constitutional limitations, bicameralism, and the political environment.

Constitutional Limitations

One of the nation's most important political principles is to divide power. The Constitution is replete with provisions that underscore this principle. Wary of concentrating too much power in the central government, the Founding Fathers created a system of separate institutions sharing and competing for power as a way to safeguard individual liberty. An essential corollary of separation of powers is "checks and balances." The framers realized that ambitious individuals in each branch might seek to aggrandize power at the expense of the other branches. To restrain each branch, the framers devised a system allowing each of the nationally elective branches to protect itself from encroachments by the others. As James Madison famously phrased it in *Federalist No. 51*: "Ambition must be made to counteract ambition."

Congressional checks on the president, however, are not self-enforcing, and they may erode and wither away if not exercised. During the two terms of the Bush-Cheney administration, for example, the president took an expansive view of executive authority, especially in the exercise of war powers after the 9/11 terrorist attacks. As commander in chief under the Constitution, President Bush asserted virtually unlimited authority to wage a global war on terrorism. At his urging, Congress passed legislation in October 2002 that many interpreted as authorizing an invasion of Iraq, which occurred in March 2003. (Congress has the constitutional authority to declare war, but that authority has not been exercised since the World War II declaration.) What James Madison did not expect or foresee was that Congress might lack the requisite "ambition" to challenge an overly assertive and ambitious president. Legislative prerogatives left undefended often migrate to the executive branch and can be difficult for Congress to reclaim.

The Constitution outlines an intricate system of governance. Power is divided among the branches and between levels of government and popular opinion is reflected differently in each. Congress and the president—each with different constituencies, terms of office, and times of election—can both claim to represent majority sentiment on national issues. Conflict among the branches, especially the elective units, inheres in our constitutional system just as the framers intended. On the major issues of the day, the advantage often goes to those who want to frustrate or obstruct policy making. Enacting consequential legislation typically requires a complex three-branch bargaining process with any one of the three—the House, the Senate, and the White House—able to "veto" passage of potential laws. How well President Obama manages this three-way relationship will influence significantly the success of his administration. The constitutional reality is that neither the legislative nor the executive branch can enact laws without the other's concurrence. As former Speaker J. Dennis Hastert (R-IL, 1999–2007) once said: "The art of what is possible is what you can get passed in the House, what you can get passed in the Senate and signed by the president. It is a three-sided game."[4]

Bicameralism

Another constitutional element merits separate attention: bicameralism. In creating the Congress, the Founding Fathers, as Alexander Hamilton wrote in *Federalist No. 60*, deliberately employed "dissimilar modes" of constituting the House and Senate to "permanently nourish different propensities and inclinations." Size, term of office, and constituency are among the many differences that distinguish the House from the Senate. There is one other significant interchamber difference—their rules and procedures—that will surely influence President Obama's ability to pass his legislative program.

The House

The House of Representatives is a "majority rule" institution. Its rules, precedents, and practices are geared toward enabling a majority to govern and to pass its legislative priorities. This principle applies whether the majority is composed exclusively from members of the dominant party—the preference, for example, of Speaker Hastert—or forged via a bipartisan coalition.[5] However a House majority is created, if the winning coalition of 218 lawmakers (half the House plus one) is determined and stays united, it can roll over any minority obstructionism. To cite Speaker Hastert, the rules of the House "insure that the will of the majority" will prevail.[6]

What this means is that President Obama will likely look first to the House to advance his agenda. No doubt there will be plenty of times that President Obama will move legislation by following the practice of his immediate predecessor in the White House during the period when Republicans controlled the Congress. "Bush's core legislative strategy has been to pass bills that track his preferences through the GOP-controlled House," wrote a well-known journalist. "Then the White House tries to get whatever it can through the [Republican] Senate, hoping to tilt the final product further in its direction in House-Senate negotiations."[7]

Speaker Nancy Pelosi (D-CA, 2007–), commands an array of parliamentary tools that she can employ to shepherd President Obama's agenda through the House. Foremost among these tools is her control of the Rules Committee. She appoints the nine majority party members, including the chair. This panel reports special rules—House resolutions that establish the conditions for debating and amending legislation. Special rules almost always attract majority support, usually on a party-line vote.

A fundamental feature of special rules is that they structure the amending process, either permitting, limiting, or preventing amendments to the bill made in order by the special rule. The fundamental goal of the Rules Committee is to establish a procedural playing field that advantages the majority party. For example, rules can report procedural resolutions that protect administration-backed measures from troublesome amendments. In short, the shape of the special rule, along with the mobilization of the required votes for passage of the underlying legislation, can help to ensure House enactment of the president's initiatives. Setting the agenda and the terms of debate goes a long way toward determining the outcome.

The Senate

The Senate is a "minority rule" institution. Its rules and practices grant every senator large procedural authority, such as unlimited freedom of debate (the filibuster) and unlimited opportunities to offer amendments, including nongermane amendments to pending legislation. There are ways to curb both of these prerogatives, but, fundamentally, the Senate is an institution where it is possible for one senator, a small group of senators, or minority party lawmakers to block action preferred by the majority. As Senator Byron Dorgan (D-ND) underscored, "The only thing it's easy to do in the Senate is slow things down. The Senate is 100 human brake pads."[8] Added Senator Judd Gregg (R-NH), "The Founding Fathers intended us to be inert, and we've expanded that ability to a point where a single senator can block action."[9]

The filibuster (extended debate) is the Senate's most famous dilatory tactic. A three-fifths vote of the entire Senate is required to invoke cloture and end a filibuster (if no vacancies, 60 of 100 as prescribed by Senate Rule XXII). If the Senate is ideologically polarized and narrowly divided, it is often impossible to attract 60 votes. The strategy of Senate Republicans in the 110th Congress was to use the threat and sometimes the reality of the filibuster to slow down or frustrate action on Democratic agenda items. As a result, Majority Leader Harry Reid (D-NV) filed a record number of cloture petitions (over ninety), a dramatic indicator of the difficulty of moving legislation or nominations through the Senate. For their part, Republicans criticized Reid for trying to make the Senate function like the House: limiting debate and blocking unwanted minority party amendments.[10] Given the ideological divide between the two parties, it is perhaps no surprise that each side has employed procedural hardball tactics in service to their political and policy goals.

The November 2008 elections did not produce a 60-vote majority for Senate Democrats. However, at some point it is likely that the 111th Senate will have 60 Democrats (Independents Joe Lieberman, Conn., and Bernard Sanders, Vt., affiliate with the majority party) and 40 Republicans.[11] There are also opportunities for the majority party to attract GOP moderates, such as Olympia Snowe and Susan Collins of Maine, to achieve or exceed the 60-vote cloture requirement to end a filibuster. But losing Democratic votes could be costly because it was mainly GOP moderates who were toppled by Democrats in the November 2008 elections. As a result, Senate Republicans are likely to stay united and utilize, or threaten to employ, a large array of dilatory tools to give themselves a bargaining edge in dealing with Majority Leader Reid and the Obama administration.

Sometimes more than one cloture vote is required on a measure. Even when Democrats are able to invoke cloture, thirty hours of additional debate is still allowed. If the Senate's most precious commodity is time, then various stalling tactics can be used to run out the clock and prevent important legislation or nominations from making it through the Senate. GOP senators might also offer amendments the size of the Manhattan telephone directory and require that they be read in full. In effect, the reading clerk would conduct a "virtual filibuster" on their behalf. In short, strategic use of parliamentary rules and maneuvers by the minority party can effectively stymie action on various parts of President Obama's agenda. It is in the "minority rule" Senate where the president will find the going tough compared to the "majoritarian" House.

Political Environment

A large number of topics that bear upon the Obama presidency are subsumed under the rubric *political*. Among the most significant factors to lawmaking are the following: the budget deficit, the role of interest groups, and the advent of a 24/7 news media.

Budget Deficit

The stark reality facing President Obama is the surge of red ink in both the near- and long-term that might constrain his legislative program. "A president can't do a lot of . . . things if the economic foundations of this country [are] going to hell," exclaimed Leon Panetta, former chief of staff to President

Clinton and President Obama's director of the Central Intelligence Agency.[12] Several numbers make the point about the dismal fiscal picture facing the president. Near-term, the 2009 fiscal deficit was once estimated to be $455 billion, the highest ever projection at the time. That figure has been modified upward by the Congressional Budget Office to $1.2 trillion—with the debt (in January 2009, $10.7 trillion) projected to rise by $2 trillion by the end of the year[13]—given costs associated with the financial bailout, a slumping economy, rising unemployment, and the resulting drop in tax revenue.

With an ailing economy, many economists believe that now is not the time for balancing budgets. In their view, renewed government spending and tax cutting is required to boost a recessionary economy whose depth and duration remain unknown.[14] Accordingly, Congress and the Obama administration passed a major economic recovery package carrying a price tag of nearly $800 billion as the first priority of the 111th Congress.

The cost of the crisis will boost interest payments on the debt, an estimated $260 billion in 2008. Interest payments crowd out money that could be used for education, health care, or other important purposes. Increasingly, interest payments are sent abroad to foreign nations, which own about 45 percent of the publicly held debt, "up from 15 percent in 1985."[15] The federal debt—the accumulation of annual deficits—is soon expected to surpass $13 trillion given the government's rescue plan to stabilize various financial firms and banks. Long-term, there are unfunded commitments (Social Security, Medicare, environmental cleanup, government pensions, etc.) that by some estimates exceed $55 trillion.[16] Thus, the budget outlook for President Obama is grim. He faces "a fiscal and economic mess of historic proportions," stated Senate Budget chairman Kent Conrad (D-ND). "It will take years to dig our way out."[17]

Interest Groups

The nation's capital is filled with lobbying groups and associations, although the exact number varies based on who is doing the counting. A well-connected lobbyist wrote that "there are now more than 35,000 registered lobbyists in Washington,"[18] and the latest figures show that they spent nearly $2.8 billion in 2007 lobbying Congress and the federal executive branch—about $200 million more than they spent in 2006.[19]

Looking in the Washington telephone directory under "associations" reveals as much about what moves Congress and the president as does the Constitution. Protected by various constitutional provisions—for example, the right of the people to petition their government for redress of grievances—lobbying and lawmaking have been twin phenomena from the nation's beginning. Lobbying "has been so deeply woven into the American political fabric that one could, with considerable justice, assert that the history of lobbying comes close to being the history of American legislation."[20]

Recent years have witnessed an explosion in the number and types of groups organized to pursue their ends on Capitol Hill. Compared with a few decades ago, many more industry associations, public affairs lobbies, single-issue groups, political action committees, and foreign agents are engaged in lobbying. Various factors account for the proliferation of groups, such as the government's large regulatory role and the competition for federal dollars. Many of these groups employ innovative technological lobbying techniques to mobilize for or against various policy initiatives, the so-called netroots—the online version of grassroots activists. Advocacy groups for the National Institutes of Health (NIH), for example, created a website to mobilize its allies in the scientific community "to attempt to reverse the shrinking budget increases at the NIH."[21] Many victories today are won in Washington because of sophisticated lobbying campaigns back in senators' home states or the districts of House members.

The universe of clashing and competing interests can make it difficult to move legislation through the House and Senate. Any consequential policy change inevitably creates winners and losers among various groups. Yet these groups are major policy-making players. They provide information and analysis to lawmakers, draft legislation and amendments, and provide campaign contributions and support. In the view of a top House committee staff aide, "We shouldn't blame companies for spending a lot of money on lobbying because it's an investment strategy."[22]

A significant issue for the Obama administration is that these many interest groups are positioned either to advance or, alternatively, to block, modify, or defeat the policy goals of the president. Many interest groups are informally affiliated with one party or the other, and their demands for "loyalty make it difficult for lawmakers to compromise."[23] Members, too, engage in "reverse lobbying"—pressuring lobbyists to support their legislative goals, which may contradict those of the administration. In sum, lobbyists can help or hinder the enactment of legislation. In the judgment of a top lobbyist, most lobbying activity is "negative stuff"—to stop things from happening.[24] The challenge for the president and his allies inside and outside the legislative branch is to overcome the obstacle course called "the Congress."

The Advent of a 24/7 Media

During the 1960s and 1970s, most Americans—and many to this day—received their news from the three major networks (ABC, CBS, and NBC).[25] Walter Cronkite, the CBS evening news anchor, was among the most trusted and respected individuals in American society. The network broadcasts were politically balanced, in large measure because the major networks were watched by a broad and diverse cross-section of the general public. Political bias in reporting was thought to hurt viewership, although there were commentators who did allege the networks provided slanted political news. Many scholars view the bias of the networks as financial rather than political; that is, they focus more on conflict, scandal, and political personalities because those topics attract and engage larger audiences.[26]

Major media changes came with the advent of cable television, the Internet, blogs, podcasting, text messaging, YouTube, Twitter, and more. Cable television, for example, provides viewers with scores of around-the-clock news channels and public affairs programming. The proliferation of media means that people can select the kind of news or public affairs broadcasting that suits their political predilections. The Fox New Channel generally presents political analysis from a conservative viewpoint, as do many talk radio programs such as Rush Limbaugh's. CNN (NBC's Cable News Network) attracts a different, more liberally-oriented audience, as does National Public Radio. As one analyst noted: "People are increasingly picking their media on the basis of partisanship. If you're Republican and conservative, you listen to talk radio and watch the Fox News Channel. If you're liberal and Democratic, you listen to National Public Radio and watch the *NewsHour with Jim Lehrer*."[27]

The media has splintered into so many smaller and smaller segments— dubbed "narrowcasting" (a fundamental difference from the "broadcasting" period of the Cronkite years)—that people can select a variety of alternative sources of information that bolster and reinforce their political biases or points of view. With so many competing and conflicting sources of information and analysis, voters often have a hard time separating fact from opinion, reality from misperception. What this can mean for Congress and the president is greater difficulty in forging the public consensus and support required to win enactment of consequential policy initiatives.

The drumbeat of 24/7 news accounts about scandal, strife, stalemate, and partisan infighting makes it difficult for elective leaders to set aside their differences to produce policy achievements. "In order to get on the nightly news or to get on those talk shows that people listen to, you have to do or say something that is outrageous or newsworthy," said Senator Michael Crapo (R-ID). "One way to do that is to be partisan."[28] The Internet, too, is filled with liberal and conservative websites and bloggers of every ideological stripe. Numerous online activists, for example, "from across the political spectrum" lobbied against Treasury Secretary Hank Paulson's initial 2008 plan for a $700 billion bailout of numerous financial institutions.[29]

An overlay to the structures of American politics—the Constitution, interests groups, the media, and so on—is the increased enmity in Congress between the two political parties. Various long- and short-term developments produced this result; they have been analyzed and discussed in numerous sources, but a few major ones merit brief mention.[30] Heightened partisan feelings between Democrats and Republicans are due in large measure to a significant demographic development. A national resorting of the two parties' constituency bases has produced large policy differences between them. The outcome, as journalist David S. Broder wrote, is two parties "more cohesive internally and further apart from each other philosophically."[31] Or as a GOP senator put it, "Today, most Democrats are far left; most Republicans are to the right; and there are very few in between."[32]

Little surprise, therefore, that we see a large number of party-line votes (a majority of one party facing off against a majority of the other party) and an increase in party cohesion on those votes. "Both Republicans and Democrats are standing with their own party against the other on about 90 percent of the [contested] votes, a level of lockstep uniformity unimaginable only a generation or two ago."[33] One result of the sharper partisanship is a tendency for "civility to lose out to conflict, compromise to deadlock, deliberation to sound bites, and legislative product to campaign issues."[34]

PRESIDENTIAL RELATIONS WITH CONGRESS

Scholars and journalists have been enamored with the honeymoon period, the first one hundred days of a new administration, ever since FDR's tremendous success in advancing his far-reaching agenda to deal with the Great Depression.[35] A president's accomplishments during the honeymoon period and beyond largely hinge on two key factors: his own leadership skills and the environmental context in which he operates. Leadership skills inhere in the person elected to serve as president. If politics is called the art of the possible, it is often the president who is instrumental in defining and shaping the possibilities. For example, does the president have a set of goals and a vision that can inspire Congress and the country to support him? Can he adapt to the context in which he finds himself—both the broad environment and that unique to each major priority—to win congressional approval of his ideas? Does he have certain qualities—intelligence, integrity, determination, good judgment, strategic and tactical skills, and so on—to achieve his goals in the give-and-take of hard bargaining with lawmakers? Can he rally public support for his objectives? Lessons from three previous administrations are especially instructive.

Presidents Franklin Roosevelt, Lyndon Johnson, and Ronald Reagan enjoyed significant successes in their dealings with Congress. It is no coincidence that each took office during a national crisis, enjoyed sizable majorities in Congress,[36] and orchestrated a skillful communications strategy. We discuss these factors as they apply to the three presidents, recognizing that many other conditions influence a chief executive's initial success with Congress (the experience and ability of his key White House staff, for example). Are these same three factors broadly in play for President Obama? Might these factors enable Obama to overcome the challenges of governance?

FDR

Franklin Delano Roosevelt was inaugurated on March 4, 1933, the third year of the Great Depression: the nation's greatest economic calamity. The banking system had collapsed, unemployment approached 25 percent, and scores of individuals and families were suffering. Still, the president acted with optimism and determination to deal with the crisis and requested Congress to follow his lead. As FDR said in his inaugural address: "I shall ask the Congress for the one remaining instrument to meet the crisis—broad Executive power to wage a war against the emergency, as great as the power that would be given to use if we were in fact invaded by a foreign foe."

The 73d Congress, meeting in a special session on March 9, 1933, per the call of the president, responded swiftly to Roosevelt's New Deal program.[37] That same day the House passed the Emergency Banking Act to give Roosevelt broad authority to deal with the banking crisis. Members had no copies of the text of the measure. Instead, Speaker Henry Rainey (D-IL) read the bill to them. After no more than forty minutes of debate, the House passed the bill (H.R. 1491) without a recorded vote. Later that day, at around 7:30 p.m., the Senate agreed to the House-passed bill by a 73 to 7 vote.[38] The measure was then sent to President Roosevelt who, a little over an hour later, signed the bill into law. It was unusual, indeed, for the inherently slow-moving Congress to act with such speed. As House GOP leader Bertrand Snell (NY) explained, "The House is burning down, and the President of the United States says this is the way to put out the fire."[39] Important to note is that Roosevelt's party enjoyed large majorities in both the House (310D, 122R) and the Senate (60D, 36R).

President Roosevelt's honeymoon period and his first year in office witnessed a pace of activity rarely seen in American history. During the first three months of the special legislative session, "Franklin Roosevelt sent fifteen messages to Congress, guided fifteen major laws to enactment, delivered ten speeches, held press conferences and cabinet meetings twice a week, conducted talks with foreign heads of state, sponsored an international conference, made all the major decisions in domestic and foreign policy, and never displayed fright or panic and rarely even bad temper."[40] His success in dealing with Congress, according to an analyst of the one-hundred-day period, occurred because of the president's "picking up cross-party support where available, threatening veto in cases where sufficient support was unattainable and compromise considered unacceptable, and compromising adroitly when necessary and feasible."[41]

Roosevelt also used radio to reach millions of Americans. Called "fireside chats," FDR made his first such address to the nation on March 12, 1933, just a week after being sworn into office. Radio addresses accomplished a number of objectives, such as explaining to the people in clear and understandable language what was being done to resolve the crisis and bolstering hope and optimism that Congress and the president were acting quickly and in a bipartisan manner to do so. For example, in the first fireside chat, FDR began by saying: "I want to tell you what has been done in the last few days, why it was done, and what the next steps are going to be." He explained the origins of the banking crisis in terms reminiscent of today's financial meltdown:

> We had a bad banking situation. Some of our bankers had shown themselves either incompetent or dishonest in their handling of the people's funds. They had used the money entrusted to them in speculation and unwise loans. This was, of course, not true in the vast majority of banks, but it was true in enough of them to shock the people into a sense of insecurity. . . . It was Government's job to straighten out this situation and do it as quickly as possible. And the job is being performed.[42]

FDR also used his fireside chats to enlist the people's help in persuading members of Congress to back the administration's programs, an appeal for popular support that Professor Samuel Kernell calls "going public."[43]

LBJ

Vice President Lyndon Baines Johnson succeeded to the presidency on November 23, 1963, the day President John F. Kennedy was assassinated. The next year Johnson won a landslide popular (61 percent) and Electoral College (486 to 52) victory over GOP Senator Barry Goldwater. In comparison to the economic crisis during the Great Depression, this period was a time of societal tension. In 1963 Dr. Martin Luther King Jr. delivered his "I have a dream" speech at the Lincoln Memorial before 250,000 people who supported King's March on Washington for Freedom and Jobs. The next year the House and Senate passed the Gulf of Tonkin Resolution, which allowed Johnson to expand the Vietnam War.

When the 89th Congress convened on January 4, 1965, Democrats controlled the House (295 to 140) and the Senate (68 to 32). No president since FDR has enjoyed such large congressional majorities, which helped Johnson win substantial support from congressional Democrats and moderate and progressive Republicans for his top priorities. Importantly, the election of so many new Democrats to the House and Senate weakened the conservative coalition (southern Democrats and conservative Republicans) that previously had stymied action on civil rights, health care, and other presidential initiatives. As a renowned former Senate majority leader, Johnson knew the intricacies and strategies of legislative procedures and politics, as well as the personal likes and dislikes of the members, perhaps better than any other chief executive in history. As he stated, "There is but one way for a President to deal with Congress, and that is continuously, incessantly, and without interruption."[44] If Johnson's policy achievements of 1964 and 1965 are combined, they nearly rival those of FDR's first year: Medicare, the Voting Rights Act of 1965, and federal aid to elementary and secondary schools were all part of Johnson's Great Society agenda, which he first articulated in a 1964 graduation speech at the University of Michigan.

Johnson's oratorical skills were not equal to those of FDR or Ronald Reagan. He had a "peculiar [speaking] style," wrote Harry McPherson, LBJ's special counsel (1964–1969), "which invited caricature. . . . Sometimes it took off into the clouds, driven by populist energy of his youth; sometimes it was as grave as a bishop's; sometimes it was impatient, quick with the hustle of a man who had much to do in a little time."[45] Johnson recognized that the bully pulpit was not his strength. I lack the ability, he said, "to stimulate, inspire, and unite all the public in the country."[46]

Molding and shaping popular opinion to promote the president's agenda in Congress, a component of the "rhetorical presidency," can be accomplished in ways that extend beyond formal public speeches.[47] Johnson was a skillful persuader, bargainer, and negotiator one-on-one or in small groups. During his presidency, House and Senate committee chairs dominated substantive policy making in Congress. They were called the "dukes" and "barons" of Capitol Hill. Winning their support, along with other key lawmakers, facilitated the achievement of the legislative results Johnson wanted. "Johnson and his people," wrote a government professor, "were talking to members of Congress and important staff people all the time, constantly cultivating and fertilizing the legislative domain."[48] In short, Johnson's behind-the-scenes persuasion (dubbed the "Johnson Treatment") of key lawmakers underscores the notion that major legislative successes can speak louder than words alone in defining presidential leadership of Congress.

Ronald Reagan

For President Reagan, 1981 was akin to the huge successes enjoyed by FDR and LBJ in advancing their first-year programs through Congress. First, Reagan won an unexpected landslide Electoral College victory in 1980, winning 489 electoral votes to just 49 for President Jimmy Carter. Reagan won 51 percent of the popular vote in a three-way contest—Independent John Anderson also contended for the White House—but his victory was interpreted as both a landslide and mandate for conservative change by the president-elect and his aides; most lawmakers, including Democrats; pundits; and the press.

Second, the country was experiencing an economic downturn. *Stagflation*—double-digit inflation coupled with high unemployment—gripped the country. By Election Day 1980, many people believed that the nation had "the least satisfactorily performing economy since the Great Depression."[49] Reagan hammered this point home during the 1980 campaign, regularly posing this question to voters: "Are you better off today than you were four years ago?" The Iran hostage crisis also contributed to the country's glum mood. Fifty-two American diplomatic personnel were held hostage by Iranian militants who took over the U.S. Embassy in Teheran on November 4, 1979. The Americans were held hostage for 444 days until their release on January 20, 1981, Inauguration Day for Reagan. Carter's aides contended that the hostage crisis "focused voter frustration on the nation's problems and triggered a late [voter] surge to Reagan."[50]

Third, Reagan's coattails contributed to the GOP's takeover of the Senate, the first time in twenty-six years that Republicans held the majority (53 to 47) in that chamber. Most Senate Republicans had never served in the majority, believed their new status occurred because of Reagan, and wanted to do all they could to help their new president push his program through Congress. In the judgment of political analyst Norman Ornstein, the GOP Senate was the most important factor in Reagan's 1981 success with Congress. "The Republican Senate gave the president much more leverage over the political agenda and the timing of events than he ever would have possessed on his own." He added that had "Republicans moved into majority status in Congress two or four years before Reagan's election, or had majority status been less novel to them, they probably would have displayed less party unity on key votes."[51]

Republicans also gained 33 House seats and with their mainly southern Democratic allies (called boll weevils), they constituted the real majority in the House. Reagan's adroitness in dealing with Congress and the skill of his congressional liaison team produced several significant policy accomplishments by the August 1981 legislative recess. On May 7, 1981, for example, the House adopted the president's controversial program to slash federal spending for social programs and increase military spending. On the key House vote, all 191 GOP members and 63 Democrats backed the president's plan.

Fourth, the public and political discontent in the country and on Capitol Hill was conducive to change. People wanted action to revive the economy and to restore their confidence in the executive's ability to solve problems. Reagan acted quickly to capitalize on this favorable environment. He limited his top priorities and focused public and congressional attention to them. The result: the political firepower of the White House and administration supporters could be effectively mobilized to move Reagan's preferred priorities—tax and spending cuts, defense hikes—successfully through the House and Senate. Some analysts suggest that Reagan's legislative successes by summer 1981 compare favorably with those of FDR and LBJ.[52]

Finally, Reagan, a former movie actor and television personality, was "the Great Communicator." Professor Charles O. Jones referred to Reagan's style of relating to Congress as "communicator in chief."[53] He excelled at lobbying Congress and its members in scores of ways, such as inviting lawmakers to the White House, dispatching his top aides to discuss issues with key members, or going to Capitol Hill to meet with congressional leaders. In addition, Reagan was a master at using television to mobilize popular support for his programs in Congress. In Professor Peterson's view:

> Reagan in 1981 demonstrated considerable skill in using the communications technology of the modern era. He was the first president since JFK to be so completely at home in front of the cameras, and thus the first president to consummate the relationship between the media and politics at a time when nearly every American had access to a television set and most people obtained the bulk of their political information from TV news. Members of the White House staff viewed Reagan's capacity to communicate with the public as one of their greatest assets.[54]

Both congressional Democrats and Republicans acknowledged Reagan's skill in using the media to mobilize public support for his programs. As a House Republican said, "He's catalyzed the people who can really get things done up here—our constituents. After his [nationally televised] tax cut speech, the phones rang off the walls to support his program." A House Democrat stated: "He is especially strong on television and has had a great impact on American attitudes."[55]

PRESIDENT OBAMA AND THE 111TH CONGRESS

President Obama enters office with significant political capital: a big electoral victory, Democratic control of both legislative chambers, popular support among diverse groups, and recognition among Democrats that his political and communication skills strengthened their majorities in the House and Senate. Crises, partisan majorities, and communication skills are among the central components that appear to encourage productive presidential relations with Congress. Using these analytic components, we can make some inferences at this early stage about the prospects for collaboration between President Obama and the Democratic Congress. To be sure, these components do not guarantee smooth relations between the branches, but they do seem to create a favorable context for achieving policy results.

Obama and Crisis

Barack Obama became president in the midst of an economic crisis with global ramifications that raises the specter of another Great Depression. The country has been in a recession since December 2007, and the economic slump is predicted to be the longest and most severe since World War II.[56] Recessionary signs abound:

- The nation lost 1.25 million jobs in three months (September, October, and November 2008) with no end in sight to job losses.[57]
- The stock market is on a downward track and subject to some of the most erratic swings in U.S. history.
- Giant financial institutions, such as Lehman Bros., Wachovia Corp., Bear Stearns, Fannie Mae and Freddie Mac (mortgage agencies) and American International Group (an insurance entity), either went out of business or required a bailout by the federal government.
- Peoples' retirement pensions and 401(k) plans plummeted $2.5 trillion in fifteen months because of the "prolonged tumble" of the stock market.[58]
- The "big three" automobile companies—General Motors, Ford, and Chrysler—require federal loans to avoid bankruptcy. On June 1, 2009, the unthinkable happened and General Motors went bankrupt.[59]

The causes of the economic meltdown are many, but the roots of the crisis involve the subprime mortgage debacle and the bursting of the housing bubble. During the early 2000s, scores of people bought homes they could not afford because lenders were giving them low interest rates and easy credit terms, even when individuals had bad credit ratings. "More and more loans to more and more people helped send home values to unsustainable highs," wrote a journalist. He continues:

> Rising home prices made people feel richer, so they borrowed against the equity in their homes. Banks bought up securities based on those loans. But when the housing market collapsed, those securities were suddenly worth much less and so the balance sheets of the banks were greatly weakened. Banks now are trying to strengthen themselves by hoarding their assets, rather than making loans. So now you need a sterling credit rating to get a loan. This has a spiraling effect. Orders for new cars have fallen dramatically, which means that auto companies are laying off workers. Those workers have less money to spend, affecting other businesses—and the problem just keeps getting worse. If there are few loans and little spending, the country [falls into a recession that it is in today].[60]

Many other factors contributed to the economic downturn in addition to the housing problem. They include the lack of financial oversight by Congress and the erroneous belief that market forces would prompt self-regulation by lenders, brokers, realtors, traders, and others.[61] The complexity of creative financial instruments like "credit default swaps" (insurance contracts on various assets) made it difficult for investors and government auditors and regulators to understand the risks associated with these instruments. Credit rating agencies gave triple A values to securities that ended up in the junk category. There was also failure on the part of business leaders.[62]

The Democratic 110th Congress and the Bush administration (principally the secretary of the treasury and the Federal Reserve chairman) tried all manner of initiatives to get the economy back on track. On October 3, 2008, President Bush signed a $700 billion financial bailout package into law, which granted wide discretion to the treasury secretary "to buy up troubled mortgage-related securities in a desperate attempt to unclog credit markets and clean up the balance sheets of banks and other financial institutions teetering on collapse."[63] A few weeks later the treasury secretary decided a better way to deal with the crisis was to shift from purchasing bad mortgage securities to injecting $250 billion directly into banks to recapitalize them so they could make loans to people and businesses.[64] The $700 billion program was called by some "a New New Deal, [government intervention] in private markets to an extent not seen since the days of the Great Depression."[65]

Despite these various initiatives, the economy continues to contract.[66] President Obama and his economic team, working with congressional Democratic leaders, developed their own economic stimulus plan, a top priority for rapid enactment. He presented congressional Democrats with a stimulus proposal costing at least $800 billion over two years (roughly $300 billion in tax cuts and $500 billion in spending).[67] The package would include "middle-class tax cuts, aid to strapped state governments and investments in domestic priorities such as infrastructure, health-care technology and education."[68] The stimulus plan is expected to create or preserve in the neighborhood of three to four million jobs over two years. As Obama said with respect to his public works program, "We will create millions of jobs by making the single-largest new investment in our national infrastructure since the creation of the federal highway system [under President Dwight Eisenhower] in the 1950s."[69] Obama also cautioned that there are no quick fixes to an economy in recession. "We are facing a crisis of historic proportions," he said. "The economy is likely to get worse before it gets better. Full recovery will not happen immediately."[70]

Critics of federal spending maintain that economic growth comes from the productivity of workers and American businesses, not from the federal government. "What we cannot do is borrow and spend our way into prosperity, building up huge federal deficits and calling it 'stimulus,'" wrote Wisconsin representative Paul Ryan, the ranking Republican on the Budget Committee.[71] With federal deficits estimated to be over $1.8 trillion in 2009 and entitlement expenditures (Social Security, Medicare, and Medicaid) escalating because of the retirement of more and more senior citizens, people might wonder if the government eventually might need bailing out. The president and many lawmakers recognize these fiscal realities, but believe that spending too little is a greater risk than spending too much, especially if the new spending refurbishes our aging infrastructure and goes to fund investments that can produce tax revenues over time that stem the tide of red ink. Obama's first-year "report card" as president is likely to be significantly influenced by whether the stimulus plan works to produce, as he said, the "change we need" to resolve our economic woes.

Obama and Democratic Majorities in Congress

The 111th Congress (2009–2011) convened on January 6, and is under Democratic control: 257 Democrats and 178 Republicans in the House and 60 Democrats—including Independents Joe Lieberman (CT) and Bernard Sanders (VT), as majority party members—and 40 Republicans in the Senate. A Democratic Congress is certainly a plus for President Obama. With unified government, it is generally easier to negotiate differences and reach agreements with members who are on the same party team than with lawmakers on the opposing team. Congressional Democrats want their president to succeed, in large part because good policy outcomes are likely to produce good political outcomes in 2010. As Representative Chris Van Hollen (D-MD), the chair of the Democratic Congressional Campaign Committee, stated: "Our political fortunes are tied to Barack Obama's. [The 2010 midterm elections] will be a midterm report card not only on Congress but on the White House, too."[72]

History suggests, however, that unified government is no guarantee of a smooth relationship between the legislative and executive branches, as the Carter and Clinton administrations can attest to. After all, the House, Senate, and White House are filled with individuals who have their own policy goals, political objectives, and ideological preferences. Forging winning coalitions on priority issues is no easy task for either congressional leaders or presidents. A fundamental issue for Democrats, then, is how to "strike a balance between separation of powers and intraparty cooperation, and between one-party hegemony and bipartisan cooperation."[73] This balance, at times, may not be easy to achieve for at least three reasons. First, for the past eight years, whether in the minority or majority, congressional Democrats were often in the position of challenging and criticizing the Republican-led administration. Now, with Obama in the White House, they bear large responsibility for shepherding the administration's priorities to enactment.

Second, there is less need for congressional Democrats to develop an alternative agenda to the president's, although with large pent-up demand for policy action on a number of issues Democrats will not be reluctant to initiate legislation of their own.[74] For example, two Senate chairmen, Max Baucus (D-MT) and Edward Kennedy (D-MA), have been working quietly for months to prepare the policy and political groundwork for a major overhaul of health care in the 111th Congress. "They are far ahead of the House, and Barack Obama's . . . administration appears content to let them lead on the issue—counting on Congress to use its own political capital to drive an overhaul as the Obama team focuses on other priorities."[75]

Third, to function effectively, unified government requires bicameral and interbranch cooperation, consultation, and communication between and among the majority party leaders of the House and Senate and the occupant of the White House. During the previous eight years, Democratic leaders of the House and Senate were the face and voice of their party and did not work closely with the Bush II White House. Now it is Obama's megaphone that will be communicating the party's message and agenda to the citizenry, while congressional Democratic leaders amplify, explain, justify, or critique the president's or their own decisions. Just as the presidency is in transition following the November elections, so too is the relationship between legislative leaders and the White House.

Another transition in the 111th Congress is that for congressional Republicans. Without their president in the White House, they will have a much harder time delivering their message to the nation. Senate Republican leader Mitch McConnell (KY) and House GOP leader John Boehner (OH) now are the party's national messengers. Their challenge is at least three-fold: deciding when to cooperate and when to oppose Democratic initiatives, determining when and how to use the lawmaking process to achieve their ultimate political aim—reclaiming majority status and defining their party's message. Should the party return to doctrine articulated by President Reagan (limited government, deregulation, lower taxes, and fiscal restraint, for example), or should it focus instead on craft policies that appeal to diverse and growing demographic groups (Hispanics, Asians, young people, independents, etc.) located across the nation? To set their party agenda and messaging themes, House and Senate Republican leaders are preparing to significantly "expand their coordination efforts" in the 111th Congress.[76]

The political planets appear aligned for major policy enactments at the outset of the 111th Congress. Obama and members of Congress have heard, they say, the public's message that excessive partisanship must end. These public messages and promises of bipartisan cooperation are usually not observed for long. This time might be different, however. Early on, the odds favor an inclusive approach to policy making. As congressional Democratic leaders said, they "hope to use the first several months of 2009 warming Republicans to the idea of working with a Democratic White House and solid majorities in the House and Senate."[77] Interestingly, bipartisanship can be an effective partisan strategy at a time when the country is craving for unity of purpose in dealing with the struggling economy. In a crisis, people want a "Yes we can," not a "No we can't" style of governance.

Obama and Communications

The 44th president is a skilled and eloquent speaker. His speechmaking talent brought him national prominence when he gave a stirring keynote address at the 2004 Democratic National Convention. During his 2008 presidential campaign, Obama's political oratory and use of language rallied voters to his side, refuted criticisms from opponents, and convinced many voters that he was ready to lead. If presidential power is the "power to persuade," as Professor Richard Neustadt wrote in his classic 1960 study *Presidential Power*, then Obama has demonstrated an ability through the power of his oratory to inform, motivate, excite, and persuade people to support his policy agenda. In the view of Winston Churchill, the British prime minister during World War II, "Of all the talents bestowed upon [modern leaders], none is so precious as the gift of oratory."[78] Obama has that gift and, in combination with his intellect and reassuring demeanor, he appears able to use his talents to mold and shape national politics and policy making.

President Obama launched a twenty-first-century style of campaigning and governing unlike any seen before. On the campaign trail, he employed cutting-edge, interactive technologies to mobilize the largest volunteer army of campaigners in electoral history. Obama used e-mail, YouTube videos, blogs, social networking sites (Twitter, Facebook, MySpace), text messaging, webcasting, and more to reach and recruit some thirteen million volunteers across the country who campaigned vigorously on his and vice president Joe Biden's behalf. Obama even announced his candidacy for the White House via a Web video and his selection of Senator Biden as vice president via text messaging.

The president's digital campaign techniques raised record sums of money (over $750 million) from over three million donors.[79] His technology-driven voter registration and turnout operation enabled Obama, a northern liberal, to become the first Democratic president to win a majority of the popular vote (53%) since Jimmy Carter in 1976. He also reconfigured the "red-blue" electoral map by making inroads in states that had long been GOP bastions. Obama carried Virginia, something that had not happened since LBJ's 1964 landslide victory, as well as Indiana and North Carolina, the first Democrat to win those states in over forty years. As one veteran journalist said of Obama's 2008 campaign: "It has rewritten the rules on how to reach voters, raise money, organize supporters, manage the news media, track and mold public opinion, and wage—and withstand—political attacks, including many carried by blogs that did not exist four years ago."[80]

As for governing, the Obama White House appears to have a two-part plan. One part is to keep his nationwide army of supporters active on his behalf and to employ them in various ways. Obama's grassroots operation includes "13 million e-mail addresses, 4 million cellphone contacts and 2 million active supporters."[81] Those volunteers can help Obama generate public support for his congressional agenda, raise money for the 2010 congressional elections, and provide volunteer services to those in need of assistance, such as the victims of natural disasters.[82] Some say that they do not want to be viewed as adjuncts of the Democratic Party (young people and independents, for example). The view is firm, however, that Obama, a former community organizer, sees grassroots activism and technological sophistication "not only as instrumental but also as a way of transforming democracy."[83] As David Axelrod, Obama's senior political adviser, said: "One of the fundamental precepts of our campaign was to use the new technology to reinvigorate our democracy. That's a commitment we will bring to this administration."[84]

As for the second part, President Obama plans to use the Internet to transform governance by promoting participatory democracy as never before seen at the national level.[85] He is not the first president to employ online techniques ("e-government," for instance), but his ideas for an interactive government are pathbreaking. In brief, Obama wants more transparency, accountability, and grassroots engagement in policy making. Several examples of Obama's intentions merit mention.[86]

- Broadcast federal meetings and hearings over the Internet.
- Post lobbying contacts with the federal government in online databases.
- Put nonemergency bills awaiting presidential signature online for five days to permit public view and input.
- Use social networking technologies to encourage citizen engagement in government programs.
- Encourage top federal executives to solicit public suggestions and input via interactive cyber-conversations.
- Conduct presidential Internet "fireside chats."
- Solicit ideas from people for new policies, such as a "Health Corp" of volunteers modeled on President Kennedy's Peace Corps.

Obama also encouraged all Americans to host informal gatherings to discuss how to improve the health system. As he stated: "In order for us to reform our health care system, we must first begin reforming how government communicates with the American people. These Health Care Community Discussions are a great way for the American people to have a direct say in our health reform efforts."[87]

The fundamental goal of this two-way communicative process is to get people to "buy-in" to programs that they had a hand in shaping. "It will be a lot easier to get the American public to adopt any new health-care system if they were part of the process of creating it," claimed one analyst.[88] Another objective of the participatory approach is to circumvent and overcome the many special interests that have stopped major health reform in the past by mobilizing grassroots supporters. It has been suggested that the new technologies could permit President Obama to speak differently to the world by, for example, using Web videos translated into various languages for transmission over the Internet.[89] In brief, Obama is our first Internet president, a chief executive who wants people to share their ideas and speak their mind about the numerous challenges facing this country. Encouraging citizens to play an active role in policy discussions also represents a shrewd political strategy.

PROSPECTS FOR "YES WE CAN" GOVERNANCE

Textbook versions of legislative-executive relations often state, "The president initiates, and the Congress responds." However, where do presidents get their ideas before they propose them to Congress? One of the principal sources is Congress itself. Creative ideas are often born and kept alive through the years and decades within Congress by such devices as hearings and floor debates. Presidents often tailor their proposals to meet anticipated congressional responses to them. Moreover, lawmakers are not reluctant to make changes to executive branch initiatives, to reformulate presidential proposals to make them their own, or to take the lead in advancing policy initiatives. How the president and congressional leaders utilize their respective prerogatives, or comparative advantages, will influence the record of both the 111th Congress and the new administration. Our perspective on "Yes we can" comes to two issues: institutional and political.

Institutionally, one of the most dramatic developments in the modern era is a huge expansion of executive power and influence. If the Founding Fathers returned to observe their handiwork, they might be shocked by the role and reach of today's president and the creation of a "presidential branch" of government. This expansion has been decades in the making, at least since the start of the twentieth century with Presidents Theodore Roosevelt and Woodrow Wilson and later with chief executives such as FDR, LBJ, and Reagan.

The Bush-Cheney administration accelerated this trend after 9/11, especially in national security matters. There are numerous analyses and commentaries about the return of the "imperial presidency."[90] One definition of an imperial presidency is an executive structure "in which enormous discretionary power to respond to national security crises and perceived dangers is concentrated in the office of the president. In this scheme, Congress, willingly or not, is only a bit player."[91] Congress, in our view, needs to reassert its formidable legislative powers, especially in the area of oversight. Only in this way might Congress prevent misjudgments by the president, provide alternative initiatives and perspectives, and hold executive officials accountable for their actions and decisions.

The assertions of executive authority after 9/11 by President George W. Bush are well-known, and include such things as domestic wiretapping; blocking White House aides from testifying before congressional committees; the practice of rendition; the creation of secret prisons abroad; interpreting, or not enforcing, certain provisions of laws as he sees fit; and so on.[92] In defense of the wartime decisions, Vice President Dick Cheney stated that "it would have been unethical or immoral for us not to do everything we could in order to protect the nation."[93] There was some push-back by the Congress against executive claims of authority, such as revising the Foreign Intelligence Surveillance Act (FISA) to provide additional guidelines regarding warrantless surveillance,[94] as well as decisions by federal courts. For instance, the Supreme Court's June 2004 decisions in *Hamdi v. Rumsfeld* and *Rasul v. Bush* constrained executive power even in wartime.

Overall, however, the GOP-controlled Congress largely supported President Bush and generally avoided hard-hitting investigations of administration transgressions. During that period of mainly unified government (2001–2007),[95] Congress was reluctant to conduct hearings and investigations that might embarrass the administration. As one GOP lawmaker explained: "Our party controls the levers of government. We're not about to go out and look beneath a bunch of rocks and try and cause heartburn. Unless [executive officials] really screw up, we're not going to go after them."[96] Another GOP lawmaker said: "We ended up functioning like a parliament, not a Congress. We confused wanting a joint agenda with not doing oversight."[97] Added journalist Ronald Brownstein, the Republican Congress "viewed itself less as an independent branch of government than as a junior partner to the White House in the American equivalent of a parliamentary system."[98]

There was large criticism during this period about the lack of assertive legislative oversight of the administration and complaints about a Congress too willing to go along with the administration's plans and policies. As Representative Barney Frank (D-MA) stated: "I believe we have seen an overreaching by the President. I believe we have seen a seizing of power that should not have been seized by the executive branch. But executive overreaching could not have succeeded as much as it has without congressional dereliction of duty."[99] A key issue for the 111th Congress is whether it will conduct, when warranted, hard-hitting investigations of its own administration.

History demonstrates that unified government is no bar to rigorous oversight. Moreover, when the nation faces a national security threat or a severe economic crisis, Congress and the public often grant new or expanded powers to the administration. Witness, for example, Congress's actions in October 2008 granting one person in the executive branch, the treasury secretary, huge discretionary authority to manage the $700 billion bailout of the financial industry with minimal accountability to the legislative branch. If alive today, James Madison might wonder why Congress granted so much unfettered authority to one executive branch official who was not selected by the public.

Two major ingredients are necessary for Congress to exercise effective oversight: committed lawmakers and a cooperative administration. Given both elements, the chances improve significantly that Congress can restore the constitutional balance between the branches, correcting the "unchecks" and the "imbalances" of the past. Obama's goals of governmental transparency and accountability, if achieved, can help reinvigorate congressional oversight.

Recall Woodrow Wilson's famous quote in his 1885 classic *Congressional Government* that the "informing function" of the legislature is to be preferred even to its legislative or lawmaking function. If Congress does not perform its informing function, then it and the citizenry will remain in "embarrassing and crippling ignorance" of the very public affairs that both need to know and learn about. On this point, "yes we can" boils down to Congress exercising its institutional responsibility to review critically administrative performance and ensure that laws are faithfully executed by the president.

Politically, "yes we can" is about the ability of the House, Senate, and White House to manage the high expectations of the American people and to produce policy enactments that achieve positive results. Most people recognize that the nation is in an economic crisis, and they will likely give the president and Congress some leeway to test various solutions. From a political perspective, this means that congressional leaders and the president must deal with the concerns and interests of different lawmakers and factions. For instance, conservative Democrats may urge tougher border enforcement and expulsion as the way to curb illegal immigration. Conversely, the Congressional Hispanic Caucus might advocate a pathway to citizenship for undocumented individuals. The demonstrated consensus-building skills of Speaker Pelosi will be critically important to the achievement of the president's goals. In combination with the majority rule character of House rules, Pelosi's political acumen will surely mean more policy successes than failures inside that chamber.

The challenge for the president will be the Senate where every senator has the capacity to block legislation, either temporarily or permanently. As Obama said, "Big changes don't happen without big Senate majorities."[100] Senate Majority Leader Reid and President Obama will work diligently to reach the 60 votes required to shut down extended debate in that chamber. Of course, Reid may have to attract GOP support if several of his more conservative Democrats vote against cloture.

Reid is aware that Senate rules provide scores of other dilatory options to senators who want to stymie action on legislation that they oppose. In the judgment of veteran Senator Christopher Dodd (D-CT), "Anybody who wants to do anything meaningful in the Senate—if they're thinking about doing it with one party, they're kidding themselves. It doesn't happen. If you neglect to deal with your counterparts, if you neglect to deal with the other party, you will not achieve much."[101] Lawmaking is typically slow and hard work because it takes time for consultation and deliberation to achieve bipartisan compromises. The Democratic-led House can ram legislation through its chamber but the Senate cannot. The incentive, therefore, will be for Obama and Senate Democrats to give Republicans a genuine chance to present their alternatives at the various lawmaking stages. Asked how he will get things done in the Congress, Obama responded:

> Look, there's always a strategy that has to be put in place in order to get things done, and so how we shape our agenda, how we time it, who we work with, how do we build coalitions, how do we persuade the American people. . . . Yes, we're sitting there, trying to plan out how to get all this stuff done. And, you know, we're inheriting probably the most crowded agenda that any president has inherited in a very, very long time. So, yeah, we're going to have to prioritize, but I don't think people should make assumptions until they actually see what we do, what we're going to be prioritizing and how we're going to do it.[102]

In sum, there are at least five basic conditions necessary for Obama to be the "Yes we can" president. First, the public must want change, and it is plain that they do. The status quo is simply not attractive to most citizens. Second, the president must have the rhetorical and bargaining skills to rally the citizenry and the Congress to his side. Third, the president and congressional leaders must use their political acumen to implement a governing vision that resonates with members of Congress and the public. Fourth, the president must respond aggressively to the economic crisis because lawmakers and citizens alike have a propensity to defer to the president and accept bold decisions during periods of upheaval. To White House chief of staff Rahm Emanuel, "This [economic] crisis provides the opportunity for us to do things that you could not do before."[103]

Lastly, as several presidents have noted, "do it early." The irony is that when presidents are just starting their first term and getting adjusted to a position for which there is no real prior training, they need to act quickly to maximize their chances for large early successes. Reflecting on his time in the White House, President Jimmy Carter urged Obama to act with haste in trying to get top priorities through the Congress, including an energy bill. "I think he can prevail if he does it early and with a great deal of dedication and enthusiasm—and with tenacity."[104] "A president's most effective year is his first," stated Senator Richard Durbin (D-IL), Obama's close friend and confidant. "He is brand new to the office, has a national mandate of varying degrees, and

Congress is usually more open to working with him. After that first year, an election year [2010] is under way and people look at him differently."[105]

NOTES

1. Brian Friel, "Cardboard Hearts, Beware," *National Journal*, August 2, 2008, 47–48.

2. Charles E. Lindblom, *The Intelligence of Democracy* (New York: Free Press, 1965).

3. Earl Latham, "The Group Basis of Politics," *American Political Science Review* (June 1952): 390.

4. Mark Wegner, "Hastert's GOP to Take Political Offense," *National Journal's CongressDailyAM*, March 15, 2004, 5.

5. J. Dennis Hastert, "Reflections on the Role of the Speaker in the Modern Day House of Representatives," in *The Cannon Centenary Conference: The Changing Nature of the Speakership* (Washington, DC: U.S. Government Printing Office, 2004), 62. As Representative Ron Kind (D-WI) pointed out, given the GOP's party discipline during their recent period of House control (1995–2007), Republicans seem "more interested in a 218 [vote] strategy" than in reaching across the aisle to win minority party votes. See Hans Nichols, "New House Democrats Plan a Revised Strategy," *The Hill*, April 29, 2003, 8.

6. Hastert, "Reflections on the Role of the Speaker."

7. Ronald Brownstein, "Bush Is a Surprise Hard-Liner," *Los Angeles Times*, March 2, 2003, A14.

8. Associated Press, "Democrats to Forgo Control in Brief Edge," *Washington Times*, November 29, 2000, A4.

9. David Rogers, "The Senate's Moment," *Politico*, June 5, 2008, 6.

10. One way for the majority leader to control the floor is to "fill the amendment tree." An amendment tree is a chart or diagram that displays the number and types of amendments that may be pending to a measure. There is a maximum number of amendments permitted by a particular chart or diagram (i.e., the tree), and once that number is reached the tree is "filled." After that, no further amendments are in order until one of the so-called limbs (or amendments) on the tree is disposed of. The Senate majority leader can fill the tree easily, because he is granted preferential recognition by the Senate's presiding officer. The result: the majority leader is recognized by the presiding officer to propose amendments back-to-back until a tree is filled. No further amendments are in order, especially those unwanted by the majority leader, until a limb is disposed of in some manner. As Senator Christopher Bond (R-MO) lamented as he sought to call up his amendment to the defense authorization bill, "I should note that he has filled up the tree, a procedural move that denies a vote on any non-majority leader-approved amendment." *Congressional Record*, September 15, 2008, S8507. Also see *Congressional Record*, May 6, 2008, S3754–S3757.

11. We assume that Minnesota Democrat Al Franken, after legal challenges are resolved, will be officially certified as the winner over incumbent GOP Senator Norm Coleman. Minnesota's election canvassing board reported that Franken had a 225-vote lead after a lengthy and final recount of the votes.

12. Victoria McGrane and Lisa Lere, "Economy Likely to Put a Crimp in Goals," *Politico*, October 20, 2008, 6.

13. Lori Montgomery, "U.S. Debt Expected to Soar This Year," *Washington Post*, January 3, 2009, A1.

14. See, for example, Robert B. Reich, "Saved by the Deficit?" *New York Times*, October 9, 2008, A33; Paul Krugman, "Let's Get Fiscal," *New York Times*, October 17, 2008, A27; and David R. Sands, "Economists Prescribe a Deeper Deficit," *Washington Times*, October 17, 2008, A1.

15. David M. Dickson, "A Country in the Red," *Washington Times*, September 22, 2008, B4.

16. Richard Wolf, "New League of 'Deficit Hawks' Revive Attacks," *USA Today*, June 25, 2008, 5A; and Clea Benson, "For Deficit Hawks, Better Dead Than Red," *CQ Weekly*, July 28, 2008, 2035–36.

17. Louise Uchitelle and Robert Pear, "Deficit Rises, and Consensus Is to Let It Grow," *New York Times*, October 20, 2008, A1.

18. Tom C. Korogolos, "In Defense of Lobbyists," *Wall Street Journal*, May 30, 2008, A15. See Debra Mayberry, "37,000? 39,402? 11,500?" *Washington Post*, January 29, 2006, B3. Another analyst reported 16,000 active registered lobbyists, and 261,000 if everyone is counted in the influence-lobbying complex, such as "public relations consultants, advertising managers, Internet advisers and policy experts." See Robert J. Samuelson, "An Obama Gift for K Street," *Washington Post*, December 15, 2008, A21.

19. Kenneth Doyle, "Lobby Spending at $2.8 Billion in 2007, Up 78.7% from 2006, CRP Summary Says," *Daily Report for Executives*, April 11, 2008, A–4.

20. Edgar Lane, *Lobbying and the Law* (Berkeley: University of California Press, 1964), 18.

21. Jeffrey Young, "Science Lobby Creates NIH Info 'Clearinghouse,'" *The Hill*, September 19, 2008, 13.

22. Jonathan D. Salant, "The Lobbying Game Today," in *Extensions*, A Journal of the Carl Albert Congressional Research and Studies Center (Fall 2006): 17.

23. Dan Carney, "Transforming the Nation by Fits and Starts," *CQ Weekly*, January 29, 2000, 162–63.

24. *CQ Monitor*, January 26, 1998, 3.

25. The principal feature of the "period from the late 1940s to the mid-1980s was the overwhelming dominance of the three major commercial networks. More then 80 percent of the commercial stations affiliated with them; network programs regularly attracted more than 90 percent of viewers." See Austin Ranney, "Broadcasting, Narrowcasting, and Politics," in Anthony King, ed., *The New American Political System* (Washington, DC: AEI Press, 1990), 178–79.

26. Ranney, "Broadcasting, Narrowcasting, and Politics," 180–83.

27. Robert J. Samuelson, "Bull Market for Media Bias," *Washington Post*, June 23, 2004, A21.

28. Llan Graff and Mary Lynn F. Jones, "Lessons about Congress not taught in school," *The Hill*, August 7, 2002, 13.

29. Micah L. Sifry and Andrew Rasiej, "Online Activists Rise Up Against the Bailout," *Politico*, September 29, 2008, 22.

30. See, for example, Ronald Brownstein, *The Second Civil War: How Extreme Partisanship Has Paralyzed Washington and Polarized America* (New York: Penguin Press, 2007); Bill Bishop, *The Big Sort: Why the Clustering of Like-Minded America Is Tearing Us Apart* (Boston: Houghton Mifflin, 2008); and Nelson W. Polsby, *How Congress Evolves: Social Bases of Institutional Change* (New York: Oxford University Press, 2004).

31. David S. Broder, "Don't Bet on Bipartisan Niceties," *Washington Monthly*, January 1, 2002, A19. Two political scientists, John Aldrich and David Rhode, describe the bimodal distribution of party preferences as "conditional party government." Those scholars state that members of Congress are more inclined to allow party leaders to act on their behalf when the two parties are internally unified and distinct from one another.

32. Kathy Kiely and Wendy Koch, "Committees Shaped by Party Ties," *USA Today*, October 5, 1998, 2A.

33. Brownstein, *The Second Civil War*, 14.

34. See David Brady and Morris Fiorina, "Congress in the Era of Permanent Campaigns," in *The Permanent Campaign and Its Future*, eds., Norman J. Ornstein and Thomas E. Mann (Washington, DC: American Enterprise Institute and The Brookings Institution, 2000), 156. Of course, it is worth remembering that partisanship has many virtues. As Representative Barney Frank (D-MA) stated, partisanship is "a much unfairly maligned concept. Partisanship is essential to a healthy democracy," *Congressional Record*, January 29, 2008, H502. For example, vigorous partisanship clarifies choices for voters, encourages turnout, promotes political and policy debate among the citizenry, and provides substantive options and alternatives for lawmakers to consider. The downside is when partisanship fosters bitter acrimony and personal attacks.

35. For an excellent summary of the honeymoon period, see Casey Byrne Knudsen Dominguez, "Is It a Honeymoon? An Empirical Investigation of the President's First Hundred Days," *Congress & the Presidency* (Spring 2005): 63–78. Also see William Safire, "100 Hours," *New York Times Magazine*, January 28, 2007, 20. When a new president inherits a country in crisis, it seems something of a misnomer to call his first months in office a "honeymoon."

36. We recognize that Reagan faced a Democratically controlled House in 1981, with the Senate in GOP hands. Although Democrats had a numerical majority in the House, the ideological or voting majority was in the hands of a conservative coalition consisting of Republicans and "Reagan Democrats." We should note that scholars have devoted considerable attention to the implications of divided government, but assessments remain mixed. David Mayhew (1991) tracks outcomes on the most consequential pieces of legislation considered between 1945 and 1990 and finds no

evidence to suggest that major policy initiatives are any more likely to pass during periods of unified government. Sarah Binder (1999) conducted a similar analysis and her results suggest that the ability of Congress and the president to address prominent issues of the day depends to a degree on whether the same party controls both the legislative and executive branches of government. Austin Ranney and other proponents of "responsible parties" also tend to associate divided government with legislative gridlock.

37. FDR's New Deal produced a large outpouring of legislation that dramatically increased the size and scope of the national government. Several examples include Social Security, rural electrification, public works, and unemployment compensation.

38. *Congressional Record*, March 9, 1933, 67.

39. *Congressional Record*, March 9, 1933, 76.

40. Arthur M. Schlesinger Jr., *The Coming of the New Deal* (Boston: Houghton Mifflin, 1959), 21.

41. Sylvia Snowiss, "Presidential Leadership in Congress: An Analysis of Roosevelt's First Hundred Days," *Publius* 1 (1971): 83.

42. *The Public Papers and Addresses of Franklin D. Roosevelt*, vol. 2: *The Year of Crisis, 1933* (New York: Random House, 1938), 61, 64–65.

43. Samuel Kernell, *Going Public: New Strategies of Presidential Leadership*, 3rd ed. (Washington, DC: CQ Press, 1997). Rather than negotiate directly with one another, Congress and the president often "go public" by appealing to voters through the media. This approach contrasts with Professor Richard Neustadt's view of political negotiation as a bargaining relationship between Congress and the president predicated on the chief executive's ability to persuade members of Congress to follow his lead. There is also the view among scholars that presidents may go public as a last resort because they failed at persuading lawmakers to back their proposals.

44. Doris Kearns Goodwin, *Lyndon Johnson and the American Dream* (New York: Harper & Row, 1976), 226.

45. Harry McPherson, *A Political Education* (Boston: Little, Brown, 1972), 249.

46. Sidney M. Milkis and Michael Nelson, *The American Presidency*, 4th ed. (Washington, DC: CQ Press, 2003), 321.

47. See Jeffrey K. Tulis, *The Rhetorical Presidency* (Princeton, NJ: Princeton University Press, 1987).

48. Mark A. Peterson, *Legislating Together: The White House and Capitol Hill from Eisenhower to Reagan* (Cambridge, MA: Harvard University Press, 1990), 68. Professor Peterson recounts a humorous story about LBJ's penchant for telephoning lawmakers at all hours of the day. Calling a senator at 2:30 a.m., the president asked: "How are you doing?" as if it were the middle of the day. The senator responded, "I was just lying here waiting for you to call me, Mr. President."

49. Fred I. Greenstein, ed., *The Reagan Presidency* (Baltimore: Johns Hopkins University Press, 1983), 15.

50. Rhodes Cook, "Reagan Buries Carter in a Landslide," *CQ Weekly Report*, November 8, 1980, 3296–97.

51. Norman J. Ornstein, *President and Congress: Assessing Reagan's First Year* (Washington, DC: American Enterprise Institute for Public Policy Research, 1982), 91, 92. Also see *Reagan's First Year* (Washington, DC: Congressional Quarterly, Inc., 1982).

52. Samuel Kernell, *Going Public: New Strategies of Presidential Leadership*, 3rd ed. (Washington, DC: CQ Press, 1997), 143.

53. Charles O. Jones, "A New President, A Different Congress, A Maturing Agenda," in *The Reagan Presidency and the Governing of America*, eds., Lester M. Salamon and Michael S. Lund (Washington, DC: Urban Institute Press, 1984), 273.

54. Peterson, *Legislating Together*, 263.

55. Courtney R. Sheldon, "How Reagan Rates with Congress," *U.S. News & World Report*, October 12, 1981, 27.

56. Michael M. Grynbaum, "In String of Bad News, Omens of a Long Recession," *New York Times*, December 8, 2008, B1. Also see "Recession 101," *Washington Post*, October 31, 2008, A12.

57. Maura Reynolds and Catherine Ho, "1.25 Million Jobs Lost in Three Months," *Los Angeles Times*, December 6, 2008, online version.

58. Nancy Trejos, "Retirement Savings Lose $2 Trillion in 15 Months," *Washington Post*, October 8, 2008, A1.

59. Steven Mufson, "Economic Pain Spreads to Industrial Icons," *Washington Post*, December 9, 2008, D1.

60. Glenn Kessler, "Getting a Grasp On the Crisis," *Washington Post*, October 9, 2008, D1. The *Post* ran an informative three-part front-page story on the housing bubble on June 15, 16, and 17, 2008. Also see Vikas Bajaj and David Leonhardt, "1997 Tax Break on Home Sales May Have Helped Inflate Bubble," *New York Times*, December 19, 2008, A1; and Jo Becker, Sheryl Gay Stolberg, and Stephen Labaton, "White House Philosophy Stoked Mortgage Bonfire," *New York Times*, December 21, 2008, 1.

61. In congressional testimony following the sudden collapse of several major financial institutions, former Federal Reserve chairman Alan Greenspan expressed a mea culpa regarding his views toward self-regulation: "I made a mistake in presuming that the self interests of organizations, specifically banks and others, were best capable of protecting their own shareholders and their equity in the firms." See *Washington Post*, October 24, 2008, A10. For a useful summary of the causes of the financial meltdown, see a *USA Today* editorial titled "Who's to Blame for Economy?" December 17, 2008, 10A.

62. Steven Pearlstein, "A Perfect Storm? No, a Failure of Leadership," *Washington Post*, December 10, 2008, D1; and Steven Pearlstein, "Just One Real Leader, and We Could Have Avoided This Mess," *Washington Post*, December 12, 2008, D1.

63. Benton Ives and Alan K. Ota, "Financial Rescue Becomes Law," *CQ Weekly*, October 6, 2008, 2692. Also see Bruce Stokes and Corine Hegland, "Running the Rescue," *National Journal*, October 11, 2008, 16–23.

64. For a critique of this approach, see Alan S. Blinder, "Missing the Target with $700 Billion," *New York Times*, December 21, 2008, B4. Blinder is a Princeton

economics professor, former vice chair of the Federal Reserve, and adviser to Democratic officials.

65. Peter Grier and Ron Scherer, "Crisis Overturns Ideology," *Christian Science Monitor*, October 15, 2008, 1.

66. The financial costs of these various economic rescue initiatives are in the trillions of dollars. See, for example, "Tracking the Bailout: The Government's Commitments," *New York Times*, November 26, 2008, A24; "A Long Tab," *Wall Street Journal*, November 26, 2008, A12; Neil Irwin and David Cho, "U.S. Offers Citigroup Expansive Safety Net," *Washington Post*, November 24, 2008, A1; and Jim Puzzanghera, "Economic Rescue Could Cost $8.5 Trillion," *Los Angeles Times*, November 30, 2008, online version.

67. Humberto Sanchez, "Stimulus Price Might Top $1.3 Trillion," *National Journal's CongressDailyAM*, January 6, 2009, 1. On January 15, 2009, House Democrats released the details of their $825 billion economic stimulus package. It proposed $550 billion in new spending and $275 billion in tax relief. See *Wall Street Journal*, January 16, 2009, A2.

68. Lori Montgomery, "Obama Expands Stimulus Goals," *Washington Post*, December 21, 2008, A1.

69. Peter Wallsten, "Obama Pledges to Create Jobs via Public Works," *Los Angeles Times*, December 7, 2008, online version.

70. William Schneider, "Reagan's Example," *National Journal*, December 6, 2008, 66.

71. Rep. Paul Ryan, "'Stimulus' Not the Way to Reboot the Economy," *Roll Call* (The Agenda Ahead Policy Briefing), December 8, 2008, 18. Rep. Ryan suggests a number of ways to produce real growth in the economy, such as lowering the corporate income tax rate to attract more investments from abroad and getting federal spending under control, especially for earmarks and entitlement programs. Also see, for example, Peter Navarro, "The Dangers of Obama's Public-Works Juggernaut," *Christian Science Monitor*, December 9, 2008, 9; Donald L. Luskin, "Death by Rescue," *National Review*, November 17, 2008, 38, 40–41; and Stephen Spruiell, "The Specter Called 'John Maynard,'" *National Review*, November 17, 2008, 22, 24.

72. Glenn Thrush, "With the 111th, the Age of Pelosi Dawns," *Politico*, January 6, 2009, 16.

73. Richard E. Cohen and Brian Friel, "Yes, They Can . . . Govern?" *National Journal*, July 12, 2008, 26.

74. See Gary Andres, "Unified Party Control, Will Congress Adapt to White House?" *Washington Times*, December 4, 2008, A21.

75. Drew Armstrong, "Senate Leaders Set to Take Lead with Health," *CQ Weekly*, November 24, 2008, 3142.

76. John Stanton and Jackie Kucinich, "GOP Vow to Get Along," *Roll Call*, December 10, 2008, 1.

77. John Stanton and Emily Pierce, "Senators' Bad Blood May Ebb," *Roll Call*, December 9, 2008, 1.

78. Quoted in Jeff Eller, "It's Time to Rewrite the Bully Pulpit," *Politico*, November 18, 2008, 29.

79. Alec MacGillis and Sarah Cohen, "Final Fundraising Tally for Obama Exceeded $750 Million," *Washington Post*, December 6, 2008, A5. The Obama campaign's assertion that small donors dominated their contributors proved to be a myth. Many small donors contributed repeatedly to exceed the $199 or less threshold for small contributors. See Michael Luo, "The Myth of the Small Donor," *New York Times*, November 25, 2008, A16.

80. Adam Nagourney, "The '08 Campaign: A Sea Change for Politics as We Know It," *New York Times*, November 4, 2008, A1.

81. Lois Romano, "'08 Campaign Guru Focuses on Grass Roots," *Washington Post*, January 13, 2009, A13.

82. Kenneth T. Walsh, "For Obama, Governing in the Age of YouTube," *U.S. News & World Report*, December 1, 2008, 32.

83. E. J. Dionne, "What Next for Obama's Network?" *Washington Post*, November 21, 2008, A23.

84. Chris Cillizza, "Obama Makes a Point of Speaking of the People, to the People," *Washington Post*, December 14, 2008, A5.

85. Elise Castelli, "Obama Vows to Advance Government's Online Presence," *Federal Times*, January 12, 2009, 11.

86. See Gregg Carlstrom, "Obama's Bold Vision for E-Gov," *Federal Times*, November 7, 2008, 1; and Ceci Connolly, "Obama Policymakers Turn to Campaign Tools," *Washington Post*, December 4, 2008, A1.

87. Ceci Connolly, "Obama Asks Nation for Input on Reforming Health System," *Washington Post*, December 6, 2008, A7.

88. Connolly, "Obama Policymakers Turn to Campaign Tools," A8.

89. Christina Bellanoni, "Web Sites Foretell a YouTube Presidency," *Washington Times*, November 7, 2008, A10. To be sure, there are various hurdles to overcome before Obama's participatory ideas are implemented fully. There is bureaucratic inertia; the recruitment of skilled information technology specialists; the development of new administrative rules and regulations; issues of privacy, secrecy, and security; and the need for additional resources. See Alexandra Marks, "Under Obama, a Newly Interactive Government," *Christian Science Monitor*, November 14, 2008, 1. Another issue is how to minimize the "digital divide," so the voices of the disadvantaged can be heard as well as the advantaged, which includes special interests. Still another is the plethora of federal regulations, such as those associated with the Presidential Records Act, "which puts the commander-in-chief in the official record." Andrew Noyes, "Experts Debate Future of Obama's Web Communications," *National Journal's CongressDailyPM*, December 12, 2008, 4–5.

90. See, for example, Charlie Savage, *Takeover: The Return of the Imperial Presidency and the Subversion of American Democracy* (Boston: Little, Brown, 2007); and Arthur Schlesinger Jr., *The Imperial Presidency* (New York: Houghton Mifflin, 1973).

91. Paul Starobin, "The King Lives! Long Live the King?" *National Journal*, February 18, 2006, 18–27.

92. T. J. Halstead, "Presidential Signing Statements: Executive Aggrandizement, Judicial Ambivalence, and Congressional Vituperation," *Government Information*

Quarterly 25 (2008): 563–64. Also see Louis Fisher, *The Constitution and 9/11: Recurring Threats to America's Freedoms* (Lawrence: University Press of Kansas, 2008).

93. Jon Ward and John Solomon, "Cheney Defends Morality of War on Terror," *Washington Times*, December 18, 2008, A1.

94. See Tim Starks, "Bush Signs FISA Rewrite into Law," *CQ Weekly*, July 14, 2008, 1900–02; and Shane Harris, "Explaining FISA," *National Journal*, July 19, 2008, 66–70.

95. On May 24, 2001, Senator James Jeffords of Vermont announced that he was changing his party affiliation from Republican to Independent and caucusing with the Democrats. His switch shifted party control of the Senate from Republicans to Democrats. Republicans regained control of the Senate following the 2002 congressional election. The House remained in Republican control throughout this period.

96. David Nather, "Congress as Watchdog: Asleep on the Job?" *CQ Weekly*, May 22, 2004, 1190.

97. Ronald Brownstein, "Treating Oversight as an Afterthought Has Its Costs," *Los Angeles Times*, November 19, 2006, online edition.

98. Ronald Brownstein, "Who's Watching the President?" *Los Angeles Times*, March 21, 2007, online edition.

99. *Congressional Record*, July 13, 2006, H5212.

100. John Nichols, "The New Senate Majority?" *The Nation*, October 27, 2008, 13.

101. Bart Jansen, "No Magic Number, But More Muscle," *CQ Weekly*, November 10, 2008, 2979.

102. "Obama Speaks Out in His First Newspaper Interview," *Los Angeles Times*, December 10, 2008, online edition.

103. Gerald F. Seib, "In Crisis, Opportunity for Obama," *Wall Street Journal*, November 21, 2008, A2.

104. Neil King Jr., "A Past President's Advice to Obama: Act with Haste," *Wall Street Journal*, December 11, 2008, A16.

105. Dean Scott, "Next President Likely to Have Limited Chance for Passage of Emission Caps, Senator Says," *Daily Report for Executives*, August 4, 2008, A-15. See Alan K. Ota, "Being Both a Leader and a 'First Friend,'" *CQ Weekly*, July 28, 2008, 2052–53.

Chapter Twelve

Relations between the President and Congress in Wartime

The Honorable Lee H. Hamilton

The decision to go to war is the most serious decision a government makes. One would expect the U.S. Constitution to speak with clarity about this grave matter, but it does not. After more than two centuries, debates over the war-making powers of the president and the Congress are unresolved and there is no resolution in sight. The president and the Congress simply disagree, and the Supreme Court has not provided much help. Partisans on both sides point to various constitutional provisions to make their case. Advocates for presidential supremacy cite the Constitution's executive and commander-in-chief clauses. The advocates of congressional authority, who want to check presidential power, point to Congress's constitutional power "to declare war." Historical precedents are not much help either. The Founders did not always speak with one voice, and the historical record can be interpreted in different ways. The debate about these powers is persistent and intense—and likely will continue for another two centuries.

My effort in this essay is not to resolve this constitutional dilemma, but to try to help future presidents and congresses find a way forward, for surely the question of intervention and war will surface again and again in the years ahead. My view is that the president can go to war—if he wants to—and Congress cannot stop him—even if it wanted to, which rarely, if ever, has been the case. The key question thus becomes: how can we assure that the president gets the best advice possible before embarking on such a fateful enterprise, and not just from his inner circle, but also the diverse body of opinion represented in the Congress?

The Congress, unlike the president's advisers, can provide genuinely independent counsel. Therefore, I suggest in the following paragraphs that it is crucial for the president and the Congress to consult meaningfully and deliberate exhaustively before committing the nation to war. The grave decision to go to war should be made only after thorough consultation. I do not seek to refute the constitutional arguments advocates of congressional and presidential authority make about the scope of each branch's powers. I want to enhance the role of Congress in making, prosecuting, and concluding war, but I recognize that in today's world the president will make the final decisions. I want to increase the likelihood of consultation and the robustness of congressional oversight during war. I want Congress to use its power of the purse to shape the conduct and, when necessary, the termination of armed conflict.

I do not worry about the clash of the executive and legislative branches. Rather, I believe that disagreement and sharp debate generate a creative tension between the branches that ultimately produces better policy with more enduring popular support. Both branches can make errors, and both have done so in the past. But a collaborative decision-making process reduces the likelihood of missteps. Some of the means to achieve the sharing of powers are consultation, oversight, and the budgetary process. As James Madison wrote in the famous Pacificus-Helvidius debates of 1793–1794, in which he dueled with Alexander Hamilton over the legality of George Washington's Neutrality Proclamation of 1793, "Those who are to conduct a war cannot in the nature of things, be proper or safe judges, whether a war ought to be commenced, continued, or concluded."[1] Congress has a role to play in all three stages of conflict, and I will suggest what such roles might be.

There are no guarantees that the approach spelled out in these pages will lead to a future president and Congress working together productively. But the proposed framework enhances the prospects for practical and constructive cooperation. I believe it will produce more effective policy, while meeting the Constitution's demands of the president and Congress.

When the framers gathered in Philadelphia in the summer of 1787, the backdrop was the ineffectiveness of the Articles of Confederation, which they sought to amend, not replace, in the aftermath of Shays' Rebellion. What emerged from the Constitutional Convention was our republic's most ingenious form of accountability, our system of checks and balances—uniquely American and the product of our Founders' ingenuity. The Constitution makes clear that the separate branches of government *share* foreign-policy-making powers.[2] As Supreme Court Justice Robert Jackson wrote, the Constitution "enjoins upon its branches not separateness but interdependence, not autonomy but reciprocity."[3] This interdependence among the branches of government has served America well for most of the last two hundred–plus years.

However, in 2009 we find ourselves in an international environment quite different than that of the late eighteenth century. The context of the present historical moment matters, and we ignore it at our own peril. America is the world's most powerful country, as it has been since the conclusion of World

War II. Our global leadership has, more often than not, served democracy, liberty, peace, and prosperity. But that leadership, and the international system, has exerted pressures on the republic, most clearly reflected in the initiation and prosecution of war in the second half of the twentieth century. This trend began with Harry Truman's intervention in Korea in June 1950 and continues to the present day in Iraq.

The 9/11 attacks presaged a sea change in America's threat perception and national security environment. The attacks prompted invasions and occupations of Afghanistan and, more controversially, Iraq under the banner of a "war on terror." As John Yoo, then of the White House Office of Legal Counsel, put it in a March 2003 memorandum: "The United States, through its military and intelligence personnel, has a right recognized by Article 51 [of the United Nations Charter] to continue using force until such time as the threat posed by al Qaeda and other terrorist groups connected to the September 11th attacks is completely ended."[4] Following this logic, the United States has been at war since September 11, and it will remain so until every last Al Qaeda member is eliminated or no longer a security risk. Under this rubric, the Bush administration concentrated an immense amount of power in the executive branch at the expense of the legislative branch, and it has left our constitutional system of representative democracy under stress.

It would be easy to dismiss the excesses of executive power during the Bush administration as an aberration, a unique confluence of circumstances that generated negative consequences for the United States and the world. I believe such a position would be short-sighted and reckless. I am reminded of legal scholar Harold Koh's writing in the aftermath of the Iran-contra affair: "To treat the Iran-contra affair solely as an exercise in executive hubris or congressional folly is to ignore its broader historical significance: as an uncured constitutional crisis in national security decision making that waits to afflict us anew."[5] This is as true today as it was after Iran-contra. It is high time we address this major imbalance of power.

The restoration of balance to executive-legislative branch relations is in the interest of all parties—the president, the Congress, and, most important, the American people—especially in times of war.

In any discussion of the shared powers of making foreign policy, the best place to start is the Constitution itself. For the legislative branch, article I, section 8 is most relevant. Congress has several enumerated powers, among them: "To declare war, grant letters of marque and reprisal, and make rules concerning captures on land and water; To raise and support armies, but no appropriation of money to that use shall be for a longer term than two years; To provide and maintain a navy; To make rules for the government and regulation of the land and naval forces." As for the executive, article II, section 2 states: "The President shall be commander in chief of the Army and Navy of the United States, and of the militia of the several states, when called into the actual service of the United States."

These words, and contemporaneous documents such as *The Federalist Papers*, serve as the foundation for all ensuing debates about the sharing of war powers. This country's representative democracy depends upon a strong and independent Congress with multiple checks on executive power, not a Congress that is solely responsive to, a servant of, or rubber stamp for the president. Congress should force the president to deal with a body made up of diverse interests representing the American people, a body that is—in many respects—closer to them than he is. Without shared power, the system of checks and balances falls apart, and the system of governance the Founders bequeathed to us slides into disrepair.

CHANGES IN THE TWENTIETH CENTURY

America's role in international affairs changed a great deal in the twentieth century. Woodrow Wilson asked for and received a declaration of war in 1914 and led the country into World War I. But it is worth recalling that even prior to the Great War, America's foreign policy was undergoing fundamental shifts. In 1900–1901 the United States sent troops to China to suppress the Boxer Rebellion. More famous, the Spanish-American War in 1898 signaled America's arrival as a world power. Supporters of the war, Theodore Roosevelt most prominently among them, cited many justifications for military action, including defending human rights in Cuba. Congress voted three resolutions tantamount to a declaration of war for the liberation and independence of Cuba. But there were larger global forces at work. As political scientist Kenneth D. Moss writes:

[There was] a global perspective shaped by expanding commercial commitments that assigned more importance to stability. Protecting foreign nationals and property rights and preventing economic and political turmoil could invite other foreign powers to intervene and potentially undermine U.S. interests. . . . Increasingly, presidents regarded the military as an instrument of foreign policy and justified its use as necessary through their role as the nation's voice in foreign policy and as commander in chief.[6]

The actions of Roosevelt's successors reflected this broader definition of the national interest. William Howard Taft intervened militarily in Nicaragua twice and Honduras once, without congressional authorization on all three occasions. In 1916, four years after leaving the White House and five years before his appointment to the Supreme Court, Taft wrote that the president could initiate hostilities without previously securing congressional approval, "if the appropriations furnish the means of transportation."[7] Woodrow Wilson and Calvin Coolidge continued the trend and intervened in Mexico, Haiti, the Dominican Republic, and Nicaragua—all without congressional authorization. But these interventions were on a relatively small scale and restricted to the Western Hemisphere.

World War II was a more definitive marker in American history in terms of how the United States engaged the world. President Franklin Delano Roosevelt relied heavily on executive agreements in determining American policy toward Europe in the late 1930s and early 1940s, circumventing the treaty-making process and the role of the United States Senate. He oversaw the creation of the combined chiefs of staff, which heightened the military's influence on foreign policy, and consequently augmented the executive's civilian control over the armed forces relative to Congress.[8]

Roosevelt's actions prompted Republican Senator Robert Taft of Ohio, a staunch defender of Congress's role in formulating foreign policy, to criticize the president in the harshest terms. "There is no principle of subjection to the Executive in foreign policy. Only Hitler and Stalin would assert that," he said in 1939.[9] Taft was being hyperbolic—Roosevelt was no dictator—but the tension between Congress and the president reflected new strains on executive-legislative relations in a new era.

The United States emerged from World War II with unprecedented power and influence in international affairs. Great Britain had lost its empire. Years of war had decimated continental powers like France and Germany, in terms of industry, infrastructure, and human losses. Japan, too, was in ruins. The same was true of the Soviet Union, whose brutal fight against the Third Reich on the Eastern Front had cost an astounding twenty-four million lives.[10]

Unlike the aftermath of World War I, the United States did not relinquish the influence it had accrued, and institutions—both international and domestic—were necessary to exercise and maintain that influence. The Atlantic and Pacific Oceans no longer reliably insulated America from instability in Europe and Asia. As Louis Hartz wrote in 1955: "The larger forces working toward a shattering of American provincialism abroad as well as at home lie . . . in the world scene itself."[11] Furthermore, the disorganization characterizing the executive branch under Roosevelt's leadership in wartime suggested that proper management of U.S. foreign policy required structural changes and new institutions.[12]

To cope with this "world scene," the Congress passed the National Security Act of 1947, laying the foundation for our present-day national security institutions, including the Department of Defense, the Central Intelligence

Agency, and the National Security Council. The objective was to centralize the various decision-making apparatuses in the *executive branch* to combat threats in a multifaceted and coordinated manner. As for the other branches of government, the National Security Act did not even mention the legislative and judicial branches' roles in making foreign policy.[13] Over the next half-century, the National Security Council, the Department of Defense, and the CIA became dominant players in the development of U.S. foreign policy.

As the battle lines of the Cold War hardened—the Berlin airlift, the 1948 coup in Czechoslovakia—U.S. troops remained in Europe and Japan. In 1949, Secretary of State Dean Acheson negotiated the North Atlantic Treaty Organization (NATO). This was an event of great significance, both then and now. Article V of the NATO Charter appeared to bypass Congress in the initiation of hostilities. It reads:

> The Parties agree that an armed attack against one or more of them in Europe or North America shall be considered an attack against them all and consequently they agree that, if such an armed attack occurs, each of them, in exercise of the right of individual or collective self-defence recognised by Article 51 of the Charter of the United Nations, will assist the Party or Parties so attacked by taking forthwith, individually and in concert with the other Parties, such action as it deems necessary, including the use of armed force, to restore and maintain the security of the North Atlantic area.[14]

In response, Republican Senator Arthur Vandenberg of Michigan drafted a resolution bearing his name, which sought to render NATO's collective self-defense provision consistent with Congress's war powers. The resolution mentions both the U.S. "Constitutional system" and the "Constitutional process," a clear statement that there was still a key role for Congress to play in decisions to go to war in defense of a NATO ally.[15] The Vandenberg Resolution stands as an important example of how consultation between the Congress and White House can produce superior foreign policy.

Technology also played a key role in the transformation of the postwar world. The detonation of atomic bombs over Hiroshima and Nagasaki introduced weapons of unprecedented destruction into modern warfare. The Soviet test of 1949 ended the U.S. nuclear monopoly and made once-hypothetical fears of nuclear war a reality. The advent of thermonuclear weapons raised the stakes and demanded changes, both institutional and practical, in the conduct of U.S. foreign policy. Political scientist Robert Jervis writes:

> Nuclear weapons, with their danger of surprise attack and the requirement for readiness to retaliate instantly, if not to strike preemptively, meant that Congress could play little role in the ultimate decision. The need—or at least the

claim—for secrecy also removed power from Congress. Related considerations meant that Congress could do very little in the event of a serious crisis.[16]

And, as stewards of America's nuclear weapons, in addition to the maintenance of a standing army of unprecedented size and significance, the military's ascent as an actor in U.S. foreign policy during peacetime continued. As the military component of U.S. foreign policy grew, so did the power of the army, navy, and, eventually, the air force.[17] As the principal practitioner of civilian control over the military—the National Security Act stated that the Joint Chiefs of Staff were subject to "unified direction under civilian control of the Secretary of Defense"—the executive's power grew in tandem with that of the military. To the executive, a fractious Congress was not up to the task of civilian control of the military. In contrast, Congress viewed the concentration of power in the executive branch with skepticism, fearing a domineering military leadership. The legislature, after all, was more responsive to the electorate.[18]

The North Korean invasion of South Korea in June 1950 put all these issues front and center. The Cold War had turned hot, and America's national security apparatus was put to the test. Upon hearing of the invasion, Truman requested Secretary of State Dean Acheson to assemble the key executive agency and military leaders to prepare policy recommendations. When Truman first gathered his advisers at Blair House, not one of the eleven present represented the Congress.[19] Only days later did Truman brief congressional leaders to, in his words, "inform them on the events and decisions of the past few days," decisions that shaped the American response in the weeks and months ahead.[20] In Truman's mind, there was not enough time to work with the Congress, as South Korea's survival hung in the balance.

Truman eventually sent U.S. forces—under a UN flag—into battle against the North Koreans, and later the Chinese, without congressional approval. Truman believed that UN Security Council Resolution 83, which recommended that member nations "furnish such [military] assistance to the Republic of Korea as may be necessary to repel the armed attack and to restore international peace and security in the area," was sufficient based on his powers as commander in chief.[21] Once, when asked who makes U.S. foreign policy, Truman replied straightforwardly: "I do."[22] This set the standard for the first decades of the Cold War. In Vietnam, and elsewhere, the executive sent U.S. troops into harm's way without a formal congressional declaration of war, though in the Vietnam case the Gulf of Tonkin Resolution served as constitutional authorization, despite legislators' later protestations.[23] In the 1960s, Congress hardly pushed back against Lyndon Johnson's centralization of power in the White House. As former senator Thomas Eagleton later testified before Congress reflecting on the Vietnam era: "I came to the conclusion that Congress preferred the right of retrospective criticism to the right of anticipatory, participatory judgment."[24]

In response to executive overreach during the Johnson and Nixon administrations, Congress reasserted itself in the late 1960s and 1970s, culminating in the War Powers Act of 1973, passed over Richard Nixon's veto, which I will discuss in greater detail below.

But there were limits to congressional activism, most notably evidenced by the War Powers Act's ineffectiveness. Legal scholar John Hart Ely puts it nicely: "Ulysses tried, genuinely I think, to tie himself to the mast in 1973, but the knots were loose, and he was soon back to his old way of avoiding responsibility."[25] Of course, there are dissenters from this viewpoint.

Former vice president Dick Cheney often reflects upon the Bush administration's drive to centralize and expand White House power. The presidency, he argues, has been hemmed in after Vietnam and Watergate. He has said: "I think there has been over time a restoration, if you will, of the power and authority of the president." He suggests that this is just and proper, and a major accomplishment of the Bush administration. He and I served in public life over much the same period of time. But we have come to opposite conclusions.

Of course, responsibility for the sorry state of executive-legislative branch relations does not rest solely with the Bush White House. Congress has been too timid in performing its constitutional duties. The president is now the de facto chief legislator and chief budget maker. If Congress is seen as having a responsibility, it is implementing the president's agenda. The foreign policy implications of this imbalance are disconcerting. That is why I favor a strong president and a strong Congress.

As the country moves forward, it is important to note that the Bush administration did not see itself as ignoring the Constitution, but rather saw its actions as entirely consistent with it. Among legal scholars, no individual has done more than John Yoo to make this case. While Yoo and the administration he served in as a deputy assistant attorney general are not one and the same, his views were influential. His writing sheds light on how we arrived at this juncture in executive-legislative relations.

In Yoo's paradigm, the "power to declare war" is no power at all. He writes: "Declarations do simply what they say they do: they declare. To use the eighteenth-century understanding, they make public, show openly, and make known the state of international relations between the United States and another nation."[26] Congress "has chosen for itself the role of approving military actions after the fact by declarations of support and by appropriations."[27] The power to appropriate, in this view, is the single unquestionable war power Congress possesses, and historic instances in which it has not exercised this singular check on war making reflect "a lack of political will rather than a defect in the constitutional design."[28] In my view, this is not the role the Founders intended Congress to play. For example, our first president, George Washington, wrote in 1793: "The Constitution vests the power of declaring war in Congress; therefore no offensive expedition of importance can be undertaken until after they have deliberated upon the subject and authorised such a measure."[29]

A judicial ruling, not on the merits of going to war, but on the constitutionality of the process leading up to war, would be most welcome to resolve the debate. But this seems more unlikely than ever, because the courts refuse to intervene in what they consider a political matter. Exhorting a supine Congress is often unproductive. Given these realities, what recourse do we have?

A NEW PARADIGM

How can Congress be more effective in checking executive excesses and advancing its views of the national interest in times of war?[30] The best place to start is at the beginning: when the decision to initiate hostilities is made. In 2008 I served on the bipartisan National War Powers Commission, cochaired by former secretaries of state James A. Baker III and Warren Christopher. The commission concluded that institutionalizing mechanisms to ensure congressional participation, consultation, and intense deliberation was essential. The commission's report included proposed legislation to replace the ineffective War Powers Act of 1973. The proposed War Powers Consultation Act of 2009 facilitates both the executive and legislative branches' fulfillment of their constitutional responsibilities. As this chapter is being written, the bill is in the early stages of consideration by the Congress and the president.

But Congress's responsibilities do not end with the initiation of conflict. Throughout the course of a war, Congress must perform strict and comprehensive oversight of the executive branch. Without oversight, the realization of Madison's fear of a unitary executive approximating tyranny is conceivable. And finally, Congress can end—and shape—war through exercising its power of the purse.

THE IMPORTANCE OF CONSULTATION

What does it mean to "declare war," the power the Constitution assigns to Congress in article I, section 8? How is the power to declare war different than the power to "make war," wording that a previous draft of the Constitution included? How do we reconcile the legislature's powers with the president's responsibilities as "Commander in Chief," as defined in article II, section 2?

The War Powers Act of 1973 sought to insert Congress formally into the decision to go to war. The expansion of the Vietnam War into Cambodia, the Christmas bombings of North Vietnam in 1972, and the ongoing Watergate scandal provided the impetus for the Congress to rein in the president. The act reads: "It is the purpose of this joint resolution to fulfill the intent of the framers of the Constitution of the United States and insure that the collective judgment of both the Congress and the President will apply to the introduction of United States Armed Forces in hostilities. . . ." Section 3 of the act calls for consultation in "every possible instance . . . before introducing United States armed forces into hostilities," one of the few aspects of the legislation the Nixon administration praised. But the act also allows the president to prosecute a war for as long as ninety days—with the clock starting in accordance with a trigger mechanism no president has recognized as legitimate—without congressional authorization or a declaration of war.

Constitutional questions revolve around several issues, primarily related to congressional restrictions on the executive's power as commander in chief. For example, could Congress legally override a president's veto of legislation halting military action?

Clearly, the ambiguous status quo is unsatisfactory. Congressional efforts to assert itself through the War Powers Act of 1973, which I—along with over two-thirds of the House and Senate—supported, have not produced the desired results. No president in thirty-six years has recognized the legitimacy of the War Powers Act, arguing that Congress overstepped its constitutional bounds. The act's unenforceability undermines the rule of law itself.

In his concurrent opinion in the 1952 Supreme Court case *Sheet & Tube Co. v. Sawyer*, Justice Robert H. Jackson wrote: "The opinions of judges, no less than executives and publicists, often suffer the infirmity of confusing the issue of a power's validity with the cause it is invoked to promote, of confounding the permanent executive office with its temporary occupant." As a nation of laws, the question of validity is essential in decisions to go to war.

Justice Jackson's opinion referred to Executive Order 10340, Harry Truman's call for the government to seize control of the nation's steel mills due to an impending strike.[31] Truman told the country: "If steel production stops, we will have to stop making shells and bombs that are going directly to our soldiers at the front in Korea." He therefore justified the seizure of steel mills as an exercise of his power as commander in chief, which was significant because, as already noted, Truman had not obtained a congressional declaration of war. Congress fought back against Truman, and attempted to halt the steel-mill seizure through budgetary restrictions. The steel companies also took action, bringing their case to the courts, where Jackson delineated the different conditions on executive power more clearly than any justice has since.

Jackson articulated three distinct conditions on presidential power:

1. When the President acts pursuant to an express or implied authorization of Congress, his authority is at its maximum, for it includes all that he possesses in his own right plus all that Congress can delegate.
2. When the President acts in absence of either a congressional grant or denial of authority, he can only rely upon his own independent powers, but there is a zone of twilight in which he and Congress may have concurrent authority, or in which its distribution is uncertain.
3. When the President takes measures incompatible with the expressed or implied will of Congress, his power is at its lowest ebb, for then he can rely only upon his own constitutional powers minus any constitutional powers of Congress over the matter.

Jackson wrote that Truman's actions fell into the third category. He did not have proper constitutional authority to seize the steel mills because, "The Constitution expressly places in Congress power 'to raise and *support* Armies' and to '*provide* and *maintain* a Navy" (emphasis in original).[32] Today, it is not Jackson's third category, but his second, that best characterizes our dilemma. Situations in which the "President acts in absence of either a congressional grant or denial of authority" create an atmosphere of ambiguity, and in matters of war and peace, the nation's actions should proceed on solid ground and with a unity of effort.

To minimize the detrimental impact of Jackson's "zone of twilight," consultation between the executive and legislative branches is key, and this is the foundation for the recommendations of the National War Powers Commission. The commission report proposes a War Powers Consultation Act: "Our statute seeks to establish a process that will encourage cooperative consultation and participation in a fashion that we believe is both pragmatic and promotes the underlying values embodied in the Constitution."[33] By providing Congress a seat at the table, the proposed reforms facilitate consultation and consensus to prevent breakdowns in executive-legislative relations that do not serve the country's interests.

Consultation has to be sincere, a true effort to consult and work with the other branch in the decision-making process. It does not work for the president and his advisers to call the congressional leadership, announce their policy decision, and label it "consultation." It is equally unproductive for a congressional majority to gamble that it will be rewarded in the court of electoral opinion for excluding White House input into its bills. What's needed is a process that creates an ongoing relationship—not just one created to deal with an immediate crisis—that builds trust among the various players, recognizes there are always alternatives in policy disputes, and allows key negotiators to sit down and talk long before decisions are made. Trust is the coin of the realm.

Consultation often produces better policy. Intensive negotiations between Secretary of State George Marshall and Senator Arthur Vandenberg produced the Marshall Plan for the reconstruction of postwar Europe, despite the skepticism of the Republican-held Congress toward the Truman White House. After the fall of communism, President George H. W. Bush worked closely with the Congress to create new programs to provide large amounts of economic assistance to Eastern Europe and the former Soviet Union. Rather than bypassing Congress or bludgeoning it, he sought congressional assistance in the design of the aid programs.

Consultation is hardly a confession of political weakness. It is a pragmatic recognition that in our system the two branches need to talk to one another. If they don't, stalemate and the public's disenchantment with government are the end result. If they do, the creative tension produces better policy.

The central institutional innovation of the commission's proposal is the Joint Congressional Consultation Committee, on the model of the Joint Committee on Atomic Energy and the Joint Committee on Taxation. The House and Senate leadership would comprise the Joint Congressional Consultation Committee. Members would include the chairmen and ranking minority members of the House Committee on Foreign Affairs, Committee on Armed Services, Permanent Select Committee on Intelligence, and Committee on Appropriations. Members from the Senate would include the chairmen and ranking minority members of the Committee on Foreign Relations, the Committee on Armed Services, the Select Committee on Intelligence, and the Committee on Appropriations. The chairman and vice chairman positions on the committee would alternate between the Speaker of the House and the majority leader of the Senate. This committee would serve as a contact point on issues of initiating war, but also on broader national security concerns. Time and again we have seen the significant benefits of consultation and its relatively meager costs. The joint committee provides a clear avenue for such consultation to proceed in a manner somewhat insulated from the Congress's occasional fractiousness. The committee would also have its own bipartisan professional staff working under the chairman and vice chairman.

While the proposed War Powers Consultation Act encourages the president to consult the joint committee on national security matters regularly, the rubber hits the road when it comes to questions of war and peace. It requires the president to consult the joint committee prior to the deployment of the U.S. armed forces into a significant armed conflict. The act defines consultations as "the timely exchanges of views regarding whether to engage in the significant armed conflict, not merely notify the Joint Congressional Consultation Committee that the significant armed conflict is about to be initiated." The president is required to provide the Joint Congressional Consultation Committee with a classified report "setting forth the circumstances necessitating the significant armed conflict, the objectives, and the estimated scope and duration of the conflict," unless secrecy precludes such a report, in which case the report is due within three days of the initiation of hostilities. After hostilities commence, consultation is mandated at least every two months. Annual reports—on a classified basis, if necessary—to the committee on ongoing conflicts are also required.

While consultation is not the sole component of the War Powers Consultation Act, it is the most important one. Obviously, the president consults with countless advisers; at the State Department, the Defense Department, the National Security Council, and so on. But one of the unfortunate characteristics of the modern presidency is that it functions almost exclusively in a bubble. Leaving the White House requires a motorcade, there is no break from the 24/7 news cycle, too many staffers are "yes men," unwilling to challenge the boss, and the shortage of fresh ideas and perspectives can be damaging and suffocating. Congress is an independent source of criticism and support, and it is in every president's interest to seek its counsel, to have assumptions challenged, and to build the bipartisan support that any policy—and none more so than prosecuting a war—requires to succeed.

Clearly, consultation does not fulfill Congress's constitutional responsibility to declare war. James Wilson, speaking in support of the Constitution's ratification, said: "This system will not hurry us into war; it is calculated to guard against it. It will not be in the power of a single man, or a single body of men, to involve us in such distress; for the important power of declaring war is vested in the legislature at large." In this vein, section 5(A) of the War Powers Consultation Act of 2009 reads: "If Congress has not enacted a formal declaration of war or otherwise expressly authorized the commitment of United States armed forces in a significant armed conflict, then within 30 calendar days after the commitment of United States armed forces to the significant armed conflict, the Chairman and Vice Chairman of the Joint Congressional Consultation Committee shall introduce an identical concurrent resolution in the Senate and House of Representatives calling for approval."

By forcing Congress to take an up or down vote, the legislation directs Congress to state its support for or opposition to military action on the record and to assert itself in a way it has been hesitant to do in the last sixty years. If the resolution is defeated in one or both houses, any member of Congress—representative or senator—"may file a joint resolution of disapproval of the significant armed conflict, and the joint resolution shall be highly privileged, shall become the pending business of both Houses, shall be voted on within five calendar days thereafter, and shall not be susceptible to intervening motions, except that each house may adjourn from day to day." The president can veto this joint resolution, but Congress can override that veto.

This provision does not provide Congress the power to stop the president from committing U.S. troops to military action. As one critic of the proposed legislation writes, "No matter how many conditions Congress might try to place on the president's use of force in such a concurrent resolution, the president would be under no legal obligation to comply because the provisions would have no force or effect outside Congress. This is because concurrent resolutions are mere sense-of-Congress expressions."[34] However, in practice, it appears that presidents already have no obligation to engage Congress in initiating hostilities. Barring judicial intervention, there is not an enforceable legal obligation to guarantee the sharing of war powers. The joint resolution is, therefore, a mechanism to reinsert Congress into the process.

James Wilson's words—"This system will not hurry us into war"—express a core objective of the War Powers Consultation Act. It would force debates of costs and benefits of proposed military action into the public domain. The president would have to confront questions and criticisms. The executive would not be able to assume Congress's silent acceptance of his war-making authority—though Congress certainly could respond to the executive's military initiatives weakly as it has done in the past. There is, after all, no legislative panacea for an unassertive Congress. Yet in each of these respects, the War Powers Consultation Act would be an improvement over the present state of affairs.

Congressional support or opposition to proposed (or already underway) military action does not fulfill the legislative branch's obligations to the American people. Congressional oversight remains one of the most effective ways for Congress to impact the country's prosecution of war.

OVERSIGHT

Oversight has long been an essential aspect of good governance in America, but today, perhaps more than ever, it is essential given the nature of the national security threats we face. On September 14, 2001, in response to the terrorist attacks of 9/11, the Congress passed S.J. Res 23, the "Authorization for Use of Military Force." The resolution authorized President Bush "to use all necessary and appropriate force against those nations, organizations, or persons he determines planned, authorized, committed, or aided the terrorist attacks that occurred on September 11, 2001, or harbored such organizations or persons, in order to prevent any future acts of international terrorism against the United States by such nations, organizations or persons."

The scope of this authorization was broad in many ways. As the nonpartisan Congressional Research Service pointed out, the identification of "organizations or persons"—nonstate actors—was unprecedented, "with the scope of its reach yet to be determined."[35] If such broad power is to be ceded to the executive, Congress must ensure it is employed responsibly, principally through stringent oversight.

Oversight can evaluate program administration and performance, ensure compliance with Congressional intent, ferret out "waste, fraud, and abuse," eliminate ineffective programs, compel an explanation or justification of policy, and ensure that government performs in a cost-effective and efficient manner. To perform these tasks, Congress has several tools. Periodic reauthorization, personal visits by members, Government Accountability Office or inspectors general reviews, subpoenas, hearings, investigations, and reports from the executive branch to Congress. Several types of committees—authorization, appropriations, and special ad hoc committees—can all play important roles.

Today, Congress does not perform adequate executive branch oversight—every observer of the Congress I know shares this view. Its record during the Bush administration was poor. It did not adequately probe prewar claims regarding Iraq's weapons of mass destruction. It did not educate itself or the American people about how much the Iraq War was going to cost. Congress played a secondary role in uncovering prisoner abuse in Iraq, Afghanistan, and Guantanamo Bay, and has done next to nothing about the misconduct. Congress created the Department of Homeland Security, but then splintered oversight among more than eighty committees and subcommittees. Congress has intelligence committees the 9/11 Commission described as dysfunctional, because they don't have the power to oversee the budgets of the intelligence community.

This "broken oversight" can be attributed to several factors: infrequent effective oversight meetings and hearings—oversight is, after all, unglamorous, even tedious work, with little political payoff; too much concern for preserving committee "turf," and not enough concern for an effective division of oversight responsibilities; too much focus on scoring political points during oversight hearings and too little focus on policy; too much power concentrated in the hands of congressional leaders, who do not have time to conduct oversight; and a lack of focus on long-term problems. What are some of the sources of these problems? The shorter congressional workweek means that committees do not meet as often as they used to, reducing time for oversight. The power of the authorizing committees—which is where most oversight work was done—has declined over the years. Members do not consider oversight a top priority. For most members, constituent service is number one, legislation is number two, and oversight is number three. Furthermore, Congress has permitted the desire for media coverage to drive the hearing and oversight process. The media does not pay much attention to traditional oversight work, focusing instead on scandals. And there is insufficient interest in government reform. When laws and policies escape thorough scrutiny, are not fine-tuned, or improperly interpreted, the performance of government suffers. Entrusting the executive with such unchecked powers is unwise, as Congress demonstrated during World War II.

OVERSIGHT IN ACTION: THE TRUMAN COMMITTEE

Where you stand depends on where you sit, and this was especially true of Harry Truman, who in his pre–White House senatorial days in 1941 chaired the Special Committee to Investigate the National Defense Program—commonly referred to as the Truman Committee. In 1938 President Roosevelt had begun, using executive orders, to create executive offices to manage national defense policy—thirty-five in total.[36] As American involvement in World War II became increasingly probable in the second half of 1940, Congress appropriated over $10 billion for defense contracts.[37] But the country was institutionally unprepared to manage such large sums, and Senator Truman witnessed the wasteful and ineffective defense spending firsthand on visits to military bases in Jackson County, Missouri. "I got in an old broken-down Dodge and drove down there and saw for myself," Truman later explained. "There were buildings—this was all cost plus, you understand—being built, barracks, mess halls, all kinds of building, and they were costing three to four times what they should have."[38]

After Republicans called for investigations into improprieties in defense spending, the White House sought to entrust oversight responsibilities to a friendly Democrat, but Truman proved relentless and the committee was truly bipartisan, composed of "sound thinkers and honest men," in Truman's words. As the historian Theodore Wilson writes, "From small towns and middle class in background, the committee members appeared to share Truman's pragmatic approach to their job, viewing it as a vehicle for exposure and correction of abuses . . . rather than a platform for ideological disputation."[39]

Over seven years (1941–1948) the committee heard from 1,798 witnesses during 432 public hearings. It published nearly two thousand pages of documents and saved perhaps $15 billion and thousands of lives by exposing faulty airplane and munitions production.[40] The Truman Committee, though it had its shortcomings, is rightfully cited as a model of effective congressional oversight. There were times, no doubt, when the committee ruffled feathers in the White House, but the undeniable outcome was improved government policy that served the interests of the president, the Congress, and the American people throughout World War II. In old age, Truman joked that he would run for reelection to the Senate at ninety. What would he focus on upon his return to Capitol Hill? Defense spending. "That's one of the first damn things I'd look into," he said. "They'd probably try to stop me, but at ninety I'm still going to be a contrary goddamn cuss."[41]

How can Congress once more use its oversight powers to better American policy? Having a spirited and doggedly persistent legislator like Harry Truman around certainly helps. Beyond that, there are certain qualities that characterize good oversight.

Oversight works best when it is done in as bipartisan a way as possible. Certainly there will be times when the committee chairman and the ranking minority member will disagree, but they should be able to sit down at the beginning of a new Congress and agree on the bulk of the committee's oversight agenda. Oversight should be done in a regular, systematic way. Congress lacks a continuous, systematic oversight process, and thus it conducts oversight in an episodic, erratic manner. A constructive relationship between Congress and the implementing agency augments oversight's effectiveness. Of course, oversight is, by its very nature, adversarial, and that is particularly appropriate when an agency has engaged in egregious behavior. But excessive antagonism between the branches is counterproductive and hinders government's performance.

Oversight must be comprehensive. There are a vast number of federal government activities that never get into the newspaper headlines, yet it is still the task of Congress to look into them. Comprehensive oversight also means casting the net widely to look at the variety of federal agencies involved in a particular area, not just the main one (for example, not just looking at the foreign policy actions of the State Department, but also of commerce, defense, agriculture, the CIA, etc.). At the same time, there is such a thing as too much oversight. Good oversight draws the line between careful scrutiny and intervention or micromanagement.

Structural reforms and individual efforts by members can be helpful, but for oversight to really work, members must receive a clear message from the congressional leadership of both parties that oversight is a priority and that it will be done in a bipartisan, systematic, and coordinated way. The key role of the House Speaker and the Senate majority leader in the practice of successful oversight cannot be overstated. And finally, there needs to be greater public and media interest in, and demand for, rigorous congressional oversight. Constituent pressure can inspire members.

THE POWER OF THE PURSE

The final area where Congress has an opportunity to leave its mark on foreign policy and war policy is the budgetary process. The Constitution is quite clear on this. Article I, section 8 tasks Congress with the following responsibilities:

> To raise and support armies, but no appropriation of money to that use shall be for a longer term than two years; To provide and maintain a navy; To make rules for the government and regulation of the land and naval forces; To provide for calling forth the militia to execute the laws of the union, suppress insurrections and repel invasions; To provide for organizing, arming, and disciplining, the militia, and for governing such part of them as may be employed in the service of the United States, reserving to the states respectively, the appointment of the officers, and the authority of training the militia according to the discipline prescribed by Congress.

This presents opportunities for Congress to check the president's actions. Many observers often cite "the power of the purse" as Congress's greatest strength. Yet every year it is the president who delivers a budget to the Congress. The Congress rubber stamps about 90 to 95 percent of it, and shows little willingness to significantly rearrange the president's budgetary priorities. The president has become the chief budget maker. Congress could ensure that public funds are better spent to meet our foreign policy objectives with tough conditionality on spending bills.

Changes in America's role in the world, the size of its military, and its broader definition of national security interests have enervated Congress's budgetary powers. As Kenneth Moss writes:

> It was possible in 1787 to try to anticipate beforehand the specific location and scenario in which an authorized, funded, weapons system would be used, but given the diverse nature of modern conflict today, it is very unrealistic, difficult, and possibly reckless. Thus, Pentagon program managers do not regularly prepare funding requests based on projections to use a particular weapons system in a specific theater of operations. The president takes initial action with the existing military and funding when committing military force, even if he or she must request additional funds to support the deployment. Once military forces are

deployed, it is unlikely that Congress will pull them back by denying funding before shots are fired. With such a large standing military, Congress operates with serious disadvantages that it did not have 200 years ago.[42]

As the budget process evolved over many decades, it came to involve hearings and consultations by a multitude of committees, which would "authorize" spending by the federal agencies and departments for which they were responsible. Then appropriations subcommittees and the full appropriations committees would take up the task of actually approving the money to be spent, before sending separate bills for the various federal departments to the floor. It was an orderly process, gave committee members a chance to examine the operations of the federal government, and allowed ordinary House and Senate members to debate, and to amend, the appropriations bills at several steps along the way. In other words, it promoted deliberation and the democratic give-and-take essential to a free society.

These days, we're lucky if there's more than one bill. By shoving the entire budget into a single measure comprising thousands of pages, the leadership makes it virtually impossible for members of Congress to read through—let alone understand—what they're being asked to vote on; undercuts members' ability to ask hard questions and offer policy alternatives, represent their constituents, or file amendments; and makes planning ahead nearly impossible for everyone, from the people who administer federal heating assistance to local school boards to federal contractors. In a foreign-policy context, this is very dangerous. With "lump sum" arrangements, the executive branch can move money around, spend on defense programs without specific authorization, and fund wars with maximum flexibility and minimal oversight. This spending pattern is characteristic of the "global war on terrorism," in Iraq, Afghanistan, and elsewhere.[43]

Congress is capable of asserting itself. In June 1973 Congress passed the Case-Church Amendment, which ended all U.S. military involvement in Southeast Asia within two months. The Case-Church Amendment was a high point of congressional involvement in the prosecution of a war. In 1974, the Congress cut off military aid to Turkey following its invasion of Cyprus and obstructed commercial agreements with the USSR through the Jackson-Vanik Amendment, which tied more open relations with the United States to freedom of emigration. The Arms Export Control Act of 1976 brought Congress into the picture on the arms trade. Similar legislative activism could occur today. Congress could set restrictions on foreign aid or military assistance as a check on the executive and to ensure that the budget reflects the importance of all the tools of American powers and the interests of the entire country.

My view is a simple one—that members of Congress take seriously their oath of office.

The 535 members of Congress, Democrats and Republicans alike, are the politicians in Washington who have to reckon in an immediate way with the toll any war takes on the nation. They listen to their constituents' anger and heartfelt doubts; they go to the funerals of men and women killed; they field calls from anguished parents with sons and daughters in harm's way; they visit the veterans' facilities where wounded troops confront the fact that their lives will never be the same. And Congress, of course, passes the legislation that funds the military, veterans' care, and a host of other war-related services.

There is a simple step Congress could take to reinsert itself in the budget debate and play a greater role in U.S. foreign policy. It's called "the regular order." For many years, Congress took up individual appropriations bills, debated them, and passed them on time. That process evolved for a reason: it safeguarded public discourse, enhanced congressional oversight, and buttressed the vital role Congress plays in forging consensus among diverse regions and constituencies. If Congress wants to remain relevant and legitimate in these challenging times, it can start by reviving its disciplined approach to budgeting.

CONCLUSION

Congress, at its best, brings great strength to our constitutional system both in times of war and times of peace. The White House and executive agencies are far less accessible to ordinary voters than Congress, and while I am well aware that Congress can too easily be swayed by powerful interests, at least ordinary citizens have a chance to engage their representatives if they want.

Similarly, the White House simply cannot reflect the diversity of the American people. It is on Capitol Hill where the regional, class, social, ideological, racial, and ethnic variety of this nation's residents come together and, more important, where they must be taken into account. It is hard work to reconcile the diverse interests that come into play around a particular issue, but that is what Congress is for, and efforts to bypass it in the name of efficiency and speed are in reality little more than shrugging off the democratic process.

Obviously, Congress sometimes cannot get its act together to be a strong, effective, and sustained counterbalance to the power of the presidency. That is why reforming the Congress—to improve consultation, oversight, and the budget process—as difficult as it may be, is crucial. Until then, the power of the presidency will continue to grow.

While I understand the pressures that have led us here, from wars and terrorism to the complexity of the legislative process, to the natural inclination of chief executives to place a high value on their own agendas, to the difficulty of getting Congress to speak with one voice, I remain puzzled by the willingness of the Congress itself to yield power. True, Democrats and Republicans both like to bolster presidents of their own party, but they also have a responsibility under the Constitution to ensure that their own institution is at least coequal to the presidency in governing the country.

When a member of Congress is sworn in, he or she vows to support and defend the Constitution, a document that right up top says that "all legislative powers herein granted shall be vested" in Congress. It hardly seems a radical step, or even disrespectful of the presidency, for Congress to turn itself into an equal partner and start behaving as if it took those words seriously.

Congress is an extraordinarily resilient institution. It has a way of righting itself when it goes off track. Indeed, the power of Congress as a coequal branch has ebbed and flowed over the years. It is now in recession, but it will come back—indeed, may already be coming back. A key indicator of that return will be how vigorously it commits itself to fulfilling its constitutional obligations. In addition to a change in attitude on matters of oversight and budgetary powers, the War Powers Consultation Act provides a path to a better balance between the president and Congress, and a stronger country at home and abroad.

NOTES

1. *Helvidius No. 1* (1793), reprinted in *The Papers of James Madison*, vol. 15: *24 March 1793–20 April 1795*, eds. Thomas A. Mason, Robert A. Rutland, and Jeanne K. Sisson (Charlottesville: University Press of Virginia, 1985).

2. Harold Hongju Koh, *The National Security Constitution: Sharing Power after the Iran-Contra Affair* (New Haven, CT: Yale University Press, 1990), 4.

3. Quoted in Koh, *The National Security Constitution*, 6.

4. John Yoo, Memo, Office of Legal Counsel, March 14, 2003, at www.aclu. org/pdfs/safefree/yoo_army_torture_memo.pdf, 3.

5. Koh, *The National Security Constitution*, 2–3.

6. Kenneth D. Moss, *Undeclared War and the Future of U.S. Foreign Policy* (Washington, DC: Woodrow Wilson Center Press, 2008), 66–67.

7. Moss, *Undeclared War*, 68.

8. Moss, *Undeclared War*, 74.

9. James T. Patterson, *Mr. Republican: A Biography of Robert A. Taft* (Boston: Houghton Mifflin, 1972), 197.

10. See John J. Mearshimer, *The Tragedy of Great Power Politics* (New York: W.W. Norton, 2001), 443, fn 72.

11. Louis Hartz, *The Liberal Tradition in America* (New York: Harvest Books, 1955), 308. Robert Jervis, "America and the Twentieth Century: Continuity and Change," *Diplomatic History* 23, no. 2 (Spring 1999): 222.

12. Peter W. Rodman, *Presidential Command* (New York: Alfred A. Knopf, 2009), 15–16.

13. See Koh, *The National Security Constitution*, 101–4.

14. Available from NATO, at www.nato.int/docu/basictxt/treaty.htm.

15. See Robert A. Pollard, "The National Security State Reconsidered," in *The Truman Presidency*, ed. Michael J. Lacey (Washington, DC: Woodrow Wilson Center Press, 1989), 222; also see Vandenberg Resolution, available at www.nato. int/archives/1st5years/appendices/3.htm.

16. Jervis, "America and the Twentieth Century," 229.

17. Jervis, "America and the Twentieth Century," 230.

18. Samuel Huntington, *The Soldier and the State* (Cambridge, MA: The Belknap Press of Harvard University Press, 1959), 81.

19. Harry S Truman, *Memoirs*, vol. 2: *Years of Trial and Hope* (Garden City, NJ: Doubleday, 1956), 333.

20. Truman, *Years of Trial and Hope*, 338.

21. William Michael Treanor, "Fame, the Founding, and the Power to Declare War," 82 *Cornell Law Review* 695, 702 (1997). Text of the resolution is available at daccessdds.un.org/doc/RESOLUTION/GEN/NR0/064/95/IMG/NR006495. pdf?OpenElement.

22. See Lee H. Hamilton with Jordan Tama, *A Creative Tension: The Foreign Policy Roles of the President and Congress* (Washington, DC: Woodrow Wilson Center Press, 2002), 10.

23. See John Hart Ely, *War and Responsibility: Constitutional Lessons of Vietnam and Its Aftermath* (Princeton, NJ Princeton University Press, 1993).

24. Ely, *War and Responsibility*, 49.

25. Ely, *War and Responsibility*, 53.

26. John Yoo, *The Powers of War and Peace: The Constitution and Foreign Affairs After 9/11* (Chicago: University of Chicago Press, 2005), 151.

27. Yoo, *The Powers of War and Peace*, 13.

28. Yoo, *The Powers of War and Peace*, 143.

29. Treanor, "Fame, the Founding, and the Power to Declare War," 725.

30. This section relies heavily on James A. Baker III and Warren Christopher, *National War Powers Commission Report* (Miller Center of Public Affairs, University of Virginia, 2008), available at millercenter.org/dev/ci/system/application/views/_new-website/policy/commissions/warpowers/report.pdf.

31. For Truman's take on the events, see Truman, *Memoirs: Years of Trial and Hope*, 465–78.

32. *Youngstown Sheet & Tube Co. v. Sawyer*, 343 U.S. 635–637, 643 (1952) (Jackson, J., concurring).

33. Baker and Christopher, *National War Powers Commission Report*, 30.

34. Don Wolfensberger, "War Powers Proposal Give the President Even More Authority," *Roll Call*, July 14, 2008.

35. Richard F. Grimmet, *The War Power Resolution: After 34 Years*, Congressional Research Service, March 10, 2008, 46.

36. Theodore Wilson, "The Truman Committee, 1941," in *Congress Investigates: A Documented History 1792–1974,* vol. IV, eds. Roger Bruns and Arthur M. Schlesinger Jr. (New York: Chelsea House Publishers, 1975), 3118.

37. Wilson, "The Truman Committee, 1941."

38. Merle Miller, *Plain Speaking: An Oral Biography of Harry S. Truman* (New York: Berkley Publishing Corporation, 1973), 165–66.

39. Wilson, "The Truman Committee, 1941," 3123.

40. Wilson, "The Truman Committee, 1941," 3124, 3126.

41. Miller, *Plain Speaking,* 170.

42. Moss, *Undeclared War,* 110.

43. Moss, *Undeclared War,* 109.

Chapter Thirteen

Rivals Only Sometimes: Presidentialism, Unilateralism, and Congressional Acquiescence in the U.S. "War on Terror"

John E. Owens

Much has been written in recent years about heightened partisan polarization in American politics and its intensification during the administration of George W. Bush (Jacobson 2006; Fiorina 2008; Sinclair 2006). Yet, over this period and in the context of the so-called "war on terror" declared by the president, a simultaneous and related incremental shift occurred in the balance of power between the president, the executive, and the Congress: the presidency became more "politicized" (Moe 1985) and institutional power shifted further to the White House and the executive and away from the Congress. The terrorist attacks on New York and Washington, and Bush's presidency, signaled not only new directions in U.S. foreign and domestic policy but also a new presidential era in U.S. government and politics and a new phase in the *aggrandizement* of presidential power, at some cost to the system's checks and balances and to civil liberties.

UNILATERAL POLICY MAKING

Presidents make policy unilaterally by signing administrative, executive orders or executive agreements, by issuing written or verbal proclamations or presidential or national security directives, by writing memoranda, by designating officials or, more recently, by issuing "findings," some of which may be secret. They deploy these unilateral instruments for strategic purposes (Mayer 1999; 2001), including when they face crises demanding swift and decisive action (Corwin 1948, 304–05), and on occasions when they would probably not receive congressional approval for their actions.

Franklin Roosevelt claimed and obtained executive powers on this basis; on other occasions, he simply claimed delegated powers on the basis of vague references to statutes, and dared the Congress to challenge him (Corwin 1947; Roche 1952), which it frequently did not. Recent presidents have perpetrated similar power grabs—especially on national and domestic security matters (Fisher 2004b), but in other policy areas as well (Nathan 1983; Cooper 2005)—when they lacked explicit congressional approval in the first instance or were subsequently not subjected to congressional censure or prohibition (Fisher 2004a; 2004b, 134–61). In taking unilateral action, presidents effectively challenge the Congress and the courts to overturn their actions, *if they want and if they can*. And, at least in the case of the Congress, legislators usually do not—for the simple reason that they find they cannot muster majorities to overturn the president's action, even less so two-thirds majorities in both chambers if the president uses his veto.

The argument developed in this chapter is that in the context of the 9/11 calamity and the atmosphere of fear of renewed terrorist attacks in the United States that it engendered, the Bush administration not only effectively used the president's unilateral powers to advance its security agenda but more often than not successfully deterred—and often intimidated—the Congress into *not* challenging it or overturning its actions, or doing its bidding by passing new legislation. Members of Congress typically found it difficult or impossible to muster collective political will to coordinate and formulate timely and forceful rebuffs to aggressive executive claims justifying unilateral action. Many were only too ready to give away or delegate their powers to the executive.

9/11 AND BUSH'S PRESIDENTIALISM

In many respects, President Bush and his advisers did what any successful American president would have done in response to the national calamity that was 9/11; following some initial delay, they interpreted the public and congressional mood well, and, in a series of effectively choreographed public conversations with ordinary Americans and the Congress, provided the symbolic leadership that is so important in the American system. 9/11 and the ensuing, apparently limitless, "war on terror" represented what Burnham calls a "new constitutional moment" (1999, 2239; Ackerman 1999) and a new stage in the *aggrandizement* of presidential power. (Owens 2008)

Although Bush's approach to the presidency and his relations with the Congress were not invented in the crisis precipitated by 9/11, it was certainly crystallized by and made much more visible by that event and the subsequent, presidentially declared, "war on terror." The foundations of Bush's *presidentialist* philosophy lay in the perceptions of leading figures in the administration that the presidency had been emasculated by congressional actions after the *débâcles* of Vietnam, Watergate, and the Iran-Contra scandal (Goldsmith

2007, 85–88; Gellman 2008, 100–102; Simendinger 2004, 1173). Its theoretical origins lie in a legal doctrine developed by conservative constitutionalists in the 1980s and 1990s that extols the virtues and necessity of a "unitary executive" (Calabresi and Rhodes 1992; Calabresi 1995; Calabresi and Prakash 1994; Yoo and Calabresi 2003; Yoo, Calabresi, and Colangelo 2005). Its leading exponents in the Bush administration were "old hands" from previous Republican administrations and included, most notably, Vice President Cheney, Cheney's chief of staff, David Addington, and Secretary of Defense Donald Rumsfeld. The Bush administration's presidentialism, then, was a part of a bold and strategic political project that is consistent with Moe's "politicized presidency" concept (1985). Its conception of the presidency was "ultra-separationist" (Jones 2007, 401). It was a philosophy designed to extend executive and presidential power—or, in Jones' more benign phrase, "to capitalize on [Bush's] position" as chief executive (2003, 174–78) and govern "executively" (Jones 2007, 399) with or without the Congress.

Unitary power is exactly as it sounds: all embracing, indivisible, inherent, plenary, exclusive, and absolute. *All* executive powers are invested personally in the president and subject to his direct command. The doctrine effectively permits the president to define policy in any area more or less unilaterally with or without congressional consent by claiming and actually exercising unlimited and exclusive power based on "inherent" and implied discretionary, independent, and formal powers derived from a very expansive interpretation of Article II of the Constitution and from congressional statutes. As a theory of governance, almost by definition, it relegates the role of the Congress, the courts, and other important actors because it seeks to insulate the president from the constitutional checks and balances in ways unknown to and antithetical to the framers of the Constitution. It is a theory, then, which is fundamentally incompatible with notions of a Madisonian or separated system in which the different institutions share power.

The Bush administration's presidentialism not only relegated the roles of other governmental actors, it was an approach to presidential power and governing that did not attach great importance to achieving or maintaining political legitimacy, reputation, prestige, or public approval—all important sources of presidential power identified as being important by Neustadt (1990, 150) and others (Lowi 1986; Kernell 2007, 18–27). Position was almost everything for Bush and his colleagues (Jones 2007, 400–401). Political influence would follow primarily, if not exclusively, from the president's formal position as chief executive. It was a doctrine that melded well with Bush's personal leadership style. Bordering on "the hurried," it was a clear and decisive, intuitively executive, style that demanded action, "forging on, rarely looking back, scoffing at—even ridiculing—doubt and anything less than 100 percent commitment" (Woodward 2002a, 256).

LEGISLATING THE "WAR ON TERROR" TOGETHER

An analysis of executive-legislative relations that focuses exclusively on legislating against terrorism might reasonably yield a conclusion that the rivalry and give-and-take intended by the framers remained in operation during the "war on terror."

As Roosevelt had done in 1941, in the aftermath of 9/11, Bush appealed and won strong congressional support for a series of significant new legislative proposals. But, over the course of the administration's "war on terror," the president did not win approval for *all* he wanted from the Congress; there were many instances when congressional preferences were reflected to some degree in "war on terror" legislation—consistent with ongoing executive-legislative "conversations" that resulted in compromises and concessions included in final legislation (Jones 2005; Sinclair 2009). Congressional-presidential conversations can be one-sided, however. Congressionally imposed increases in emergency funding for New York City, federalization of Transportation Security Administration workers (the 2001 Aviation and Transportation Security Act), insistence on a new Department of Homeland Security, restrictions on the PATRIOT Act, the McCain torture amendment, and other legislative actions provide only part of the story. A more important question is the *preponderant balance* of relations both in respect of legislation and the *extent* to which the Congress effectively checked the Bush administration's aggressive presidentialist claims.

UNILATERAL PRESIDENTIAL ACTION

In the days and weeks after 9/11, the president issued a small avalanche of directives and executive orders: blocking property and prohibiting terrorist-related transactions (EO 13224), establishing an Office of Homeland Security and the Homeland Security Council in the White House (EO 13228), critical infrastructure protection (EO 13231), and designating Afghanistan and its airspace a combat zone (EO 13239).

None of these required congressional approval and many were not controversial. Many were, however, partly because the Bush administration sought to exploit the new opportunities presented by 9/11 and its "war on terror" to expand presidential and executive power through unilateral presidential action—sometimes in secret—on the basis of claiming that the president could exercise "exclusive, independent and inherent" powers, not subject to congressional or judicial review. On these bases, Bush issued executive orders limiting access to presidential records (EO 13233); authorized "the largest

CIA covert action program since the Cold War" (Woodward 2001, A1), the details of which were not disclosed to the Congress (Priest 2005); sanctioned a highly secret Department of Defense program giving blanket advance approval to kill or capture and, if possible, interrogate, "high value" targets in Afghanistan, Iraq, and elsewhere (Hersh 2004); and instituted a comprehensive covert program to topple Saddam Hussein (Woodward 2002b; Slavin 2002, A1; Risen 2006).

Invoking his "inherent" powers, Bush also issued a highly controversial military order in November 2001 unilaterally deeming noncitizens as "unlawful" or "enemy combatants"—rather than prisoners of war under the protections of the Third Geneva Convention. "Enemy combatants" could be incarcerated and interrogated by the military for indefinite periods without charge or access to their families or lawyers at Guantánamo Bay and elsewhere, including at secret prisons in different parts of the world, and including in countries known to practice torture. Under the same order and without congressional consent, for the first time since World War II Bush authorized the Pentagon to create secret military tribunals to try "enemy combatants." These tribunals comprising military officers who reported directly to the Pentagon could be held outside the United States, beyond the reach of U.S. judicial systems, and the ambit of U.S. constitutional protections. The president and the secretary of defense subsequently extended this military order to allow detention of U.S. citizens far from any battlefield, even if they were arrested inside the United States.

Subsequently, on the basis of legal advice from Attorney General Alberto Gonzales that "a new kind of war . . . renders obsolete Geneva's strict limitations on questioning of enemy prisoners and renders quaint some of its provisions" (2002), the president wrote a classified memorandum to administration officials insisting that, although the United States would continue to treat detainees humanely and support the Geneva Conventions, none of the Geneva Conventions would apply to Al Qaeda. Indeed, according to Gonzales, under the "inherent" powers provided the president by the U.S. Constitution, he had the authority to suspend the application of the conventions (2002). While Gonzales's memo argued that the president need not adhere to traditional principles of international law, a later opinion—the notorious (and subsequently rescinded) "torture memo" written by Jay Bybee, assistant attorney general in the OLC—went even further: the president could *choose* not to follow international law (2002). Following the enactment of the 2005 Detainee Treatment Act, the new acting head of the OLC had signed a secret legal opinion averring that even the harshest tactics used by the CIA were not "cruel, inhuman or degrading" (Johnston and Shane 2007, A1)—the phrase used in McCain's amendment.

The direct and indirect policy consequences of these orders were the torture and abuse of prisoners, extrajudicial interrogations and trials, and the use of extraordinary rendition to transfer detainees from one country to another, where they were interrogated and often abused by proxy (Hersh 2004; Jehl and Johnston 2005). The implications from an executive-legislative perspective were that the administration could ignore existing U.S. statutory and international treaty obligations and unilaterally reformulate U.S. torture policy, then or at any other time in the future, without recourse to Congress.

FOUNDATIONAL LAWMAKING: LEGITIMATING A PRESIDENTIALIST "WAR ON TERROR"

Besides taking various unilateral actions, administration officials also pursued a bold and aggressive legislative strategy designed to expand presidential power and wage a "war on terror" consistent with the unitary executive doctrine. In the aftermath of 9/11 and in the context of fear of further terrorism engendered thereafter, the administration demanded and the Congress ceded broad new discretionary powers to the executive that subsequently provided part of the legal foundation for the administration claiming further legislative authority, which the Congress was not aware it had given. Moreover, when the administration subsequently stretched congressional authority, often without telling the Congress, lawmakers typically did not oversee, challenge, or check the executive as Madison's dictum that "Ambition must be made to counteract ambition" intended.

Authorizing a Limitless "War on Terror"

Whereas Roosevelt sought and obtained a congressional declaration of war in 1941, specifying the Imperial Government of Japan as the enemy and pledging all the country's resources until "the conflict [is brought] to a successful termination" in common with the practice of previous presidents and congresses since 1950, President Bush insisted on launching his "war" only on the basis of a "use of force" resolution that granted him even broader legal authority than the 1964 Gulf of Tonkin resolution or the resolution the Congress granted Bush's father authority to launch the 1990–1991 Gulf War. In its final form, the resolution granted the president authority to use "all necessary and appropriate force against those nations, organizations, or persons *he determines* planned, authorized, committed, or aided the terrorist attacks that occurred on September 11, 2001, or harbored such organizations or persons, *in order to prevent any future acts* [my emphases] of international terrorism against the United States by such nations, organizations or persons" (PL 107-40).

Realistically, it was neither feasible nor politically advisable to identify who was responsible for the 9/11 attacks (Abramowitz 2002, 73–75), yet the resolution nevertheless allowed the president almost unlimited freedom to define unilaterally the post-9/11 contours of national security and antiterrorism policy, including the conditions under which military action could be taken. Although the resolution was intended to fall under the auspices of the War Powers Act, it did not even provide for subsequent congressional accounting or scrutiny, as the authors of the 1973 legislation intended.

On the basis of legal advice from the administration's Office of Legal Counsel (2001), at the joint session of the Congress nine days after the attacks President Bush unilaterally translated the congressional-approved "use of force" resolution into a presidential-declared "war" on terrorism: for the administration, the 9/11 attacks were "an act of war" by foreign aggressors, not mere criminal acts by individuals requiring redress by the U.S. justice system;[1] hence, U.S. military actions could be constitutionally justified as self-defense. The "war on terror" would also be indefinite and without geographical limits (Bush 2001). Without a formal congressional declaration, then, Bush's declaration effectively blurred the line between a metaphor and a legal state (war), thereby providing him with foundational authority for other nonbattlefield policies (e.g., military detention policies, suspension of *habeas corpus*, etc.) (Kassop 2007). When administration officials were subsequently asked to justify the administration's actions on illegal wiretapping, suspension of *habeas corpus* rights, extraordinary rendition, torture and prisoner abuse, they invariably quoted the congressional use of force resolution.

Extending Executive Authority through the PATRIOT Act

While the 2001 use of force resolution provided much of the foundational authority for the "war on terror" the administration wanted, other proposed administration policy required new legislation, notably intelligence gathering, law enforcement, asset seizure, monitoring and detainment by the Immigration and Naturalization Service, and transforming the Justice Department's primary mission from catching criminals to thwarting terrorism. Much of this additional authority was provided by the lengthy, complex, and highly controversial USA PATRIOT Act, which lawmakers approved by wide margins and President Bush signed seven weeks after 9/11.

Only very occasionally did congressional majorities stand up to the administration. In 2002, for example, a bipartisan coalition led by House Republican majority leader Dick Armey (R-TX) killed a Bush administration proposal for a national ID card and authorization for Operation TIPS (Terrorist Information and Prevention System).[2] The following year they approved an amendment limiting the Pentagon's controversial Total Information

Awareness (TIA) program, which used data-mining technology to scan vast amounts of personal data; in October 2003, the Congress cut off all funding for any further TIA research and development. Against these rare instances of congressional resistance, Congress members remained under constant—and, ultimately, effective—administration pressure to expand and make the PA-TRIOT legislation permanent (Lichtblau 2003a, A1; Lichtblau with Liptak 2003, A1). Willing Republican congressional leaders worked closely with the Bush administration to legislate new restrictive legislation (Lichtblau 2003b, A1; Fessenden 2003, 2912, 2914) and to kill proposals that sought to circumscribe executive discretion (Ramasastry 2003; Lichtblau 2004, A1).

Extending the "War on Terror" to Iraq

President Bush's request for a second broadly defined "use of force" authorization for the invasion and occupation of Iraq in 2002 elicited a similar response from lawmakers to his 2001 resolution. As one of President Reagan's former associate attorney generals noted at the time, "George Washington, Abraham Lincoln and Franklin Delano Roosevelt never claimed war powers close to what Bush is claiming" (Bruce Fein quoted in Allen and Eilperin 2002, A1). Despite the breadth of his request, despite strong doubts about the legality of a preemptive strike against a sovereign country, despite abundant evidence of the daunting nature and the military's misgivings about the proposed invasion and occupation, despite not undertaking meaningful scrutiny of the 2002 National Intelligence Estimate or seriously challenging the administration's case for invasion and occupation, and despite the president making his request for congressional authorization only when he was committed politically and militarily, again the Congress deferred to the White House, did not insist on a declaration of war, did not balk at the administration's refusal to provide further details of troop numbers, costs, length of engagement, or details of reconstruction plans, and reacted positively and swiftly to a request to approve a resolution before the November 2002 elections. There was some congressional opposition, primarily from Democrats, but the dominant response was strong support; most Democrats were passively resigned and accepting of symbolic concessions—on the proposed scope of the military action, on the need for multilateral action, and on postconflict reports on reconstruction, peacekeeping, and other planning efforts—that did not substantially constrain the administration's intended course of action.

Once the invasion and occupation were under way—and notwithstanding the rapidly increasing costs of the global "war on terror," across-the-board budgetary pressures, an increasingly large budget deficit—the Congress also failed to control the spiraling invasion and occupation costs. Driven by the Bush administration's ever-expanding definition of the "war on terror"—or the "Long War"—the Congress approved intact more or less all appropriation requests, which by late 2008 totaled over $864 billions (Belasco 2008). Approximately, $650 billion of this total was appropriated for Iraq, compared with an initial estimate of $50 to $60 billion provided by former Office of Management and Budget director Mitch Daniels (Bumiller 2002).

Unlike in previous wars, neither the administration nor Republican or Democratic congressional majorities proposed tax increases or encouraged substantive debates over financing the war or prioritizing budgetary demands. Instead, war spending was financed largely through borrowing that will need to be repaid. Moreover, the Congress repeatedly allowed the Bush administration to exploit a provision in the 1985 Gramm-Rudman-Hollings Balanced Budget and Emergency Deficit Control Act that permits presidents to submit piecemeal supplemental or emergency spending requests in mid-fiscal year, over and above the president's annual budget, at a time when little legislative time is available for the appropriations committees to exercise proper scrutiny.

Neither did lawmakers insist on detailed and credible "war on terror" costs, nor that outlays be used for the purposes specifically authorized. So, when administration officials unilaterally transferred monies appropriated for one purpose to funding preparations for the invasion of Iraq, or impounded funds, lawmakers resisted taking corrective action (Obey and Byrd 2004).

As a consequence of Congress's continued tolerance of supplementals, the real costs of the administration's policy choices in Iraq and Afghanistan remained obscured; overall budgetary priorities were difficult to establish, deficit spending substantially increased, and lawmakers' capacity to conduct meaningful oversight was reduced. Moreover, not only reluctant majority Republicans lacked the political will to rein in war spending. Notwithstanding their initial *bravado*, the new Democratic majority elected in 2006 was ultimately unwilling to insist on constraints and controls. After the president vetoed a Democratic-led attempt to impose a timetable on the president withdrawing U.S. troops from Iraq in May 2007, lawmakers backed off and the president won his funding request without any timetable. So that by the time Bush left office he had effectively seen off almost all congressional challenges: the president successively won almost unlimited funding for the "war on terror" for every year since 2001; had resisted congressional attempts to restrict war spending and force troop withdrawal; and, latterly, had actually increased U.S. troops in Iraq in the so-called surge and bought enough political time to continue with his policies for the duration of his presidency. The experience was almost an object lesson in congressional ineffectiveness that stands in sharp contrast to congressional efforts during the Korean, Vietnam, and Bosnian wars (U.S. Congress. House. Committee on the Budget 2007).

CORRECTIVE LAWMAKING: LEGITIMATING NEW EXTENSIONS OF EXECUTIVE POWER

The 2001 use of force resolution, the PATRIOT Act and the USA PATRIOT and Terrorism Prevention Reauthorization Act of 2005 provided the legislative foundations for the Bush administration's "war on terror," along with the 2002 Homeland Security Act, which created the Department of Homeland Security to house agencies that exercise powers authorized by the PATRIOT Act. As, however, the Bush administration implemented its "war on terror," a number of its policies were successfully challenged in the courts, notably by the U.S. Supreme Court over certain *habeas corpus* issues in *Hamdi v. Rumsfeld* (2004), *Rasul v. Bush et al.* (2004), *Hamdan v. Rumsfeld* (2006), and *Boumediene v. Bush* (2008), at which points the administration returned to the Congress for new legitimating legislation. The Congress obliged by enacting the remedial legislation the administration wanted , notably by legitimizing the administration's use of military commissions to determine the status and "try" detainees, by denying detainees habeas corpus rights (through the bipartisan Graham-Levin amendment in the 2006 Military Commissions Act), by condoning the use of torture (through the Graham-Kyl amendment to the 2005 Detainee Treatment Act), and by grandfathering the administration's use of electronic surveillance of U.S. citizens (in the Foreign Intelligence Surveillance Act of 1978 Amendments Act of 2008).

CONGRESSIONAL-PRESIDENTIAL RIVALRY?

Congressional-presidential relations in the Bush administration's "war on terror" do not provide many examples of vigorous institutional rivalry, let alone congressional dominance. To say the least, the administration's interpretation of the separated system lay some distance from traditional Madisonian theory. It went even beyond Hamilton, who stressed the importance of the "energy in the executive" (*Federalist No. 69*), but who nevertheless drew an important distinction between presidential power and the exercise of a royal prerogative. Most of the time, Congress bent its knee to the administration under Democratic as well as Republican majorities. The typical pattern of policy making was one of strong executive action, with or without congressional knowledge or consent, and invariably accompanied by aggressive administration assertions of "inherent" executive power and/or foundational congressional authorization (in the form of the 2001 use of force resolution).

Sometimes, strong executive action was followed by partial congressional or judicial challenge (primarily but not exclusively from Democrats), and a certain amount of congressional-presidential negotiation with particularly skillful tactical plays by the administration (Howell and Kriner's "skillfully and accurately gauging congressional opposition" [2007]). Regardless of whether the Congress collectively challenged the administration, ultimately, the legislature deferred to the president. Exceptions were rare; stunning congressional silences, inaction, and acquiescence were common.

Given its elite rather than popular origins (see Ackerman 1999: 2312), one obvious question is whether the transformation of presidential power will outlive Bush's presidency. Following Barack Obama's victory in the 2008 presidential elections, former Vice President Cheney opined that the new president will "appreciate" the expansions of executive power achieved during the Bush administration and "not likely . . . cede that authority back to the Congress. I think they'll find that due to the challenges they face, they'll need all the authority they can muster" (quoted in Bolton 2008). In his election campaign, however, Senator Obama strongly criticized the expansive nature of the 2001 and 2003 use of force resolutions and the Bush administration's assertion of "plenary power." Specifically, Obama rejected "the view that the President may do whatever he deems necessary to protect national security," disavowed "the use of signing statements to make extreme and implausible claims of presidential authority," and promised to "follow existing law." He also added that "when it comes to US citizens and residents, I will only authorize surveillance for national security purposes consistent with FISA and other federal statutes" (Savage 2007).[3]

In office, President Obama has rejected the "war on terror" nomenclature in favor of the "enduring struggle against terrorism and extremism" or the "ongoing struggle" (2009), and appointed as head of the OLC and solicitor general prominent constitutional lawyers fiercely critical of the Bush administration's expansive view of executive power (Lichtblau 2009, A1). In his first two days in office, the new president also signed executive orders revoking the Bush administration's severe limits on public access to presidential records, closing Guantánamo promptly "consistent with the national security and foreign policy interests of the United States and the interests of justice," creating a special task force to review detainee policy, prohibiting the CIA from maintaining its own prisons overseas, and at a stroke the new president revoked Bush's EO 13440 (2007) and every executive directive, order, and regulation relating to the detention or interrogation of individuals issued by any executive branch lawyer after 9/11. The administration has also announced that primary authority over detention policies will move from the Pentagon to the Justice Department.

However, both in his campaign and as president, Obama has also strongly supported U.S. efforts against Al Qaeda and other networks, as well as enhanced military action against the resurgent Taliban in Afghanistan and Pakistan. Some early decisions by the Obama administration suggest elements of continuity with the nonmilitary aspects of the Bush administration's policies. While he has ordered the closure of Guantánamo, following the *Boumediene* decision ruling unconstitutional the use of military tribunals, the Bush administration had previously expressed a desire to close the facility. Although it has promised to keep the Congress better apprised of the CIA's activities, the new administration has also not ruled out the use of torture. Obama's nominee for CIA director told the Senate Intelligence Committee in January 2009 that, in certain circumstances, he would seek presidential approval for the CIA to use methods that went beyond the president's new order; and left open whether such methods would amount to torture, as defined by congressional legislation (Mazzetti 2009, A1). In a case before the Ninth Circuit Appeals Court involving allegations of extraordinary rendition and torture by a Guantánamo detainee in early February 2009, the new administration also followed the Bush administration and invoked the "state secrets" doctrine to suppress evidence and shut down the case (Schwartz 2009). Even though Obama has abandoned the Bush administration's "enemy combatant" terminology, the president has apparently not ruled out indefinite military detention of terrorist suspects and their allies or "trials" by military commissions.

While it remains to be seen how the Obama administration will respond to other cases against the U.S. government involving *habeas corpus* rights brought by detainees at Guantánamo and elsewhere who allege torture and by others who allege illegal wiretapping, several senators have already challenged the administration by reintroducing a State Secrets Protection Act, which will require a court to rule whether the administration may claim state secrets privilege to suppress evidence. One indication of whether a new constitutional equilibrium (Owens 2008) has been reached may be determined by whether and to what extent the Congress collectively challenges the new president on these and other counterterrorist issues, particularly in the new context of global economic depression. Presidential power is not only the power to persuade, it is also a question of what a president can get away with—and whether the Congress and the courts will stop him or her. Ackerman (1999, 2334–35) suggested a one-year period in which to test the endurance of a constitutional transformation. By 2019, we should know the lasting legacy of George W. Bush's presidential shift of power to the executive.

REFERENCES

Abramowitz, David. 2002. The President, the Congress and the Use of Force: Legal and Political Considerations in Authorizing Use of Force against International Terrorism. *Harvard Journal of Law and Public Policy* 43, no. 1: 71–81.

Ackerman, Bruce. 1999. "Revolution on a Human Scale," *The Yale Law Journal*, 108: 2279–2349.

Allen, Mike, and Juliet Eilperin. 2002. Bush Aides Say Iraq War Needs No Hill Vote. *Washington Post*, August 26, A1.

Belasco, Amy. 2008. *The Cost of Iraq, Afghanistan, and Other Global War on Terror Operations since 9/11*. Washington, DC: CRS Report to Congress, RL33110, October 15.

Bolton, Alexander. 2008. Cheney Says Obama Should Be Grateful to Bush. *The Hill*, December 15.

Bumiller, Elisabeth. 2002. Threats and Responses: The Cost; White House Cuts Estimate of Cost of War with Iraq. *New York Times*, December 31.

Burnham, Walter Dean. 1999. Constitutional Moments and Punctuated Equilibria: A Political Scientist Confronts Bruce Ackerman's We the People. *Yale Law Journal* 108: 2237–77.

Bush, George W. 2001. Address to a Joint Session of Congress and the American People. U.S. Capitol, Washington, DC, September 20.

Bybee, Jay. 2002. "Standards of Conduct for Interrogation under 18 USC. 230-234A," *Memorandum to White House Alberto Gonzales*, 1 August. (Accessed 25 January 2007 at http://news.findlaw.com/hdocs/docs/doj/bybee80102ltr.html)

Calabresi, Steven G. 1995. Some Normative Arguments for the Unitary Executive. *Arkansas Law Review* 48, no. 23: 90–104.

Calabresi, Steven G., and Saikrishna B. Prakash. 1995. The President's Power to Execute the Laws, *Yale Law Journal* 104: 541–665.

Calabresi, Steven G., and Kevin H. Rhodes. 1992. The Structural Constitution: Unitary Executive, Plural Judiciary. *Harvard Law Review* 105: 1153–1216.

Cooper, Joseph. 2005. "From Congressional to Presidential Preeminence. Power and Politics in Late Nineteenth Century America and Today." In *Congress Reconsidered*, 8th ed., eds. Lawrence C. Dodd and Bruce I. Oppenheimer. Washington, DC: CQ Press: 363–94.

Corwin, Edward. 1947. *Total War and the Constitution*. New York: Ayer Co.

———. 1948. *The President: Office and Powers*. New York: New York University.

Delahunty, Robert J., and John C. Yoo. 2002. The President's Constitutional Authority to Conduct Military Operations against Terrorist Organizations and the Nations that Harbor or Support Them. Research Paper 93. Berkeley: University of California at Berkeley School of Law, at repositories.cdlib.org/cgi/viewcontent.cgi?article=1003&context=boaltwp Research Paper 93 (accessed June 30, 2004).

Fessenden, Helen. 2003. "Deal on Intelligence Authorization Includes Enhanced FBI Powers," *CQ Weekly*, 22 November: 2912–14.

Fiorina, P. 2008. A Divider, Not a Unifier—Did It Have to Be? In *The George W. Bush Legacy*, eds. Colin Campbell, Bert A. Rockman, and Andrew Rudalevige, 92–111. Washington, DC: CQ Press.

Fisher, Louis. 2004a. *The Politics of Executive Privilege*. Durham: Carolina Academic Press.

———. 2004b. *Presidential War Power*. 2d rev. ed. Lawrence: University Press of Kansas.

Gellman, Barton. 2008. *Angler: The Cheney Vice Presidency.* New York: Penguin Press.

Goldsmith, Jack L. 2007. *The Terror Presidency: Law and Judgment inside the Bush Administration.* New York: W.W. Norton.

Gonzales, Alberto. 2002. Decision Re Application of the Geneva Convention on Prisoners of War to the Conflict with Al Qaeda and the Taliban. Memorandum for the President, January 25 at wid.ap.org/documents/doj/gonzales.pdf (accessed December 28, 2006).

Hamilton, Alexander, James Madison, and John Jay. 1961. *The Federalist Papers.* New York and Toronto: New American Library.

Hersh, Seymour. 2004. Annals of National Security. The Gray Zone. How a Secret Pentagon Program Came to Abu Ghraib. *New Yorker,* May 24.

Howell, William G., and Douglas L. Kriner. 2007. Bending So as Not to Break: What the Bush Presidency Reveals about the Politics of Unilateral Action. In *The Polarized Presidency of George W. Bush,* eds. George C. Edwards and Desmond S. King, 96–141. Oxford and New York: Oxford University Press.

Jacobson, Gary C. 2006. *A Divider, Not a Uniter: George W. Bush and the American Public.* New York: Longman.

Jehl, Douglas, and David Johnston. 2005. Rule Change Lets C.I.A. Freely Send Suspects Abroad to Jails. *New York Times,* March 6.

Johnston, David, and Scott Shane. 2007. Debate Erupts on Techniques Used by C.I.A. *New York Times,* October 5, A1.

Jones, Charles O. 2003. "Capitalizing on Position in a Perfect Tie." In *The George W. Bush Presidency: An Early Assessment,* ed. Fred I. Greenstein, 73–96. Baltimore, MD, and London: The Johns Hopkins University Press.

———. 2005. *The Presidency in a Separated System.* 2nd ed. Washington, DC: The Brookings Institution.

———. 2007. The US Congress and Chief Executive George W. Bush. In *The Polarised Presidency of George W. Bush,* eds. George C. Edwards and Desmond S. King, 387–418. Oxford and New York: Oxford University Press.

Kassop, Nancy. 2007. A Political Question by Any Other Name. Government Litigation Strategy in the Enemy Combatant Cases of *Hamdi* and *Padilla.* In *The Political Question Doctrine and The Supreme Court of the United States,* eds. Nada Mourtada-Sabbah and Bruce E. Cain. Lanham, MD: Lexington Books.

Kernell, Samuel. 2007. *Going Public: New Strategies of Presidential Leadership.* Washington, DC: CQ Press.

Koszczuk, Jackie. 2002. "Lawmakers Struggle to Keep An Eye on Patriot Act," *CQ Weekly,* 7 September 2002: 2284–88.

Lichtblau, Eric. 2003a. Republicans Want Terror Law Made Permanent. *New York Times,* April 9, A1.

———. 2003b. "Lawmakers Approve Expansion of FBI's Antiterrorism Powers," *New York Times,* 20 November 20: A1.

———. 2004. "Veto Threatened on Bill to Restrict Powers Under Terrorism Law," *New York Times,* 30 January: A1.

———. 2009. Obama Pick to Analyze Broad Powers of President. *New York Times,* January 8, A1.

Lichtblau, Eric, with Adam Liptak. 2003. "On Terror and Spying, Ashcroft Expands Reach," *The New York Times,* 15 March: A1.

Lowi, Theodore J. 1986. *The Personal President: Power Invested, Promise Unfulfilled.* Ithaca, NY: Cornell University Press.

Mayer, Kenneth R. 1999. Executive Orders and Presidential Power, *Journal of Politics* 62, no. 2: 445–66.

———. 2001. *With the Stroke of a Pen: Executive Orders and Presidential Power.* Princeton, NJ: Princeton University Press.

Mazzetti, Mark. 2009. Panetta Open to Tougher Methods in Some C.I.A. Interrogation. *New York Times,* February 5, A1.

Moe, Terry M. 1985. "The Politicized Presidency." In *The New Direction in American Politics,* eds. John E. Chubb and Paul E. Peterson. Washington, DC: The Brookings Institution: 235–71.

Nathan, Richard P. 1983. *The Administrative Presidency.* New York: Wiley.

Neustadt, Richard E. 1990. *Presidential Power and the Modern Presidents. The Politics of Leadership from Roosevelt to Reagan.* New York: Free Press.

Obama, Barack. 2009. Interview with Al Arabiya News Channel, at www.alarabiya. net/articles/2009/01/27/65087.html#004 (accessed January 28, 2009).

Obey, David R., and Robert C. Byrd. 2004. Letter to the President, April 26, at www. house.gov/appropriations_democrats/letters.htm (accessed September 27, 2006).

Owens, John E. 2008. "Presidential *Aggrandizement* and Congressional Acquiescence in the 'War on Terror': A New Constitutional Equilibrium?" In *America's "War On Terrorism": New Dimensions in United States Government and National Security,* eds John E. Owens and John W. Dumbrell, 25–76. Lanham, MD: Lexington Books.

Priest, Dana. 2005. "Covert CIA Program Withstands New Furor. Anti-Terror Effort Continues to Grow," *The Washington Post,* 30 December: A1.

Ramasastry, Anita. 2003. "Patriot II: The Sequel. Why It's Even Scarier than the First Patriot Act," *FindLaw.com.* 17 February. http://writ.news.findlaw.com/ramasastry/20030217.html (accessed 25 Sept 2004).

Risen, James. 2006. *State of War: The Secret History of the CIA and the Bush Administration.* New York: Free Press.

Roche, John P. 1952. Executive Power and the Domestic Presidency: The Quest for Prerogative. *Western Political Quarterly* 5, no. 4 (December): 592–618.

Savage, Charlie. 2006. Bush Shuns Patriot Act Requirement. In Addendum to Law, He Says Oversight Rules Are Not Binding. *Boston Globe,* March 24.

———. 2007. "Barack Obama's Q&A," *Boston Globe,* 20 December, at http://www. boston.com/news/politics/2008/specials/CandidateQA/ (accessed 17 December 2008).

Schwartz, John. 2009 "Obama Backs Off a Reversal on Secrets," *New York Times,* 10 February.

Simendinger, Alexis. 2004. Andy Card on Power and Privilege. *National Journal,* April 17.

Sinclair, Barbara. 2006. *Party Wars, Polarization and the Politics of National Policy Making*. Norman: University of Oklahoma Press.

———. 2009. The President and the Congressional Party Leadership in a Polarized Era. In *Rivals for Power*, ed. James A.Thurber. Lanham, MD: Rowman and Littlefield.

Slavin, Barbara. 2002. U.S. Stirs Efforts to Oust Saddam, *USA Today*, February 28.

U.S. Congress. House. Committee on the Budget. 2007. Hearings. The Cost of Funding of the *Global War on Terror (GWOT)*. 110th Cong., 1st sess. January 18, at budget.house.gov/hearings/2007/Kosiak070118.pdf (accessed February 27, 2008).

U.S. Department of Justice, Office of Legal Counsel. 2001. "The President's Constitutional Authority to Conduct Military Operations Against Terrorists and Nations Supporting Them," *Memorandum: John Yoo to Timothy Flanigan, the Deputy Counsel to the President*. 25 September. Accessed January 2009 at http://www.usdoj.gov/olc/warpowers925.htm.

Woodward, Bob. 2001. CIA Told to Do "Whatever Necessary" to Kill Bin Laden; Agency and Military Collaborating at "Unprecedented" Level; Cheney Says War against Terror "May Never End." *Washington Post*, October 21, A1.

———. 2002a. *Bush at War*. New York and London: Simon & Schuster.

———. 2002b. "President Broadens Anti-Hussein Order; CIA Gets More Tools to Oust Iraqi Leader," *Washington Post*, 16 June: A1.

Yoo, Christopher S., and Steven G. Calabresi. 2003. The Unitary Executive during the Second Half-Century. *Harvard Journal of Law & Public Policy* 26, no. 3 (June): 668–802.

Yoo, Christopher S., Steven G. Calabresi, and Anthony J. Colangelo. 2004. "The Unitary Executive in the Modern Era, 1945-2004," *Iowa Law Review* 90/2: 601–732.

NOTES

I am grateful for the interview time and assistance with this project provided by various House and Senate committee staffers in June and November 2006 and the congenial intellectual home provided at the Center for Congressional and Presidential Studies by Jim Thurber.

1. In international law, the traditional definition of *war* refers to hostile actions by a state, not hostile actions by foreign individuals and groups.

2. TIPS would have allowed postal and other community workers to report suspicious activities (Koszczuk 2002, 2286–87).

3. Subsequently, however, Senator Obama voted for the Foreign Intelligence Surveillance Act (FISA) Bill in June 2008, which allowed retroactive amnesty for telecom companies for participating in Bush administration's illegal spying program on American citizens.

Chapter Fourteen

The President, Congress, Military Tribunals, and Guantanamo

Louis Fisher

On November 13, 2001, President George W. Bush authorized the creation of military tribunals to try individuals who assisted in the terrorist attacks of 9/11. Military tribunals had not been used since World War II, but the administration looked to the Supreme Court case of *Ex parte Quirin* (1942) as an "apt precedent." It also invoked "inherent" powers of the president as further legal authority. Congress acquiesced to these initiatives, but the detention of hundreds of suspects at the U.S. naval base in Guantanamo, Cuba, met repeated defeats in the courts. Using strained and false historical precedents, the administration claimed it could indefinitely hold U.S. citizens and aliens at the naval base with few procedural safeguards. As detention continued year after year, without trial or even bringing charges against the suspects, the administration's position grew progressively weaker in court, in the country, and in the eyes of the world community. During the presidential campaign in 2008, Senator Barack Obama pledged to close the detention facility at Guantanamo. In his first few days in office, on January 22, 2009, President Obama issued several executive orders related to the detainees.

SHAKY PRECEDENTS

In legal briefs filed in federal court, the Bush administration argued that military tribunals "have tried enemy combatants since the earliest days of the Republic under such procedures as the President has deemed fit."[1] What the precedents show, however, is the existence of long-standing independent *legislative* power. Military tribunals had operated under the procedures that *Congress* saw fit to spell out by statute. On June 30, 1775, the Continental Congress adopted rules and regulations for the military in a series of 69

Articles of War (legislative statutes).[2] From the very start, the punishment of offenses by the military was "wholly statutory, having been . . . enacted by Congress as the legislative power."[3] During his service as commander in chief at the time of the Revolutionary War, George Washington adhered faithfully to the Articles of War and recognized that changes in the military code "can only be defined and fixed by Congress."[4]

The Bush administration claimed that this period of American history supported presidential authority to create military tribunals: "It was well recognized when the Constitution was written and ratified that one of the powers inherent in military command was the authority to institute tribunals for punishing enemy violations of the laws of war," and that General Washington had appointed a "Board of General Officers" in 1780 to try British Major John André as a spy."[5] The administration insisted that "there was no provision in the American Articles of War providing for the jurisdiction in a court-martial to try an enemy for the offense of spying."[6] Both positions are false. The Continental Congress adopted a resolution in 1776 expressly providing that enemy spies "shall suffer death . . . by sentence of a court martial, or such other punishment as such court martial shall direct," and ordered that the resolution "be printed at the end of the rules and articles of war."[7] The previous year, Congress had made it punishable by court-martial for members of the Continental Army to "hold correspondence with" or "give intelligence to" the enemy.[8] It is not possible to locate presidential power at the time of Major André's trial in 1780. There was no president or separate executive during that period. One branch of government existed: the Continental Congress. Independent executive or judicial branches did not appear until the drafting of the Constitution in 1787 and the operation of the new government in 1789.

The Bush administration advised a federal court in 2004: "Throughout this country's history, Presidents have exercised their inherent authority as Commanders in Chief to establish military commissions, without any authorization from Congress. In April 1818, for example, military tribunals were convened, without Congressional authorization, to try two British subjects for inciting the Creek Indians to war with the United States."[9] In fact, the prosecution of two British subjects during the Seminole war in Florida underscored the abuses associated with executive-created military tribunals. After the tribunal changed its sentence for one of the men from death to corporal punishment, General Andrew Jackson ordered that the individual be shot and his order was carried out. Far from defending Jackson or claiming inherent authority over military tribunals, President James Monroe quickly distanced himself from the controversy and gave Congress documents it requested to conduct an investigation.[10]

A House committee, in a report highly critical of Jackson, found no law that authorized a military trial unless one was "acting as a spy." On that specific charge, however, the individual was found not guilty. The committee concluded there was not even "a shadow of necessity for [their] death."[11] A Senate report noted that "[h]umanity shudders at the idea of a cold-blooded execution of prisoners, disarmed, and in the power of the conqueror."[12] Military jurist William Winthrop later remarked that if an officer ordered an execution in the manner of Jackson he "would *now* be indictable for murder."[13]

As support for independent presidential authority to create military tribunals, the Bush administration referred to the Mexican War.[14] Precedents established during that period offer no such support. In carrying out his duties as commander of U.S. forces in Mexico, General Winfield Scott wanted to create military tribunals to punish misconduct by his raw and undisciplined troops.[15] He never challenged the constitutional authority of Congress to create commissions and even asked Congress to provide statutory authority. He feared that abuses by his troops would provoke guerrilla warfare. Scott knew from military history that lawless and cruel actions by American soldiers in Mexico would trigger an insurgency.[16] Far from claiming inherent or independent authority, he relied on the existing Articles of War (enacted by Congress) and practices in the States. Further, he stated that no commission "shall try any case clearly cognizable by any court martial."[17] He invited Congress at any time to pass legislation to modify his military commissions.

Military commissions during the Civil War were grounded in statutes that recognized their existence and operation as early as 1862.[18] Some of the commissions that operated during that time are stains on American legal history. Captain Henry Wirz, superintendent of the infamous Andersonville prison, was unfairly blamed by a commission for terrible camp conditions and "hurried to his death by vindictive politicians, an unbridled press, and a nation thirsty for revenge."[19] The commission created after the war to try the alleged conspirators in Lincoln's assassination was, in the words of Lincoln's former attorney general Edward Bates, "not only unlawful, but . . . a gross blunder in policy: It denies the great, fundamental principle, that ours is a government of *Law*, and that the law is strong enough, to rule the people wisely and well."[20] Bates raised points that would later apply to the commissions created after 9/11. Military tribunals are repugnant because the people who serve "are selected by the military commander *from among his own subordinates,* who are bound to obey him, and responsible to him; and therefore, they will, commonly, find the case as required or desired by the commander who selected them."[21] Courts-martial are more legitimate and constitutional because they are created by statute and therefore the members of the court "have *legal* duties and rights." Military tribunals "exist only by the will of the commander, and that will is their only known rule of proceeding."²²

THE NAZI SABOTEUR CASE

Another argument used by the Bush administration to unilaterally create military tribunals was the Supreme Court decision in *Ex parte Quirin* (1942). Eight Germans, arriving in two submarines, intended to use explosives to damage the industrial capacity of the United States. Strategic targets included bridges, railroads, and factories. After the saboteurs were apprehended, President Franklin D. Roosevelt issued a proclamation and military order to try the men by military tribunal. Much of Roosevelt's language appears in the Bush military order.²³ In 2004, a plurality of the Supreme Court refer to *Quirin* as "the most apposite precedent" on the detention of U.S. citizens.²⁴ In that same decision, a dissent by Justices Scalia and Stevens describes *Quirin* as "not this Court's finest hour." What deficiencies could they have been referring to?

One of the German saboteurs, George Dasch, turned himself into the FBI and helped the agency locate the other seven. Initially, the government planned to try them in civil court. Why were they later brought before a military tribunal? There are several reasons. The government was concerned that if Dasch appeared in open court he would say that he had turned himself in and helped the government find his colleagues. The government had given the public (and the world) the impression that the executive branch possessed uncanny capacity to detect and apprehend enemy saboteurs. The administration did not want enemy nations to understand how easily spies had infiltrated America.

The second reason for creating a military tribunal had to do with available penalties. Administration officials, in their review of federal criminal statutes, could not find a basis for sentences of more than two or three years in prison if the men were tried in civil court. Roosevelt wanted the men executed, a penalty he could impose with a military tribunal. Also, if the men had been tried in civil court or a court-martial they would have access to procedural safeguards in defending themselves. Brought before a military tribunal, they would have whatever rules and procedures the administration devised.²⁵

Consider the nature of President Roosevelt's military tribunal and ask whether it would be tolerable to have U.S. citizens tried abroad under his system. Roosevelt created the tribunal, named the generals to serve on it (all subordinate to him), named the prosecutors and defense counsel (subordinates also), and when the tribunal issued its verdict the trial record was transmitted to Roosevelt for final action. Thus was created a virtually closed circle within the executive branch. All powers of government—legislative, executive, and judicial—were concentrated in one branch. No external checks existed. Under the Articles of War, any conviction or sentence by a military court was subject to review within the military system, including the judge advocate general's office. Under Roosevelt's system, "final reviewing authority" was centered in him. The tribunal began with few rules. The tribunal created them by responding to motions made by the government and defense counsel as the trial progressed.[26] If an American were tried in this fashion by a foreign government, the procedural and legal deficiencies would be condemned.

Secretary of War Henry L. Stimson opposed Roosevelt's tribunal. He found it offensive for Attorney General Francis Biddle to devote several weeks in the middle of World War II to prosecute the case. Dozens of other attorneys in the administration could have performed that assignment.[27] Serving as coprosecutor was Maj. Gen. Myron C. Cramer, judge advocate general of the army. Stimson objected to that appointment because the judge advocate general was supposed to exercise an independent review after the trial to assure its fairness. Stimson was unable to derail the tribunal in 1942; two years later he succeeded.

The Supreme Court Enters

With the military tribunal about to reach a judgment, one of the defense attorneys for the Nazi saboteurs managed to get the dispute before the Supreme Court. On July 27, 1942, the Supreme Court publicly announced that it would begin oral argument two days later. However, there had yet to be any action by a lower court. At 8 p.m., on July 28, a federal district court dismissed a habeas petition by the defense counsel.[28] At noon the following day, the Supreme Court began to hear the case. The briefs filed by the opposing parties are dated the same day that oral argument began. The justices were therefore unprepared to analyze complex issues of military law and Articles of War rarely litigated before the Court. Oral argument continued for nine hours over two days, giving justices time to comprehend at least the main contours (legal and political) of the case.

The justices began oral argument without the benefit of any review by the appellate court, the D.C. Circuit. Several justices objected to the case coming directly from the district court. To permit oral argument to continue, defense counsel promised to submit papers to the appellate court. On July 31, after the two days of oral argument, the Court was ready to decide the case. At 11:59 a.m. it took the case from the appellate court (granted certiorari) and one minute later issued a one-page per curiam that upheld the jurisdiction of the military commission. The per curiam contained no legal justifications or reasoning. The Court merely promised, at some future date, to issue a full opinion.[29] It took the Court nearly three months to write and release the full opinion, on October 29.

The justices understood that President Roosevelt had violated several Articles of War enacted by Congress but were undecided how to handle that. In drafting the full opinion, Chief Justice Harlan Fiske Stone worked with the knowledge that on August 8, after the eight Germans had been found guilty by the military commission, six had been electrocuted pursuant to Roosevelt's order. On September 10, Stone wrote to Justice Felix Frankfurter that he found it "very difficult to support the Government's construction of the articles [of war]," adding that it "seems almost brutal to announce this ground of decision for the first time after six of the petitioners have been executed and it is too late for them to raise the question if in fact the articles as they construe them have been violated." Only years later, Stone said, would the facts be known after release of the trial transcript and related documents. The two surviving saboteurs (George Dasch and Peter Burger) could then raise disturbing legal questions, which "would not place the present Court in a very happy light."[30] If they prevailed in court, Stone said it would leave the Court "in the unenviable position of having stood by and allowed six to go to their death without making it plain to all concerned—including the President—that it had left undecided a question on which counsel strongly relied to secure petitioners' liberty."[31]

Frankfurter wrote with assurance that "there can be no doubt that the President did *not* follow" Articles 46 through 53.[32] Having released the per curiam, the justices could not publicly criticize Roosevelt for violating the Articles of War. As constitutional scholar Alpheus Thomas Mason noted, the justices "own involvement in the trial through their decision in the July hearing practically compelled them to cover up or excuse the President's departures from customary procedures."[33] Years later, Justice William O. Douglas said "it was unfortunate the Court took the case." He pointed out that although "it was easy to agree on the original per curiam," the justices "almost fell apart when it came time to write out the views."[34]

Scholarly Analysis

After the Court released the full opinion, Justice Frankfurter asked Frederick Bernays Wiener, an expert on military law, to evaluate the decision. Wiener concluded that the deficiencies of the decision flowed "in large measure" from the administration's disregard for "almost every precedent in the books" when it established the military tribunal. Wiener said that court-martial procedures had "almost uniformly been applied to military commissions," and that it was "too plain for argument" that the president could not waive or override the required review by the judge advocate general's office. The only precedent for putting the judge advocate general of the army in the role of prosecutor (the trial of the Lincoln conspirators) was one that "no self-respecting military lawyer will look straight in the eye." Even in that case, Wiener noted, "the Attorney General did not assume to assist the prosecution."[35]

During an interview held in 1962, Justice Douglas said the "experience with *Ex parte Quirin* indicated, I think, to all of us that it is extremely undesirable to announce a decision on the merits without an opinion accompanying it. Because once the search for the grounds, the examination of the grounds that had been advanced is made, sometimes those grounds crumble."[36] A study by Alpheus Thomas Mason concludes that the Court had no choice other than to uphold the jurisdiction of the military commission, being "somewhat in the position of a private on sentry duty accosting a commanding general without his pass," an outcome that put the judiciary "in danger of becoming part of an executive juggernaut."[37]

Michal Belknap's critique of *Quirin* observes that Stone went to "such lengths to justify Roosevelt's proclamation" that he preserved the "form" of judicial review while "gutt[ing] it of substance."[38] When Justices decide to march to the beat of war drums the Court "remained an unreliable guardian of the Bill of Rights."[39] Belknap describes an essay by Frankfurter ("F.F.'s Soliloquy"), written while Stone was drafting the full opinion, as the work of a judge "openly hostile to the accused and manifestly unwilling to afford them procedural safeguards."[40] David J. Danelski calls the full opinion of *Quirin* "an agonizing effort to justify a *fait accompli*." The opinion represented a "constitutional and propaganda victory" for the executive branch but "an institutional defeat" for the Supreme Court. Danelski cautions the Court to "be wary of departing from its established rules and practices, even in times of national crisis, for at such times the Court is especially susceptible to co-optation by the executive."[41]

Two years after the Court released the full opinion in *Quirin*, the Roosevelt administration decided that the procedure it followed in 1942 was so flawed that it was not a model worth repeating. On November 29, 1944, two German agents arrived by submarine, coming ashore in Maine and making their way to New York City, where they were quickly apprehended. Initially, the administration decided to repeat the 1942 process with the same coprosecutors (Biddle and Cramer). Secretary Stimson, however, lobbied forcefully within the White House to transfer the case from the Justice Department to military professionals in New York. Roosevelt would not appoint the members of the tribunal, the prosecutors, and the defense counsel. Those decisions were left to a commanding general. Instead of submitting the trial record to President

Roosevelt, as in 1942, it was sent to the judge advocate general's office, in accordance with Article of War 50 1/2. As a result of Stimson's intervention, the Roosevelt administration thought about what it had done in 1942 and decided not to do it again.[42]

In 1953, several justices looked back at what the Court did with the Nazi saboteur case and decided it was a poor model to emulate. The Court was considering whether to sit in summer session to hear the espionage case of Julius and Ethel Rosenberg. Could it take up the case and issue a per curiam immediately after oral argument, promising a full opinion later, as it did in 1942? Justice Robert Jackson objected to the procedure and Justice Frankfurter agreed, adding "that the *Quirin* experience was not a happy precedent."[43]

DETAINING "ENEMY COMBATANTS"

In the months following 9/11, a number of suspected terrorists were tried in civil court, including John Walker Lindh, "shoe-bomber" Richard Reid, and Zacarias Moussaoui.[44] Others were held in U.S. bases and designated an "enemy combatant." On November 26, 2002, the general counsel of the Defense Department defined enemy combatant as "an individual who, under the laws and customs of war, may be detained for the duration of an armed conflict." The term included "a member, agent, or associate of Al Qaida or the Taliban."[45] The Bush administration offered two legal grounds for detaining enemy combatants. One was constitutional: "Article II alone gives the President the power to detain enemies during wartime, regardless of congressional action."[46] The second was statutory: the Authorization for Use of Military Force (AUMF) Act of 2001, which supported military operations against Afghanistan and 9/11 terrorists.[47] However, no member of Congress during debate on the AUMF ever expressed support for the indefinite detention of suspected terrorists (including U.S. citizens) without trial.

The Justice Department insisted that whenever the administration decided to detain a U.S. citizen indefinitely, without access to a trial, federal courts had no right to interfere with executive judgment. Courts "may not second-guess the military's determination that an individual is an enemy combatant and should be detained as such." Courts lacked the competence and institutional expertise to "intrude upon the constitutional prerogative of the Commander in Chief (and military authorities acting at his control)," possibly creating a conflict between judicial and military opinion "highly comforting to enemies of the United States."[48]

In other briefs, the Justice Department cautioned that whatever review function a federal judge might exercise should be heavily circumscribed. If the president designated someone an enemy combatant, judicial review would be limited "to confirming based on *some evidence* the existence of a factual basis supporting the determination."[49] A court would have to accept as "some evidence" whatever documents executive officials presented without an opportunity to see the evidence or cross-examine secret informers.

These legal issues initially focused on two U.S. citizens, Yaser Esam Hamdi and Jose Padilla. Both were designated enemy combatants and held indefinitely without trial. Evidence for their detention consisted of declarations signed by Pentagon officials who had no direct knowledge of either man. They signed their name to documents prepared by intelligence analysts, often on the basis of confidential informers with a history of false statements and drug use.[50] One district judge described Hamdi's case as "the first in American jurisprudence where an American citizen has been held incommunicado and subjected to an indefinite detention in the continental United States without charges, without any findings by a military tribunal, and without access to a lawyer."[51] It was uncertain whether Hamdi was an enemy combatant "or just a bystander."[52] According to newspaper reports, some informers had a financial incentive, expecting to receive $5,000 for each person identified as "Taliban" and $20,000 for those labeled "al Qaeda."[53]

On June 28, 2004, eight justices of the Supreme Court rejected the administration's central proposition that Hamdi's detention was quintessentially a presidential decision and could not be reevaluated or overturned by the courts. Except for Justice Clarence Thomas, all members of the Court decided they had the institutional authority and competence to review and override presidential judgments in the field of national security. The Court's action was fragmented among a plurality of four (O'Connor, Rehnquist, Kennedy, Breyer), joined at times by a concurrence/dissent from Souter and Ginsburg, and at other times a dissent from Scalia and Stevens.

The plurality agreed on a core principle: "we necessarily reject the Government's assertion that separation of powers principles mandate a heavily circumscribed role for the courts in such circumstances. . . . Whatever power the United States Constitution envisions for the Executive in its exchanges with other nations or with enemy organizations in times of conflict, it most assuredly envisions a role for all three branches when individual liberties are at stake."[54] On that point the plurality was joined by Souter, Ginsburg, Scalia, and Stevens. The plurality also held that an enemy combatant "must receive notice of the factual basis for his classification, and a fair opportunity to rebut the Government's factual assertions before a neutral decisionmaker."

The plurality endorsed Hamdi's right to "a fair opportunity to rebut the Government's factual assertions before a neutral decisionmaker," referring to earlier rulings that due process requires a "neutral and detached judge." The plurality spoke about the need for "an independent tribunal," an "independent review," and an "impartial adjudicator." Having singled out those fundamental values, it expressed satisfaction with some kind of review panel within the executive branch, perhaps even "an appropriately authorized and properly constituted military tribunal." The plurality seemed to ignore how Hamdi became an enemy combatant. President Bush reached that judgment on the basis of executive branch declarations prepared by someone who had no actual knowledge of Hamdi. No review panel within the executive branch, much less within the military, could possibly possess the plurality's sought-for qualities of neutrality, detachment, independence, and impartiality in passing judgment on a presidential decision.

After the Court's ruling, the administration transferred Hamdi to Saudi Arabia rather than try him before some type of executive or military panel. Why would it release someone it had considered a dangerous terrorist if there were substantial grounds for detaining him? The case of the second U.S. citizen, Jose Padilla, raised similar questions about executive judgments. At various times the administration claimed that he intended to detonate a radiological dispersal device (a "dirty bomb") or blow up apartment buildings in the United States. As with Hamdi, declarations were prepared by executive officials who had no direct knowledge of Padilla. After holding Padilla in military detention for more than three years, the administration changed course and tried him in civil court. On August 16, 2007, a jury in Florida convicted Padilla of terrorism conspiracy charges, along with two codefendants. The case had nothing to do with allegations about a "dirty bomb" or blowing up apartment buildings. A key piece of physical evidence introduced at trial was a "mujahideen data form" that Padilla supposedly filled out to attend a terrorist training camp in Afghanistan. Padilla's fingerprints were on the form but it was impossible to determine if they were placed there in Afghanistan or after being detained by the United States and held at the naval brig.[55]

DETAINEES AT GUANTANAMO

Hundreds of terrorist suspects were picked up in Afghanistan, Pakistan, and other countries and taken to the U.S. naval base at Guantanamo Bay, Cuba. Many were designated as enemy combatants on the basis of confidential information obtained from informers whose names were not disclosed. Detainees and their legal counsel were unable to gain information in order to effectively cross-examine the administration's evidence. Over a period of years, U.S. officials acknowledged that the detainees at the naval base represented a mix of terrorist fighters and innocent people erroneously swept up. Hundreds would be released. Moazzam Begg, seized in Pakistan in January 2002, was imprisoned for three years in Bagram, Kandahar, and Guantanamo. Initially labeled an "enemy combatant," he was later released without explanation, apology, or any type of reparation.[56]

In a memo signed on February 2, 2002, President Bush stated that none of the Geneva Conventions assuring humane treatment of prisoners should apply to Al Qaeda. He claimed authority under the Constitution "to suspend Geneva as between the United States and Afghanistan, but I decline to exercise that authority at this time. Accordingly, I determine that the provisions of Geneva will apply to our present conflict with the Taliban."[57] The conditional "at this time" allowed Bush to suspend Geneva protections to the Taliban if he wanted to. In this same memo, he determined that the Taliban detainees "are unlawful combatants and, therefore, do not qualify as prisoners of war under Article 4 of Geneva." He explained that American values "call for us to treat detainees humanely, including those who are not legally entitled to such treatment." Interrogation techniques for detainees at the naval base would therefore depend not on legal obligations but rather shifting policy decisions by the Bush administration.

The administration drafted legal memos to guide U.S. interrogators. Several steps were needed to condone abusive methods. First, exclude experts who knew the most about military law, especially those in the judge advocate general corps. Second, put detainees in a place supposedly beyond the reach of federal judges (the naval base at Guantanamo). Third, conclude that existing treaties and federal statutes on the treatment of detainees are not binding on the president. Last, authorize interrogation methods that would be impermissible if used by the U.S. military on prisoners of war. These legal memos, highly classified, circulated among a small circle of executive officials.[58]

A Law-Free Zone?

An important step toward abusive detention occurred on December 28, 2002, when two attorneys in the Office of Legal Counsel (OLC), within the Justice Department, concluded that the "great weight" of legal authority indicated that a federal district court "could not probably exercise habeas jurisdiction" over noncitizens detained at Guantanamo.[59] The effect was to send a green light to U.S. interrogators to treat detainees inhumanely. The Justice Department produced a forty-two-page memo concluding that international treaties and federal laws do not apply to Al Qaeda and Taliban detainees.[60] Relying on this opinion, Attorney General John Ashcroft wrote to Bush on February 1, 2002, describing different ways of shielding U.S. interrogators from possible criminal prosecutions. If Bush determined that Afghanistan was a "failed state" and therefore unable to be a party to the Geneva Conventions, the treaty's protections would not apply and "various legal risks of liability, litigation, and criminal prosecutions are minimized."[61] If President Bush intended to treat detainees "humanely," why this concerted attempt by senior executive officials to demonstrate that federal courts would lack jurisdiction to hear grievances from detainees? Why was Ashcroft concerned that U.S. interrogators might face criminal prosecution? What techniques of interrogation did the administration contemplate?

The Bybee Memo

A decisive step in authorizing abusive interrogations was a fifty-page memo sent from OLC head Jay Bybee to White House Counsel Alberto Gonzales. The memo, dated August 1, 2002, analyzed the meaning of the U.S. statute that implements the Convention against Torture and Other Cruel, Inhuman and Degrading Treatment or Punishment (CAT). The statute defines torture as an act committed by a person "acting under the color of law specifically intended to inflict severe physical and mental pain or suffering (other than pain or suffering incidental to lawful sanctions) upon another person within his custody or physical control." The statute applies to actions by U.S. individuals "outside the United States" and includes fines and imprisonment. In view of those penalties, the Justice Department developed legal doctrines to shield abusive U.S. interrogators. Bybee advised Gonzales that for an act to constitute torture as defined by the statute "it must inflict pain that is difficult to endure" and offered this understanding of physical pain: "Physical pain amounting to torture must be equivalent in intensity to the pain accompanying serious physical injury, such as organ failure, impairment of bodily function, or even death."[62]

To shield interrogators from prosecution, Bybee analyzed the statutory meaning of "specifically intended." To act with specific intent, an interrogator "must expressly intend to achieve the forbidden act" (the infliction of pain). If an interrogator understood that severe pain or suffering was "reasonably likely to result from his action, but no more, he would have acted only with general intent" rather than specific intent. If the objective was to gain information from a detainee, not harm him or inflict severe pain, the interrogator "lacks the requisite specific intent even though the defendant did not act in good faith. Instead, a defendant is guilty of torture only if he acts with the express purpose of inflicting severe pain or suffering on a person within his custody or physical control." If the American interrogator intended to pry loose intelligence from a detainee and the questioning caused severe pain, there would be no violation of the torture statute or any treaty. The pain would be incidental, not the intended purpose.

Bybee identified other restrictions on antitorture statutes and treaties. Even if a U.S. interrogator clearly violated the torture statute, the statute would be unconstitutional "if it impermissibly encroached on the President's constitutional power to conduct a military campaign." As commander in chief, the president "has the constitutional authority to order interrogations of enemy combatants to gain intelligence information concerning the military plans of the enemy." Because this power, as interpreted by Bybee, derives from the Constitution, no statute or treaty could limit it.

OLC supplied a legal framework for the Defense Department "working groups": officials from different agencies called together to hammer out final administration policy. A Defense Department memo of October 11, 2002, discussed "more aggressive interrogation techniques than the ones presently used" at Guantanamo. Those techniques "may be required in order to obtain information from detainees that are resisting interrogation efforts and are suspected of having significant information essential to national security." The memo states that the detainees at Guantanamo "are not protected by the Geneva Conventions (GC),"[63] even though the Bush memo of February 7, 2002, concluded that the Taliban would be covered by Geneva, at least "at this time."

On January 15, 2003, Defense Secretary Rumsfeld directed his general counsel to establish a "working group" within the department "to assess the legal, policy, and operational issues relating to the interrogation of detainees held by the U.S. Armed Forces in the war on terrorism."[64] His memo was issued before the March 2003 military operations against Iraq, but its scope was broad enough to cover all detainees in Guantanamo, Afghanistan, Iraq, or other locations.

When the report of the working group was released, the influence of Bybee's memo was apparent. The working group organized its analysis to cover the Geneva Conventions, CAT, interpretations about "specifically intended," the Commander in Chief Clause, and protections accorded to a U.S. interrogator by the doctrines of necessity and self-defense.[65] The working group concluded that the torture statute "does not apply to the conduct of U.S. personnel" at Guantamamo and did not apply "to the President's detention and interrogation of enemy combatants pursuant to his Commander-in-Chief authority." An April 4 report describes some interrogation techniques that would later appear in photos from Abu Ghraib, including hooding and nudity. Clothing could be removed, "to be done by military police if not agreed to by the subject." Nudity creates "a feeling of helplessness and dependence." Anxiety could be increased in various ways, including the "simple presence of [a] dog without directly threatening action."

The April 4 report understood that America's reputation would be damaged if detainee abuse became public: "Should information regarding the use of more aggressive interrogation techniques than have been used traditionally by U.S. forces become public, it is likely to be exaggerated or distorted in the U.S. and international media accounts, and may produce an adverse effect on support for the war on terrorism." The involvement of U.S. personnel in aggressive interrogations "would constitute a significant departure from traditional U.S. military norms and could have an adverse impact on the cultural self-image of U.S. military forces."[66]

Abu Ghraib

In April 2004, three national security cases reached the Supreme Court for oral argument: the *Hamdi* and *Padilla* cases (involving U.S. citizens) and the issue of holding detainees at Guantanamo (*Rasul*). During the *Hamdi* and *Padilla* arguments, justices asked Deputy Solicitor General Paul Clement if "anything in the law" limited the method of interrogating detainees. He assured the Court that the United States had signed treaties that prohibit torture and the United States would honor its treaty obligations. Those who conduct interrogations, he pointed out, understood that using coercion or torture was likely to yield unreliable information. The best way to get reliable information is "to develop a relationship of trust." During the *Padilla* oral argument, justices also asked if detainees were being tortured or abused. Clement at first cautioned that the president needed to exercise discretionary judgments in applying military force and courts should not attempt to interfere. One justice objected: "if the law is what the executive says it is, whatever is necessary and appropriate in the executive's judgment," the result was an "executive, unchecked by the judiciary." Clement reminded the Court that the president was limited by treaty obligations. Also, if a U.S. military person committed a war crime "on a harmless, you know, detained enemy combatant or a prisoner of war," the government would prosecute the individual in a court-martial.

The *Hamdi* and *Padilla* oral arguments began at 10:19 a.m. on April 28 and concluded at 12:20 p.m. Later that evening, the public began to see photos of U.S. abuse of detainees held at the Abu Ghraib prison in Iraq. Viewers from around the world saw prisoners forced to conduct simulated sex acts and assume positions of sexual humiliation. In one photo, a prisoner was shown standing on a box, his head covered, with wires attached to his fingers, toes, and penis. He was told if he fell off the box he would be electrocuted. Female

U.S. soldiers, grinning with cigarettes in their mouths, stood next to naked Iraqi prisoners, pointing at their genitals.[67]

The U.S. military had already begun an inquiry into these abuses. A report by Maj. Gen. Antonio M. Taguba began circulating on websites in early May 2004. He described "numerous incidents of sadistic, blatant, and wanton criminal abuses" inflicted on detainees, referring to the abuses as "systemic and illegal."[68] Several American soldiers had committed "egregious acts and grave breaches of international law." His report detailed such actions as keeping detainees naked for several days at a time, a male military police guard having sex with a female detainee, using unmuzzled dogs to intimidate and terrify detainees, and sodomizing a detainee with a chemical light and perhaps a broomstick. Taguba's report, highly professional and analytic, told only part of the story. His investigation was limited to the 800th Military Police Brigade and the Abu Ghraib prison. Abusive U.S. treatment of detainees occurred in other prisons in Iraq and Afghanistan. Documentary records detail the deliberate planning of abusive interrogation by Bush administration officials.[69]

Worldwide condemnation of conditions at Abu Ghraib and other prisons forced the White House to withdraw Bybee's memo. At a press briefing on June 22, 2004, Gonzales met with reporters to explain changes in administration policy. To the extent that legal memos explored broad theories, such as the scope of the president's power as commander in chief, they were "irrelevant and unnecessary to support any action taken by the President." These "over-broad" and "abstract legal theories" invited misinterpretation and would be replaced by "more concrete guidance addressing only those issues necessary for the legal analysis of actual practices."[70] Gonzales did not repudiate Bybee's analysis of the Commander in Chief Clause. Those passages were simply unnecessary and too easy to misread. To that extent, Bybee's language was temporarily shelved. Second, Gonzales did not prohibit all abusive interrogations. When asked by a reporter how the change to the Bybee memo related to CIA interrogation, he said his briefing "does not include CIA activities." Later disclosures revealed that the CIA could do what the military could not.

At the end of 2004, the OLC issued a new memo to replace Bybee's. The memo forthrightly states that torture "is abhorrent both to American law and values and to international norms" and that the repudiation of torture "is reflected in our criminal law, for example, 18 U.S.C. §§ 2340-2340A; international agreements, exemplified by the United Nations Convention Against Torture (the 'CAT'); customary international law; centuries of Anglo-American law; and the longstanding policy of the United States, repeatedly and recently reaffirmed by the President."[71] Withdrawing Bybee's memo was not the same as repudiating its interpretations of presidential power. Parts of Bybee's analysis would reappear a year later when Congress passed new legislation on torture.

THE COURT DECIDES *RASUL*

In OLC memos, the administration argued that the U.S. naval base in Guantanamo was outside the United States and therefore beyond the jurisdiction of federal judges to hear cases brought by detainees. That legal theory prevailed in district court on July 30, 2002.[72] The judge relied heavily on a decision by the Supreme Court in *Johnson v. Eisentrager* (1950), but the facts of that case were quite different from the situation in Guantanamo. Unlike the detainees at the naval base, the individuals in *Eisentrager* had been charged, given counsel, tried, found guilty, and sentenced.

Was the naval base outside the jurisdiction of federal courts? The United States occupies the naval base under a lease entered into with the Cuban government in 1903. The lease states that the United States recognizes the "ultimate sovereignty" of Cuba over the military base, but Cuba consented that the United States "shall exercise complete jurisdiction and control over and within said areas." In short, the United States possessed full jurisdiction but not sovereignty.

The D.C. Circuit agreed with the district court that *Eisentrager* prevented the detainees at Guantanamo from seeking habeas relief in federal court.[73] Several cases in the Ninth Circuit explored the right of the detainees to file a habeas petition.[74] In one case, the Ninth Circuit denied that the government could keep detainees at the naval based outside the reach of courts. Detainees were entitled to some kind of judicial forum and legal counsel.[75] The Ninth Circuit decided that *Eisentrager* did not control the case of the detainees held at Guantanamo. The crucial issue was not "sovereignty" but rather "territorial jurisdiction."[76]

The Supreme Court did not take the Ninth Circuit case but did agree to hear the consolidated cases out of the D.C. Circuit (*Rasul* and *Al Odah*). When the case was argued on April 20, 2004, several justices expressed concern about the scope of power sought by the administration. To Justice Breyer, it "seems rather contrary to an idea of a Constitution with three branches that the executive would be free to do whatever they want, whatever they want without a check." Also, "several hundred years of British history" interpreting habeas corpus ran against the administration's argument. Moreover, *Eisentrager* did not fit the conditions at the naval base. The 1950 decision covered admitted enemy aliens who had received a hearing before a military tribunal. The detainees at Guantanamo did not admit to being enemy aliens and had never received a hearing.

Solicitor General Ted Olson advised the justices that the question of whether the naval base was outside the jurisdiction of federal courts was a "political decision." It would be "remarkable," he said, for the judiciary "to start deciding where the United States is sovereign and where the United States has control." If he hoped to convince the Court on that point he was mistaken. Why give alien detainees in the continental United States (and Hawaii) some rights while keeping others offshore in a law-free zone? Olson compared the naval base with detainees held in prisons in Afghanistan, but justices found the analogy unpersuasive. Afghanistan, they pointed out, "is not a place where American law is, and for a century, has customarily been applied to all aspects of life," as was true of the naval base.

On June 28, 2004, in a 6 to 3 decision, the Court rejected *Eisentrager* as an automatic bar on detainee access to a habeas petition. It ruled that federal courts have jurisdiction to consider challenges to the legality of detaining foreign nationals captured abroad, in connection with hostilities, and held at Guantanamo. Writing for the majority in *Rasul v. Bush*, Justice Stevens explained why the prisoners in *Eisentrager* differed from the detainees at the naval base. The 1950 case involved enemy aliens captured outside U.S. territory and held as POWs. They were tried and convicted by a military tribunal sitting outside the United States for offenses against laws of war. The detainees at Guantanamo were not nationals of countries at war with the United States, denied being engaged in or plotting acts of aggression against the United States, had no access to any tribunal, were never charged with or convicted of wrongdoing, and for two years had been detained in a territory over which the United States exercised exclusive jurisdiction and control.[77]

In a concurrence, Kennedy agreed that Guantanamo was "in every practical respect a United States territory" and expressed concern that the detainees at the naval base were "being held indefinitely, and without benefit of any legal proceeding to determine their status." Scalia's dissent, joined by Rehnquist and Thomas, claimed that the majority "overrules *Eisentrager*" even though Stevens had explained why several elements of *Eisentrager* differed from the detainees at the naval base.

HAMDAN REJECTS INHERENT AUTHORITY

The administration responded to *Rasul* by establishing a Combatant Status Review Tribunal (CSRT). A panel of three military officers would provide a hearing for each detainee. Each detainee was assigned a "personal representative" (a military officer, not a lawyer) who had access to information in agency files. Information that the personal representative gained from a detainee could be passed on to the government. The detainee had a right to appear before the panel to present evidence and call witnesses if "reasonably available."[78] There was no obligation on the part of the administration to share with the detainee classified evidence used to place him in the category of enemy combatant.

The administration understood that it had picked up detainees from Afghanistan and other countries by relying on informants who could have made mistakes or might have had financial incentives in wanting to label someone "Taliban" or "Al Qaeda." Unaware of who had accused them, detainees did not know if information about them flowed from malice, vengeance, or ignorance. One of these detainees brought before the CSRT was Salim Ahmed Hamdan, whose case would reach the Supreme Court in 2006 and test the bounds of inherent presidential power.

Detainee Treatment Act

Disclosures about Abu Ghraib and abuses at Guantanamo prompted Congress to pass legislation that would prohibit (once again) cruel and inhumane treatment of detainees. Islamic extremists were using reports of detainee abuse to recruit new members. An amendment by Senator John McCain, barring all U.S. government agencies from "cruel, inhuman, or degrading" treatment of detainees, passed the Senate by a vote of 90 to 9. The administration initially opposed the amendment but consented after McCain agreed to add language giving civilian interrogators legal protections already afforded to military interrogators.[79] The Detainee Treatment Act (DTA) placed some limits on detainee access to federal courts through habeas action and appeared to allow U.S. agencies to transfer persons to other countries for "cruel, inhuman, or degrading treatment or punishment" if those individuals were not technically in U.S. custody.

In signing the bill, President Bush implied that he need not carry out the law. He said he would construe the DTA "in a manner consistent with the constitutional authority of the President to supervise the unitary executive branch and as Commander in Chief and consistent with the constitutional limitations on the judicial power." He said that his administration "is committed to treating all detainees held by the United States in a manner consistent with our Constitution, laws, and treaty obligations, which reflect the values we hold dear." Promising to be "consistent with" is not the same as complying with the law. The rule of law means that the president will carry out the law as enacted by Congress and not—through a signing statement—convert statutory law into some type of discretionary administration policy.

Hamdan and the Military Commissions Act

On June 29, 2006, the Supreme Court in *Hamdan v. Rumsfeld* decided several legal issues. It rejected the position of the Bush administration that the president possessed "inherent" powers under article II and could unilaterally create military commissions. The Court held that Bush's action was not authorized by Congress and was contrary to existing law in the Uniform Code of Military Justice (UCMJ). Nor was there anything in the DTA or in the text or legislative history of the Authorization for Use of Military Force (AUMF) that intended to expand or alter what the UCMJ authorized. The type of commission established by Bush "risk[ed] concentrating in military hands a degree of adjudicative and punitive power in excess of that contemplated either by statute or by the Constitution." The Court further pointed out that the military commission established under the Bush military order violated the Geneva Conventions.

The UCMJ provides that any rule adopted for a military commission must be the same as those applied to a court-martial unless the president can show that such uniformity is impracticable. The Court expressed concern that the accused and his civilian counsel could be excluded from learning about evidence presented during a closed proceeding. Under the commission rules developed by the Bush administration, neither "live testimony nor witnesses' written statements need be sworn." The rules failed "to apply one of the most fundamental protections afforded not just by the Manual for Courts-Martial but also by the UCMJ itself: the right to be present."

In response to *Hamdan*, the administration went to Congress to seek statutory authority. At a Senate hearing on July 11, 2006, acting OLC head Steven Bradbury claimed that the Court "did not address the President's constitutional authority and did not reach any constitutional question."[80] In fact, the Court decided two constitutional issues. First, it rejected the argument that the president possessed inherent authority under article II to create military commissions. Second, it affirmed the constitutional authority of Congress under article I to limit the president to the procedural constraints of the UCMJ. At congressional hearings, attorneys from the military services objected to the use of evidence derived from hearsay or coercion, the exclusion of defendants from their trials, and allowing classified evidence to be provided to a defense lawyer but not to the defendant.[81] To John D. Hutson, the navy's top uniformed lawyer from 1997 to 2000, the administration's proposed rules allowed the government to tell a detainee: "We know you're guilty. We can't tell you why, but there's a guy, we can't tell you who, who told us something. We can't tell you what, but you're guilty."[82]

When the administration's bill (S. 3861) was introduced in the Senate on September 7, it included this language: "The President's authority to convene military commissions arises from the Constitution's vesting in the President of the executive power and the power of the Commander in Chief of the Armed Forces." Of course that is what the Supreme Court had just rejected in *Hamdan*. The language on inherent authority was stripped from the bill. The Military Commissions Act (MCA) of 2006 sets forth new structures and procedures for military commissions and defines "unlawful enemy combatant" to include a person "who has engaged in hostilities or who has purposefully and materially supported hostilities against the United States or its co-belligerents," and a person "who, before, on, or after the date" of the enactment of the Military Commissions Act "has been determined to be an unlawful enemy combatant by a Combatant Status Review Tribunal or another competent tribunal established under the authority of the President or the Secretary of Defense."

Another Visit to the Supreme Court

The MCA provided that no person may invoke the Geneva Conventions in any habeas action in court to which the United States is a party. An alien unlawful enemy combatant was subject to trial by military commission. The statute also dealt with statements obtained by coercion, access to witnesses, informers, classified information, and the president's obligation to comply with the Geneva Conventions. Several provisions bear on torture and interrogations, attempting to define the liability of U.S. officers who interrogate detainees.

Hamdan and the MCA sparked new litigation, including the legitimacy of the Combatant Status Review Tribunals. On February 20, 2007, the D.C. Circuit held that the MCA denied jurisdiction to federal courts to consider the habeas petitions filed by detainees at Guantanamo previous to the date of the statute.[83] In this manner the court revived the issue whether Guantanamo was "sovereign" U.S. territory or merely under the "jurisdiction" of the United States. The D.C. Circuit denied that a "*de facto* sovereignty" existed at the naval base. A dissent by Judge Judith Rogers agreed that it was the intent of Congress, in passing the MCA, to withdraw jurisdiction from federal courts, but held that the statute offended the Suspension Clause. Because the statute was void it did not deprive federal courts of jurisdiction. She rejected the majority's reasoning that Congress may suspend habeas corpus for alien detainees because they have no individual rights under the Constitution. The Suspension Clause, she noted, "makes no reference to citizens or even persons."

On June 12, 2008, the Supreme Court in *Boumediene v. Bush* held that both the MCA and the DTA operated as an unconstitutional suspension of the writ. The Court reviewed the situation of detainees at Guantanamo who had been designated an "enemy combatant" by the CSRTs. Although captured in Afghanistan and elsewhere, the detainees represented in *Boumediene* denied membership in the Al Qaeda network or the Taliban regime. Divided 5 to 4, the Court concluded that they had a right to file habeas petitions and be heard in federal court. The procedures provided by Congress in the DTA were not an "adequate and effective" substitute for habeas corpus.

Writing for the majority, Justice Kennedy pointed out that the privilege of habeas corpus was placed in the Constitution before adoption of the Bill of Rights. The framers "viewed freedom from unlawful restraint as a fundamental precept of liberty, and they understood the writ of habeas corpus as a vital instrument to secure that freedom." The Constitution's structure of separated powers "protects persons as well as citizens." Underscoring what had been decided by the Court in *Rasul*, Justice Kennedy said that the United States, "by virtue of its complete jurisdiction and control over the base, maintains de facto sovereignty over this territory."

Because of the DTA and MCA, detainees at Guantanamo faced restrictions on their access to classified information and could be found guilty on the basis of hearsay evidence. Congress had allowed detainee access to the D.C. Circuit, but it appeared that the court could not consider any evidence outside the CSRT record. Kennedy concluded by saying that the laws and the Constitution "are designed to survive, and remain in force, in extraordinary times. Liberty and security can be reconciled; and in our system they are reconciled within the framework of the law."

PLANS TO CLOSE GUANTANAMO

In one of his first actions as president, Barack Obama on January 22, 2009, signed a series of executive orders directing that the detention camp at Guantanamo be closed within a year. At the same time, he directed the CIA to shut down whatever secret prisons might remain. Current military commission proceedings would be halted to permit the administration to conduct a full review of the 245 detainees held at the naval base. Options included their release, transfer, or prosecution. If the latter, action might be taken in federal court or by court-martial. About 60 of the detainees had already been cleared for release but the Bush administration was unable to locate countries willing to accept them. A separate executive order required that interrogations comply with federal torture statutes, the Convention against Torture, and the Geneva Conventions. All interrogations shall follow the noncoercive methods described in the Army Field Manual. President Obama directed the CIA to expeditiously close any detention facilities and not to operate them in the future.

NOTES

1. Brief for Appellants, *Hamdan v. Rumsfeld*, No. 04-5393 (D.C. Cir. December 8, 2004), 53.

2. William Winthrop, *Military Law and Precedents*, 2d ed. (Washington, DC: Government Printing Office, 1920), 953–60.

3. Winthrop, *Military Law and Precedents*, 21.

4. *The Writings of George Washington* (John C. Fitzpatrick ed., 1931), 13:136–40; 17:239.

5. Brief for Appellants, *Hamdan v. Rumsfeld*, No. 04-5393 (D.C. Cir. December 8, 2004), 58.

6. Brief for Appellants, *Hamdan v. Rumsfeld.*.

7. *Journals of the Continental Congress*, 1774–1789, 5:693.

8. American Articles of War of 1775, art. 28, reprinted in Winthrop, *Military Law and Precedents*, 955.

9. Winthrop, *Military Law and Precedents*, 59.

10. *A Compilation of the Messages and Papers of the Presidents* (James D. Richardson ed., 1925), 2:612; *Annals of Congress* (1818), 15:2135–50.

11. *American State Papers: Military Affairs* (1819), 1:735.

12. *Annals of Congress* (1819), 15:267.

13. Winthrop, *Military Law and Precedents*, 465 (emphasis in original). For more on Jackson's troubles with tribunals in Florida and New Orleans, see Louis Fisher, *Military Tribunals and Presidential Power* (Lawrence: University Press of Kansas, 2005), 25–31.

14. Brief for Appellants, *Hamdan v. Rumsfeld*, No. 04-5393 (D.C. Cir. December 8, 2004).

15. Winfield Scott, *Memoirs of Lieut.-General Scott, LL.D.* (Freeport, NY: Books for Libraries Press, 1864), vol. 2, 392–93.

16. Timothy D. Johnson, *Winfield Scott: The Quest for Military Glory* (Lawrence: University Press of Kansas, 1968), 166–70.

17. Johnson, *Winfield Scott*, 544. For additional details on Scott's actions in Mexico, see Fisher, *Military Tribunals and Presidential Power*, 32–35.

18. 12 Stat. 598, sec. 5 (1862). See also 12 Stat. 736, sec. 30 (1863) and 13 Stat. 356, sec. 1 (1864).

19. Darrett B. Rutman, "The War Crimes and Trial of Henry Wirz," *Civil War History* 6 (1960): 117–18; Fisher, *Military Tribunals and Presidential Power*, 62–65.

20. Howard K. Beale, ed., *The Diary of Edward Bates, 1859–1866* (Washington, DC: Government Printing Office, 1933), 483 (emphasis in original).

21. Beale, *Diary of Edward Bates*, 502 (emphasis in original).

22. Beale, *Diary of Edward Bates* (emphasis in original). See Fisher, *Military Tribunals and Presidential Power*, 65–70.

23. For similarities between the Bush and Roosevelt orders, see Louis Fisher, *Nazi Saboteurs on Trial: A Military Tribunal and American Law* (Lawrence: University Press of Kansas, 2003), 159–60.

24. *Hamdi v. Rumsfeld*, 542 U.S. 507, 523 (2004) (plurality opinion by Justice O'Connor).

25. Fisher, *Nazi Saboteurs on Trial*, 45–49.

26. Fisher, *Nazi Saboteurs on Trial*, 48–49, 52–53; Fisher, *Military Tribunals and Presidential Power*, 111–12.

27. *Diary of Henry L. Stimson*, July 1, 1942, Roll 7, 136, Manuscript Room, Library of Congress.

28. *Ex parte Quirin*, 47 F.Supp. 431 (D.D.C. 1942).

29. *Ex parte Quirin*, 317 U.S. 1, 11 (1942). For further details on the Court's procedures, see Louis Fisher, *The Constitution and 9/11: Recurring Threats to America's Freedoms* (Lawrence: University Press of Kansas, 2008), 178–79.

30. Letter from Chief Justice Stone to Justice Frankfurter, September 10, 1942, Papers of Felix Frankfurter, Part III, Reel 43, Manuscript Room, Library of Congress.

31. "Memorandum re Saboteur Cases," September 25, 1942, Papers of Harlan Fiske Stone, Manuscript Room, Library of Congress, 2.

32. "Memorandum of Mr. Justice Frankfurter, In re Saboteur Cases," (emphasis in original), Papers of William O. Douglas, Box 77, Manuscript Room, Library of Congress, 1.

33. Alpheus Thomas Mason, "*Inter Arma Silent Leges*," *Harvard Law Review* 69 (1956): 806, 826.

34. William O. Douglas, *The Court Years, 1939–1975* (New York: Vintage Books, 1980), 138–39.

35. "Observations of *Ex parte Quirin*," signed "F.B.W.," November 5, 1942, Papers of Felix Frankfurter, Part III, Reel 43, Manuscript Room, Library of Congress, 1, 8, 9. For more detailed criticism by Wiener, see Fisher, *Nazi Saboteurs on Trial*, 129–34.

36. Conversation between Justice Douglas and Professor Walter Murphy, June 9, 1962, Seeley G. Mudd Manuscript Library, Princeton University, 204–5.

37. Alpheus Thomas Mason, *Harlan Fiske Stone: Pillar of the Law* (New York: Viking Press, 1956), 665, 666.

38. Michal Belknap, "The Supreme Court Goes to War: The Meaning and Implications of the Nazi Saboteur Case," *Military Law Review* 89 (1980): 59.

39. Belknap, "The Supreme Court Goes to War," 95.

40. Michael Belknap, "Frankfurter and the Nazi Saboteurs," *Yearbook 1982: Supreme Court Historical Society*, 66. For the language of the Soliloquy, see Fisher, *Nazi Saboteurs on Trial*, 117–21.

41. David J. Danelski, "The Saboteurs' Case," *Journal of Supreme Court History* 1 (1996): 61, 80.

42. Fisher, *Nazi Saboteurs on Trial*, 138–44.

43. "Memorandum Re: *Rosenberg v. United States*, Nos. 111 and 687, October Term 1952," June 4, 1953, Frankfurter Papers, Harvard Law School, Part I, Reel 70, Library of Congress, 8.

44. For details on the Moussaoui trial, see Fisher, *Military Tribunals and Presidential Power*, 211–20.

45. Letter from William J. Haynes II, General Counsel, Department of Defense, to Senator Carl Levin, November 26, 2002, 1–2.

46. Letter from William J. Haynes II, General Counsel, Department of Defense, to Alfred P. Carlton Jr., President, American Bar Association, September 23, 2002, 2.

47. Respondent's Answer to the Petition for Writ of Habeas Corpus, *Padilla v. Hanft*, C/A No. 02:04-2221-26AJ (D. S.C. 2004), 1–2, 10–12, 18–22.

48. Brief for Respondents-Appellants, *Hamdi v. Rumsfeld*, No. 02-6895 (4th Cir. 2002), 29–30, 31.

49. Respondents' Response to, and Motion to Dismiss, the Amended Petition for a Writ of Habeas Corpus, *Padilla v. Bush*, 02 CIV. 4445 (MBM) (S.D. N.Y. 2002), 15 (emphasis added).

50. For analysis of the *Hamdi* and *Padilla* cases, see Fisher, *The Constitution and 9/11*, 190–209.

51. *Hamdi v. Rumsfeld*, Civil Action No. 2:02cv439 (E.D. Va. 2002), at 1.

52. *Hamdi v. Rumsfeld*, Civil Action No. 2:02cv439 (E.D. Va. 2002), 5.

53. Petition for Writ of Certiorari, *Hamdi v. Rumsfeld*, No. 03-7338, U.S. Supreme Court, 9, note 8.

54. *Hamdi v. Rumsfeld*, 542 U.S. 507, 535–36 (2004).

55. Peter Whoriskey, "Jury Convicts Jose Padilla of Terror Charges," *Washington Post*, August 17, 2007, A1; Abby Goodnough and Scott Shane, "Padilla Is Guilty on All Charges in Terror Trial," *New York Times*, August 17, 2007, A1.

56. Moazzam Begg, *Enemy Combatant: My Imprisonment at Guantánamo, Bagram, and Kandahar* (New York: New Press, 2006).

57. "Humane Treatment of al Qaeda and Taliban Detainees," memorandum of February 7, 2002, from President Bush to the Vice President, the Secretary of State, the Secretary of Defense, the Attorney General, Chief of Staff to the President, Director of Central Intelligence, Assistant to the President for National Security Affairs, and Chairman of the Joint Chiefs of Staff, 1–2.

58. For closer analysis of the preparation of administration memos on interrogation of detainees, see Fisher, *The Constitution and 9/11*, 216–26.

59. Memorandum for William J. Haynes II, General Counsel, Department of Defense, from Patrick F. Philbin, Deputy Assistant Attorney General, and John C. Yoo, Deputy Assistant Attorney General, December 28, 2001, 1.

60. Memorandum for William J. Haynes II, General Counsel, Department of Defense, from John Yoo, Deputy Assistant Attorney General, and Robert J. Delahunty, Special Counsel, January 9, 2002.

61. Letter from Ashcroft to Bush, February 1, 2002, 1. In this letter, Ashcroft refers to a Supreme Court decision in *Clark v. Allen*, 331 U.S. 503 (1947), to conclude

that when the president makes a determination about a treaty, it becomes a political question a court will not decide. Yoo and Delahunty had cited that case in their memo to Haynes.

62. "Re: Standards of Conduct for Interrogation under 18 U.S.C. §§ 2340-2340A," memorandum from Bybee to Gonzales, August 1, 2002, 1 (hereafter "Bybee Memo").

63. Department of Defense, "Legal Brief on Proposed Counter-Resistance Strategies," memorandum for Commander, Joint Task Force 170, JTF 170-SJA, October 11, 2002, 1 (paragraphs 1 and 2), declassified June 21, 2004.

64. Office of the Secretary of Defense, "Detainee Interrogations," memorandum for the General Counsel of the Department of Defense, January 15, 2003, declassified June 21, 2004.

65. "Working Group Report on Detainee Interrogations in the Global War on Terrorism: Assessment of Legal, Historical, Policy, and Operational Considerations," March 6, 2003 (draft); "Working Group Report on Detainee Interrogations in the Global War on Terrorism: Assessment of Legal, Historical, Policy, and Operational Considerations," April 4, 2003 (final report).

66. "Working Group Report on Detainee Interrogations in the Global War on Terrorism." For a review of the drafting of the OLC and working group memos, see Jane Mayer, "The Memo," *New Yorker*, February 27, 2006, 32–41.

67. "Photos Show U.S. Troops Abusing Iraqi Prisoners," *Los Angeles Times*, April 29, 2004, A4; James Risen, "G.I.'s Are Accused of Abusing Iraqi Captives," *New York Times*, April 29, 2004, A13; "Photographs Reveal Atrocities by U.S. Soldiers," *Washington Times*, April 29, 2004, A5.

68. Article 15-6 Investigation of the 800th Military Police Brigade, 16.

69. Jameel Jaffer and Amrit Singh, *Administration of Torture: A Documentary Record from Washington to Abu Ghraib and Beyond* (New York: Columbia University Press, 2007).

70. Fisher, *The Constitution and 9/11*, 229–31.

71. Office of Legal Counsel, U.S. Department of Justice, "Re: Legal Standards Applicable under 18 U.S.C. §§ 2340-2340A," memorandum for James B. Comey, Deputy Attorney General, December 30, 2004, 1 (citations omitted).

72. *Rasul v. Bush*, 215 F.Supp.2d 55 (D.D.C. 2002).

73. *Al Odah v. United States*, 321 F.3d 1134 (D.C. Cir. 2003).

74. *Coalition of Clergy v. Bush*, 189 F.Supp.2d 1036 (C.D. Cal. 2002); *Coalition of Clergy, Lawyers, & Professors v. Bush*, 310 F.3d 1153 (9th Cir. 2002); *Gherebi v. Bush*, 262 F.Supp.2d 1064 (C.D. Cal. 2003); *Gheribi v. Bush*, 352 F.3d 1278 (9th Cir. 2003).

75. *Gheribi v. Bush*, 352 F.3d at 1283.

76. *Gheribi v. Bush*, 352 F.3d, 1287–88, 1289–90.

77. *Rasul v. Bush*, 542 U.S. 466, 475–76 (2004).

78. Department of Defense, News Transcript, "Defense Department Background Briefing on the Combatant Status Review Tribunal," July 7, 2004, 1–2.

79. Josh White, "President Relents, Backs Torture Ban," *Washington Post*, December 16, 2005, A1.

80. "The Supreme Court's Decision in *Hamdan v. Rumsfeld*," hearing before the Senate Committee on the Judiciary, 109th Cong. (2006), available at judiciary.senate.gov/print_testimony.cfm?id=1986&wit_id=5505.

81. R. Jeffrey Smith, "Top Military Lawyers Oppose Plan for Special Courts," *Washington Post*, August 3, 2006, A11.

82. Smith, "Top Military Lawyers Oppose Plan."

83. *Boumediene v. Bush*, 476 F.3d 981, 989 (D.C. Cir. 2007).

Chapter Fifteen

The President and Congress: Separate, Independent, and Completely Equal

The Honorable Mickey Edwards

Less than four weeks after he became president of the United States, Barack Obama achieved a major legislative victory. With the nation's economy reeling, the new administration had advocated, and the Congress had passed, a nearly $800 billion economic "stimulus" package that was described by its opponents as the single largest spending bill in the history of the world.[1] Journalists on one Sunday morning television program, just days after the bill's passage, said Obama had achieved more in those three short weeks than the last previous Democratic president, Bill Clinton, had achieved in the eight years of his presidency.

There is no question that the enactment of such a massive new infusion of federal dollars into the private sector was a direct result of Obama's victory in the 2008 elections. For one thing, Obama's Republican opponent, John McCain, would certainly not have proposed legislation nearly so expensive or far-reaching; indeed, having returned to his seat in the United States Senate, McCain was a leader in opposition to the bill's passage.[2] And without Obama's victory, in which he carried or nearly carried states that had long been traditionally Republican, there would have been more Republicans in both houses of Congress. Since every Republican in the House and all but three in the Senate voted against the stimulus package, it is likely that the Republicans who would have been elected without Obama's presence on the ballot would have also opposed spending at the level the new administration proposed.[3]

But presidents—even very popular presidents—have a limited ability to affect the ultimate shape of legislation. As Republicans were quick to point out, the stimulus package that passed the House of Representatives, and shaped the ensuing debate, was less the handiwork of the Obama administration than of Nancy Pelosi, the House Speaker, and David Obey, the chairman of the

House Appropriations Committee. Critics argued that the legislation went beyond the original framework for an economic shot in the arm (legislation that Obama adviser Larry Summers envisioned as "targeted" and "temporary") and included spending projects that had long been on Democrats' legislative wish list but which had no chance of enactment with a Republican president in the White House.[4]

With polls showing the economic stimulus legislation far less popular than the president himself, Obama took to the hustings, taking his message directly to voters where they lived and worked. He was received enthusiastically. And nothing changed. In the end, not one single House Republican voted for the legislation. In the Senate, only three—Olympia Snowe and Susan Collins of Maine and Arlen Specter of Pennsylvania—supported the bill, and only after winning significant concessions from the Democratic majority. As for the Democrats, all had already been supportive of the legislation before the president began his traveling sales tour.[5]

To the cynic, or the dispassionate scholar, Obama may have only been "another president"; true, he had made history by virtue of his racial identity and he had surprised most observers by his rapid ascent through the political system, but having won, he was now to be just one more in the line of chief executives, a position nearly half a hundred other men had held before him, not all of them exemplary. But in fact many in the public saw him as something different: the combination of his calm demeanor and his rousing rhetoric suggested that he might actually be a transcendent figure, somebody whose personality and character would bring change not only in policy but in the very nature of governance. That may eventually prove to be the case, but it is hard to be transcendent in a system of government that divides, and limits, authority.

Part of what was supposed to be "transcendent" about this new presidency was Obama's emphasis on bridging the partisan gap that had made cooperative governing so difficult. Obama did his part: he traveled to Capitol Hill to meet with members of the Republican minority; he dined at George Will's home with conservative columnists and commentators; he invited Republicans as well as Democrats to watch the Super Bowl in the White House. He advocated a new commitment to working together.[6] In the meantime, the Speaker of the House, Nancy Pelosi, announced that since Democrats had won the election, they would write the bill, leaving Republicans like McCain and House Republican leader John Boehner, of Ohio, to grumble that they had to be part of writing the legislation if they were to be expected to support it.

If the final stimulus package reflected the will of Democrats in Congress more than the initiatives of the presidency that was not the first time this new president had run up against the realities of Washington. Members of Congress, even of the president's own party, understand that while the president of the United States may be the most visible of American public officials, and represents the nation among world leaders, he is not, in fact, the head of government: even the most popular occupant of the White House is the head of one of three coequal branches of a highly decentralized government.

This congressional "independence" was revealed repeatedly in the early days of the Obama presidency: Obama's choice for secretary of health and human services, former Senate majority leader Tom Daschle, withdrew from consideration after the Senate continued to press him for details about a failure to properly report income to the Internal Revenue Service. When Obama's treasury secretary, Timothy Geithner, won an internal White House battle that resulted in limiting federal interference with compensation packages for corporate executives whose firms had received federal assistance, the Senate, led by Connecticut Senator Christopher Dodd, wrote stricter compensation limits into the law over the White House's objections.

Eager to move forward with his own agenda, Obama repeatedly signaled that he would prefer that the Congress not spend its time investigating possible wrongdoing by the departed Bush administration, especially in regard to such issues as extraordinary rendition, treatment of prisoners at Guantanamo, warrantless electronic surveillance, invoking of state secrets authority, and dismissal of U.S. attorneys. Michigan Congressman John Conyers, chairman of the House Judiciary Committee, and Vermont Senator Patrick Leahy, chairman of the Judiciary Committee in the Senate, announced plans to conduct hearings into allegations of Bush administration abuses.[7]

It is with these early reminders of the challenge of leadership that Obama set out to undertake the other great challenges that faced the nation as he assumed his new office.

When Barack Obama took office as the forty-fourth president of the United States, he was faced with a challenge unlike any faced by his most recent predecessors. First, there was the scope of the issues with which his new administration would have to contend. When Franklin Roosevelt was elected, the nation was in the midst of a great depression marked by soup lines and suicides but Hitler had not yet taken power in Germany, Japan had not yet begun its bloody march through Asia, and America was at peace. Presidents who came to office with the nation at war—Truman, Eisenhower, Nixon, and Johnson—were not required to simultaneously deal with the massive economic crisis Roosevelt had faced. But Obama was inheriting a presidency in which both war and economic recession demanded immediate attention and creative action.

As terrible as they are, wars come to an end. And economic downturns, even ones as severe as that of the late 1920s, eventually run their course. But Obama's second challenge—potentially of even greater and more lasting significance—was unprecedented.

It is in the nature of politics, and perhaps of human nature, that power once grasped is seldom surrendered. The presidency Barack Obama came to was one that had, for nearly eight years, claimed and exercised authority beyond anything granted by the Constitution or asserted by any earlier occupant of the White House. In more than eleven hundred signing statements President George W. Bush had claimed the right to determine how and whether he was bound to obey legislation he himself had signed into law.[8] In authorizing electronic surveillance of American citizens without a judicial warrant, he had deliberately violated clear federal law, asserting that his powers as commander in chief of the armed forces contained an inherent authority to act in the national defense with or without legal sanction. Although the Constitution places with the Congress, not the executive, the power to decide the treatment of prisoners of war, the Bush administration had ordered suspected terrorists held indefinitely without trial or charges, a violation of a specific constitutional prohibition against suspension of habeas corpus rights. For several years, Obama and other Democrats had vigorously attacked these broad claims of presidential authority, denouncing them as unconstitutional. When Obama became president, with great challenges and facing almost certain resistance to many of his proposed solutions, there would undoubtedly be many occasions when the exercise of such powers, never specifically repudiated by Congress, would be tempting. For Barack Obama, a former professor of constitutional law, no decision would have greater long-lasting impact than whether to renounce the powers he might otherwise claim. George Washington had done so; could Obama, in a much different age, surrender the authority that might lie within his grasp to the Congress, his constitutional rival for power?[9]

The Madisonian structure of American government created powers specifically delegated to one or another of the three branches of government, but it also left ample room for struggle between the branches. As a result, when one branch claimed authority and that claim was not challenged, the established precedent effectively changed the reality—the classic case being the Supreme Court's famous decision in *Marbury v. Madison*, which effectively made the Court the recognized final arbiter of constitutionality, a power not conferred by the Constitution itself. Obama's repudiation of the Bush administration's assertions would help undermine the claims of a super-empowered presidency that might prove tempting to future presidents. His failure to renounce those claims might have the opposite effect, strengthening the presidency and further weakening the Congress as the effective collective voice of the people.[10]

On the morning of January 23, 2009, less than forty-eight hours after George W. Bush left the White House and returned to Texas, Admiral Dennis Blair, the new president's choice to serve as director of national intelligence, traveled to Capitol Hill to seek the Senate's approval of his appointment. By coincidence, the committee that would pose the first hurdle for the nomination was chaired by the same senator—and fellow Democrat—who had earlier presided over Barack Obama's inauguration. One might have expected her to be enthusiastic at the prospect of supporting President Obama's nominee, and she was. But to her credit and in a departure from the habit of some members of Congress to automatically defer to whatever a president might want if he were of the same political party, this senator added something new.

Diane Feinstein opened the hearing by asking Blair a series of questions, customary in such hearings and designed to elicit pledges of openness in dealings with Congress. But then she asked a question that had not been part of the historic pattern: would Blair, she asked, assure the Senate that intelligence officials would henceforth share information with all the members of the Intelligence Committee, not just the chairman and cochairman as had been the previous practice? Blair said he would. Senator Feinstein said she hoped that question would become standard in the future.

The Congress writes America's laws. Under the Constitution, it alone determines when and whether the United States will go to war; the president may command the country's military forces when called into action, having the constitutional final word over strategy and tactics, but it is still the Congress, not the White House, that sets the rules, even the rules for how the military is to be regulated and how prisoners of war are to be treated. These are heavy responsibilities and ones that require that members of Congress have all the information they need to decide wisely. Yet, increasingly, as the nature of war has changed, the Congress has chosen to defer to presidential leadership on questions relating to national security. One result of that deference has been a procedure, embodied in formal legislation, which permits the executive branch to share highly classified information only with a very limited number of legislators (known informally as the Gang of Eight), who are often forbidden from sharing what they've learned either with members of their staffs—many of whom are quite expert in security and defense matters—or other members of Congress.

During one meeting of the Senate Judiciary Committee, Senator Sheldon Whitehouse of Rhode Island complained that executive branch officials could choose to declassify information when it might suit their purposes but that members of Congress were prohibited by law from revealing that same information, thus limiting their ability to debate, or block, presidential initiatives. There was an obvious answer to that dilemma: the Congress could simply change the law. Absent the acquiescence of the Congress—a separate, independent, and completely equal branch of government—the executive branch would not have the authority to deny the peoples' representatives the information they need to act intelligently on the public's behalf. It may be prudent to limit access to highly classified national security information even among elected members of Congress (even if that information is known to many thousands of federal bureaucrats) but that is a decision for the Congress, not the executive, to make. If members of the Senate are frustrated by their inability to get the information they need to make decisions, they simply need to get their colleagues to change the rules.

This is the dilemma Senator Whitehouse would face: while most essential powers of government are actually vested in Congress, not the president—going to war, setting tax rates, establishing spending priorities—the realities are often more complicated. Take, for example, the management of war, or the sharing of secret information. As a member of Congress, it might be my right under the Constitution to interpose my views and even to insist, with the support of my colleagues, on a particular course of action. But I would also be aware that much is at stake—the lives of many thousands of Americans, perhaps—and that the president has access to sources of information (highly trained military officers, intelligence agencies, embassies and consulates, and so on). It takes a great deal of self-assurance to insist that one's own judgment is superior to that which presumably flows from all those streams of information and analysis.

Nor is military action the only arena in which such a dilemma occurs. As the theme of this book makes clear, the executive and legislative branches of government are rivals; each has a case to make for supremacy in the decision-making process.

Ronald Reagan was enormously popular for much of his presidency and is regarded by a number of prominent historians, some of them quite hostile to his political views, as one of the most significant presidents in American history. Even in a Congress in which his fellow Republicans were outnumbered, there were enough conservative Boll Weevil Democrats to often provide a working majority in support of his proposals. It is assumed that federal spending decisions will be set, at least initially, by the White House; in 1921 the Congress delegated to the president the responsibility for submitting an annual national budget, and since that time it has generally been the president's proposed priorities that have established the baseline from which budget debates began. Yet Reagan once had the distinction of having one of his budget proposals cast aside with barely an acknowledgment that it had been submitted. And when Reagan reluctantly agreed to a tax increase as part of a broader agreement with House and Senate Democrats, many members of his own party, including members of the Republican leadership, voted against the increase, even after he invited congressional Republicans to the White House and there made a personal, and emotional, plea for support.

Similarly, when President George W. Bush's treasury secretary, Henry Paulson, urged the Congress to adopt his initial proposals to provide federal funds to struggling financial institutions, the plan was defeated in the House of Representatives largely because of opposition from members of the president's own party.

One gets a clearer picture of the tenuous relationship between the White House and the Congress, and the differences between the attitudes toward security and economic issues, when looking at the interaction between the Bush administration and the president's fellow Republicans over an eight-year period. Almost regardless of the boldness of presidential proposals, Republicans in Congress could usually be counted upon to give their support if the issue was somehow couched in terms of the ongoing "war on terror." Whether it was passage of the PATRIOT Act, creation of special military tribunals, providing immunity guarantees for companies that shared private customer information with government agencies, or rewriting laws to facilitate electronic surveillance, the president could generally be assured his fellow party members would stand with him (even as many, and often most, Democrats did not).

But when it came to matters that were not related to national security, party-line support was less certain. In the most dramatic example, the proposal to provide a federal bailout in light of the economic crisis that hit the country late in 2008, Republicans voted against the administration's proposal by better than two-to-one (65 in favor, 133 opposed).

One might reasonably expect, given the partisan nature of the political system, that members of the opposition party (that is, the party that does not control the White House) would have sufficient philosophical disagreement with the president that their resistance to presidential requests would be the norm, but congressional opposition even to same-party presidents has a long history.

During Jimmy Carter's presidency, his fellow Democrats not only controlled both houses of Congress, but often did so with quite substantial margins. But it did Carter little good. He proposed elimination of a number of congressionally approved water projects; the proposal went nowhere, opposed even by some of his party's most prominent leaders.[11] He threatened to veto another bill containing nineteen projects he considered wasteful; Congress called his hand, approved the projects anyway, and Carter, rather than lose the entire bill, reluctantly agreed to sign it. He proposed a new consumer protection law and a labor reform package; Congress gutted both bills.

But many observers consider Carter's to have been a failed presidency. One cannot say that about Bill Clinton, the first Democrat elected to two consecutive terms since Franklin Roosevelt. True, Clinton had to deal with a Republican Congress after his first years in office, but that was not the case when he unveiled his first major initiative, the creation of a far-reaching federal health care plan. At that point, Clinton had come straight from an election in which he defeated an incumbent president. And he had Democratic majorities in both the House and Senate. He put enormous muscle behind his health care plan and put his own wife, Hillary Clinton, a formidable figure in her own right, in charge of the effort. But the plan was defeated. (Harry Truman, who had Democratic majorities for most of his presidency, wrote in his autobiography that his single greatest disappointment as president was the Congress's refusal to pass a national health insurance bill).[12]

Clearly, being president isn't all that it's cracked up to be, especially when it comes to getting laws passed. Why is that?

In 2008, George W. Bush prepared to head overseas. A columnist for the *Washington Post*, Dana Milbank, explained that the president was for a short time stepping out of his role as head of government to function in his other role, as head of state. That would undoubtedly seem to most Americans a reasonable distinction; after all, on foreign trips presidents concern themselves with basing rights, treaties, cooperative agreements, and other nondomestic issues. Political scientists, lawyers, journalists, and even many public officials accept this delineation—the two hats of the presidency—without a second thought. But—and this is something many members of Congress understand—while the president of the United States is, for international purposes, this nation's head of state, on a full par with kings and queens, prime ministers, and the like, he or she is not the head of government. The United States has no head of government; rather a president is the head of one of three separate, independent, and completely equal branches of government. What's more, the part of the government the president heads is, constitutionally, the weaker of the two nonjudicial branches (remember, it is the Congress that decides on war, on taxes, on spending; as the saying goes, "the president proposes; the Congress disposes").

Thus, the conflicts. Presidents have an enormous base of power. While their actual authority may be tightly circumscribed by the Constitution, they alone take office with the approval of the entire nation. If a member of the House of Representatives were to receive a full 100 percent of the vote in his or her district, and if every eligible citizen in that district voted, he or she would still have the support of no more than one four-hundred-and-thirty-fifth of the national electorate (and even less if one counts the votes of jurisdictions such as the District of Columbia, Puerto Rico, Guam, the Virgin Islands, which have no voting representation in Congress). Likewise, a member of the Senate, even from the very largest states, would have a small constituency compared to that of a president. That is no minor distinction. Constitution or no Constitution, presidents believe themselves to be head of government, and most Americans probably see it the same way. Further, the one area in which the president has constitutional primacy—commanding the troops in the field—is of such consequence that his or her position is automatically magnified in public perception.

The president has other advantages, too. Because he directs the various federal departments and agencies, the presidential reach is enormous, affecting policy in almost every walk of life, from farming to driving on an interstate highway. President George W. Bush famously interpreted the theory of the unitary executive (which originally meant only that there was one president at a time instead of a three-part joint presidency) to mean that the agencies and bureaus of the federal government worked only for him and thus could not be directed by Congress, even though it was Congress that wrote the laws and appropriated the money to implement them.

The news media is complicit in the expansion of presidential power, though the press's role is completely understandable. There is one president. A presidential initiative is much easier to cover and report on than the activities of 535 voting members of Congress. The power, and authority, of members of Congress is collective; individual representatives and senators have less influence and thus understandably receive less public notice. Every congressional member's constituents will have more familiarity with presidential perspectives than that of their own delegates to the national legislature. It is not uncommon for members of Congress to find themselves forced to defend opposition to a presidential initiative since that is the perspective voters will be most familiar with. It is a reversal of the situation in the early days of the republic, before mass communication systems began to shrink the country; then, it was the member of Congress who was close by and the president who was distant. Today the president is in every citizen's living room night after night.

Presidents also have the advantage of distance from their own constituencies. Interest groups that try to influence presidential decision making generally have to get their arguments placed before the president in an indirect way, passed through an array of gatekeepers; they seldom get a chance to walk up to a president at a town meeting or civic club luncheon to press their case. Presidents are insulated from direct pressure. George W. Bush often boasted of his firmness, his resolve, his obvious certitude. But whether desirable or not, that is a far easier position for a president to maintain than it would be for a member of Congress.

While the president has access to the work product of tens of thousands of executive branch employees, the typical House member who is not a member of the congressional or party leadership will generally have no more than twenty or so staff members, including those whose primary function is to answer constituent mail, answer the phones, help constituents resolve problems with federal agencies, interact with community leaders, and so forth. A number of those staff members will not be in Washington at all, but in the home district, trying to maintain as close as possible a relationship with a community of more than six hundred thousand citizens. A House member, who occupies a relatively safe seat (that is, one who is reasonably certain of avoiding defeat) and can thus give greater attention to sponsoring or analyzing legislation, may still have no more than three or four staff members whose primary function is to deal with actual legislation. The size of a senator's staff is determined by the population of the state the senator represents, but even the most heavily staffed senators—and in the House and Senate the larger committee staffs—are at a distinct disadvantage in competing with entire executive branch bureaucracies.

Members of Congress, like the president, have distinctive political philosophies to fall back on in making their decisions. But unlike the president, they have a unique duality of purpose. Political scientists call these two distinct purposes the "delegate" function and the "trustee" function. What they mean is, most members of Congress feel a clear responsibility to represent the view of their constituents (that is, to be their delegates to the national legislature), at least so far as they are able to do so without violating their own deeply held convictions. And at the same time, they take seriously the obligation to use their own greater familiarity with the issues, and their broader perspectives of national, rather than purely local, concerns, to do what they think is in the best interests of the nation as a whole, rather than just what the folks back home might prefer. This is a conundrum presidents don't face, and it is at the root of the struggle for power, the rivalry this book describes.

Consider the pulls on senators and representatives. Most will want to be supportive of a president of their own party or of their own party's leaders. That is not because they put partisan loyalties above other considerations but because there are commonly held perspectives that cause one to join one party or another. They will also want to be as true as possible to that philosophy, as they see it; thus, when a president—even one of their own party—diverges from that philosophical path, they will often withdraw their support.

Or they may withdraw their support because their constituents feel strongly that the party's, or the president's, position is wrong. If this is truly a system of self-government, no member of Congress should cavalierly disregard his or her constituents' strongly held sentiments.

The rivalry between the Congress and the president is thus not merely a matter of struggles over constitutional interpretation or the natural human inclination to seek enhancement of one's own ability to shape events. The rivalry flows also from the very different nature of the offices: nearness or distance from constituent pressures, whether one represents half a million or three hundred million citizens, the extent of available expertise, and so on.

But while the system creates an intentional tension between the branches— the very heart of the Madisonian concept of branches and factions and levels of government each checking the other—the Constitution, hailed for its liberty-enhancing constraints on governmental power, empowers as well. It is a government, not merely a debating society, and as such, it must act.

Here there develops a further aspect of the continuing rivalry between the branches. It has become common in recent years for scholars and journalists, disaffected by the often nasty partisanship of public decision making, to advocate for the rise of a new "centrist" politics. Thus a pressure for the Congress to seek middle ground, a consensus. Because the president's is the loudest voice in the public debate, one might suppose that the starting point for this search for consensus might be the position enunciated from the White House. Knock a bit off the edges, amp up here, cut back there, and come together.

The problem with that scenario, as with all utopias, is that utopia is often not all it's cracked up to be. In her short story "The Ones Who Walked Away from Omelas," Ursula LeGuin describes a utopia of sorts: a community in which one child is intentionally left to suffer great deprivation because by sacrificing her, the rest of the populace is able to enjoy a life of bounty and beauty. On first reading, one comes to most appreciate those few citizens who refuse to participate and leave the town, and its utopian features, behind. Ultimately, though, one comes to be less appreciative of those who walk away rather than dismantling the system.[13] All utopias, including those of consensual harmony, miss something important. The search for consensus is no different.

American democracy is designed not for happy harmony but for deliberate conflict. Democracy is dependent on the full consideration of alternatives; on the ability of the people, through their representatives, to weigh options and consider which best serve the interests of the nation. There are obvious examples to illustrate why conflict is better than a search for some sort of "common ground." What, for example, is a proper middle position on slavery? What is a middle position on women's equality? There are rights and wrongs and decisions to be made. For every major advance in American democracy, there has been a need to engage in serious argument.

Given this necessity of vigorous debate, it is easy to see why the executive and Congress come into such regular conflict. No matter the initiative—lower taxes (does that mean higher debt?), more regulation (stifled innovation?), education reform (sacrificing the study of civics to enhance mastery of mathematics?), the Congress, if it is to be the heart of a public participation in the decision-making process, must be able to put issues squarely on the table and engage in serious discussion about their relative merits. Merely following the advice of a chief executive diminishes democracy; it doesn't enhance it.

It has been said that whether a presidency attains a high level of significance depends in great part on circumstance: it is hard to make a lasting mark on history if one serves during a period when all is relatively calm and uneventful. If that's the case, Barack Obama has an opportunity to achieve a singular place in America's story, well beyond the matter of his racial heritage. When the Chinese speak of living in interesting times, these are the times they have in mind. The Obama years may be successful or they may fall short, but they will not be boring.

The Obama administration will grapple with the nation's economic difficulties, the unique nature of the terrorist threat to the United States and the Western world, the winding down of ongoing wars in Iraq and Afghanistan, a sobering level of federal debt, struggling state and local governments, and the disturbing presence of hyperpartisanship and animus in the public discourse. But by following the presidency of George W. Bush, with his expansionist view of the presidential role, President Obama will also have an opportunity to put his own stamp on the nature of the rivalry between the legislative and executive branches of government.

Consider George Bush's use of presidential signing statements. Almost since the beginning of the republic, presidents have chosen to signal their reaction to legislation presented to them by the Congress. In some cases they have praised the newly signed laws and the new legal paths they created—new protections, new entitlements, and new social compacts. At other times they have used their signing statements to express their regret that the legislation they were signing fell short of their hopes; the new laws were merely the best they could manage to get the Congress to enact. In either case, though, once signed the new laws were binding on every American citizen, with the president no exception. This was simply because the Constitution provides a president only two options on receiving legislation: to sign it into law or exercise a presidential veto, returning the bill to Congress where it might attempt to override his veto and enact the new law anyway. This is not a minor presidential prerogative: a president needs the support of only one-third of one house of Congress to prevail. Thus if the House of Representatives votes 435–0 to enact the legislation notwithstanding the president's objections, and if the Senate agrees by an overwhelming vote of 66–34, the president nonetheless wins—having won one-third of the Senate. What the president cannot do, however, is choose a third course: to sign a bill into law but declare that he would decide for himself whether he was to be bound by it.

It is inevitable that at some point in his presidency, Barack Obama will be presented with legislation he does not like very much. That will be his opportunity to clearly express a commitment to follow the strictures of the Constitution. If he chooses to sign the bill notwithstanding his concerns, he can declare his understanding that while he might have preferred a different course, he would thenceforth be constitutionally bound to obey the law he had just signed. If, on the other hand, he exercises his veto, he can make clear that he is doing so only because if he were to sign the legislation he would have no choice but to follow its mandates. In either case, he would have struck a potentially fatal blow to the ambitions of future presidents who might wish to establish a third course setting the occupant of the White House above the law.

President Obama will have similar opportunities to challenge, in his own way, each of President Bush's extraordinary claims to "inherent" authority. If he were to reverse his early positions and seek to use "enhanced interrogation" techniques in an attempt to elicit information from captives in the war on terror he could appeal directly to Congress for the authority to do so, acknowledging that such decisions were within the constitutional purview of the legislative branch. And so on, for each area in which the Bush administration sought to create or establish presidential powers beyond that authorized by federal statute or the Constitution.

For the purposes of this chapter, and to illustrate the opportunities now present, it is convenient to point to the claims of George W. Bush's presidency that being the most recent attempt to rewrite the rules of the great rivalry this book seeks to explain. But it should be clear that attempts to enhance presidential authority did not begin with George Bush and likely will not end with the ending of his presidential tenure. Abraham Lincoln understood the general constitutional prohibition against the suspension of habeas corpus rights and that in the only circumstances under which such a suspension was permitted—in the case of invasion or insurrection—that choice would have to be made not by the president but by Congress. Even though Lincoln did, in fact, seek, and receive, retroactive congressional approval, his request and the

Congress's action were not contemporaneous. Franklin Roosevelt famously attempted to enlarge the size of the Supreme Court in a vain attempt to win rulings that would permit him to enact policies the Court had found to be unconstitutional. This, then, is not a matter of repudiating one president (George W. Bush) or one set of extraconstitutional policy decisions, but of considering how a path might be found to continue the separations and checks the Founders saw as essential to preserving essential liberties of the kind most easily lost when power accrues too readily in too few hands.

The presidential scholar Richard Neustadt argued for a strong executive, a vigorous and energetic and effective president. He believed, however, that strength in the executive was to be found in creative vision and in the ability to persuade and motivate.[14] Such a presidency would enable a rivalry that served American liberty rather than threatening it; the Congress and the president would contend for primacy in the court of public opinion, conducting their battle for policy primacy in an arena bounded by the constraints of the Constitution. It would be a rivalry but it would serve us well.

NOTES

1. The final package, reached as a result of compromise between the House and Senate versions of the legislation, totaled $787 billion, including various short-term and long-term spending programs, aid to state governments, and a variety of tax cuts. A number of economists suggested that the bill's greatest impact would not be felt until 2010 and that further spending would be needed. When the final version of the bill was passed, President Obama had been in office for only twenty-five days.

2. McCain described the legislation as "big on giveaways for the special interests and corporate high rollers, yet short on help for ordinary working Americans" and urged supporters to sign an online petition opposing the bill.

3. Florida, Indiana, Ohio, North Carolina, Virginia, Nevada—states Republicans had long counted on—were suddenly battleground states. Helped by Obama's popularity, new Democratic senators were elected in Alaska, Colorado, New Hampshire, New Mexico, North Carolina, Oregon, and Virginia, and perhaps (uncertain at the time of this writing), Minnesota. All voted for the stimulus package.

4. "(The) President has put emphasis in this package on measures that are temporary," Summers on Fox News on February 9, four days before the final legislation was enacted.

5. Obama's trips to Illinois, Florida, and Indiana produced headlines and television news coverage but changed no votes.

6. Obama also made personal phone calls to Republican leaders and sent his chief of staff, Rahm Emanuel, to Capitol Hill for meetings with House Republicans. At the same time, Obama encouraged Democrats to drop from the legislation some

provisions that had drawn particularly sharp criticism from its Republican opponents, including funding for family planning.

7. According to *Politico*, a Washington newspaper, Leahy suggested that doing nothing was not an acceptable option.

8. The Bush administration's use of signing statements to declare the president's authority to determine whether he was bound by the legislation he had signed into law was revealed in a series of articles in the *Boston Globe* by Charlie Savage, whose discoveries resulted in his receiving a Pulitzer Prize. In the wake of the discovery, both the American Bar Association and The Constitution Project appointed bipartisan task forces to investigate the practice. Both task forces found unanimously that the practice was unconstitutional. The Constitution provides, in article 1, section 7, that when a president receives legislation duly passed by Congress his only two options are to sign it into law or veto it.

9. The power to declare war, to make rules concerning captures on land and water, and to make rules governing and regulating the military are all found in article 1, section 8 of the Constitution. The prohibition against the suspension of habeas corpus, except in cases of invasion or insurrection, is in article 1, section 9.

10. Madison, in "Federalist No. 51," wrote that "the great security against a gradual concentration of the several powers (of government) in the same department, consists in giving to those who administer each department, the necessary constitutional means . . . to resist encroachments of the others."

11. Future Speaker Jim Wright, then the house majority leader, was perhaps the most vigorous opponent of his fellow Democrat's proposals.

12. President Truman proposed a national health insurance plan in November 1945, when his presidency was only seven months old. He made it a centerpiece of his so-called Fair Deal legislative agenda.

13. Included in a collection of short stories (*The Wind's Twelve Quarters*), this wrenching tale of moral dilemma won the Hugo Award for short stories in 1974.

14. An adviser to Presidents Truman, Kennedy, and Johnson, and a founding faculty member of Harvard's Kennedy School of Government, Neustadt believed that the American presidency was essentially a weak office and argued in his book *Presidential Power*, published in 1960, that a president's real power rested in the ability to persuade.

Index

About the Contributors

Gary Andres is vice chairman of research for Dutko Worldwide. He also previously worked in senior positions in the White House for Presidents George H. W. Bush and George W. Bush. Mr. Andres is the author of *Lobbying Reconsidered: Under the Influence* (2008). He earned his Ph.D. in public policy analysis at the University of Illinois, Chicago. He writes regularly about politics, Congress, and the presidency for the *Weekly Standard* and *Politico*.

Richard S. Conley is associate professor of political science at the University of Florida. He specializes in the U.S. presidency and executive-legislative relations, as well as in comparative executives and legislatures (in Canada, France, Ireland). He is author of *The Presidency, Congress, and Divided Government: A Post War Assessment* (2002), *Historical Dictionary of the Reagan-Bush Era* (2007), *Historical Dictionary of the George W. Bush Era* (forthcoming 2009), and editor of *Reassessing the Reagan Presidency* (2003) and *Transforming The American Polity: The Presidency of George W. Bush and the War on Terrorism* (2004). His journal articles have appeared in *American Politics Research, Comparative Political Studies, Congress and the Presidency, Politics and Policy, Political Research Quarterly, Political Science Quarterly, Polity, Presidential Studies Quarterly*, and *White House Studies*.

Roger H. Davidson is professor emeritus of government and politics at the University of Maryland and visiting professor of political science at the University of California, Santa Barbara. His recent books include *Workways of Governance* (2003), *Understanding the Presidency*, 5th ed., coedited with James P. Pfiffner (2008), and *Congress and Its Members*, 12th ed., with

Walter J. Oleszek and Frances E. Lee (forthcoming 2010). He is a fellow of the National Academy of Public Administration. In spring 2008, for the U.S. State Department, he toured four South Pacific nations to present lectures, seminars, and media appearances explaining the U.S. presidential nomination and election system.

The **Honorable Mickey Edwards** was a member of Congress for sixteen years and was a member of the House Republican leadership (Policy Committee chairman), ranking member of Appropriations subcommittees on foreign operations and military construction, and member of the House Budget Committee. Since leaving Congress he has taught government at Harvard, Princeton, and Georgetown. He has been a political columnist for the *Los Angeles Times*, *Chicago Tribune*, and *Boston Globe* and a regular commentator on NPR's *All Things Considered*. He is also a vice president of the Aspen Institute. His most recent book, *Reclaiming Conservatism*, was published in 2008.

Louis Fisher is a specialist in constitutional issues for the Law Library of the Library of Congress, after earlier working for the Congressional Research Service as a specialist in separation of powers. In 1987 he was research director of the House Iran-Contra Committee, writing major sections of the final report. He testifies frequently before congressional committees and is the author of nineteen books and four hundred articles. His most recent book is *The Constitution and 9/11: Recurring Threats to America's Freedoms* (2008).

Patrick Griffin is a partner in Griffin Williams LLC, a management consulting firm that helps public and private sector clients navigate developmental transitions, organizational crisis, and political challenges. Mr. Griffin's public sector career has included serving as a top adviser to the president of the United States and to two Senate Democratic leaders. Prior to cofounding his current company, Mr. Griffin founded the government relations firm of Griffin, Johnson, Madigan, and Peck. Mr. Griffin also currently serves as the academic director for the Public Affairs and Advocacy Institute in the School of Government at American University. Before coming to Washington, Mr. Griffin was an assistant professor at the University of Wisconsin, Milwaukee. Mr. Griffin's education background includes a Ph.D. in education, as well as master's and bachelor's degrees in urban affairs and policy.

The **Honorable Lee H. Hamilton** is president and director of the Woodrow Wilson International Center for Scholars and director of the Center on Congress at Indiana University. He represented Indiana's 9th District in the

House of Representatives from 1964 to 1999. He served on the National War Powers Commission in 2008. He also served as cochair of the Iraq Study Group and vice chair of the 9/11 Commission.

Mark J. Oleszek is a doctoral candidate in American politics at the University of California, Berkeley. His research focuses on social dynamics inherent to lawmaking in the U.S. Senate, an interest born from work as a legislative aide to the Senate Democratic Policy Committee.

Walter J. Oleszek is a senior specialist in the legislative process at the Congressional Research Service. He has been at CRS since 1968 and has served as either a full-time professional staff aide or as a consultant to numerous House and Senate congressional reform committees or commissions. He is a long-time adjunct faculty member at the American University and the author or coauthor of several books on the Congress.

John E. Owens is professor of U.S. government and politics at the University of Westminster and a faculty fellow in the Center for Congressional and Presidential Studies at the American University in Washington, D.C., and associate fellow at the Institute for the Study of the Americas in the University of London's School of Advanced Study. He is the author of numerous articles on the U.S. Congress, congressional-presidential relations, and comparative legislative politics. His most recent book, coedited with John W. Dumbrell, is *America's "War" on Terrorism: New Dimensions in United States Government and National Security*, which was published in 2008. His previous publications include *Congress and the Presidency: Institutional Politics in a Separated System*, coauthored with Michael Foley; *Leadership in Context*, coedited with Erwin C. Hargrove; and *The Republican Takeover of Congress*, coedited with Dean McSweeney.

James P. Pfiffner is university professor in the School of Public Policy at George Mason University. He has written or edited twelve books on the presidency and American national government, including *Power Play: The Bush Administration and the Constitution* (2008). His professional experience includes service in the Director's Office of the U.S. Office of Personnel Management (1980–1981), and he has been a member of the faculty at the University of California, Riverside, and California State University, Fullerton.

Mark J. Rozell is professor of public policy at George Mason University and the author of nine books and editor of seventeen additional books on various aspects of American government and politics. He has testified before

Congress on executive privilege issues on several occasions and presently is preparing the third edition of his book on that topic, *Executive Privilege: Presidential Power, Secrecy and Accountability.*

Andrew Rudalevige is Walter E. Beach '56 Chair of Political Science at Dickinson College and, in 2008–2009, director of the Dickinson Humanities Program at the University of East Anglia, Norwich, England. Most recently the coeditor of *The George W. Bush Legacy*, he is author of various essays and books on interbranch relations, including *Managing the President's Program* (2002), which won the Richard E. Neustadt Prize, and *The New Imperial Presidency: Renewing Presidential Power after Watergate* (2006).

Barbara Sinclair is Marvin Hoffenberg Professor Emerita of Political Science at UCLA. She specializes in American politics and primarily does research on the U.S. Congress. Her publications include articles in the *American Political Science Review*, the *American Journal of Political Science*, the *Journal of Politics*, and *Legislative Studies Quarterly*, and the following books: *Congressional Realignment* (1982), *Majority Leadership in the U.S. House* (1983), *The Transformation of the U.S. Senate* (1989), *Legislators, Leaders, and Lawmaking: The U.S. House of Representatives in the Postreform Era* (1995), *Unorthodox Lawmaking: New Legislative Processes in the U.S. Congress* (1997, 2000, 2007), and *Party Wars: Polarization and the Politics of National Policy Making* (2006). She has served as chair of the Legislative Studies Section of the American Political Science Association, president of the Western Political Science Association, and vice president of the American Political Science Association. She is an elected member of the American Academy of Arts and Sciences.

Mitchel A. Sollenberger is an assistant professor of political science at the University of Michigan, Dearborn, and the author of *The President Shall Nominate: How Congress Trumps Executive Power* (2008).

James A. Thurber is University Distinguished Professor of Government, founder (1979) and director of the Center for Congressional and Presidential Studies (american.edu/ccps) at American University, Washington, D.C. Under his direction, CCPS organizes biannually the Campaign Management Institute and the Public Affairs and Advocacy Institute over the last two decades. He was the principal investigator of a seven-year grant from the Pew Charitable Trusts to study campaign conduct. He was the principal investigator of a four-year study of lobbying and ethics funded by the Committee for Economic Development. He is a fellow of the National Academy of Public

Administration and is a former APSA congressional fellow. He is author of books and articles on Congress, congressional-presidential relations, interest groups and lobbying and ethics, and campaigns and elections. He is an author or editor of *Campaigns and Elections: American Style,* with Candice J. Nelson (2009, 3d ed.); *Congress and the Internet,* with Colton Campbell (2002); *The Battle for Congress: Consultants, Candidates, and Voters* (2001); *Crowded Airwaves: Campaign Advertising in Elections,* with Candice J. Nelson and David A. Dulio (2000); *Campaign Warriors: Political Consultants in Elections* (2000); *Remaking Congress: The Politics of Congressional Stability and Change,* with Roger Davidson (1995); and *Divided Democracy: Cooperation and Conflict between Presidents and Congress* (1991). He coproduced three BBC-TV documentaries on the U.S. Congress and elections.

Stephen J. Wayne is a well-known author and lecturer on the American presidency, presidential elections, and the psychology of political leadership. A professor of government at Georgetown University since 1988, Wayne has written or edited eleven books, many in multiple editions, and authored numerous articles, chapters, and reviews in professional journals, scholarly compilations, newspapers, and magazines. His best-known works include *The Road to the White House, The Legislative Presidency,* and *Presidential Leadership,* with George Edwards.

Joseph White is Luxenberg Family Professor of Public Policy and chair of the Department of Political Science at Case Western Reserve University. He earned his Ph.D. in political science from the University of California, Berkeley; and before coming to CWRU spent the largest part of his career with the Governmental Studies Program of the Brookings Institution. His research has focused on the federal budget and appropriations processes, budget and entitlement policy, and health policy both in the United States and other advanced industrial democracies. His budgeting publications include *The Deficit and the Public Interest: The Search for Responsible Budgeting in the 1980s,* with Aaron Wildvasky (1991), as well as numerous journal articles and book chapters.